CONTENTS

JAPANESE
Vocabulary

Second Edition

by

Nobuo Akiyama

Professorial Lecturer, Japanese Language
The Paul H. Nitze School of Advanced International Studies
The Johns Hopkins University

and

Carol Akiyama

Language Training Consultant
Washington, D.C.

BARRON'S

All inquiries should be addressed to:
Barron's Educational Series, Inc.
250 Wireless Boulevard
Hauppauge, NY 11788
www.barronseduc.com

Library of Congress Catalog Card No. 2008927160

ISBN-13: 978-0-7641-3973-4
ISBN-10: 0-7641-3973-8

PRINTED IN CHINA
9 8 7 6

CONTENTS

HOW TO USE THIS BOOK

THIS IS NOT JUST ANOTHER DICTIONARY!

Though called *Japanese Vocabulary*, this book offers you much more than its title implies. A dictionary lists words in alphabetical order. This book, on the other hand, organizes words by category—from basic numbers to the advanced high-tech language of the twenty-first century.

OVERALL DESIGN

The book begins with an easy pronunciation guide. The main body consists of nine chapters, followed by an English-Japanese Wordfinder.

Each chapter is divided into parts that deal with a particular aspect or function of human experience. For example, the chapters of daily life (Sections 23 through 29) deal with seven themes: At Home, Eating and Drinking, Shopping and Errands, Banking and Commerce, Games and Sports, The Arts, Holidays and Going Out. This organization enables you to locate related terms about a particular topic without having to look up each alphabetically.

USING THIS BOOK FOR DIFFERENT LEARNING GOALS

Beginners or advanced students of Japanese alike can use this book successfully. If you are a beginner, you will find the text user friendly, an easy system for acquiring basic vocabulary. If you already know some Japanese, you will appreciate the convenient arrangement of the words into categories. It gives you instant access to the expressions you need for discussing or reporting on specific topics.

FEATURES

Within each category, the English word is on the left side of the page, the Japanese equivalent is in the middle column, and the pronunciation is in the column on the right. The English items are arranged in alphabetical order, unless the nature of the theme requires some other logical system of organization. Related items, concepts, or specific uses are indented under the main item.

Special *FOCUS* sections deal with specific parts of a category by providing more information about it. Idiomatic expressions and other useful material are boxed for easy reference.

The English-Japanese Wordfinder at the back of the book lists the reference section for each word, and also provides the Japanese characters for each entry.

Nobuo Akiyama
Carol Akiyama

ABBREVIATIONS

n	noun. Since nouns are the largest number of items, most nouns are *not* identified. This abbreviation is used only in certain cases for clarity.
v	verb
vi	intransitive verb
vt	transitive verb
adj	adjective, adjectival phrase
adv	adverb, adverbial phrase
conj	conjunction
inf	informal usage
~	denotes that something additional must be supplied, and where. For example:

almost never	hotondo	~nai	**every, each**	dono	~mo
	hotondo	<u>ika</u>nai		dono	<u>hon</u> mo
		go			book
	(almost never go)		(each book, every book)		

PRONUNCIATION GUIDE

Japanese is not difficult to pronounce if you follow a few simple guidelines. Take the time to read this section, and try out each sound presented.

Let's start with the vowels. If you have studied Spanish, it may help you to know that Japanese vowels are more like those of Spanish than those of English.

VOWELS

The following vowels are short and pure, with *no glide*—that is, they are not diphthongs.

Japanese Vowel	English Equivalent	Example
a	as in father	akai (*ah-kah-ee*) red
e	as in men	ebi (*eh-bee*) shrimp
i	as in see	imi (*ee-mee*) meaning
o	as in boat	otoko (*oh-toh-koh*) male
u	as in food	uma (*oo-mah*) horse

The following vowels, called long vowels, are like the ones above, but lengthened.

Japanese Vowel	English Equivalent	Example
ā	as in father, but lengthened	batā (*bah-tah*) butter
ei	as in men, but lengthened	eigo (*eh-goh*) English
ii	as in see, but lengthened	iiharu (*ee-hah-roo*) insist
ō	as in boat, but lengthened	ōsama (*oh-sah-mah*) king
ū	as in food, but lengthened	yūbin (*yoo-been*) mail

And keep in mind these points:

- Long vowels are important. Pronouncing a long vowel incorrectly can result in a different word or even an unintelligible one. For example,

obasan	(*oh-bah-sahn*)	means aunt
obāsan	(*oh-bah̄-sahn*)	means grandmother
ojisan	(*oh-jee-sahn*)	means uncle
ojiisan	(*oh-jēē-sahn*)	means grandfather
seki	(*seh-kee*)	means seat
seiki	(*seh-kee*)	means century

- Sometimes the **i** and the **u** are not pronounced. This usually occurs between voiceless consonants (p, t, k, ch, f, h, s, sh), or at the end of a word following a voiceless consonant. Here's an example you may already know:

  sukiyaki (*skee-yah-kee*)

  This word for a popular Japanese dish begins with **skee**, not **soo**. The **u** is not pronounced.
  One more example:

  tabemashita (*tah-beh-mahsh-tah*) I ate

  The **i** is not pronounced.

CONSONANTS

With a few exceptions, Japanese consonants are similar to those of English. Note those that are different:

f The English **f** is pronounced with a passage of air between the upper teeth and the lower lip. To make the Japanese **f**, blow air lightly between your lips as if you were just beginning a whistle.

g Always pronounced as in *go*, never as in *age*. You may also hear it pronounced as the **ng** sound in *sing*, but not at the beginning of a word.

r This is different from the English **r**. To make the Japanese **r**, lightly touch the tip of your tongue to the bony ridge behind the upper teeth, almost in the English **d** position. It's more like the Spanish **r**, but it's not trilled.

s Always hissed, as in *so*; never voiced, as in *his* or *pleasure*.

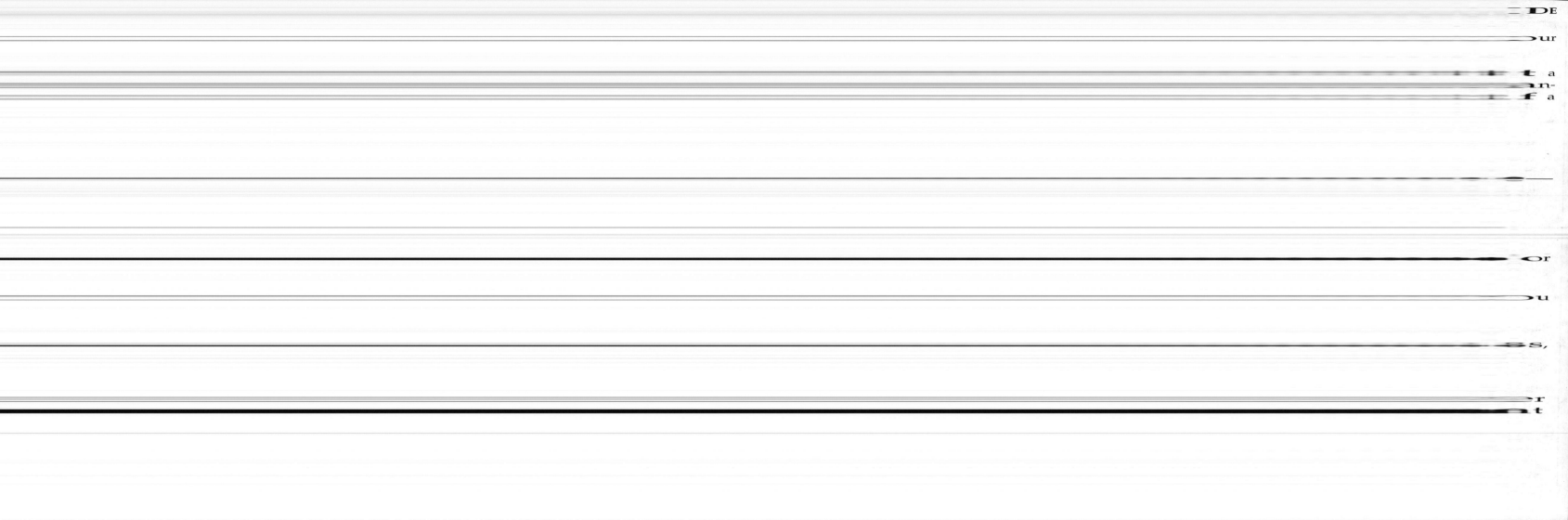

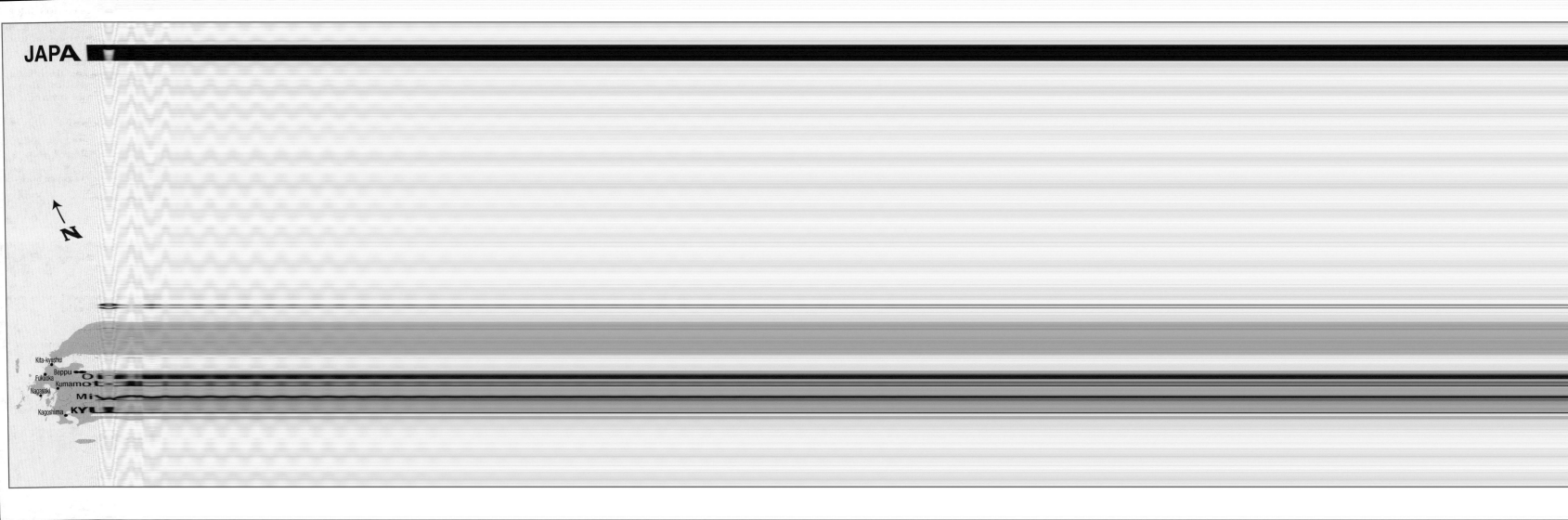

BASIC INFORMATION

1. ARITHMETIC

a. CARDINAL NUMBERS

zero	zero / rei	*zeh-roh/reh*
one	ichi	*ee-chee*
two	ni	*nee*
three	san	*sahn*
four	shi / yon	*shee/yohn*
five	go	*goh*
six	roku	*roh-koo*
seven	shichi / nana	*shee-chee/nah-nah*
eight	hachi	*hah-chee*
nine	ku / kyū	*koo/kyoo*
ten	jū	*joo*
eleven	jūichi	*joo-ee-chee*
twelve	jūni	*joo-nee*
thirteen	jūsan	*joo-sahn*
fourteen	jūshi / jūyon	*joo-shee/joo-yohn*
fifteen	jūgo	*joo-goh*
sixteen	jūroku	*joo-roh-koo*
seventeen	jūshichi	*joo-shee-chee*
	jūnana	*joo-nah-nah*
eighteen	jūhachi	*joo-hah-chee*
nineteen	jūku / jūkyū	*joo-koo/joo-kyoo*
twenty	nijū	*nee-joo*
twenty-one	nijūichi	*nee-joo-ee-chee*
twenty-two	nijūni	*nee-joo-nee*
twenty-three	nijūsan	*nee-joo-sahn*
twenty-four	nijūshi / nijūyon	*nee-joo-shee/nee-joo-yohn*
twenty-five	nijūgo	*nee-joo-goh*
twenty-six	nijūroku	*nee-joo-roh-koo*
twenty-seven	nijūshichi	*nee-joo-shee-chee*
	nijūnana	*nee-joo-nah-nah*
twenty-eight	nijūhachi	*nee-joo-hah-chee*
twenty-nine	nijūku	*nee-joo-koo*
	nijūkyū	*nee-joo-kyoo*
thirty	sanjū	*sahn-joo*
thirty-one	sanjūichi	*sahn-joo-ee-chee*
thirt-two	sanjūni	*sahn-joo-nee*
thirty-three	sanjūsan	*sahn-joo-sahn*
...		
forty	yonjū	*yohn-joo*

forty-one	yonjūichi	*yohn-jōo-ee-chee*
forty-two	yonjūni	*yohn-jōo-nee*
forty-three	yonjūsan	*yohn-jōo-sahn*
...		
fifty	gojū	*goh-jōo*
fifty-one	gojūichi	*goh-jōo-ee-chee*
sixty	rokujū	*roh-koo-jōo*
seventy	nanajū	*nah-nah-jōo*
eighty	hachijū	*hah-chee-jōo*
ninety	kyūjū	*kyōo-jōo*
one hundred	hyaku	*hyah-koo*
one hundred and one	hyakuichi	*hyah-koo-ee-chee*
one hundred and two	hyakuni	*hyah-koo-nee*
one hundred ten	hyakujū	*hyah-koo-jōo*
one hundred twenty	hyakunijū	*hyah-koo-nee-jōo*
two hundred	nihyaku	*nee-hyah-koo*
two hundred and one	nihyakuichi	*nee-hyah-koo-ee-chee*
two hundred ten	nihyakujū	*nee-hyah-koo-jōo*
three hundred	sanbyaku	*sahn-byah-koo*
four hundred	yonhyaku	*yohn-hyah-koo*
five hundred	gohyaku	*goh-hyah-koo*
six hundred	roppyaku	*rohp-pyah-koo*
seven hundred	nanahyaku	*nah-nah-hyah-koo*
eight hundred	happyaku	*hahp-pyah-koo*
nine hundred	kyūhyaku	*kyōo-hyah-koo*
one thousand	sen	*sehn*
one thousand and one	sen-ichi	*sehn-ee-chee*
one thousand ten	senjū	*sehn-jōo*
one thousand three hundred	sensanbyaku	*sehn-sahn-byah-koo*
two thousand	nisen	*nee-sehn*

two thousand and one	nisen-ichi	nee-sehn-ee-chee
two thousand four hundred	nisen-yonhyaku	nee-sehn-yohn-hyah-koo
three thousand	sanzen	sahn-zehn
...		
four thousand	yonsen	yohn-sehn
...		
five thousand	gosen	goh-sehn
...		
six thousand	rokusen	roh-koo-sehn
...		
seven thousand	nanasen	nah-nah-sehn
...		
eight thousand	hassen	hahs-sehn
...		
nine thousand	kyūsen	kyōō-sehn
...		
ten thousand	ichiman	ee-chee-mahn
ten thousand and one	ichiman-ichi	ee-chee-mahn-ee-chee
ten thousand ten	ichimanjū	ee-chee-mahn-jōō
ten thousand two hundred	ichiman-nihyaku	ee-chee-mahn-nee-hyah-koo
eleven thousand	ichimansen	ee-chee-mahn-sehn
...		
twelve thousand	ichimannisen	ee-chee-mahn-nee-sehn
thirteen thousand	ichimansanzen	ee-chee-mahn-sahn-zehn
fourteen thousand	ichiman-yonsen	ee-chee-mahn-yohn-sehn
fifteen thousand	ichimangosen	ee-chee-mahn-goh-sehn
sixteen thousand	ichimanrokusen	ee-chee-mahn-roh-koo-sehn
seventeen thousand	ichimannanasen	ee-chee-mahn-nah-nah-sehn
eighteen thousand	ichimanhassen	ee-chee-mahn-hahs-sehn
nineteen thousand	ichimankyūsen	ee-chee-mahn-kyōō-sehn
twenty thousand	niman	nee-mahn
thirty thousand	sanman	sahn-mahn
forty thousand	yonman	yohn-mahn
fifty thousand	goman	goh-mahn
sixty thousand	rokuman	roh-koo-mahn
seventy thousand	nanaman	nah-nah-mahn
eighty thousand	hachiman	hah-chee-mahn
ninety thousand	kyūman	kyōō-mahn
one hundred thousand	jūman	jōō-mahn
two hundred thousand	nijūman	nee-jōō-mahn
one million	hyakuman	hyah-koo-mahn
one million and one	hyakuman-ichi	hyah-koo-mahn-ee-chee

one million and two	hyakuman-ni	*hyah-koo-mahn-nee*
...		
two million	nihyakuman	*nee-hyah-koo-mahn*
...		
three million	sanbyakuman	*sahn-byah-koo-mahn*
ten million	senman	*sehn-mahn*
...		
one hundred million	ichioku	*ee-chee-oh-koo*
...		
one billion	jūoku	*j $\overline{oo}$ -oh-koo*
...		
two billion	nijūoku	*nee-j $\overline{oo}$ -oh-koo*
...		
ten billion	hyakuoku	*hyah-koo-oh-koo*
one hundred billion	sen-oku	*sehn-oh-koo*
...		
one trillion	itchō	*eet-ch $\overline{oh}$*
...		
two trillion	nichō	*nee-ch $\overline{oh}$*

Another system for cardinal numbers from one through ten is listed below. From eleven on, they are the same as the previous set of cardinal numbers.

one	hitotsu	*hee-TOH-tsoo*
two	futatsu	*foo-TAH-tsoo*
three	mittsu	*meet-TSOO*
four	yottsu	*yoht-TSOO*
five	itsutsu	*ee-TSOO-tsoo*
six	muttsu	*moot-TSOO*
seven	nanatsu	*nah-NAH-tsoo*
eight	yattsu	*yaht-TSOO*
nine	kokonotsu	*koh-KOH-noh-tsoo*
ten	tō	*toh*

FOCUS: Counting Different Kinds of Things

people
one (person)	hitori	*hee-toh-ree*
two (persons)	futari	*foo-tah-ree*
three (persons)	sannin	*sahn-neen*

integer	seisū	_seh-soo_
irrational number	murisū	_moo-ree-soo_
natural number	shizensū	_shee-zehn-soo_
negative number	fusū	_foo-soo_
odd number	kisū	_kee-soo_
ordinal number	josū	_joh-soo_
positive number	seisū	_seh-soo_
prime number	sosū	_soh-soo_
rational number	yurisū	_yoo-ree-soo_
real number	jissū	_jees-soo_
reciprocal number	gyakusū	_gyah-koo-soo_
Roman numeral	Rōma sūji	_roh-mah soo-jee_

e. BASIC OPERATIONS

arithmetical operations	enzan	_ehn-zahn_
add	kuwaeru (v)/tasu (v)	_koo-wah-eh-roo/tahs_
• addition	tashizan	_tah-shee-zahn_
• plus	purasu kigō	_poo-rahs kee-goh_
• two plus two equals four	ni tasu ni wa yon	_nee tahs nee wah yohn_
subtract	hiku (v)	_hee-koo_
• subtraction	hikizan	_hee-kee-zahn_
• minus	mainasu kigō	_mah-ee-nahs kee-goh_
• three minus two equals one	san hiku ni wa ichi	_sahn hee-koo nee wah ee-chee_
multiply	kakeru (v)	_kah-keh-roo_
• multiplication	kakezan	_kah-keh-zahn_
• multiplication table	kuku no hyō	_koo-koo noh hyoh_
• three times two equals six	san kakeru ni wa roku	_sahn kah-keh-roo nee wah roh-koo_
divide	waru (v)	_wah-roo_
• division	warizan	_wah-ree-zahn_
• six divided by three equals two	roku waru san wa ni	_roh-koo wah-roo sahn wah nee_
raise to a power	ruijōsuru (v)	_roo-ee-joh-soo-roo_
• to the power of	ruijō	_roo-ee-joh_
• squared	nijō no	_nee-joh noh_
• cubed	sanjō no	_sahn-joh noh_
• to the fourth power	yonjō	_yohn-joh_
• to the nth power	enujō	_eh-noo-joh_
• two squared equals four	ni no nijō wa yon	_nee no nee-joh wah yohn_
extract a root	kon o hiraku (v)	_kohn oh hee-rah-koo_
• square root	heihōkon	_heh-hoh-kohn_
• cube root	rippōkon	_reep-poh-kohn_

Approximate Numbers

about, around, nearly	yaku	yah-koo
about, around, almost, practically	hobo	hoh-boh
almost, nearly, all but	ōyoso	ōh-yoh-soh
almost, nearly, all but	daitai	dah-ee-tah-ee
almost, nearly, all but, practically	hotondo	hoh-tohn-doh

These words are placed before numbers or amounts to show approximation.

about 10	yaku jū	yah-koo jōō
almost 20	hobo nijū	hoh-boh nee-jōō
nearly 30	ōyoso sanjū	oh-yoh-soh sahn-jōō
all but 40	daitai yonjū	dah-ee-tah-ee yohn-jōō
practically 50	hotondo gojū	hoh-tohn-doh goh-jōō

There are some exceptions. Some words to show approximation are placed after numbers or amounts.

around, on or around	zengo	zehn-goh
around 60	rokujū zengo	roh-koo-jōō zehn-goh
around (used with time factors)	koro	koh-roh
on or around 7 o'clock	shichiji koro	shee-chee-jee koh-roh

d. TYPES OF NUMBERS

number	kazu / sūji	kah-zoo/sōō-jee
• number	bangō o tsukeru (v)	bahn-goh oh tsoo-keh-roo
• numeral	sūji	sōō-jee
• numerical	kazu no (adj)	kah-zoo noh
Arabic numeral	Arabia sūji	ah-rah-bee-ah sōō-jee
cardinal number	kisū	kee sōō
complex number	fukusosū	foo-koo soh-sōō
digit	sūji	sōō-jee
even number	gūsū	gōō-sōō
fraction	bunsū	boon-sōō
• fractional	bunsu no (adj)	boon-sōō noh
imaginary number	kyosū	kyoh-sōō

1c FRACTIONS

eighth	daihachi	*dah-ee-hah-chee*
ninth	daiku	*dah-ee-koo*
tenth	daijū	*dah-ee-jōo*
eleventh	daijūichi	*dah-ee-jōo-ee-chee*
twelfth	daijūni	*dah-ee-jōo-nee*

For another system of cardinal numbers, the ordinal numbers through ninth are formed by adding -me to the end of the corresponding number. Tenth works with -banme or dai-.

first	hitotsume	*hee-toh-tsoo-meh*
second	futatsume	*foo-tah-tsoo-meh*
third	mittsume	*meet-tsoo-meh*
fourth	yottsume	*yoht-tsoo-meh*
fifth	itsutsume	*ee-tsoo-tsoo-meh*
sixth	muttsume	*moot-tsoo-meh*
seventh	nanatsume	*nah-nah-tsoo-meh*
eighth	yattsume	*yaht-tsoo-meh*
ninth	kokonotsume	*koh-koh-noh-tsoo-meh*
tenth	jūbanme/daijū	*jōo-bahn-meh/dah-ee-jōo*

c. FRACTIONS

Formation Rule

Use cardinal numbers.
Put the divisor or denominator first, followed by **bun no**, and then add the dividend or a numerator.

Example: divisor 8, dividend 5
hachibun no go
hah-chee-boon noh goh

one-half	nibun no ichi	*nee-boon noh ee-chee*
one-third	sanbun no ichi	*sahn-boon noh ee-chee*
one-fourth	yonbun no ichi	*yohn-boon noh ee-chee*
one-fifth	gobun no ichi	*goh-boon noh ee-chee*
two-thirds	sanbun no ni	*sahn-boon noh nee*
three-fourths	yonbun no san	*yohn-boon noh sahn*
four-ninths	kyūbun no yon	*kyōo-boon noh yohn*

small objects not in the categories listed above		
one	ikko/hitotsu	EEK-koh/hee-TOH-tsoo
two	niko/futatsu	NEE-koh/foo-TAH-tsoo
three	sanko/mittsu	SAHN-koo/meet-TSOO

b. ORDINAL NUMBERS

One way of forming the ordinal numbers is by adding -banme to the end of the corresponding cardinal number.

first	ichibanme	ee-chee-bahn-meh
second	nibanme	nee-bahn-meh
third	sanbanme	sahn-bahn-meh
fourth	yobanme	yoh-bahn-meh
fifth	gobanme	goh-bahn-meh
sixth	rokubanme	roh-koo-bahn-meh
seventh	nanabanme	nah-nah-bahn-meh
eighth	hachibanme	hah-chee-bahn-meh
ninth	kyūbanme	kyoo-bahn-meh
tenth	jūbanme	joo-bahn-meh
eleventh	jūichibanme	joo-ee-chee-bahn-meh
twelfth	jūnibanme	joo-nee-bahn-meh
thirteenth	jūsanbanme	joo-sahn-bahn-meh
twenty-third	nijūsanbanme	nee-joo-sahn-bahn-meh
hundredth	hyakubanme	hyah-koo-bahn-meh
thousandth	senbanme	sehn-bahn-meh
ten thousandth	ichimanbanme	ee-chee-mahn-bahn-meh
millionth	hyakumanbanme	hyah-koo-mahn-bahn-meh
billionth	jūokubanme	joo-oh-koo-bahn-meh

Another way of forming the ordinal numbers is by attaching dai- to the front of the corresponding cardinal number.

first	daiichi	dah-ee-ee-chee
second	daini	dah-ee-nee
third	daisan	dah-ee-sahn
fourth	daiyon	dah-ee-yohn
fifth	daigo	dah-ee-goh
sixth	dairoku	dah-ee-roh-koo
seventh	dainana	dah-ee-nah-nah

nth root	enujōkon	*eh-noo-jōh-kohn*
• (the) square root of nine is three	kyū no heihōkon wa san	*kyōō noh heh-hoh-kohn wah sahn*
ratio	hirei	*hee-reh*
• twelve is to four as nine is to three	jūni tai yon wa kyū tai san	*jōō-nee tah-ee yohn wah kyōō tah-ee sahn*

FOCUS: Arithmetical Operations

Addition—tashizan
$2 + 3 = 5$ two plus three equals five   ni tasu san wa go

Subtraction—hikizan
$9 - 3 = 6$ nine minus three equals six   kyū hiku san wa roku

Multiplication—kakezan
$4 \times 2 = 8$ four times two equals eight   yon kakeru ni wa hachi
$4 \cdot 2 = 8$

Division—warizan
$10 \div 2 = 5$ ten divided by two equals five   jū waru ni wa go

Raising to a power—ruijō
$3^2 = 9$ three squared (or to the second power) equals nine   san no nijō wa kyū
$2^3 = 8$ two cubed (or to the third power) equals eight   ni no sanjō wa hachi
$2^4 = 16$ two to the fourth power equals sixteen   ni no yonjō wa jūroku
x^n x to the nth power   ekkusu no enujō

Extraction of root—kon no kaihō
$\sqrt[2]{4} = 2$ the square root of four is two   yon no heihōkon wa ni
$\sqrt[3]{27} = 3$ the cube root of twenty-seven is three   nijūnana no rippōkon wa san
$\sqrt[n]{x}$ the nth root of x   ekkusu no enujōkon

Ratio—hirei
$12:4 = 9:3$ twelve is to four as nine is to three   jūni tai yon wa kyū tai san

f. ADDITIONAL MATHEMATICAL CONCEPTS

algebra	daisū	*dah-ee-sōo*
• algebraic	daisū no *(adj)*	*dah-ee-sōo noh*
arithmetic	sansū	*sahn-sōo*
• arithmetical	sansū no *(adj)*	*sahn-sōo noh*
average	heikin	*hēh-keen*
calculate	keisansuru *(v)*	*keh-sahn-soo-roo*
• calculation	keisan	*keh-sahn*
constant	teisū	*teh-sōo*
count	kazoeru *(v)*	*kah-zoh-eh-roo*
• countable	kazoerareru *(adj)*	*kah-zoh-eh-rah-reh-roo*
decimal	shōsū	*shoh-sōo*
difference	sa	*sah*
equality	dōtō	*doh-toh*
• equals	hitoshii	*hee-toh-shēē*
• does not equal	hitoshikunai	*hee-toh-shee-koo-nah-ee*
• is equivalent to	sōtōsuru	*soh-toh-soo-roo*
• is greater than	yori ōkii	*yoh-ree ōh-kēē*
• is less than	yori chiisai	*yoh-ree chēē-sah-ee*
• is similar to	ruijishiteiru	*roo-ee-jee-jeeshteh-ee-roo*
equation	hōteishiki	*hoh-teh-shkee*
exponent	beki shisū	*beh-kee shee-sōo*
factor	insū	*een-sōo*
• factor	insū ni bunkaisuru *(v)*	*een-sōo nee boon-kah-ee-soo-roo*
• factorization	insūbunkai	*een-sōo-boon-kah-ee*
function	kansū	*kahn-sōo*
logarithm	taisū	*tah-ee-sōo*
• logarithmic	taisū no *(adj)*	*tah-ee-sōo noh*
minus	mainasu	*mah-ee-nah-soo*
multiple	baisū	*bah-ee-sōo*
percent	pāsento	*pāh-sehn-toh*
• percentage	ritsu	*ree-tsoo*
plus	purasu	*poo-rah-soo*
problem	mondai	*mohn-dah-ee*
• problem to solve	kaiketsusuru mondai	*kah-ee-keh-tsoo-soo-roo mohn-dah-ee*
product	seki	*seh-kee*
proposition	meidai / teiri	*meh-dah-ee/teh-ree*
quotient	shō	*shoh*
set	shūgō	*shōo-goh*
solution	kaiketsuhō	*kah-ee-keh-tsoo-hōh*
• solve	kaiketsusuru *(v)*	*kah-ee-keh-tsoo-soo-roo*
statistics	tōkei	*toh-keh*
• statistical	tōkei no *(adj)*	*toh-keh noh*
sum	gōkei	*goh-keh*
• sum up	gōkeisuru *(v)*	*goh-keh-soo-roo*

symbol	kigō	*kee-gōh*
theorem	teiri	*teh-ree*
unknown	michisū	*mee-chee-sōo*
variable	hensū	*hehn-sōo*

2. GEOMETRY

a. FIGURES

plane figures	heimen zukei	*heh-mehn zoo-keh*
triangle	sankakukei	*sahn-kah-koo-keh*

a lovers' triangle (*lit.* triangle relation)	sankaku kankei	*sahn-kah-koo kahn-keh*
to look daggers at someone (*lit.* make one's eyes triangular)	me o sankaku ni suru	*meh oh sahn-kah-koo nee soo-roo*

• acute-angled	eikaku *(adj)*	*eh-kah-koo*
• equilateral	tōhen *(adj)*	*toh-hehn*
• isoceles	nitōhen *(adj)*	*nee-toh-hehn*
• obtuse-angled	donkaku *(adj)*	*dohn-kah-koo*
• right-angled	chokkaku *(adj)*	*chohk-kah-koo*
• scalene	futōhen/sha *(adj)*	*ftoh-hehn/shah*
four-sided figures	shihenkei	*shee-hehn-keh*
• parallelogram	heikōshihenkei	*heh-koh-shee-hehn-keh*
• rectangle	chōhōkei	*choh-hoh-keh*
• rhombus	hishigata	*hee-shee-gah-tah*
• square	seihōkei	*seh-hoh-keh*
• trapezoid	daikei	*dah-ee-keh*
n-sided figures	enuhenkei	*eh-noo-hehn-keh*
• pentagon	gokakukei	*goh-kah-koo-keh*
• hexagon	rokkakukei	*rohk-kah-koo-keh*
• heptagon	nanakakukei	*nah-nah-kah-koo-keh*
• octagon	hakkakukei	*hahk-kah-koo-keh*
• decagon	jukkakukei	*jook-kah-koo-keh*
circle	en	*ehn*

a happy home (*lit.* round and full home)	enman na katei	*ehn-mahn nah kah-teh*

• center	chūshin	*chōo-sheen*
• circumference	enshū	*ehn-shōo*
• diameter	chokkei	*chohk-keh*

• radius	hankei	*hahn-keh*
• tangent	sessen	*sehs-sehn*
solid figures	rittai	*reet-tah-ee*
prism	kakuchū	*kahk-chōō*
• right prism	chokkakuchū	*chohk-kahk-chōō*
parallelepiped	heikōrokumentai	*heh-kōh-roh-koo-mehn-tah-ee*
cube	seirokumentai	*seh-roh-koo-mehn-tah-ee*
pyramid	kakusui	*kahk-soo-ee*
polyhedron	tamentai	*tah-mehn-tah-ee*
• tetrahedron	shimentai	*shee-mehn-tah-ee*
• octahedron	hachimentai	*hah-chee-mehn-tah-ee*
• dodecahedron	jūnimentai	*jōō-nee-mehn-tah-ee*
• icosahedron	nijūmentai	*nee-jōō-mehn-tah-ee*
cylinder	enchū	*ehn-chōō*
cone	ensuitai	*ehn-soo-ee-tah-ee*
sphere	kyūkei	*kyōō-keh*

b. CONCEPTS

angle	kakudo	*kah-koo-doh*
• acute angle	eikaku	*eh-kah-koo*
• adjacent angle	rinsetsukaku	*reen-seh-tsoo-kah-koo*
• bisector	nitōbunsen	*nee-toh-boon-sehn*
• complementary angle	yokaku	*yoh-kah-koo*
• concave angle	ōkaku	*ōh-kah-koo*
• convex angle	tokkaku	*tohk-kah-koo*
• obtuse angle	donkaku	*dohn-kah-koo*
• one turn (360°)	ichi kaiten	*ee-chee kah-ee-tehn*
• opposite angle	taichōkaku	*tah-ee-chōh-kah-koo*
• right angle	chokkaku	*chohk-kah-koo*
• side	hen	*hehn*
• straight angle	heikaku	*hēh-kah-koo*
• supplementary angle	hokaku	*hoh-kah-koo*
• vertex	chōten	*chōh-tehn*
axis	jiku	*jee-koo__*
coordinate	zahyō	*zah-hyōh*
• abscissa coordinate	yoko zahyō	*yoh-koh zah-hyōh*
• ordinate coordinate	tate zahyō	*tah-teh zah-hyoh*
degree	do	*doh*
draw	sen o hiku (v)	*sehn oh hee-koo*
drawing instruments	seizu kigu	*seh-zoo kee-goo*
• compass	konpasu	*kohn-pahs*
• eraser	keshigomu	*keh-shee-goh-moo*
• pen	pen	*pehn*

FOCUS: Geometrical Figures

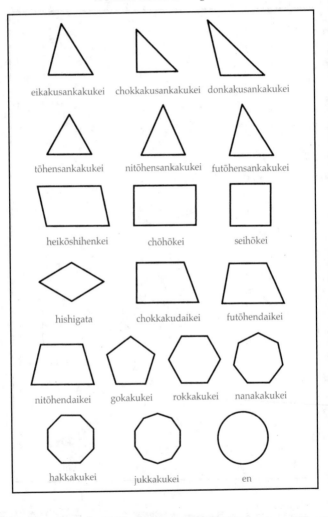

eikakusankakukei   chokkakusankakukei   donkakusankakukei

tōhensankakukei   nitōhensankakukei   futōhensankakukei

heikōshihenkei   chōhōkei   seihōkei

hishigata   chokkakudaikei   futōhendaikei

nitōhendaikei   gokakukei   rokkakukei   nanakakukei

hakkakukei   jukkakukei   en

FOCUS: Geometrical Solids

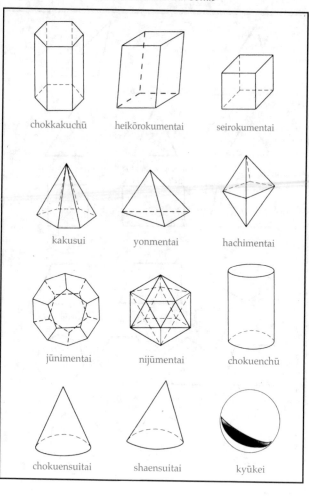

chokkakuchū

heikōrokumentai

seirokumentai

kakusui

yonmentai

hachimentai

jūnimentai

nijūmentai

chokuenchū

chokuensuitai

shaensuitai

kyūkei

FOCUS: Angles

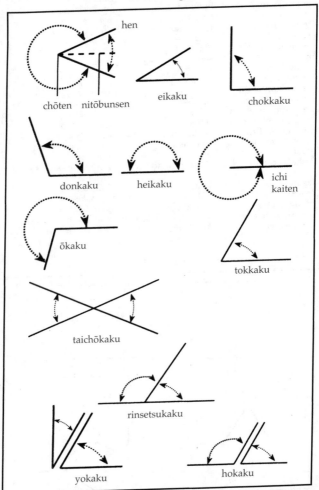

• **pencil**	enpitsu	*ehn-pee-tsoo*
• **protractor**	bundoki	*boon-doh-kee*
• **ruler**	jōgi	*jōh-gee*
• **template**	tenpurēto	*tehn-poo-rēh-toh*
geometry	kika	*kee-kah*
• **geometrical**	kika no *(adj)*	*kee-kah noh*
line	sen	*sehn*
• **broken line**	hasen	*hah-sehn*
• **curved line**	kyokusen	*kyohk-sehn*
• **horizontal line**	suiheisen	*soo-ee-hēh-sehn*
• **parallel lines**	heikōsen	*hēh-kōh-sehn*
• **perpendicular line**	suisen	*soo-ee-sehn*
• **segment line**	senbun	*sehn-boon*
• **straight line**	chokusen	*chohk-sehn*
• **vertical line**	suichokusen	*soo-ee-chohk-sehn*
point	ten	*tehn*
Pythagorean theorem	Pitagorasu no teiri	*pee-TAH-goh-rah-soo noh teh-ree*
segment	kyūkei	*kyōo-keh*
space	kūkan	*kōo-kahn*
trigonometry	sankakuhō	*sahn-kah-koo-hōh*
• **trigonometric**	sankakuhō no *(adj)*	*sahn-kah-koo-hoh noh*
• **cosecant**	kosekanto	*koh-seh-kahn-toh*

FOCUS: Lines

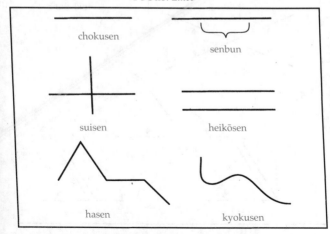

• **cosine**	kosain	*koh-sah-een*
• **cotangent**	kotanjento	*koh-tahn-jehn-toh*
• **secant**	sekanto	*seh-kahn-toh*
• **sine**	sain	*sah-een*
• **tangent**	tanjento	*tahn-jehn-toh*
vector	do-kei	*doh-keh*

3. QUANTITY AND SPACE

a. WEIGHTS AND MEASURES

area	menseki	*mehn-seh-kee*
• **acre**	ēkā	*eh-kah*
• **hectare**	hekutāru	*hehk-tah-roo*
• **square centimeter**	heihōsenchi	*heh-hoh-sehn-chee*
• **square inch**	heihōinchi	*heh-hoh-een-chee*
• **square foot**	heihōfīto	*heh-hoh-fee-toh*
• **square kilometer**	heihōkiro	*heh-hoh-kee-roh*
• **square meter**	heihōmētoru	*heh-hoh-meh-toh-roo*
• **square mile**	heihōmairu	*heh-hoh-mah-ee-roo*
• **square millimeter**	heihōmiri	*heh-hoh-mee-ree*
length	nagasa	*nah-gah-sah*
• **centimeter**	senchi	*sehn-chee*
• **inch**	inchi	*een-chee*
• **foot/feet**	fīto	*fee-toh*
• **kilometer**	kiro	*kee-roh*
• **meter**	mētoru	*meh-toh-roo*
• **mile**	mairu	*mah-ee-roo*
• **millimeter**	miri	*mee-ree*
speed	sokudo	*sohk-doh*
• **per hour**	jisoku	*jee-soh-koo*
• **per minute**	funsoku	*foon-soh-koo*
• **per second**	byōsoku	*byoh-soh-koo*
volume	taiseki/yōseki	*tah-ee-seh-kee/yoh-seh-kee*
• **cubic centimeter**	rippōsenchi	*reep-poh-sehn-chee*
• **cubic kilometer**	rippōkiro	*reep-poh-kee-roh*
• **cubic meter**	rippōmētoru	*reep-poh-meh-toh-roo*
• **cubic millimeter**	rippōmiri	*reep-poh-mee-ree*
• **gallon**	garon	*gah-rohn*
• **liter**	rittoru	*reet-toh-roo*
• **ounce**	onsu	*ohn-soo*
• **pint**	painto	*pah-een-toh*
• **quart**	kuōto	*koo-oh-toh*
weight	jūryō	*joo-ryoh*
• **gram**	guramu	*goo-rah-moo*
• **kilogram**	kiroguramu	*kee-roh-goo-rah-moo*
• **milligram**	miriguramu	*mee-ree-goo-rah-moo*

• ounce	onsu	*ohn-soo*
• pound	pondo	*pohn-doh*
• ton	ton	*tohn*

b. WEIGHING AND MEASURING

dense	mitsudo ga takai *(adj)*	*mee-tsoo-doh gah tah-kah-ee*
• density	mitsudo / nōdo	*mee-tsoo-doh/noh-doh*
dimension	jigen	*jee-gehn*
extension	enchō / kakuchō	*ehn-choh/kahk-choo*
heavy	omoi *(adj)*	*oh-moh-ee*
high	takai *(adj)*	*tah-kah-ee*
• height	takasa	*tah-kah-sah*
light	karui *(adj)*	*kah-roo-ee*
long	nagai *(adj)*	*nah-gah-ee*
• length	nagasa	*nah-gah-sah*
mass	ryoh	*ryoh*
• massive	tairyō no *(adj)*	*tah-ee-ryoh noh*
maximum	saidai no *(adj)*	*sah-ee-dah-ee noh*
measure	hakaru *(v)*	*hah-kah-roo*
measuring cup	keiryō kappu	*keh-ryoh kahp-poo*
measuring tape	tēpumejā	*teh-poo-meh-jah*
medium	chūgurai no *(adj)*	*choo-goo-rah-ee noh*
minimum	saishō no *(adj)*	*sah-ee shoh noh*
narrow	semai *(adj)*	*seh-mah-ee*
short	mijikai *(adj)*	*mee-jee-kah-ee*
size	saizu	*sah-ee-zoo*
tall	takai *(adj)*	*tah-kah-ee*
thick	atsui *(adj)*	*ah-tsoo-ee*
thin	usui *(adj)*	*oo-soo-ee*
weigh	mekata o hakaru *(v)*	*meh-kah-tah oh hah-kah-roo*
• weight	jūryō	*joo-ryoh*
wide	hiroi *(adj)*	*hee-roh-ee*
• width	hirosa	*hee-roh-sah*

c. CONCEPTS OF QUANTITY

a lot, much	takusan	*tahk-sahn*
all, everything	subete *(adv)*	*soo-beh-teh*
	zenbu	*zehn-boo*
• everyone	daremo	*dah-reh-mo*
almost, nearly	hotondo *(adv)*	*hoh-tohn-dah*
approximately	ōyoso	*oh-yoh-soh*
as much as	dake	*dah-keh*
big, large	ōkii *(adj)*	*oh-kee-ee*

• become big	ōkiku naru (v)	ōh-kee-koo nah-roo
both	ryōhō	ryoh-hoh
capacity	yōryō / yōseki / teiin (persons)	yoh-ryoh/yoh-seh-kee/teh-een
decrease	genshō	gehn-shoh
• decrease	genshōsuru (vi)	gehn-shoh-soo-roo
	genshōsaseru (vt)	gehn-shoh-sah-seh-roo
double	nibai no (adj)	nee-bah-ee noh
• double	nibai ni suru (vt)	nee-bah-ee nee soo-roo
empty	kara no (adj)	kah-rah noh
• empty	kara ni suru (v)	kah-rah nee soo-roo
enough	jūbun na (adj)	jōo-boon nah
	jūbun ni (adv)	jōo-boon ni
entire	zentai no (adj)	zehn-tah-ee noh
every, each	dono ~mo	doh-noh ~moh
fill	mitasu (v)	mee-tah-soo
• full	ippai no (adj)	eep-pah-ee noh
grow	fueru (vi)	foo-eh-roo
	fuyasu (vt)	foo-yah-soo
• growth	zōdai	zoh-dah-ee
half	hanbun no (adj)	hahn-boon noh
• halve	nitōbunsuru (v)	nee-toh-boon-soo-roo
how much	dono kurai	doh-noh koo-rah-ee
how much (money)	ikura	ee-koo-rah
increase	zōka / zōdai	zoh-kah/zoh-dah-ee
• increase	zōkasuru (vi)	zoh-kah-soo-roo
	zōkasaseru (vt)	zoh-kah-sah-seh-roo
less	yori sukunai	yoh-ree skoo-nah-ee
little	chiisai (adj)	chēe-sah-ee
• a little	sukoshi	skoh-shee
lot	takusan (adv)	tahk-sahn
massive	tairyō no (adj)	tah-ee-ryoh noh
more	motto (adv)	moht-toh
no one	dare mo ~nai	dah-reh moh ~nah-ee
nothing	nani mo ~nai	nah-nee moh ~nah-ee
pair	kumi / tsui	koo-mee/tsoo-ee
part	bubun	boo-boon
piece	shōhen / ko	shoh-hehn/koh
portion	bubun	boo-boon
quantity	ryō	ryoh
several	ikutsuka no (adj)	ee-koots-kah noh
small	chiisai (adj)	chēe-sah-ee
• become small	chiisakunaru (v)	chēe-sah-koo-nah-roo
some	ikuraka no (adj)	ee-koo-rah-kah noh
sufficient	jūbun nah (adj)	jōo-boon nah
too much	ōsugi	oh-soo-gee
triple	sanbai no (adj)	sahn-bah-ee noh
• triple	sanbai ni suru (vt)	sahn-bah-ee nee soo-roo

3d CONCEPTS OF LOCATION

d. CONCEPTS OF LOCATION

above	ue no *(adj)*	oo-eh noh
	ue ni *(adv)*	oo-eh nee
across	mukōgawa no *(adj)*	moo-koh-gah-wah noh
	mukōgawa ni *(adj)*	moo-koh-gah-wah nee
ahead, forward	saki no *(adj)* / mae no *(adj)*	sah-kee noh/mah-eh noh
	saki ni *(adv)* / mae ni *(adv)*	sah-kee nee/mah-eh nee
among	naka ni *(adv)*	nah-kah nee
around	mawari ni *(adv)*	mah-wah-ree nee
away	hedatatta *(adj)*	heh-dah-taht-tah
	hedatatte *(adv)*	heh-dah-taht-teh
back, backward	ushiro no *(adj)*	oo-shee-roh noh
	ushiro ni *(adv)*	oo-shee-roh nee
beside, next to	tonari no *(adj)*	toh-nah-ree noh
	tonari ni *(adv)*	toh-nah-ree nee
between	aida no *(adj)*	ah-ee-dah noh
	aida ni *(adv)*	ah-ee-dah nee
beyond	koeta *(adj)*	koh-eh-tah
	koete *(adv)*	koh-eh-teh
bottom	soko	soh-koh
• at the bottom	soko ni *(adv)*	soh-koh nee
center	chūō	choo-oh
• at the center	chūō ni *(adv)*	choo-oh nee
compass	rashinban / konpasu	rah-sheen-bahn/KOHN-pahs_
direction	hōkō	hoh-koh
distance	kyori	kyoh-ree
down	shita no *(adj)*	shtah noh
	shita ni *(adv)*	shtah nee
east	higashi	hee-gah-shee
• eastern	higashi no	hee-gah-shee noh
• to the east	higashi e	hee-gah-shee eh
edge	hashi	hah-SHEE
at the edge of	hashi ni	hah-shee nee
far	tōku no *(adj)*	toh-koo noh
	tōku ni *(adv)*	toh-koo nee
fast	hayai *(adj)*	hah-yah-ee
	hayaku *(adv)*	hah-yah-koo
from	kara	kah-rah
front	mae	mah-eh
• in front of	mae ni	mah-eh nee
here	koko	koh-koh_
horizon	suihei	soo-ee-heh_
• horizontal	suihei no *(adj)*	soo-ee-heh_ noh
in	naka no *(adj)*	nah-kah noh

English	Japanese	Pronunciation
• inside	naka ni *(adv)*	*nah-kah nee*
left	naka ni *(adv)*	*nah-kah nee*
• to the left	hidari	*hee-dah-ree*
level	hidari ni	*hee-dah-ree nee*
middle	heimen	*heh-mehn*
• in the middle	chūkan	*choo-kahn*
near	chūkan ni	*choo-kahn nee*
	chikai *(adj)*	*chee-kah-ee*
north	chikaku ni *(adv)*	*chee-kah-koo nee*
• northeast	kita	*kee-tah*
• northern	hokutō	*hohk-toh*
• northwest	kita no	*kee-tah noh*
• to the north	hokusei	*hohk-seh*
nowhere	kita ni	*kee-tah nee*
on	dokonimo *(adv)*	*doh-koh-nee-moh*
	ue no *(adj)*	*oo-eh noh*
outside	ue ni *(adv)*	*oo-eh nee*
	soto no *(adj)*	*soh-toh noh*
over there	soto ni *(adv)*	*soh-toh nee*
place	asoko	*ah-soh-koh*
position	basho	*bah-shoh*
right	ichi	*ee-chee*
• to the right	migi	*mee-gee*
somewhere	migi ni	*mee-gee nee*
south	dokoka	*doh-koh-kah*
• southeast	minami	*mee-nah-mee*
• southern	nantō	*nahn-toh*
• southwest	minami no *(adj)*	*mee-nah-mee noh*
• to the south	nansei	*nahn-seh*
surface	minami ni	*mee-nah-mee nee*
there	hyōmen	*hyoh-mehn*
through	soko	*soh-koh*
	shite *(adj)*	*toh-shteh*

FOCUS: Compass Points

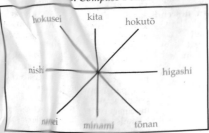

to, at	ni/de	nee/deh
top	ichiban ue	ee-chee-bahn oo-eh
• at the top	ichiban ue de	ee-chee-bahn oo-eh deh
toward	ni taishite	nee tah-ee-shteh
under	shita no *(adj)*	shtah noh
	shita ni *(adv)*	shtah nee
up	ue no *(adj)*	oo-eh noh
	ue ni *(adv)*	oo-eh nee
vertical	suichoku no *(adj)*	soo-ee-choh-koo noh
west	nishi	nee-shee
• western	nishi no *(adj)*	nee-shee noh
• to the west	nishi ni	nee-shee nee
where	doko ni *(adv)*	doh-koh nee

e. MOVEMENT

accelerate	kasokusuru *(v)*	kah-soh-koo-soo-roo
approach	sekkinsuru *(v)*	sehk-keen-soo-roo
arrive	tsuku *(v)*	tskoo
climb	noboru *(v)*	noh-boh-roo
crash	butsukaru *(v)*	boo-tsoo-kah-roo
crawl	hau *(v)*	hah-oo
come	kuru *(v)*	koo-roo
descend	kudaru *(v)*	koo-dah-roo
dive	tobikomu *(v)*	too-bee-koh-moo
drive	untensuru *(v)*	oon-tehn-soo-roo
enter	hairu *(v)*	hah-ee-roo
fall	ochiru *(v)*	oh-chee-roo
fast	hayai *(adj)*	hah-yah-ee
• fast	hayaku *(adv)*	hah-yah-koo
flee	nigeru *(v)*	nee-geh-roo
fly	tobu *(v)*	toh-boo
follow	shitagau *(v)*	shtah-gah-oo
get up, rise	okiru *(v)*	oo-kee-roo
go	iku *(v)*	ee-koo
• go away	saru *(v)*	sah-roo
• go down, descend	sagaru *(vi)*	sah-gah-roo
	kudaru *(vt)*	koo-dah-roo
• go on foot	aruite iku *(v)*	ah-roo-ee-teh ee-koo
• go out, exit	deru *(v)*	deh-roo
• go up, climb	noboru *(vt)*	noh-boh-roo
hurry	isogu *(v)*	ee-soh-goo
jump	tobiagaru *(v)*	toh-bee-ah-gah-roo
leave, depart	shuppatsusuru *(v)*	shoop-pah-tsoo-soo-r
lie down	yokotawaru *(v)*	yoh-koh-tah-wah-ro
lift	mochiageru *(v)*	moh-chee-ah-geh-re
march	kōshinsuru *(v)*	koh-sheen-soo-roo
motion	ugoki	oo-goh-kee

move	ugoku *(vi)*	oo-goh-koo
	ugokasu *(vt)*	oo-goh-kah-soo
• movement	undō	oon-doh
pass by	tōrisugiru *(v)*	toh-ree-soo-gee-roo
pull	hipparu *(v)*	heep-pah-roo
put	oku *(v)*	oh-koo
• put down	oku *(v)*	oh-koo
quickly	hayaku *(adv)*	hah-yah-koo
reach	tassuru *(v)*	tahs-soo-roo
return	kaeru *(vi)*	kah-eh-roo
	kaesu *(vt)*	kah-eh-soo
run	hashiru *(v)*	hah-shee-roo
send	okuru *(v)*	oh-koo-roo
shake	yureru *(vi)*	yoo-reh-roo
sit down	suwaru *(v)*	soo-wah-roo
slide	suberu *(v)*	soo-beh-roo
slow	osoi *(adj)*	oh-soh-ee
• slowly	osoku *(adv)*	oh-soh-koo
stand	tachiagaru *(v)*	tah-chee-ah-gah-roo
stop	tomaru *(vi)*	toh-mah-roo
	tomeru *(vt)*	toh-meh-roo
turn	magaru *(v)*	mah-gah-roo
walk	aruku *(v)*	ah-roo-koo
• walk	sanpo	sahn-poh
• take a walk	sanpro ni iku *(v)*	sahn-poh nee ee-koo

4. TIME

a. GENERAL EXPRESSIONS OF TIME

	gogo	goh-goh
afternoon	gogo	goh-goh
• in the afternoon	gogo ni	goh-goh nee
• this afternoon	kyō no gogo	kyoh noh goh-goh
• tomorrow afternoon	ashita no gogo	ahsh-tah noh goh-goh
dawn	yoake	yoh-ah-keh
day	ichinichi	ee-chee-nee-chee
	hi	hee
• all day	ichinichijū	ee-chee-nee-chee-joo
evening	ban	bahn
• in the evening	ban ni	bahn nee
• this evening	konban	kohn-bahn
• tomorrow evening	ashita no ban	ahsh-tah noh bahn
midnight	mayonaka	mah-yoh-nah-kah
• at midnight	mayonaka ni	mah-yoh-nah-kah nee
morning	asa	ah-sah
• in the morning	gozenchū ni	goh-zehn-choo nee

• this morning	kesa	*keh-sah*
• tomorrow morning	ashita no asa	*ahsh-tah noh ah-sah*
night	yoru	*yoh-roo*
• at night	yoru ni	*yoh-roo nee*
• last night	yūbe	*yōo-beh*
• this night	konya	*kohn-yah*
• tomorrow night	ashita no yoru	*ahsh-tah noh yoh-roo*
• tonight	konban	*kohn-bahn*
noon	hiruma	*hee-roo-mah*
• at noon	shōgo ni	*shoh-goh nee*
sunrise	hinode	*hee-noh-deh*
sunset	hinoiri	*hee-noh-ee-ree*
time (in general)	jikan	*jee-kahn*
• time (hour)	ji	*jee*
• time (as in every time)	toki	*toh-kee*

Time is money.	**Toki wa kane nari.**	*toh-kee wah kah-neh nah-ree*
now and then	**tokidoki**	*toh-kee-doh-kee*

today	kyō	*kyōh*
tomorrow	ashita	*ahsh-tah*
• day after tomorrow	asatte	*ah-saht-teh*
yesterday	kinō	*kee-nōh*
• day before yesterday	ototoi	*oh-toh-toh-ee*
• yesterday afternoon	kinō no gogo	*kee-nōh noh goh-goh*
• yesterday morning	kinō no asa	*kee-nōh noh ah-sah*

b. TELLING TIME

What time is it?	Nanji desu ka.	*NAHN-jee dehs kah*
• It's 1:00.	Ichiji desu.	*ee-CHEE-jee dehs*
• It's 2:00.	Niji desu.	*nee-jee dehs*
• It's 3:00.	Sanji desu.	*SAHN-jee dehs*
• It's exactly 3:00.	Chōdo san ji desu.	*chōh-doh SAHN-jee dehs*
• It's 3:00 on the dot.	Sanji kikkari desu.	*SAHN-jee keek-kah-ree dehs*
• It's 1:10.	Ichiji juppun desu.	*ee-CHEE-jee joop-poon dehs*
• It's 4:25.	Yoji nijūgofun desu.	*yoh-jee nee-jōo-goh-foon dehs*

• It's 3:15.	Sanji jūgofun desu.	*SAHN-jee jōō-goh-foon dehs*
• It's 3:30.	Sanji han desu.	*SAHN-jee hahn dehs*
• It's 2:45.	Niji yonjūgofun desu.	*nee-jee yohn-jōō-goh-foon dehs*
	Sanji jūgofun mae desu.	*SAHN-jee jōō-goh-foon mah-eh dehs*
• It's 5:50.	Rokuji juppun mae desu.	*roh-koo-jee joop-poon mah-eh dehs*
• It's 5:00 A.M.	Gozen goji desu.	*goh-zehn goh-jee dehs*
• It's 5:00 P.M.	Gogo goji desu.	*goh-goh goh-jee dehs*
• It's 10:00 A.M.	Gozen jūji desu.	*goh-zehn jōō-jee dehs*
• It's 10:00 P.M.	Gogo jūji desu.	*goh-goh jōō-jee dehs*
At what time?	Nanji ni.	*NAHN-jee nee*
• At 1:00.	Ichiji ni.	*ee-CHEE-jee nee*
• At 2:00.	Niji ni.	*nee-jee nee*
• At 3:00.	Sanji ni.	*SAHN-jee nee*

c. UNITS OF TIME

century	seiki	*sēh-kee*
• a half century	hanseiki	*hahn-sēh-kee*
• a quarter century	shihanseiki	*shee-hahn-sēh-kee*
day	ichinichi	*ee-chee-nee-chee*
	hi	*hee*
• daily	mainichi no *(adj)*	*mah-ee-nee-chee noh*
decade	jūnenkan	*jōō-nehn-kahn*
hour	jikan	*jee-kahn*
• hourly	jikangoto no *(adj)*	*jee-kahn-goh-toh noh*
	jikangoto ni *(adv)*	*jee-kahn-goh-toh nee*
instant	shunji/shunkan	*shoon-jee/shoon-kahn*
minute	fun	*foon*
moment	shunkan	*shoon-kahn*
month	tsuki	*tskee*
• monthly	maitsuki no *(adj)*	*mah-ee-tskee noh*
second	byō	*byōh*
week	shū	*shōō*
• weekly	maishū no *(adj)*	*mah-ee-shōō noh*
year	toshi	*toh-shee*
• yearly, annually	maitoshi no *(adj)*	*mah-ee-toh-shee noh*
• the year two thousand	nisennen	*nee-sehn-nehn*

> It is common to divide a month into three periods. Also, the last days of each month and each year have special designation.

the first third of the month	jōjun	jōh-joon
the second third of the month	chūjun	choo-joon
the last third of the month	gejun	geh-joon
the last day of the month	misoka	mee-soh-kah
the last day of the year	ōmisoka	oh-mee-soh-kah

d. TIMEPIECES

alarm clock	mezamashi	meh-zah-mah-shee
clock	okidokei	oh-kee-doh-keh
dial	mojiban	moh-jee-bahn
digital watch/clock	dejitaru no tokei	DEH-jee-tah-roo noh toh-keh
grandfather clock	hakogata ōdokei	hah-koh-gah-tah oh-doh-keh
hand of a clock	tokei no hari	toh-keh noh hah-ree
hourglass	sunadokei	soo-nah-doh-keh
pocket watch	kaichūdokei	kah-ee-choo-doh-keh
stopwatch	sutoppuwotchi	soo-TOHP-poo-woht-chee
sundial	hidokei	hee-doh-keh
table clock	okidokei	oh-KEE-doh-keh
timer	taimā	TAH-ee-mah
wall clock	kakedokei	kah-KEH-doh-keh
watch	tokei	toh-keh
• The watch is fast.	Tokei ga, susumigachi desu.	toh-keh gah, soo-soo-mee-gah-chee dehs
• The watch is slow.	Tokei ga, okuregachi desu.	toh-keh gah, oh-koo-reh-gah-chee dehs
watchband	tokei no bando	toh-keh noh bahn-doh
watch battery	tokei no denchi	toh-keh no dehn-chee
wind	neji o maku (v)	neh-jee oh mah-koo
wristwatch	udedokei	oo-deh-doh-keh

e. CONCEPTS OF TIME

after	ato de (adv)	ah-toh deh
again	mata (adv)	mah-tah
ago	mae ni (adv)	mah-eh nee
almost always	daitai itsumo	dah-ee-tah-ee EE-tsoo-moh
almost never	hotondo ~nai (adv)	hoh-tohn-doh ~nah-ee
already	sude ni (adv)/mō (adv)	soo-deh nee/moh
always	itsumo (adv)	ee-tsoo-moh
as soon as	sugu ni (adv)	soo-goo nee

at the same time	dōji ni	*dōh-jee nee*
be about to, be on the point/verge of	~kaketeiru	*kah-keh-teh-ee-roo*
be on time	jikandōri ni	*jee-kahn-dōh-ree nee*
become	~ni naru (v)	*~nee nah-roo*
before	mae ni (adv)	*mah-eh nee*
begin	hajimaru (vi)	*hah-jee-mah-roo*
	hajimeru (vt)	*hah-jee-meh-roo*
• beginning	hajimari	*hah-jee-mah-ree*
brief	kantan na (adj)	*kahn-tahn nah*
• briefly	kantan ni (adv)	*kahn-tahn nee*
change	kawaru (vi)	*kah-wah-roo*
	kaeru (vt)	*kah-eh-roo*
continue	tsuzuku (vi)	*tsoo-zoo-koo*
	tsuzukeru (vt)	*tsoo-zoo-keh-roo*
• continually	tsuzukete (adv)	*tsoo-zoo-keh-teh*
during	aida ni (adv)	*ah-ee-dah nee*
early	hayai (adj)	*hah-yah-ee*
	hayaku (adv)	*hah-yah-koo*
end, finish	owaru (v)	*oh-wah-roo*
• end	owari	*oh-wah-ree*
every time	maikai	*mah-ee-kah-ee*
frequent	hinpan na (adj)	*heen-pahn nah*
• frequently	shibashiba	*shee-bah-shee-bah*
future	shōrai / mirai	*shoh-rah-ee/mee-rah-ee*
happen, occur	okoru (vi)	*oh-koh-roo*
in the meanwhile	sono kan ni	*soh-noh kahn nee*
in time	maniatte	*mah-nee-aht-teh*
just now	tatta ima	*taht-tah ee-mah*
last	tsuzuku (vi)	*tsoo-zoo-koo*
• last a long time	nagai aida tsuzuku	*nah-gah-ee ah-ee-dah tsoo-zoo-koo*
• last a short time	tankikan tsuzuku	*tahn-kee-kahn tsoo-zoo-koo*
last	saigo no (adj)	*sah-ee-goh noh*
	mae no (adj)	*mah-eh noh*
• last month	sengetsu	*sehn-geh-tsoo*
• last year	kyonen	*kyoh-nehn*
late	osoi (adj)	*oh-soh-ee*
	osoku (adv)	*oh-soh-koo*
• to be late	osokunaru	*oh-soh-koo-nah-roo*
long-term	chōkiteki na (adj)	*choh-kee-teh-kee nah*

Better late than never.	Shinai yori osoi hō ga mashi.	*shee-nah-ee yoh-ree oh-soh-ee hoh gah mah-shee*

look forward to	kitaisuru (v)	kee-tah-ee-soo-roo
never	kesshite ~nai (adv)	kehs-shteh ~nah-ee
• almost never	hotondo ~nai (adv)	hoh-toh-doh ~nah-ee
now	ima / genzai	ee-mah/gehn-zah-ee
• by now	imagoro wa	ee-mah-goh-roh wah
• for now	ima no tokoro	ee-mah noh toh-koh-roh
• from now on	korekara	koh-reh-kah-rah
nowadays	genzai dewa	gehn-zah-ee deh-wah
now and then	tokidoki (adv)	toh-kee-doh-kee
occasionally	tokidoki (adv)	toh-kee-doh-kee
often	yoku (adv)	yoh-koo
once	katsute (adv)	kah-tsoo-teh
• once in a while	tokidoki	toh-kee-doh-kee
• once upon a time	mukashimukashi	moo-kah-shee-moo-kah-shee
only	dake	dah-keh
past	kako	kah-koh
present	genzai	gehn-zah-ee
previous	mae no (adj)	mah-eh noh
• previously	mae ni (adv)	mah-eh nee
rare	mare na (adj)	mah-reh nah
• rarely	mare ni (adv)	mah-reh nee
recent	saikin no (adj)	sah-ee-keen noh
• recently	chikagoro (adv)	chee-kah-goh-roh
right away	sugu ni (adv)	soo-goo nee
schedule	yoteihyō / sukejūru	yoh-teh-hyoh/skeh-joo-roo
short-term	tanki no (adj)	tahn-kee noh
simultaneous	dōji no	doh-jee noh
• simultaneously	dōji ni	doh-jee nee
since	kara	kah-rah
• since Monday	getsuyōbi kara	gehts-yoh-bee kah-rah
• since yesterday	kinō kara	kee-noh kah-rah
slow	osoi (adj)	oh-soh-ee
• slowly	osoku (adv)	oh-soh-koo
soon	mōsugu (adv)	moh-soo-goo
• as soon as	sugu ni	soo-goo nee
• sooner or later	sonouchi	soh-noh-oo-chee
spend (time)	sugosu (v)	soo-goh-soo
sporadic	tokiori no (adj)	toh-kee-oh-ree noh
• sporadically	tokiori (adv)	toh-kee-oh-ree
still	mada (adv)	mah-dah
take place	okoru (vi)	oh-koh-roo
temporary	ichijiteki na (adj)	ee-chee-jee-teh-kee nah
• temporarily	ichijiteki ni (adv)	ee-chee-jee-teh-kee nee
then	sorekara (conj)	soh-reh-kah-rah
	sono toki	soh-noh toh-kee
timetable	jikokuhyō	jee-koh-koo-hyoh
to this day	konnichi made	kohn-nee-chee mah-deh

until	made *(adv)*	*mah-deh*
usually	itsumo wa *(adv)*	*ee-tsoo-moh wah*
wait	matsu *(v)*	*mah-tsoo*
when	itsu *(adv)*	*ee-tsoo*
while	no aida ni	*noh ah-ee-dah nee*
within	inai ni	*ee-nah-ee nee*
yet	mada *(adv)*	*mah-dah*

5. DAYS, MONTHS, AND SEASONS

a. DAYS OF THE WEEK

day of the week	yōbi	*yoh-bee*
• **Monday**	getsuyōbi	*geh-tsoo-yoh-bee*
• **Tuesday**	kayōbi	*kah-yoh-bee*
• **Wednesday**	suiyōbi	*soo-ee-yoh-bee*
• **Thursday**	mokuyōbi	*moh-koo-yoh-bee*
• **Friday**	kinyōbi	*keen-yoh-bee*
• **Saturday**	doyōbi	*doh-yoh-bee*
• **Sunday**	nichiyōbi	*nee-chee-yoh-bee*
• **on Mondays**	getsuyōbi ni	*geh-tsoo-yoh-bee nee*
• **on Saturdays**	doyōbi ni	*doh-yoh-bee nee*
• **on Sundays**	nichiyōbi ni	*nee-chee-yoh-bee nee*
holiday	kyūjitsu	*kyoo-jee-tsoo*
weekend	shūmatsu	*shoo-mah-tsoo*

a weekend carpenter (*lit.* a Sunday carpenter)	**nichiyō daiku**	*nee-chee-yoh dah-ee-koo*

What day is it?	Kyō wa naní yōbi desu ka.	*kyoh wah nah-nee yoh-bee dehs kah*
workday	heijitsu	*heh-jee-tsoo*

b. MONTHS OF THE YEAR

month of the year	ichinen no tsuki	*ee-chee-nehn noh tskee*
• **January**	ichigatsu	*ee-chee-gah-tsoo*
• **February**	nigatsu	*nee-gah-tsoo*
• **March**	sangatsu	*sahn-gah-tsoo*
• **April**	shigatsu	*shee-gah-tsoo*
• **May**	gogatsu	*goh-gah-tsoo*
• **June**	rokugatsu	*roh-koo-gah-tsoo*
• **July**	shichigatsu	*shee-chee-gah-tsoo*
• **August**	hachigatsu	*hah-chee-gah-tsoo*
• **September**	kugatsu	*koo-gah-tsoo*
• **October**	jūgatsu	*joo-gah-tsoo*

• November	jūichigatsu	*jōo-ee-chee-gah-tsoo*
• December	jūnigatsu	*jōo-nee-gah-tsoo*
calendar	karendā	*kah-rehn-dāh*
leap year	uruudoshi	*oo-roo-oo-doh-shee*
month	tsuki	*tskee*
• monthly	maitsuki no *(adj)*	*mah-ee-tskee noh*
school year	gakunen	*gah-koo-nehn*
What month is it?	Nangatsu desu ka.	*NAHN-gah-tsoo dehs kah*

c. SEASONS

season	kisetsu	*kee-seh-tsoo*
• spring	haru	*hah-roo*
• summer	natsu	*nah-tsoo*
• fall	aki	*ah-kee*
• winter	fuyu	*foo-yoo*
equinox	bunten	*boon-tehn*
• autumnal equinox	shū bun	*shōo-boon*
• vernal equinox	shunbun	*shoon-boon*
moon	tsuki	*tskee*
solstice	shiten	*shee-tehn*
• summer solstice	geshi	*geh-shee*
• winter solstice	tōji	*toh-jee*
sun	taiyō	*tah-ee-yōh*

FOCUS: The Seasons

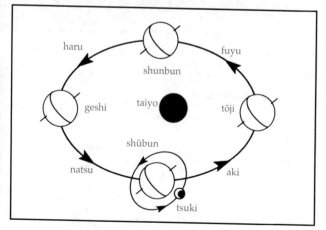

| to be as different as chalk from cheese (*lit.* the moon and a terrapin) | tsuki to suppon | *tskee toh soop-pohn* |

d. THE ZODIAC

horoscope	hoshiuranai	*hoh-shee-oo-rah-nah-ee*
zodiac	jūnikyūzu	*j$\overline{oo}$-nee-ky$\overline{oo}$-zoo*
• **signs of the zodiac**	jūnikyūzu no sain	*j$\overline{oo}$-nee-ky$\overline{oo}$-zoo noh sah-een*
• **Aries**	ohitsujiza	*oh-hee-tsoo-jee-zah*
• **Taurus**	oushiza	*oh-oo-shee-zah*
• **Gemini**	futagoza	*foo-tah-goh-zah*
• **Cancer**	kaniza	*kah-nee-zah*
• **Leo**	shishiza	*shee-shee-zah*
• **Virgo**	otomeza	*oh-toh-meh-zah*
• **Libra**	tenbinza	*tehn-been-zah*
• **Scorpio**	sasoriza	*sah-soh-ree-zah*
• **Sagittarius**	iteza	*ee-teh-zah*
• **Capricorn**	yagiza	*yah-gee-zah*
• **Aquarius**	mizugameza	*mee-zoo-gah-meh-zah*
• **Pisces**	uoza	*oo-oh-zah*

e. THE TRADITIONAL TWELVE-ANIMAL CALENDAR

Year of the Rat	nezumidoshi	*neh-zoo-mee-doh-shee*
Year of the Ox	ushidoshi	*oo-shee-doh-shee*
Year of the Tiger	toradoshi	*toh-rah-doh-shee*
Year of the Hare	udoshi	*oo-doh-shee*
Year of the Dragon	tatsudoshi	*tah-tsoo-doh-shee*
Year of the Serpent	midoshi	*mee-doh-shee*
Year of the Horse	umadoshi	*oo-mah-doh-shee*
Year of the Sheep	hitsujidoshi	*hee-tsoo-jee-doh-shee*
Year of the Monkey	sarudoshi	*sah-roo-doh-shee*
Year of the Cock	toridoshi	*toh-ree-doh-shee*
Year of the Dog	inudoshi	*ee-noo-doh-shee*
Year of the Boar	idoshi	*ee-doh-shee*

f. EXPRESSING THE DATE

What's today's date?	Kyō wa nannichi desu ka.	*kyoh wah NAHN-nee-chee dehs kah*
• **It's October first.**	Jūgatsu tsuitachi desu.	*j$\overline{oo}$-gah-tsoo tsoo-ee-tah-chee dehs*

• It's January second.	Ichigatsu futsuka desu.	*ee-chee-gah-tsoo foo-tsoo-kah dehs*
• It's May third.	Gogatsu mikka desu.	*goh-gah-tsoo meek-kah dehs*
What year is it?	Kotoshi wa nannen desu ka.	*koh-toh-shee wah NAHN-nehn dehs kah*
It's 2008.	Nisen hachi nen desu.	*nee-sehn hah-CHEE nehn dehs*
When were you born?	Itsu umaremashita ka.	*EE-tsoo oo-mah-reh-mahsh-tah kah*
• I was born in 19...	Sen kyūhyaku ... nen ni umaremashita.	*sehn kyōō-hyahk ... nehn nee oo-mah-reh-mahsh-tah*

g. IMPORTANT DATES

(*indicates a national holiday.)

the New Year	shinnen	*sheen-nehn*
New Year's Day (January 1)*	ganjitsu	*gahn-jee-tsoo*
New Year's Eve	ōmisoka no ban	*ōh-mee-soh-kah noh bahn*
the first government business day (January 4)	goyō hajime	*goh-yōh hah-jee-meh*
Adulthood Day (second Monday in January)*	seijin no hi	*sēh-jeen noh hee*
National Foundation Day (February 11)*	kenkoku kinenbi	*kehn-kohk kee-nehn-bee*
Vernal Equinox Day (March 20 or 21)*	shunbun no hi	*shoon-boon noh hee*
Showa Day (April 29)*	shōwa no hi	*shōh-wah noh hee*
Constitution Day (May 3)*	kenpō kinenbi	*kehn-pōh kee-nehn-bee*
Greenery Day (May 4)*	midori no hi	*mee-doh-ree noh hee*
Children's Day (May 5)*	kodomo no hi	*koh-doh-moh noh hee*
Marine Day (third Monday in July)*	umi no hi	*OO-mee noh hee*
Bon Festival (August 12 ~ 16)	obon	*oh-bohn*
Respect for the Aged Day (third Monday in September)*	keirō no hi	*kēh-rōh noh hee*
Autumnal Equinox Day (September 23 or 24)*	shūbun no hi	*shōō-boon noh hee*

Health-Sports Day (second Monday in October)*	taiiku no hi	tah-ee-ee-koo noh hee
Culture Day (November 3)*	bunka no hi	boon-kah noh hee
Labor Thanksgiving Day (November 23)*	kinrō kansha no hi	keen-roh kahn-shah noh hee
Emperor's Birthday (December 23)*	tennō tanjōbi	tehn-noh tahn-joh-bee
the last government business day (December 28)	goyō osame	goh-yoh oh-sah-meh

6. TALKING ABOUT THE WEATHER

a. GENERAL WEATHER VOCABULARY

air	kūki	koo-kee
atmosphere	taiki	tah-ee-kee
• atmospheric conditions	kiatsu	kee-ah-tsoo
awful	hidoi (adj)	hee-doh-ee
• awful weather	hidoi tenki	hee-doh-ee tehn-kee
beautiful	subarashii (adj)	soo-bah-rah-shee
• beautiful weather	subarashii tenki	soo-bah-rah-shee tehn-kee
clear	harewatatta (adj)	hah-reh-wah-taht-tah
• The sky is clear.	Kaisei desu.	kah-ee-seh dehs
climate	kikō	kee-koh
• continental	tairikusei no (adj)	tah-ee-ree-koo-seh noh
• dry	kansōshita (adj)	kahn-soh-shtah
• humid	shikke ga takai (adj)	sheek-keh gah tah-kah-ee
• tropical	nettaisei no (adj)	neht-tah-ee-seh noh
cloud	kumo	koo-moh

| to sit on the fence (*lit.* watch the direction of the cloud moving) | kumoyuki o miru | koo-moh-yoo-kee oh mee-roo |

• cloudy	kumotta (adj)	koo-moht-tah
cold	samui (adj)	sah-moo-ee
• I am cold.	Samui desu.	sah-moo-ee dehs
cool	suzushii (adj)	soo-zoo-shee
damp	jimejime shita (adj)	jee-meh-jee-meh shtah
dark	kurai (adj)	koo-rah-ee
• It's dark already.	Mō kurai desu.	moh koo-rah-ee dehs

dew	tsuyu	TSOO-yoo
drizzle	kirisame	kee-ree-sah-meh
dry	kansō shita (adj)	kahn-soh shtah
El Niño	eru nīnyo	eh-roo-NEE-nyoh
fine	ii (adj)	ee
• It's fine.	Ii tenki desu.	ee tehn-kee dehs
fog	kiri	kee-ree
• foggy	kiri noh (adj)	kee-ree noh
foul	warui (adj)	wah-roo-ee
• foul weather	akutenkō	ah-koo-tehn-koh
freeze	kōru (vi)	koh-roo
• below freezing	hyōtenka no (adj)	hyoh-tehn-kah noh
• freezing point	hyōten	hyoh-tehn
• freezing rain	hisame	hee-sah-meh
• frozen	kootta (adj)	koh-oht-tah
front	zensen	zehn-sehn
• cold front	kanrei zensen	kahn-reh zehn-sehn
• stationary front	teitai zensen	teh-tah-ee zehn-sehn
• warm front	ondan zensen	ohn-dahn zehn-sehn
frost	shimo	shee-moh
hail	arare	ah-rah-reh
• hail	arare ga furu (vi)	ah-rah-reh gah foo-roo
heat	nekki	nehk-kee
• heat wave	neppa	nehp-pah
high (atmospheric) pressure	kōkiatsu	koh-kee-ah-tsoo
hot	atsui (adj)	ah-tsoo-ee
• hot and humid	mushiatsui (adj)	moo-shee-ah-tsoo-ee
How's the weather?	Donna tenki desu ka.	DOHN-nah tehn-kee dehs kah
• It's a bit cold.	Chotto samui desu.	choht-toh sah-moo-ee dehs
• It's a bit hot.	Chotto atsui desu.	choht-toh ah-tsoo-ee dehs
• It's awful.	Hidoi tenki desu.	hee-doh-ee tehn-kee dehs
• It's beautiful.	Subarashii tenki desu.	sbah-rah-shee tehn-kee dehs
• It's cloudy.	Kumori desu.	koo-moh-ree dehs
• It's cold.	Samui desu.	sah-moo-ee dehs
• It's fine.	Ii tenki desu.	ee tehn-kee dehs
• It's foul.	Warui tenki desu.	wah-roo-ee tehn-kee dehs
• It's hot.	Atsui desu.	ah-tsoo-ee dehs
• It's humid.	Shikke ga takai desu.	sheek-keh gah tah-kah-ee dehs
• It's mild.	Atatakai desu.	ah-tah-tah-kah-ee dehs
• It's muggy.	Mushiatsui desu.	moo-shee-ah-tsoo-ee dehs
• It's pleasant.	Kaiteki desu.	kah-ee-teh-kee dehs
• It's raining.	Ame ga futte imasu.	ah-meh gah foot-teh ee-mahs

• It's snowing.	Yuki ga futte imasu.	yoo-kee gah foot-teh ee-mahs
• It's sunny.	Hi ga tette imasu.	hee gah teht-teh ee-mahs
• It's thundering.	Kaminari ga natte imasu.	kah-mee-nah-ree gah naht-teh ee-mahs
• It's very cold.	Totemo samui desu.	toht-teh-moh sah-moo-ee dehs
• It's very hot.	Totemo atsui desu.	toht-teh-moh ah-tsoo-ee dehs
• It's windy.	Kaze ga tsuyoi desu.	kah-zeh gah tsoo-yoh-ee dehs
• There's lightning.	Inazuma ga hikatte imasu.	ee-nah-zoo-mah gah hee-kaht-teh ee-mahs
humid	shikke ga takai (adj)	sheek-keh gah tah-kah-ee
humidity	shikke	sheek-keh
hurricane	harikēn	hah-ree-kehn
ice	kōri	koh-ree
• icy	kōri ga hatta (adj)	koh-ree gah haht-tah
jet-stream	jetto kiryū / henseifū	jeht-toh kee-ryoo/hehn-seh-foo
La Niña	ranīnya	rah-nee-nyah
low (atmospheric) pressure	teikiaitsu	teh-kee-ah-tsoo
light	akari	ah-kah-ree
lightning	inazuma	ee-nah-zoo-mah
• flash/bolt of lightning	inazuma no hikari	ee-nah-zoo-mah noh hee-kah-ree
melt	tokeru (v)	toh-keh-roo
mild	atatakai (adj)	ah-tah-tah-kah-ee
mist	kasumi	kah-soo-mee
moon	tsuki	tskee
muggy	mushiatsui (adj)	moo-shee-ah-tsoo-ee
rain	ame	ah-meh
• acid rain	sanseiu	sahn-seh-oo
• heavy rain	ōame	oh-ah-meh
• icy rain	hisame	hee-sah-meh
• light rain	kosame	koh-sah-meh
• pouring rain	doshaburi	doh-shah-boo-ree
• torrential rain	gōu	goh-oo
• rain	ame ga furu (v)	ah-meh gah foo-roo
• rainy season	tsuyu	tsoo-yoo
• It's rainy.	Ame ga futte imasu.	ah-meh gah foot-teh ee-mahs
sea	umi	oo-mee
shadow/shade	kage	kah-geh
shower	niwakaame	nee-wah-kah-AH-meh
sky	sora	soh-rah
sleet	mizore	mee-zoh-reh

snow	yuki	*yoo-kee*
• snow	yuki ga furu *(v)*	*yoo-kee gah foo-roo*
• snow accumulation	sekisetsu	*seh-kee-seh-tsoo*
• snowfall	kōsetsu	*koh-seh-tsoo*
• snowflake	seppen	*sehp-pehn*
• snowstorm	fubuki	*foo-boo-kee*
star	hoshi	*hoh-shee*
storm	bōfūu	*boh-fōo-oo*
• stormy	arashi no *(adj)*	*ah-rah-shee noh*
sun	taiyō	*tah-ee-yoh*
• sunny	jōtenki no *(adj)*	*joh-tehn-kee noh*
thunder	kaminari	*kah-mee-nah-ree*
• clap of thunder	raimei	*rah-ee-meh*
• thunder	kaminari ga naru *(v)*	*kah-mee-nah-ree gah nah-roo*
• thunderstorm	raiu	*rah-ee-oo*

to scold someone severely (*lit.* drop thunder on someone)	kaminari o otosu	*kah-mee-nah-ree oh oh-toh-soo*

tornado	tatsumaki	*tah-tsoo-mah-kee*
typhoon	taifū	*tah-ee-fōo*
weather	tenki	*tehn-kee*
• bad weather	warui tenki	*wah-roo-ee tehn-kee*
• good weather	ii tenki	*ēe tehn-kee*
• The weather is beautiful.	Subarashii tenki desu.	*soo-bah-rah-shēe tehn-kee dehs*

a fickle person (*lit.* a weather-like person)	otenkija	*oh-ten-kee-yah*
weather permitting (*lit.* if the weather is good)	tenki ga yokereba	*tehn-kee gah yoh-keh-reh-bah*

wet	nureta *(adj)* / shimetta *(adj)*	*noo-reh-tah/shee-meht-tah*
wind	kaze	*kah-zeh*
• be windy	kaze ga tsuyoi	*kah-zeh gah tsoo-yoh-ee*
• wind velocity	fūryoku	*fōo-ryoh-koo*

b. REACTING TO THE WEATHER

cold	samui (adj)	sah-moo-ee
• I am cold.	Samui desu.	sah-moo-ee dehs
have chills	samuke ga suru	sah-moo-keh gah soo-roo
• I have chills.	Samuke ga shimasu.	sah-moo-keh gah shee-mahs
hot	atsui (adj)	ah-tsoo-ee
• I am hot.	Atsui desu.	ah-tsoo-ee dehs
I can't stand the cold.	Samusa ni yowai desu.	sah-moo-sah nee yoh-wah-ee dehs
I can't stand the heat.	Atsusa ni yowai desu.	AH-tsoo-sah nee yoh-wah-ee dehs
I love the cold.	Samui no ga suki desu.	sah-moo-ee noh gah skee dehs
I love the heat.	Atsui no ga suki desu.	ah-tsoo-ee noh gah skee dehs
perspire	ase o kaku (v)	ah-seh oh kah-koo
warm up	atatakakunaru (v)	ah-tah-tah-kah-koo-nah-roo

c. WEATHER-MEASURING INSTRUMENTS AND ACTIVITIES

barometer	kiatsukei	kee-ahts-keh
• barometric pressure	kiatsu	kee-ahts
Celsius	sesshi	sehs-shee
centigrade	sesshi	sehs-shee
degree	do	doh
Fahrenheit	kashi	kah-shee
minus	mainasu	mah-ee-nahs
plus	purasu	poo-rahs
temperature	kion	kee-ohn
• high	takai (adj)	tah-kah-ee
• low	hikui (adj)	hee-koo-ee
• maximum	saiko (no) (adj)	sah-ee-koh (noh)
• minimum	saitei (no) (adj)	sah-ee-teh (noh)
thermometer	ondokei	ohn-doh-keh
• boiling point	futtōten	foot-toh-tehn
• freezing point	hyōten	hyoh-tehn
• melting point	yūten	yoo-tehn
thermostat	jidō chōon sōchi	jee-doh choh-ohn soh-chee
weather forecast	tenki yohō	tehn-kee yoh-hoh
weather forecaster (radio, TV)	tenki yohō gakari	tehn-kee yoh-hoh gah-kah-ree
zero	reido/hyōten	reh-doh/hyoh-tehn
• above zero	reido ijō no	reh-doh ee-joh noh
• below zero	hyotenka	hyoh-tehn-kah

• Chinese character	kanji	*kahn-jee*
• Japanese character	kana	*kah-nah*
• phonetic character in words of Japanese origin	hiragana	*hee-rah-gah-nah*
• phonetic character in words of foreign origin	katakana	*kah-tah-kah-nah*
clause	setsu	*seh-tsoo*
• main	shu *(adj)*	*shoo*
• relative	kankei *(adj)*	*kahn-keh*
• subordinate	jūzoku *(adj)*	*jōō-zoh-koo*
comparison	hikaku	*hee-kah-koo*
conjunction	setsuzokushi	*sehts-zohk-shee*
counter	mono o kazoeru kotoba	*moh-noh oh kah-zoh-eh roo koh-toh-bah*
discourse	wahō	*wah-hoh*
• direct	chokusetsu *(adj)*	*chohk-seh-tsoo*
• indirect	kansetsu *(adj)*	*kahn-seh-tsoo*
gender	sei	*seh*
• masculine	dansei	*dahn-seh*
• feminine	josei	*joh-seh*
• neuter	chūsei	*chōō-seh*
grammar	bunpō	*boon-poh*
interrogative	gimonshi	*gee-mohn-shee*
mood	dōshi no hō	*doh-shee noh hoh*
• conditional mood	jōkenhō	*joh-kehn-hoh*
• imperative mood	meireihō	*meh-reh-hoh*
• indicative mood	chokusetsuhō	*chohk-sehts-hoh*
• subjunctive mood	kateihō	*kah-teh-hoh*
noun	meishi	*meh-shee*
number	kazu	*kah-zoo*
• plural number	fukusū	*fkoo-sōō*
• singular number	tansū	*tahn-sōō*
object	mokutekigo	*mohk-teh-kee-goh*
• direct	chokusetsu *(adj)*	*chohk-seh-tsoo*
• indirect	kansetsu *(adj)*	*kahn-seh-tsoo*
participle	bunshi	*boon-shee*
• past	kako *(adj)*	*kah-koh*
• present	genzai *(adj)*	*gehn-zah-ee*
particle	joshi	*joh-shee*
person	ninshō	*neen-shoh*
• first person	ichininshō	*ee-chee-neen-shoh*
• second person	nininshō	*nee-neen-shoh*
• third person	sanninshō	*sahn-neen-shoh*
predicate	jutsubu	*joo-tsoo-boo*
preposition	zenchishi	*zehn-chee-shee*
pronoun	daimeishi	*dah-ee-meh-shee*

• demonstrative	shiji *(adj)*	*shee-jee*
• indefinite	futei *(adj)*	*foo-teh*
• interrogative	gimon *(adj)*	*gee-mohn*
• personal	ninshō *(adj)*	*neen-shoh*
• possessive	shoyū *(adj)*	*shoh-yoo*
• reflexive	saiki *(adj)*	*sah-ee-kee*
• relative	kankei *(adj)*	*kahn-keh*
sentence	bun	*boon*
• affirmative	kōtei *(adj)*	*koh-teh*
• declarative	heijo *(adj)*	*heh-joh*
• interrogative	gimon *(adj)*	*gee-mohn*
• negative	hitei *(adj)*	*hee-teh*
subject	shugo	*shoo-goh*
tense	jisei	*jee-seh*
• future	miraikei	*mee-rah-ee-keh*
• past	kakokei	*kah-koh-keh*
• past perfect	kakokanryōkei	*kah-koh-kahn-ryoh-keh*
• past progressive	kakoshinkōkei	*kah-koh-sheen-koh-keh*
• present	genzaikei	*gehn-zah-ee-keh*
• present perfect	genzaikanryōkei	*gehn-zah-ee-kahn-ryoh-keh*
• present progressive	genzaishinkōkei	*gehn-zah-ee-sheen-koh-keh*
verb	dōshi	*doh-shee*
• active	nōdōtai no *(adj)*	*noh-doh-tah-ee noh*
• conjugation	dōshi no katsuyō	*doh-shee noh kah-tsoo-yoh*
• gerund	dōmeishi	*doh-meh-shee*
• infinitive	futeishi	*fteh-shee*
• intransitive verb	jidōshi	*jee-doh-shee*
• irregular verb	fukisokudōshi	*fkee-sohk-doh-shee*
• modal	johō no *(adj)*	*joh-hoh noh*
• passive	ukemi no *(adj)*	*oo-keh-mee noh*
• reflexive verb	saikidōshi	*sah-ee-kee-doh-shee*
• regular verb	kisokudōshi	*kee-soh-koo-doh-shee*
• transitive verb	tadōshi	*tah-doh-shee*

b. DEMONSTRATIVE ADJECTIVES

this	kono	*koh-noh*
these	korera no	*koh-reh-rah noh*
that	sono	*soh-noh*
those	sorera no	*soh-reh-rah noh*
that (over there)	ano	*ah-noh*
those (over there)	arera no	*ah-reh-rah noh*

c. PERSONAL PRONOUNS: SUBJECT

I	watakushi ga/wa	*wah-tahk-shee gah/wah*
you	anata ga/wa	*ah-nah-tah gah/wah*
he	kare ga/wa	*kah-reh gah/wah*

she	kanojo ga/wa	*kah-noh-joh gah/wah*
we	watakushitachi ga/wa	*wah-tahk-shee-tah-chee gah/wah*
you	anatatachi ga/wa	*ah-nah-tah-tah-chee gah/wah*
they (all male, or male and female)	karera ga/wa	*kah-reh-rah gah/wah*
they (all female)	kanojotachi ga/wa	*kah-noh-joh-tah-chee gah/wah*

d. PERSONAL PRONOUNS: POSSESSIVE

my, mine	watakushi no	*wah-tahk-shee noh*
your, yours	anata no	*ah-nah-tah noh*
his	kare no	*kah-reh noh*
her, hers	kanojo no	*kah-noh-joh noh*
our, ours	watakushitachi no	*wah-tahk-shee-tah-chee noh*
your, yours	anatatachi no	*ah-nah-tah-tah-chee noh*
their, theirs (all male, or male and female)	karera no	*kah-reh-rah noh*
their, theirs (all female)	kanojotachi no	*kah-noh-joh-tah-chee noh*

e. PERSONAL PRONOUNS: DIRECT OBJECT

me	watakushi o	*wah-tahk-shee oh*
you	anata o	*ah-nah-tah oh*
him	kare o	*kah-reh oh*
her	kanojo o	*kah-noh-joh oh*
us	watakushitachi o	*wah-tahk-shee-tah-chee oh*
you	anatatachi o	*ah-nah-tah-tah-chee oh*
them (all male, or male and female)	karera o	*kah-reh-rah oh*
them (all female)	kanojotachi o	*kah-noh-joh-tah-chee oh*

f. PERSONAL PRONOUNS: INDIRECT OBJECT

(to) me	watakushi ni	*wah-tahk-shee nee*
(to) you	anata ni	*ah-nah-tah nee*
(to) him	kare ni	*kah-reh nee*
(to) her	kanojo ni	*kah-noh-joh nee*
(to) us	watakushitachi ni	*wah-tahk-shee-tah-chee nee*
(to) you	anatatachi ni	*ah-nah-tah-tah-chee nee*
(to) them (all male, or male and female)	karera ni	*kah-reh-rah nee*
(to) them (all female)	kanojotachi ni	*kah-noh-joh-tah-chee nee*

g. REFLEXIVE PRONOUNS

myself	watakushi jishin	*wah-tahk-shee jee-sheen*
yourself	anata jishin	*ah-nah-tah jee-sheen*
himself	kare jishin	*kah-reh jee-sheen*
herself	kanojo jishin	*kah-noh-joh jee-sheen*
ourselves	watakushitachi jishin	*wah-tahk-shee-tah-chee jee-sheen*
yourselves	anatatachi jishin	*ah-nah-tah-tah-chee jee-sheen*
themselves (all male, or male and female)	karera jishin	*kah-reh-rah jee-sheen*
themselves (all female)	kanojotachi jishin	*kah-noh-joh-tah-chee jee-sheen*

> The Japanese expression jibun de can be considered an all-purpose reflexive pronoun:
>
> | | | |
> |---|---|---|
> | **one's self** | jibun | *jee-boon* |
> | **by one's self** | jibun de | *jee-boon deh* |
>
> | | |
> |---|---|
> | I'm going myself. | Watakushi wa, jibun de ikimasu. |
> | She's doing it herself. | Kanojo wa, jibun de shite imasu. |
> | Can you do it yourself? | Jibun de dekimasu ka. |

h. INTERROGATIVE PRONOUNS

who	dare ga	*dah-reh gah*
what	nani ga / no / ni	*nah-nee gah/noh/nee*
whom	dare o	*dah-reh oh*
to whom	dare ni	*dah-reh nee*
whose	dare no	*dah-reh noh*
which	dore ga / dono / dore o	*doh-reh gah/doh-noh/doh-reh oh*

i. OTHER PRONOUNS

all	zenbu	*zehn-boo*
everyone	daremo	*dah-reh-moh*
everything	nandemo mina	*nahn-deh-moh mee-nah*
nobody	daremo ~nai	*dah-reh-moh ~nah-ee*
no one	daremo ~nai	*dah-reh-moh ~nah-ee*
none	daremo ~nai	*dah-reh-moh ~nah-ee*
nothing	nanimo ~nai	*nah-nee-moh ~nah-ee*
one	hito	*hee-toh*
others	hoka no hito	*hoh-kah noh hee-toh*

some (*people*)	aru hito	*ah-roo hee-toh*
someone	dareka	*dah-reh-kah*
something	nanika	*nah-nee-kah*

j. PARTICLES

> Japanese contains many particles—short words which are often called postpositions because they come after other words. These particles help to identify the relationship of the words they follow to other important parts of the sentence.
>
> Some particles (such as the following) function as *markers* to identify grammatical elements, while others convey meaning.
>
> | wa/ga | Subject markers. They occur with words that translate the English subject. More accurately, **wa** is a topic marker, and **ga** is the grammatical subject marker. Sometimes a sentence can have both. |
> | o | Direct object marker. Sometimes, for emphasis, **ga** has this function. |
> | ni | Indirect object marker |
> | no | Possessive marker |
> | ka | Question marker |

and (*between nouns*)	to	*toh*
at	ni/de	*nee/deh*
by	de	*deh*
by means of	de	*deh*
(direct object marker)	o	*oh*
from	kara	*kah-rah*
in	ni/de	*nee/deh*
(indirect object marker)	ni	*nee*
of, ~ 's	no	*noh*
on	ni/de	*nee/deh*
(possessive marker)	no	*noh*
(question marker)	ka	*kah*
(subject marker)	ga/wa	*gah/wah*
(topic marker)	wa	*wah*
to	e/ni/made	*eh/nee/mah-deh*
until	made	*mah-deh*
with	to/de	*toh/deh*

k. CONJUNCTIONS

also	soshite/mata	*sohsh-teh/mah-tah*
and (at the beginning of a sentence)	soshite	*sohsh-teh*
because	nazenara	*nah-zeh-nah-rah*

but	dakedo	*dah-keh-doh*
	demo	*deh-moh*
	keredomo	*keh-reh-doh-moh*
	shikashi	*shee-kah-shee*
furthermore	sarani	*sah-rah-nee*
	sonoue	*soh-noh-oo-eh*
however	keredomo	*keh-reh-doh-moh*
	shikashi	*shkah-shee*
	tokoroga	*toh-koh-roh-gah*
moreover	shikamo	*shee-kah-moh*
or	aruiwa	*ah-roo-ee-wah*
	matawa	*mah-tah-wah*
	soretomo	*soh-reh-toh-moh*
so, therefore	sorede	*soh-reh-deh*
	shitagatte	*shtah-gaht-teh*
then	sorekara	*soh-reh-kah-rah*
	suruto	*soo-roo-toh*
thus	sorede	*soh-reh-deh*

9. REQUESTING INFORMATION

answer	kotae	*koh-tah-eh*
• answer	kotaeru *(v)*	*koh-tah-eh-roo*
ask someone	dareka ni kiku	*dah-reh-kah nee kee-koo*
ask for	tanomu *(v)*	*tah-noh-moo*
• ask for something	nanika o tanomu	*nah-nee-kah oh tah-noh-moo*
Can you tell me ...?	...o, oshiete moraemasu ka.	*...oh, oh-shee-eh-teh moh-rah-eh-mahs kah*
How?	Do yatte. *(inf)*	*doh yaht-teh*
How come?	Naze.	*nah-zeh*
How do you say that in Japanese?	Nihongo de, sore o nan to iimasu ka.	*nee-hohn-goh deh, soh-reh oh NAHN toh ee-mahs kah*
How much?	Dono kurai desu ka.	*doh-noh koo-rah-ee dehs kah*
How much? (money)	Ikura desu ka.	*EE-koo-rah dehs kah*
I don't understand.	Wakarimasen.	*wah-kah-ree-mah-sehn*
So?	Sorede.	*soh-reh-DEH*
What?	Nani. *(inf)*	*NAH-nee*
What does it mean?	Sore wa, donna imi desu ka.	*soh-reh wah, DOHN-nah ee-mee dehs kah*
When?	Itsu. *(inf)*	*EE-tsoo*
Where?	Doko. *(inf)*	*DOH-koh*
Which (*one*)?	Dore. *(inf)*	*DOH-reh*
Who?	Dare. *(inf)*	*DAH-reh*
Why?	Naze. *(inf)*	*NAH-zeh*

PEOPLE

10. FAMILY AND FRIENDS

a. FAMILY MEMBERS

> Japanese has two sets of words for family members.
>
> One set is used as follows:
> - talking *about* members of your own family *to* someone outside the family
>
> Another set is used as follows:
> - talking *to* members of your own family
> - talking *about* members of someone else's family
>
> The two sets are given below.

Talking About One's Own Family to Others

aunt	oba	*oh-bah*
brothers	kyōdai	*kyoh-dah-ee*
brothers and sisters (*pl*)	kyōdai to shimai	*kyoh-dah-ee toh shee-mah-ee*
• brother-in-law (spouse's elder brother, or elder sister's husband)	gikei	*gee-keh*
• brother-in-law (spouse's younger brother, or younger sister's husband)	gitei	*gee-teh*
• elder brother	ani	*AH-nee*
• younger brother	otōto	*oh-toh-toh*
cousin	itoko	*ee-toh-koh*
daughter	musume	*moo-soo-meh*
• daughter-in-law	musuko no yome	*moos-koh noh yoh-meh*
family	kazoku	*kah-zoh-koo*
• family relationship	kazoku kankei	*kah-zoh-koo kahn-keh*
father	chichi	*chee-chee*
• father-in-law	gifu	*GEE-foo*
grandchildren	mago	*mah-goh*

grandfather	sofu	*SOH-foo*
grandmother	sobo	*SOH-boh*
husband	otto	*oht-toh*
mother	haha	*hah-hah*
• mother-in-law	gibo	*GEE-boh*
nephew	oi	*oh-ee*
niece	mei	*meh-ee*
parent	oya	*oh-yah*
parents	ryōshin	*ryoh-sheen*
relatives	shinseki	*sheen-seh-kee*
sisters	shimai	*shee-mah-ee*
• sister-in-law (spouse's elder sister, or elder brother's wife)	giri no ane	*gee-ree noh ah-neh*
• sister-in-law (spouse's younger sister, or younger brother's wife)	giri no imōto	*gee-ree noh ee-moh-toh*
• elder sister	ane	*ah-neh*
• younger sister	imoto	*ee-moh-toh*
son	musuko	*moos-koh*
• son-in-law	musume no otto	*moo-soo-meh noh oht-toh*
twin	futago	*ftah-goh*
uncle	oji	*oh-jee*
wife	tsuma	*tsoo-mah*

Talking to One's Own Family or About Someone Else's Family

aunt	obasan	*oh-bah-sahn*
brothers	gokyōdai	*goh-kyoh-dah-ee*
brothers and sisters (*pl*)	gokyōdai to goshimai	*goh-kyoh-dah-ee toh goh-shee-mah-ee*
• brother-in-law (spouse's elder brother, or elder sister's husband)	giri no oniisan	*gee-ree noh oh-nee-sahn*
• brother-in-law (spouse's younger brother, or younger sister's husband)	giri no otōtosan	*gee-ree noh oh-toh-toh-sahn*
• elder brother	oniisan	*oh-nee-sahn*
• younger brother	otōtosan	*oh-toh-toh-sahn*
cousin	itokosan	*ee-toh-koh-sahn*
daughter	ojōsan	*oh-joh-sahn*
• daughter-in-law	musukosan no oyomesan	*moos-koh-sahn noh oh-yoh-meh-sahn*

family	gokazoku	*goh-kah-zoh-koo*
family relationship	gokazoku kankei	*goh-kah-zoh-koo kahn-keh*
father	otōsan	*on-toh-sahn*
• father-in-law	giri no otōsan	*gee-ree noh oh-toh-sahn*
grandchildren	omagosan	*oh-mah-goh-sahn*
grandfather	ojiisan	*oh-jee-sahn*
grandmother	obāsan	*oh-bah-sahn*
husband	goshujin	*goh-shoo-jeen*
mother	okāsan	*oh-kah-sahn*
• mother-in-law	giri no okāsan	*gee-ree noh oh-kah-sahn*
nephew	oigosan	*oh-ee-goh-sahn*
niece	meigosan	*meh-ee-goh-sahn*
parents	goryōshin	*goh-ryoh-sheen*
relatives	goshinseki	*goh-sheen-seh-kee*
sisters	goshimai	*goh-shee-mah-ee*
• sister-in-law (spouse's elder sister, or elder brother's wife)	giri no onēsan	*gee-ree noh oh-neh-sahn*
• sister-in-law (spouse's younger sister, or younger brother's wife)	giri no imōtosan	*gee-ree noh ee-moh-toh-sahn*
• elder sister	onēsan	*oh-neh-sahn*
• younger sister	imōtosan	*ee-moh-toh-sahn*
son	musukosan	*moos-koh-sahn*
• son-in-law	ojōsan no goshujin	*oh-joh-sahn noh goh-shoo-jeen*
twin	futago	*ftah-goh*
uncle	ojisan	*oh-jee-sahn*
wife	okusan	*ohk-sahn*

b. FRIENDS

acquaintance	chijin	*chee-jeen*
boyfriend	otoko tomodachi	*oh-toh-koh toh-moh-dah-chee*
	bōi furendo	*boh-ee foo-rehn-doh*
chum	nakayoshi	*nah-kah-yoh-shee*
colleague	dōryō	*doh-ryoh*
enemy	teki	*teh-kee*
fiancé	konyakusha	*kohn-yahk-shah*
fiancée	konyakusha	*kohn-yahk-shah*
friend	tomodachi	*toh-moh-dah-chee*
• become friends	tomodachi ni naru (v)	*toh-moh-dah-chee nee nah-roo*

• best friend	dai no shinyū	*dah-ee noh sheen-yōō*
• between friends	tomodachi no aida no/ni/de	*toh-moh-dah-chee noh ah-ee-dah noh/nee/deh*
• break off a friendship	zekkōsuru *(v)*	*zehk-koh soo-roo*
• childhood friend	osananajimi	*oh-sah-nah-nah-jee-mee*
• close friend	shinyū	*sheen-yōō*
• dear friend	shinyū	*sheen-yōō*
• family friend	kazoku no tomodachi	*kah-zoh-koo noh toh-moh-dah-chee*
• friendship	yūkō	*yōō-koh*
girlfriend	onna tomodachi	*ohn-nah toh-moh-dah-chee*
	gāru furendo	*gah-roo foo-rehn-doh*
lover	koibito	*koh-ee-bee-toh*
• love affair	renai	*rehn-ah-ee*

11. DESCRIBING PEOPLE

a. GENDER AND APPEARANCE

attractive	miryokuteki na *(adj)*	*mee-ryohk-teh-kee nah*
beautiful	utsukushii *(adj)*	*oots-koo-shēē*
• beauty	bijin	*bee-jeen*
big	ōkii *(adj)*	*oh-kēē*
• become big	ōkikunaru *(v)*	*oh-kee-koo-nah-roo*
blond	kinpatsu no *(adj)*	*keen-pahts noh*
• blond	kinpatsu no hito	*keen-pahts noh hee-toh*
body	karada	*kah-rah-dah*
• bodily physique	taikaku	*tah-ee-kah-koo*
boy	otoko no ko	*oh-toh-koh noh koh*
• boyish	shōnen no yō na *(adj)*	*shoh-nehn noh yoh nah*
childish	kodomoppoi *(adj)*	*koh-doh-mohp-poh-ee*
clean	kirei na *(adj)*	*kee-reh nah*
cool	seiketsu na *(adj)*	*seh-kehts nah*
	kakkō ii *(adj)*	*kahk-koh ēē*
curly-haired	chijirege no *(adj)*	*chee-jee-reh-geh noh*
cute	kawaii *(adj)*	*kah-wah-ēē*
dark-haired	kuroi kaminoke no *(adj)*	*koo-roh-ee kah-mee-noh-keh noh*
dirty	kitanai *(adj)*	*kee-tah-nah-ee*
elegance	yūga/jōhin	*yōō-gah/joh-heen*
• elegant	yūga na/jōhin na *(adj)*	*yōō-gah nah/joh-heen nah*
• elegantly	yūga ni *(adv)*/jōhin ni *(adv)*	*yōō-gah nee/joh-heen nee*
fat	futotta *(adj)*	*ftoht-tah*
• become fat	futoru *(v)*	*ftoh-roo*
• obesity	himan	*hee-mahn*

female	josei	*joh-seh*
• feminine	josei no *(adj)*	*joh-seh noh*
• feminine (womanly)	joseiteki na *(adj)*	*joh-seh-teh-kee nah*
gentleman	shinshi	*sheen-shee*
• gentlemanly	shinshiteki na *(adj)*	*sheen-shee-teh-kee nah*
girl	onna no ko	*ohn-nah noh koh*
handsome (masculine)	hansamu na *(adj)*	*hahn-sah-moo nah*
health	kenkō	*kehn-koh*
• healthy	kenkōteki na *(adj)*	*kehn-koh-teh-kee nah*
height	se no takasa	*seh noh tah-kah-sah*
• How tall are you?	Anata no se no takasa wa dono kurai desu ka.	*ah-nah-tah noh SEH noh tah-kah-sah wah doh-noh koo-rah-ee dehs kah*
• I am ... tall.	Watakushi no se no takasa wa ... desu.	*Wah-tahk-shee noh SEH no tah-kah-sah wah ... dehs*
• medium (average) height	chūgurai no se no takasa	*choo-goo-rah-ee noh seh noh tah-kah-sah*
• short	se ga hikui	*seh gah hee-koo-ee*
• tall	se ga takai	*seh gah tah-kah-ee*
lady	fujin	*foo-jeen*
large	ōkii *(adj)*	*oh-kee*
look	yōbō	*yoh-boh*
male	dansei	*dahn-seh*
• masculine	dansei no *(adj)*	*dahn-seh noh*
• virile	danseiteki na *(adj)*	*dahn-seh-teh-kee nah*
man	dansei	*dahn-seh*
• young man	wakamono	*wah-kah-moh-noh*
nasty	inken na *(adj)*	*een-kehn nah*
red-haired	akai kaminoke no *(adj)*	*ah-kah-ee kah-mee-noh-keh noh*
sex	sei	*seh*
shabby	misuborashii *(adj)*	*mee-soo-boh-rah-shee*
sick	byōki no *(adj)*	*byoh-kee noh*
• become sick	byōki ni naru *(v)*	*byoh-kee nee nah-roo*
• sickness	byōki	*byoh-kee*
skinny	yasekoketa *(adj)*	*yah-seh-koh-keh-tah*
slender	hossorishita *(adj)*	*hohs-soh-ree-shtah*
slim	hossorishita *(adj)*	*hohs-soh-ree-shtah*
small, little	chiisai *(adj)*	*chee-sah-ee*
strength	chikara / tsuyosa	*chee-kah-rah/tsyoh-sah*
• strong	tsuyoi *(adj)*	*tsyoh-ee*
stylish	iki na *(adj)*	*ee-kee nah*
thin	yaseta *(adj)*	*yah-seh-tah*
• become thin	yaseru *(vi)*	*yah-seh-roo*
ugly	minikui *(adj)*	*mee-nee-koo-ee*

weak	yowayowashii *(adj)*	*yoh-wah-yoh-wah-shee*
• weakness	yowayowashisa	*yoh-wah-yoh-wah-shsah*
• become weak	yowakunaru *(v)*	*yoh-wah-koo-nah-roo*
weight	omosa / taijū / mekata	*oh-moh-sah/tah-ee-jōō/meh-kah-tah*
• heavy	omoi *(adj)*	*oh-moh-ee*
• How much do you weigh?	Anata no taijū wa dono kurai desu ka.	*ah-nah-tah noh tah-ee-jōō wah doh-noh koo-rah-ee dehs kah*
• I weigh ...	Watakushi no mekata wa, ... desu.	*wah-tahk-shee noh meh-kah-tah wah, ... dehs*
• gain weight	futoru *(vi)*	*foo-toh-roo*
• light	karui *(adj)*	*kah-roo-ee*
• lose weight	yaseru *(v)*	*yah-seh-roo*
• weigh oneself	jibun no taijū o hakaru	*jee-boon noh tah-ee-jōō oh hah-kah-roo*
woman	josei	*joh-seh*

b. CONCEPTS OF AGE

adolescence	shishunki	*shee-shoon-kee*
• adolescent	shishunki no *(adj)*	*shee-shoon-kee noh*
• teenager	tīnējā	*tēēn-eh-jah*
adult	otona	*oh-toh-nah*
age	toshi / nenrei	*toh-shee/nehn-reh*
• age	toshitoru *(v)*	*tohsh-toh-roo*
• aged	kōreisha	*koh-reh-shah*
baby	akachan	*ah-kah-chahn*
child	kodomo	*koh-doh-moh*
elderly person	nenpai no hito	*nehn-pah-ee noh hee-toh*
• have white hair	shiraga ga aru	*shee-rah-gah gah ah-roo*
grow up	sodatsu *(vi)*	*soh-dah-tsoo*
infant	nyūji	*nyōō-jee*
middle age	chūnen	*chōō-nehn*
old	toshitotta *(adj)*	*tohsh-toht-tah*
• become old	toshitoru *(v)*	*tohsh-toh-roo*
• old age	rōgo	*roh-goh*
• older	toshiue no *(adj)*	*toh-shee-oo-eh noh*
• older brother	ani	*AH-nee*
• older sister	ane	*ah-neh*
• How old are you?	Toshi wa, ikutsu desu ka.	*toh-shee wah, EE-koots dehs kah*
• I am ... old.	... sai desu.	*... sah-ee dehs*
toddler	yōji	*YOH-jee*
young	wakai *(adj)*	*wah-kah-ee*
• younger	toshishita no *(adj)*	*toh-shee-shtah noh*
• younger brother	otōto	*oh-tōh-toh*

- **younger sister** imōto *ee-moh-toh*
- **youth** seinen jidai *seh-nehn jee-dah-ee*
- **youthful** wakawakashii *(adj)* *wah-kah-wah-kah-shee*

c. MARRIAGE AND THE HUMAN LIFE CYCLE

anniversary	kekkon kinenbi	*kehk-kohn kee-nehn-bee*
• diamond anniversary	kekkon nanajūgoshūnen kinenbi	*kehk-kohn nah-nah-jōo goh-shōo-nehn kee-nehn-bee*
• golden anniversary	kekkon gojusshūnen kinenbi	*kehk-kohn goh-joos-shōo-nehn kee-nehn-bee*
• silver anniversary	kekkon nijūgoshūnen kinenbi	*kehk-kohn nee-jōo-goh-shōo-nehn kee-nehn-bee*
bachelor	dokushin	*dohk-sheen*
birth	tanjō	*tahn-jōh*
• birthday	tanjōbi	*tahn-jōh-bee*
• celebrate one's birthday	tanjōbi o iwau	*tahn-jōh-bee oh ee-wah-oo*
• Happy birthday!	Tanjōbi omedetō.	*tahn-jōh-bee oh-meh-deh-toh*
• be born	umareru *(v)*	*oo-mah-reh-roo*
• I was born on ...	Watakushi wa, ... ni umaremashita.	*wah-tahk-shee wah, ... nee oo-mah-reh-mahsh-tah*
bride	hanayome	*hah-nah-yoh-meh*
death	shi	*shee*
	shibō	*shee-boh*
• die	shinu *(v)*	*shee-noo*
• die	nakunaru *(v, pol)*	*nah-koo-nah-roo*
divorce	rikon	*ree-kohn*
• divorce	rikonsuru *(v)*	*ree-kohn-soo-roo*
• divorced	rikonshita *(adj)*	*ree-kohn-shtah*
engagement	konyaku	*kohn-yah-koo*
• become engaged	konyakusuru *(v)*	*kohn-yahk-soo-roo*
• engaged	konyakushita *(adj)*	*kohn-yahk-shtah*
fiancé	konyakusha	*kohn-yahk-shah*
fiancée	konyakusha	*kohn-yahk-shah*
gift	okurimono	*oh-koo-ree-moh-noh*
• give a gift	okurimono o ageru	*oh-koo-ree-moh-noh oh ah-geh-roo*
go to school	gakkō ni iku	*gahk-koh nee ee-koo*
groom (bridegroom)	hanamuko	*hah-nah-moo-koh*
heredity	iden	*ee-dehn*
• inherit	iden de uketsugu *(v)*	*ee-dehn deh oo-keh-tsoo-goo*
honeymoon	shinkonryokō	*sheen-kohn-ryoh-koh*

husband	otto	*oht-toh*
kiss	seppun, kisu	*sehp-poon, kees*
• kiss	kisusuru *(v)*	*kees-soo-roo*
	seppunsuru *(v)*	*sehp-poon-soo-roo*
life	jinsei	*jeen-seh*
• live	sumu *(v)*	*soo-moo*
love	ai	*ah-ee*
• love	aisuru *(v)*	*ah-ee-soo-roo*
• fall in love	sukininaru *(v)*	*skee-nee-nah-roo*
• in love	renai chū	*rehn-ah-ee chōō*
marital status	kekkon shikau	*kehk-kohn shee-kah-koo*
marriage, matrimony	kekkon	*kehk-kohn*
• get married	kekkonsuru *(v)*	*kehk-kohn-soo-roo*
• married	kikon no *(adj)*	*kee-kohn noh*
• (to) marry (someone)	kekkonsuru *(v)*	*kehk-kohn soo-roo*
• unmarried	mikon no *(adj)*	*mee-kohn noh*
newlyweds	shinkon fusai	*sheen-kohn fsah-ee*
pregnancy	ninshin	*neen-sheen*
• abort (pregnancy)	chūzetsusuru *(v)* / dataisuru *(v)*	*chōō-zeh-tsoo-soo-roo/dah-tah-ee-soo-roo*
• abortion	chūzetsu / datai	*chōō-zeh-tsoo/dah-tah-ee*
• be pregnant	ninshin chū desu	*neen-sheen chōō dehs*
• get pregnant	ninshinsuru *(v)*	*neen-sheen-soo-roo*
• give birth	umu *(v)*	*oo-moo*
• have a baby	kodomo ga umareru	*koh-doh-moh gah oo-mah-reh-roo*
raise (someone)	sodateru *(v)*	*soh-dah-teh-roo*
reception (wedding)	hirōen	*hee-roh-ehn*
separation	bekkyo	*behk-kyoh*
• separate	bekkyosuru *(v)*	*behk-kyoh-soo-roo*
• separated	bekkyoshita *(adj)*	*behk-kyoh-shtah*
spouse	haigūsha	*hah-ee-gōō-shah*
wedding	kekkonshiki	*kehk-kohn-shkee*
• wedding invitation	kekkonshiki e no shōtai	*kehk-kohn-shkee eh noh shoh-tah-ee*
• wedding ring	kekkon yubiwa	*kehk-khon yoo-bee-wah*
widow	mibōjin	*mee-boh-jeen*
widower	yamome	*yah-moh-meh*
wife	tsuma	*tsmah*

d. RELIGION AND RACE

animism	seirei shinkō	*sēh-rēh sheen-koh*
Arab	Arabujin	*ah-rah-boo-jeen*
archbishop	daishikyō	*dah-ee-shkyoh*
atheism	mushinron	*moo-sheen-rohn*

• atheist	mushinronsha	moo-sheen-rohn-shah
baptism	senrei	sehn-reh
belief	shinnen	sheen-nehn
• believe	shinjiru (v)	sheen-jee-roo
• believe in	shinjiru (v)	sheen-jee-roo
• believer	shinja	sheen-jah
bishop	shikyō	shee-kyoh
black	kokujin	koh-koo-jeen
Buddhism	bukkyō	book-kyoh
• Buddhist	bukkyō no shinja	book-kyoh noh sheen-jah
• Buddhist	bukkyō no (adj)	book-kyoh noh
• Buddhist priest	obōsan	oh-boh-sahn
• Bhuddhist temple	otera	oh-teh-rah
Catholic	katorikkukyōto	kah-toh-reek-koo-kyoh-toh
	katorikkukyō no (adj)	kah-toh-reek-koo-kyoh noh
• Catholicism	katorikkukyō shinkō	kah-toh-reek-koo-kyoh sheen-koh
Christian	kirisutokyōto	kee-rees-toh-kyoh-toh
• Christianity	kirisutokyō	kee-rees-toh-kyoh
church	kyōkai	kyoh-kah-ee
confirmation	kenshinrei	kehn-sheen-reh
Confucianism	jukyō	joo-kyoh
• Confucian	jusha	joo-shah
faith	shinkō	sheen-koh
• faithful	shinkōshin ga atsui (adj)	sheen-koh-sheen gah ah-tsoo-ee
god	kamisama	kah-mee-sah-mah
Hebrew, Jewish	Yudayajin no (adj)	yoo-dah-yah-jeen noh
Hindu	Hinzūkyōto	heen-zoo-kyoh-toh
human	ningen no (adj)	neen-gehn noh
• humanity	ningensei	neen-gehn-seh
Islam (religion)	kaikyō	kah-ee-kyoh
• Islamic	kaikyō no (adj)	kah-ee-kyoh noh
• Muslim	kaikyōto	kah-ee-kyoh toh
Judaism	Yudayakyō	yoo-dah-yah-kyoh
• Jew	Yudayajin	yoo-dah-yah-jeen
• Jewish	Yudayajin no (adj)	yoo-dah-yah-jeen noh
lay person	hirashinto	hee-rah-sheen-toh
Mass	misa	mee-sah
meditation	mokusō	mohk-soh
• meditate	mokusōsuru (v)	mohk-soh-soo-roo
minister	bokushi	bohk-shee
monk	shūdōshi	shoo-doh-shee
mosque	mosuku	mohs-koo
myth	shinwa	sheen-wah
nun	nisō	nee-soh
Occidental	seiōjin	seh-oh-jeen

Oriental	Ajiajin	ah-jee-ah-jeen
pagan	ikyōto	ee-kyoh-toh
pray	oinorisuru (v)	oh-ee-noh-ree-soo-roo
• prayer	oinori	oh-ee-noh-ree
priest	seishokusha	seh-shohk-shah
Protestant	shinkyōto	sheen-kyoh-toh
Protestant	shinkyō	sheen-kyoh
• Protestantism	Yudayakyō no	yoo-dah-yah-kyoh noh
rabbi	rippō hakase	reep-poh-hah-kah-seh
	minzoku	meen-zoh-koo
race	shūkyō	shoo-kyoh
religion	shinkōbukai (adj)	sheen-koh-boo-kah-ee
• religious	gishiki	gee-shkee
rite	gishiki	gee-shkee
ritual	shintō	sheen-toh
Shintoism	shintō no shinja	sheen-toh noh sheen-jah
• Shintoist	kannushi	kahn-noo-shee
• Shinto priest	jinja	jeen-jah
• Shinto shrine	miko	mee-koh
• shrine assistant (female)		
soul	tamashii	tah-mah-shee
spirit	seishin	seh-sheen
• spiritual	seishinteki (adj)	seh-sheen-teh-kee
synagogue	Yudayakyō jiin	yoo-dah-yah-kyoh jee-een
temple	jiin	jee-een
western	seiō no (adj)	seh-oh noh
Zen Buddhism	zenshū	zehn-shoo

e. CHARACTERISTICS AND SOCIAL TRAITS

active	katsudōteki na (adj)	kah-tsoo-doh-teh-kee nah
• activity	katsudō	kah-tsoo-doh
adapt	tekigōsaseru (vt)	teh-kee-goh-sah-seh-roo
• adaptable	tekigōsei ga aru (adj)	teh-kee-goh-seh gah ah-roo
affection	aijō	ah-ee-joh
• affectionate	aijō no fukai (adj)	ah-ee-joh noh fkah-ee
aggressive	kōgekiteki na (adj)	koh-geh-kee-teh-kee nah
• aggressiveness	kōgekisei	koh-geh-kee-seh
ambition	taibō	tah-ee-boh
• ambitious	nozomi ga takai (adj)	noh-zoh-mee gah tah-kah-ee
anger	ikari	ee-kah-ree
• angry	okotta (adj)	oh-koht-tah
• become angry	okoru (v)	oh-koh-roo
anxious	shinpai na (adj)	sheen-pah-ee nah
• anxiety	fuankan	foo-ahn-kahn

arrogance	gōman	góh-mahn
• arrogant	gōman na *(adj)*	góh-mahn nah
artistic	geijutsuteki na *(adj)*	geh-joo-tsoo-teh-kee nah
astute	kibin na *(adj)*	kee-been nah
attractive	miryokuteki na *(adj)*	mee-ryohk-teh-kee nah
avarice, greed	donyoku	dohn-yoh-koo
• avaricious, greedy	yoku no fukai *(adj)*	yoh-koo noh fkah-ee
bad	warui *(adj)*	wah-roo-ee
brash	sekkachi na *(adj)*	sehk-kah-chee nah
brilliant	sainō ni michita *(adj)*	sah-ee-nóh nee mee-chee-tah
calculating	keisandakai *(adj)*	kéh-sahn-dah-kah-ee
calm	odayaka na *(adj)*	oh-dah-yah-kah nah
• calmness	odayakasa	oh-dah-yah-kah-sah
character	seikaku	séh-kah-koo
• characteristic	dokutoku na *(adj)*	dohk-tohk nah
• characterize	seikakuzukeru *(v)*	séh-kah-koo-zoo-keh-roo
charisma	karisuma	kah-ree-soo-mah
• charismatic	karisuma no aru *(adj)*	kah-ree-soo-mah noh ah-roo
cheerful	akarui *(adj)*	ah-kah-róo-ee
clever	kenmei na *(adj)*	kehn-méh nah
comical	kokkei na *(adj)*	kohk-kéh nah
conformist	junnōsha	joon-nóh-shah
• nonconformist	hijunnōsha	hee-joon-nóh-shah
conscience	ryōshin	ryóh-sheen
• conscientious	ryōshinteki na *(adj)*	ryóh-sheen-teh-kee nah
conservative	hoshuteki na *(adj)*	hoh-shoo-teh-kee nah
courage	yūki	yóo-kee
• courageous	yūki ga aru *(adj)*	yóo-kee gah ah-roo
courteous	reigi tadashii *(adj)*	réh-gee tah-dah-shée
• courtesy	reigi	réh-gee
• discourteous	shitsurei na *(adj)*	shtsoo-réh nah
creative	sōzōteki na *(adj)*	soh-zóh-teh-kee nah
critical	hihanteki na *(adj)*	hee-hahn-teh-kee nah
cry	naku *(v)*	nah-koo
cultured	kyōyō no aru *(adj)*	kyóh-yóh noh ah-roo
curiosity	kōkishin	kóh-kee-sheen
• curious	kōkishin no tsuyoi *(adj)*	kóh-kee-sheen noh tsoo-yoh-ee
delicate	sensai na *(adj)*	sehn-sah-ee nah
diligence	kinben	keen-behn
• diligent, hard-working	kinben na *(adj)*	keen-behn nah
diplomatic	gaikōteki na *(adj)*	gah-ee-kóh-teh-kee nah
disgusting	hakike o moyōsu *(adj)*	hah-kee-keh o moh-yóh-soo
dishonest	fushōjiki na *(adj)*	fshóh-jee-kee nah
disingenuous	inken na *(adj)*	een-kehn nah

dull	taikutsu na	*tah-ee-koo-tsoo nah*
dumb	gudon na	*goo-dohn nah*
dynamic	seiryokuteki na *(adj)*	*seh-ryohk-teh-kee nah*
eccentric	fūgawari na *(adj)*	*foo-gah-wah-ree nah*
egoism	rikoshugi	*ree-koh-shoo-gee*
• egoist	rikoshugisha	*ree-koh-shoo-gee-shah*
• egoistic	rikoteki na *(adj)*	*ree-koh-teh-kee nah*
elegance	yūga	*yoo-gah*
• elegant	yūga na *(adj)*	*yoo-gah nah*
eloquence	yūben	*yoo-behn*
• eloquent	yūben na *(adj)*	*yoo-behn nah*
energetic	enerugisshu na *(adj)*	*eh-neh-roo-gees-shoo nah*
envious	urayamashii *(adj)*	*oo-rah-yah-mah-shee*
• envy	urayamu *(v)*	*oo-rah-yah-moo*
faithful	chūjitsu na *(adj)*	*choo-jee-tsoo nah*
fascinate	miwakusuru *(vt)*	*mee-wahk-soo-roo*
• fascinating	miwakuteki na *(adj)*	*mee-wahk-teh-kee nah*
• facination	miwaku	*mee-wah-koo*
fool	bakamono	*bah-kah-moh-noh*
• foolish, silly	bakageta *(adj)*	*bah-kah-geh-tah*
friendly	shitashige na *(adj)*	*shtah-shee-geh nah*
funny	omoshiroi *(adj)*	*oh-moh-shee-roh-ee*
fussy	kourusai *(adj)*	*koh-oo-roo-sah-ee*
generosity	kandaisa	*kahn-dah-ee-sah*
• generous	kandai na *(adj)*	*kahn-dah-ee nah*
gentle	yasashii *(adj)*	*yah-sah-shee*
gloomy	inkina *(adj)*	*een-kee-nah*
good	ii *(adj)*	*ee*
• goodness	zenryōsa	*zehn-ryoh-sah*
good at (something)	jōzu na *(adj)*	*joh-zoo nah*
graceful	yūga na *(adj)*	*yoo-gah nah*
habit	shūkan	*shoo-kahn*
happiness	shiawase	*shee-ah-wah-seh*
• happy	shiawase na *(adj)*	*shee-ah-wah-seh nah*
hate	ken-o	*kehn-oh*
• hate	totemo kirau *(v)*	*toh-teh-moh kee-rah-oo*
• hateful	iya na *(adj)*	*ee-yah nah*
honest	shōjiki na *(adj)*	*shoh-jee-kee nah*
• honesty	shōjikisa	*shoh-jee-kee-sah*
horrible	hidokute zotto suru	*hee-doh-koo-teh zoht-toh soo-roo*
humanitarian	jindōshugi no *(adj)*	*jeen-doh-shoo-gee noh*
humble	hikaeme na *(adj)*	*hee-kah-eh-meh nah*
• humility	kenson	*kehn-sohn*
humor	yūmoa	*yoo-moh-ah*
• humorous	kokkei na *(adj)*	*kohk-keh nah*
• sense of humor	yūmoa no kankaku	*yoo-moh-ah noh kahn-kah-koo*

idealism	risōshugi	ree-soh-shoo-gee
• idealist	risōshugisha	ree-soh-shoo-gee-shah
• idealistic	risōshugiteki na	ree-soh-shoo-gee-teh-kee nah
imagination	sōzōryoku	soh-zoh-ryoh-koo
• imaginative	sōzōryoku ni tonda (adj)	soh-zoh-ryoh-koo nee tohn-dah
impudence	atsukamashisa	ahts-kah-mah-shsah
• impudent	atsukamashii (adj)	ahts-kah-mah-shee
impulse	shōdō	shoh-doh
• impulsive	shōdōteki na (adj)	shoh-doh-teh-kee nah
independent	jishuteki na (adj)	jee-shoo-teh-kee nah
individualist	kojinshugisha	koh-jeen-shoo-gee-shah
ingenious	dokusōteki na (adj)	dohk-soh-teh-kee nah
• ingenuity	dokusōsei	dohk-soh-seh
innocence	mujaki	moo-jah-kee
• innocent	mujaki na (adj)	nwo-jah-kee nah
insane	shōki dewa nai	shoh-kee deh-wah nah-ee
insolence	ōhei	oh-heh
• insolent	ōhei na (adj)	oh-heh nah
intellectual	chishikijin	chee-shee-kee-jeen
	chiteki na (adj)	chee-teh-kee nah
intelligence	chisei	chee-seh
• intelligent	chiseiteki na (adj)	chee-seh-teh-kee nah
irony	hiniku	hee-nee-koo
• ironical	hiniku na (adj)	hee-nee-koo nah
irritable	tanki na (adj)	tahn-kee nah
jealous	shittobukai (adj)	sheet-toh-boo-kah-ee
• jealousy	shitto	sheet-toh
kind	shinsetsu na (adj)	sheen-seh-tsoo nah
• kindness	shinsetsu	sheen-seh-tsoo
laid back	nonbirishita (adj)	nohn-bee-ree-shtah
laugh	warau (v)	wah-rah-oo
laziness	bushō	boo-shoh
• lazy	bushō na (adj)	boo-shoh nah
liar	usotsuki	oo-soh-tsoo-kee
liberal	kakushinshugisha	kahk-sheen-shoo-gee-shah
	kakushinteki na (adj)	kahk-sheen-teh-kee nah
lively	ikiikishita (adj)	ee-kee-ee-kee-shtah
	ikiikito (adv)	ee-kee-ee-kee-toh
love	ai	ah-ee
• love	aisuru (v)	ah-ee-soo-roo
• lovable	airashii (adj)	ah-ee-rah-shee
madness	kyōki	kyoh-kee
• crazy, mad	kichigaijimita (adj)	kee-chee-gah-ee-jee-mee-tah
malicious	akui ni michita (adj)	ah-koo-ee nee mee-chee-tah

manipulative	zurugashikoi (adj)	zoo-roo-gah-shkoh-ee
mean	ijiwaru na (adj)	ee-jee-wah-roo nah
mischievous	itazurazuki na (adj)	ee-tah-zoo-rah-zoo-kee nah
mood	kigen	kee-gehn
• be in a good mood	kigen ga ii	kee-gehn gah ēē
• be in a bad mood	kigen ga warui	kee-gehn gah wah-roo-ee
nasty	tachi no warui (adj)	tah-chee noh wah-roo-ee
neat	sapparishaita (adj)	sahp-pah-ree-shtah
nervous	shinkeishitsu na (adj)	sheen-keh-shee-tsoo nah
nice	ii (adj)	ēē
not nice, odious	iya na (adj)	ee-yah nah
obnoxious	fukai kiwamarinai (adj)	fkah-ee kee-wah-mah-ree-nah-ee
obstinate	gōjō na (adj)	goh-jōh nah
optimism	rakutenshugi	rahk-tehn-shoo-gee
• optimist	rakutenshugisha	rahk-tehn-shoo-gee-shah
• optimistic	rakutenteki na (adj)	rahk-tehn-teh-kee nah
original	sōsakuteki na (adj)	soh-sahk-teh-kee nah
patience	nintai	neen-tah-ee
• patient	nintaizuyoi (adj)	neen-tah-ee-zoo-yoh-ee
• impatient	kimijika na (adj)	kee-mee-jee-kah nah
perfection	kanzen	kahn-zehn
• perfectionist	kanzenshugisha	kahn-zehn-shoo-gee-shah
personality	seikaku	sēh-kah-koo
pessimism	hikanshugi	hee-kahn-shoo-gee
• pessimist	hikanshugisha	hee-kahn-shoo-gee-shah
• pessimistic	hikanteki na (adj)	hee-kahn-teh-kee nah
picky	kuchiyakamashii (adj)	koo-chee-yah-kah-mah-shēē
pleasant, likeable	tanoshii (adj)	tah-noh-shēē
• like	konomu (v)	koh-noh-moo
poor	misuborashii (adj)	mee-soo-boh-rah-shēē
possessive	shoyūyoku ga tsuyoi (adj)	shoh-yōō-yoh-koo gah tsoo-yoh-ee
presumptuous	buenryo na (adj)	boo-ehn-ryoh nah
pretentious	mie o hatta (adj)	mee-eh oh haht-tah
proud	hokori no takai (adj)	hoh-koh-ree noh tah-kah-ee
prudent	shinchō na (adj)	sheen-chōh nah
quiet	shizuka na (adj)	shee-zoo-kah nah
rebellious	hankōteki na (adj)	hahn-kōh-teh-kee nah
refined	jōhin na (adj)	jōh-heen nah
reserved	uchiki na (adj)	oo-chee-kee nah
restless	ochitsukanai (adj)	oh-chee-tskah-nah-ee
rich	yūfuku na (adj)	yōō-fkoo nah
ridiculous	matomo ja nai (adj)	mah-toh-moh jah nah-ee
romantic	romanchikku na (adj)	roh-mahn-cheek-koo nah
rough	soya na (adj)	soh-yah nah

rude	burei na *(adj)*	*boo-reh nah*
sad	kanashige na *(adj)*	*kah-nah-shee-geh nah*
sarcasm	hiniku	*hee-nee-koo*
• sarcastic	hiniku na *(adj)*	*hee-nee-koo nah*
scheming	zurui *(adj)*	*zoo-roo-ee*
seduction	yūwaku	*yoo-wah-koo*
• seductive	miwakuteki na *(adj)*	*mee-wahk-teh-kee nah*
selfish	rikoteki na *(adj)*	*ree-koh-teh-kee nah*
self-sufficient	jiritsu shiteiru *(adj)*	*jee-ree-tsoo shteh-ee-roo*
sensitive	binkan na *(adj)*	*been-kahn nah*
sentimental	kanshōteki na *(adj)*	*kahn-shoh-teh-kee nah*
serious	majime na *(adj)*	*mah-jee-meh nah*
shrewd	nukemenonai *(adj)*	*noo-keh-meh-noh-nah-ee*
shy	uchiki na *(adj)*	*oo-chee-kee nah*
simple	tanjun na *(adj)*	*tahn-joon nah*
sincere	seijitsu na *(adj)*	*seh-jee-tsoo nah*
sloppy, disorganized	darashinai *(adj)*	*dah-rah-shee-nah-ee*
sly	warugashikoi *(adj)*	*wah-roo-gah-shkoh-ee*
smart	rikō na *(adj)*	*ree-koh nah*
smile	hohoemi	*hoh-hoh-eh-mee*
• smile	hohoemu *(v)*	*hoh-hoh-eh-moo*
snobbish	kidotta *(adj)*	*kee-doht-tah*
stingy	kechi na *(adj)*	*keh-chee nah*
strong	takumashii *(adj)*	*tahk-mah-shee*
stubborn	ganko na *(adj)*	*gahn-koh nah*
stupid	oroka na *(adj)*	*oh-roh-kah nah*
superstitious	meishinbukai *(adj)*	*meh-sheen-boo-kah-ee*
sweet	yasashii *(adj)*	*yah-sah-shee*
talkative	oshaberi na *(adj)*	*oh-shah-beh-ree nah*
traditional	dentōteki na *(adj)*	*dehn-toh-teh-kee nah*
tricky	zurugashikoi *(adj)*	*zoo-roo-gah-shee-koh-ee*
troublemaker	monchaku o okosu hito	*mohn-chah-koo oh oh-kohs hee-toh*
vain	mieppari no *(adj)*	*mee-ehp-pah-ree noh*
versatile	tagei na *(adj)*	*tah-geh nah*
vulnerable	kizutsukiyasui *(adj)*	*kee-zoo-tskee-yah-soo-ee*
weak	yowayowashii *(adj)*	*yoh-wah-yoh-wah-shee*
well-mannered	reigitadashii *(adj)*	*reh-gee-tah-dah-shee*
wisdom	kenmei	*kehn-meh*
• wise	kenmei na *(adj)*	*kehn-meh nah*

tango tango タンゴ 28c

tape recorder tēpu rekōdā テープレコーダー 20b

tariff kanzei 関税 31

taro satoimo 里芋 14e, 24e

tartar shiseki 歯石 40b

taste ajiwau *(v)* 味わう 12c

tasty oishii *(adj)* 美味しい 24p

Taurus oushiza 牡牛座 5d

tax zeikin 税金 24m

taxi takushī タクシー 33a

taxi driver takushī no untenshu タクシーの運転手 38a

tea (Japanese) ocha お茶 24k

tea (western) kōcha 紅茶 24k

tea store ocha ya お茶屋 24n

teach oshieru *(v)* 教える 37f

teacher kyōshi 教師 37d, 38a

teacup (Japanese) yunomijawan 湯飲み茶碗 23d

teacup saucer chataku 茶托 24l

team chīmu チーム 27b

teapot tīpotto ティーポット 23d

tears namida 涙 21a

teaspoon kosaji 小さじ 23d, 24l

technical book senmonsho 専門書 25o

technical/vocational school shokugyō gakkō 職業学校 37a

technology gijutsu 技術 42a

teenager tīnējā ティーンエージャー 11b

tee-shirt tīshatsu Tシャツ 25k

telecommunication enkyori tsūshin 遠距離通信 18a, 42a

telecommunications satellite Tsūshin eisei 通信衛星 18a

teleconferencing terekonfarensu テレコンファレンス 42a

telephone denwa 電話 18a, 18b, 23e, 35c, 38c

telephone bill denwa ryōkin no seikyūsho 電話料金の請求書 18b

telephone call denwa 電話 18b

telephone card terefon kādo テレフォンカード 18a

telephone number denwabangō 電話番号 11f, 18b, 38b

telescopic lens bōen renzu 望遠レンズ 25d

television terebi テレビ 20b

television set terebi テレビ 20b, 23d, 35c

tell tsugeru *(v)* 告げる 17a

tell a joke jōdan o iu *(v)* 冗談を言う 17a

tell a story itsuwa o hanasu *(v)* 逸話を話す 17a

teller's window madoguchi 窓口 26

temperate ondan na *(adj)* 温暖な 13e

temperature kion 気温 6c

temperature (fever) netsu 熱 40a

template tenpurēto テンプレート 2b

temple jiin 寺院 11d

temple otera お寺 36a

temporarily ichijiteki ni *(adv)* 一時的に 4e

temporary ichijiteki na *(adj)* 一時的な 4e

temporary rinji yatoi 臨時雇い 38d

ten jū 十 1a

ten tō 十 1a

ten billion hyakuoku 百億 1a

ten million senman 千万 1a

ten thousand ichiman 一万 1a

ten thousand and one ichiman-ichi 一万一 1a

ten thousand ten ichiman-jū 一万十 1a

ten thousand two hundred ichiman-nihyaku 一万二百 1a

ten thousandth ichimanbanme 一万番目 1b

tenant kyojūsha 居住者 23g

tender yasashii *(adj)* 優しい 21a

tendon ken 腱 12a

tennis tenisu テニス 27b

tense kinchōshita *(adj)* 緊張した 21a

tense (grammar) jisei 時制 8a

tent tento テント 36b

tenth daijū 第十 1b

tenth jūbanme 十番目 1b

tenth jūbanme/daijū 十番目／第十 1b

terminal (computer) tāminaru ターミナル 42b

terminal (transportation) tāminaru ターミナル 32a

termite shiroari 白蟻 15d

terrace terasu テラス 23a

territory ryōdo 領土 13e

terrorism tero/tero kōi テロ／テロ行為 44b

test tesuto テスト 37f

testicle kōgan 睾丸 12a

testify shōgensuru *(v)* 証言する 17a, 41

testimony shōgen 証言 41

tetrahedron shimentai 四面体 2a

text honbun 本文 19c, 19f, 20a

text messaging tekisuto messēji テキストメッセージ 18a

textbook kyōkasho 教科書 25o, 37b

textile orimono 織物 13c

Thai Taijin タイ人 30d

Thai (language) Taigo タイ語 30d

Thailand Taikoku タイ国 30b

thank kanshasuru *(v)* 感謝する 17a, 21a

Thank goodness! Arigatai. *(inf)* ありがたい。 21c

Thank you! Arigatō gozaimasu. ありがとうございます。 16c

thankful kansha no *(adj)* 感謝の 21a

thankfulness kansha 感謝 21a

that sono その 8b

that (over there) ano あの 8b

that is to say sunawachi すなわち 44c

the first government business day (January 4) goyō hajime 御用始め 5g

the last government business day (December 28) goyō osame 御用納め 5g

the New Year shinnen 新年 5g

The pleasure is mine! Kochirakoso. こちらこそ。 16b

The sky is clear. Kaisei desu. 快晴です。 6a

The watch is fast. Tokei ga, susumigachi desu. 時計が、進みがちです。 4d

The watch is slow. Tokei ga, okuregachi desu. 時計が、遅れがちです。 4d

The weather is beautiful Subarashii tenki desu. 素晴らしい天気です。 6a

the year two thousand nisennen 二千年 4c

theater gekijō 劇場 28e

theater kangeki 観劇 27a

their (all female) kanojotachi no 彼女達の 8d

their (all male, or male and female) karera no **彼らの** 8d

them (all female) kanojotachi o 彼女達の 8e

them (all male, or male and female) karera o 彼らの 8e

theme tēma テーマ 28d

themselves (all females) kanojotachi jishin 彼女達自身 8g

themselves (all male, or male and female) karera jishin 彼ら自身 8g

then sono toki その時 4e

then sorekara *(conj)* それから 4e, 8k

then suruto *(conj)* すると 8k

theorem teiri **定理** 1f

theory of relativity sōtaisei genri 相対性原理 42a

there soko ni そこに 36c

there soko そこ 3d

There is no class today. Kyō wa, gakkō ga arimasen. 今日は、学校がありません。 37f

There's lightning. Inazuma ga hikatte imasu. 稲妻が光って います。 6a

There's no doubt that... ...wa, utagai no yochi mo arimasen. ···は、疑いの余地もありませ ん。 44c

There's nothing to declare. Nani mo, shinkokusuru mono ga arimasen. 何も、申告する物 がありません。 31

There's something to declare. Shinkokusuru mono ga arimasu. 申告する物があ ります。 31

therefore soreyue それゆえ 44c

thermal energy netsu enerugī 熱エネルギー 44a

thermometer ondokei 温度計 6c

thermometer taionkei 体温計 25h, 40a

thermostat jidō chōon sōchi 自動調温装置 6c, 35c

these korera no これらの 8b

thesis ronbun 論文 37f

they (all female) kanojotachi ga/wa 彼女達が/は 8c

they (all male, or male and female) karera ga/wa 彼らが/は 8c

thick atsui *(adj)* 厚い 3b, 13d

thief dorobō 泥棒 39b

thigh futomomo 太もも 12a

thin usui *(adj)* 薄い 3b, 13d

thin yaseta *(adj)* 痩せた 11a

think kangaeru *(v)* 考える 22b

third daisan 第三 1b

third mittsume 三つ目 1b

third sanbanme ３番目 1b

third person sanninshō 三人称 8a

Third World daisansekai 第三世界 43

thirteen jūsan 十三 1a

thirteen thousand ichimansanzen 一万三千 1a

thirteenth jūsanbanme 十三番目 1b

thirty sanjū 三十 1a

thirty thousand sanman 三万 1a

thirty-one sanjūichi 三十一 1a

thirty-two sanjūni 三十二 1a

this kono この 8b

this afternoon kyō no gogo 今日の午後 4a

this evening konban 今晩 4a

this evening kyō no yūgata 今日の夕方 4a

This is... Watakushi wa, ...desu ga. 私は、…ですが。 18b

This line is busy. Hanashichū desu. 話し中です。 18b

this morning kesa 今朝 4a

this night konban 今晩 4a

this night konya 今夜 4a

thorn toge とげ 14a

those sorera no それらの 8b

those (over there) arera no あれらの 8b

thought kangae 考え 22a

thousandth senbanme 千番目 1b

threat odokashi 脅かし 17a

threaten odokasu (v) 脅かす 17a

three mittsu 三つ 1a

three san 三 1a

three (bound objects) sansatsu 三冊 1a

three (floors) sangai 三階 1a

three (liquid or dry measure) sanbai 三杯 1a

three (long, thin objects) sanbon 三本 1a

three (persons) sannin 三人 1a

three (small objects) sanko/mittsu 三個／三つ 1a

three (thin, flat objects) sanmai 三枚 1a

three hundred sanbyaku 三百 1a

three million sanbyakuman 三百万 1a

three thousand sanzen 三千 1a

three-fourths yonbun no san 四分の三 1c

three-piece suit mitsuzoroi 三つ揃い 25k

throat nodo 喉 12, 40a

through tōshite (adv) 通して 3d

through... ... o tootte …を通って 36c

throw nageru (v) 投げる 27b

throw up haku (v) 吐く 40a

thumb oyayubi 親指 12a

thumbtack gabyō 画鋲 25c, 37b, 38c

thunder kaminari ga naru (v) 雷が鳴る 6a

thunder kaminari 雷 6a

thunderstorm raiu 雷雨 6a

Thursday mokuyōbi 木曜日 5a

thus sorede (conj) それで 8k

tick dani ダニ 15d

ticket ken 券 27b, 30a, 32a, 34

ticket counter kippu uriba 切符売り場 34

tide chōryū 潮流 13b

tie nekutai ネクタイ 25k

tie (score) dōten 同点 27b

tiger tora 虎 15a

tight kitsui (adj) きつい 25l

tighten pittarisaseru (v) ピッタリさせる 25m

tights taitsu タイツ 25k

till tagayasu (v) 耕す 14a

time (as in every time) toki とき 4a

time (hour) ji 時 4a

time (in general) jikan 時間 4a

time difference jisa 時差 32c

time for breakfast chōshoku no jikan 朝食の時間 35c

time for dinner yūshoku no jikan 夕食の時間 35c

time for taking a bath ofuro no jikan お風呂の時間 35c

timer taimā タイマー 4d

timetable jikokuhyō 時刻表 4e, 34

timid okubyō na (adj) 臆病な 21a

timpani tinpanī ティンパニー 28c

tint iroai o tsukeru (v) 色合いをつける 7c

tint iroai 色合い 7c

tip chippu o ageru (v) チップを上げる 24m

tip chippu チップ 24m

tire taiya タイヤ 33a, 33e

tissues tisshū ティッシュー 25f

title shōgō 称号 11f, 16b

title (books, movies, etc.) daimei 題名 20a

to e/ni/made へ／に／まで 8j

to her kanojo ni 彼女に 8f

to him kare ni 彼に 8f

to me watakushi ni 私に 8f

to sum up ... ... o yōyakusureba, ・・・を要約すれば、 17b

to the east higashi e (ni) 東へ（に）3d, 36c

to the fourth power yonjō 四乗 1e

to the left hidari ni 左に 3d, 36c

to the north kita ni 北に 3d, 36c

to the nth power enujō n乗 1e

to the power of ruijō 累乗 1e

to the right migi ni 右に 3d, 36c

to the south minami ni 南に 3d, 36c

to the west nishi ni 西に 3d, 36c

to them (all female) kanojotachi ni 彼女達に 8f

to them (all male or male and female) karera ni 彼らに 8f

to this day konnichi made 今日まで 4e

to us watakushitachi ni 私達に 8f

to whom dare ni 誰に 8h

To Whom It May Concern kankeisha kakui dono 関係者各位殿 19a

to you anata ni あなたに 8f

to you (plural) anatatachi ni あなた達に 8f

to, at ni/de に／で 3d

toad hikigaeru ひきがえる 15c

toast kanpai 乾杯 17a

toast kanpaisuru (v) 乾杯する 17a

toast kongari yaku (v) こんがり焼く 24o

toaster tōsutā トースター 23d

tobacco kizami tabako 刻みタバコ 25e

tobacco shop tabako senmonten タバコ専門店 25e

today kyō 今日 4a

toddler yōji 幼児 11b

toe ashiyubi 足指 12a

toenail ashi no tsume 足の爪 12a

toilet otearai お手洗い 23a, 23b

toilet toire トイレ 32c, 35c, 37c

toilet paper toiretto pēpā
トイレットペーパー 35c

toiletries senmenyōgu 洗面用具
12d, 25f

Tokyo Tōkyō 東京 30c

tolerance kanyō 寛容 21a

tolerant kanyō na *(adj)* 寛容な
21a

Toll (road sign) ryōkinsho
料金所 33d

toll booth ryōkinsho 料金所 33c

toll road yūryō dōro 有料道路
33c

toll-free torufurī no *(adj)* / muryō
no *(adj)* トルフリーの／無料の
18b

tomato tomato トマト 14e, 24e

tomorrow ashita 明日 4a

tomorrow afternoon ashita no
gogo 明日の午後 4a

tomorrow evening ashita no ban
明日の晩 4a

tomorrow evening ashita no
yūgata 明日の夕方 4a

tomorrow morning ashita no asa
明日の朝 4a

tomorrow night ashita no ban
明日の晩 4a

tomorrow night ashita no yoru
明日の夜 4a

ton ton トン 3a

tongue shita 舌 12a, 40b

tongue tan タン 24c

tonight konban 今晩 4a

tonsils hentōsen 扁桃腺 40a

Too bad! Zannen. 残念。 21c

too much ōsugi 多過ぎ 3c

tool daikudōgu 大工道具 23b,
25b

tool dōgu 道具 33c

tooth ha 歯 12a, 40b

toothache shitsū 歯痛 40b

toothbrush haburashi 歯ブラシ
12d, 25f, 40b

toothpaste nerihamigaki
練り歯磨き 12d, 25f, 40b

toothpick yōji 楊枝 24l

topaz topāzu トパーズ 25i

tornado tatsumaki 竜巻き 6a

torrential rain gōu 豪雨 6a

torture gōmon 拷問 44b

total eclipse kaikishoku 皆既蝕
13a

touch fureru *(v)* 触れる 12c

touch shokkan 触感 12c

tough katai *(adj)* 固い 13d, 24p

tour kankō ryokō 観光旅行 30a

tour bus kankō basu 観光バス
30a

tour guide kankō gaido
観光ガイド 30a

tour guide tsuā gaido
ツアーガイド 38a

tourist kaknō kyaku 観光客 30a

tournament tōnamento
トーナメント 27b

tow truck rekkāsha レッカー車
33a

toward ... ...no hō e ・・・の方へ
36c

toward ni taishite に対して 3d

Tow-Away Zone ken-in chiiki
牽引地域 33d

towel taoru タオル 12d, 23d, 35c

tower tō 塔 36a

town machi 町 11f

toxic dokusei no *(adj)* 毒性の
44a

track (railroad) sen 線 34

track (sports) torakku トラック
27b

track and field rikujōkyōgi
陸上競技 27b

tracking number tsuiseki bangō
追跡番号 19e

trackpad torakkupaddo
トラックパッド 42b

traditional dentōteki na (adj)
伝統的な 11e

traffic kōtsū 交通 33c

traffic accident kōtsū jikō
交通事故 39c

traffic jam kōtsū jūtai 交通渋滞
33c

traffic light shingō 信号 33c, 36a

traffic police kōtsū junsa
交通巡査 33b

tragedy higeki 悲劇 20a, 28e

trailer torērā トレーラー 33a

train kisha 汽車 34

train station eki 駅 34

train ticket kisha no kippu
汽車の切符 30a

trainer torēnā トレーナー 27b

training torēningu トレーニング
27b

transformer henatsuki 変圧器
25b

transitive verb tadōshi 他動詞
8a

translate honyakusuru 翻訳する
17a

translation honyaku 翻訳 17a

transmission sōshin 送信 20b

transparent tōmei na (adj)
透明な 7b, 13d

transplant ishoku 移植 14a

transplant ishokusuru (v)
移植する 14a

transporter jidōsha unpansha
自動車運搬車 33a

trapezoid daikei 台形 2a

trash gomibako ゴミ箱 19f

travel ryokō 旅行 30a

travel ryokōsuru (v) 旅行する
38

travel agency ryokō dairiten
旅行代理店 30a

traveler's check toraberā chekku
トラベラーチェック 26, 35b

tray obon お盆 23d, 24l

tray (plane) tēburu テーブル 32c

tree ki 木 14c

trenchcoat torenchikōto
トレンチコート 25k

trial saiban 裁判 41

trial lawyer hotei bengoshi
法廷弁護士 41

triangle sankakukei 三角形 2a

tricky zurugashikoi (adj)
ずる賢い 11e

trigonometric sankakuhō no (adj)
三角法の 2b

trigonometry sankakuhō 三角法
2b, 37e

trim (plants) karikomu (v)
刈り込む 14a

trio torio トリオ 28c

trip, journey ryokō 旅行 30a,
36b

triple sanbai ni suru (vt)
三倍にする 3c

triple sanbai no (adj) 三倍の 3c

tripod sankyaku 三脚 25k

trolley torōrīkā トローリーカー
33a

trombone toronbōn トロンボーン
28c

tropic kaikisen 回帰線 13e

Tropic of Cancer kitakaikisen
北回帰線 13e

Tropic of Capricorn
minamikaikisen 南回帰線 13e

tropical nettai no *(adj)* 熱帯の
13b, 13e

tropical nettaisei no *(adj)*
熱帯性の 6a

tropical zone nettaichitai
熱帯地帯 13e

troublemaker monchaku o okosu
hito 悶着を起こす人 11e

trousers zubon ズボン 25k

trout masu 鱒 15c, 24d

truck torakku トラック 33a

truck driver torakku no
untenshu トラックの運転手
38a

true honmono no *(adj)* 本物の 25i

trumpet toranpetto *(adj)*
トランペット 28c

trunk (car) toranku トランク 33e

trunk (tree) miki 幹 14a

trust shinraisuru *(v)* 信頼する
21a

trustworthy shinrai dekiru *(adj)*
信頼出来る 21a

try on tamesu *(v)* 試す 25m

tuba chūba チューバ 28c

Tuesday kayōbi 火曜日 5a

tulip chūrippu チューリップ 14b

tumor shuyō 腫瘍 40a

tuna maguro 鮪 15c, 24d

tuner chūnā チューナー 20b

tunnel tonneru トンネル 33c

turbulence rankiryū 乱気流 32c

Turk Torukojin トルコ人 30d

turkey shichimenchō 七面鳥
15b, 24c

Turkey Toruko トルコ 30b

Turkish (language) Torukogo
トルコ語 30d

turn magaru *(v)* 曲がる 3e, 33c,
36c

turn off kesu *(v)* 消す 20b, 35c

turn on tsukeru *(v)* つける 20b,
35c

turn pages, leaf through pēji o
mekuru *(v)* ページをめくる
20a

turn signal hōkō shijiki
方向指示器 33e

turn to the left hidari ni magaru
(v) 左に曲がる 33c

turn to the right migi ni magaru
(v) 右に曲がる 33c

turnip kabu 蕪 14e, 24e

turntable tāntēburu
ターンテーブル 20b

turtle kame 亀 15c

tweezers kenuki 毛抜き 25f

twelfth daijūni 第十二 1b

twelfth jūnibanme 十二番目 1b

twelve jūni 十二 1a

twelve thousand ichimannisen
一万二千 1a

twenty nijū 二十 1a

twenty thousand niman 二万 1a

twenty-eight nijūhachi 二十八
1a

twenty-five nijūgo 二十五 1a

twenty-four nijūshi/nijūyon
二十四 1a

twenty-nine nijūku/nijūkyū
二十九 1a

twenty-one nijūichi 二十一 1a

twenty-seven nijūshichi/
nijūnana 二十七 1a

twenty-six nijūroku 二十六 1a

twenty-third nijūsanbanme
二十三番目 1b

twenty-three nijūsan 二十三 1a

twenty-two nijūni 二十二 1a

twig koeda 小枝 14a

twin futago 双子 10a

two futatsu 二つ 1a

two ni 二 1a

two (bound objects) nisatsu
二冊 1a

two (floors) nikai 二階 1a

two (liquid or dry measure)
nihai 二杯 1a

two (long, thin objects) nihon
二本 1a

two (persons) futari 二人 1a

two (small objects) niko/futatsu
二個／二つ 1a

two (thin, flat objects) nimai
二枚 1a

two billion nijūoku 二十億 1a

two hundred nihyaku 二百 1a

two hundred and one
nihyakuichi 二百一 1a

two hundred ten nihyakujū
二百十 1a

two hundred thousand nijūman
二十万 1a

two million nihyakuman 二百万
1a

two thousand nisen 二千 1a

two thousand and one nisen-ichi
二千一 1a

two trillion nichō 二兆 1a

two-thirds sanbun no ni
三分の二 1c

typewriter taipuraitā
タイプライター 19d

typhoon taifū 台風 6a

U

Ugh! Wā, yada. わあ、やだ。
21c

ugly minikui (adj) 醜い 11a, 25l

ukulele ukurere ウクレレ 28c

ulcer ikaiyō 胃潰瘍 40a

ultraviolet light shigaisen
紫外線 13a

unacceptable ukeiregatai (adj)
受け入れ難い 21b

unbearable taegatai (adj)
耐え難い 21a

Unbelievable! Shinjirarenai. (inf)
信じられない。 21c

uncle oji 叔父 10a

uncle ojisan 叔父さん 10a

under shita ni (adv) 下に 3d

under shita no (adj) 下の 3d

underlining andārain
アンダーライン 19c

understand rikaisuru (v)
理解する 22b, 37f

underwear shitagi 下着 25k

undress mugu (v) 脱ぐ 25m

unemployment shitsugyō 失業
38d

unemployment compensation
shitsugyō teate 失業手当 38d

Unfortunately! Un waruku.
運悪く。 21c

unilateral ippōteki na (adj)
一方的な 43

union member kumiaiin 組合員
38d

United States of America
Amerika アメリカ 30b

universal suffrage futsū
senkyoken 普通選挙権 43

universe uchū 宇宙 13a

university daikagu 大学 11f, 37a, 38b

university degree gakushigō 学士号 11f

unknown michisū 未知数 1f

unlawful, illegal ihō no (adj) 違法の 41

unleaded gas muen gasorin 無鉛ガソリン 33c

unmarried mikon no 未婚の 11c

unpleasant fuyukai na (adj) 不愉快な 21b

unreserved seat jiyū seki 自由席 34

until made (adv) まで 4e, 8j

up ue ni (adv) 上に 3d

up ue no (adj) 上の 3d

uppercase ōmoji 大文字 19c

upright piano tategata piano 縦型ピアノ 28c

Uranus tennōsei 天王星 13a

urinary system hinyō keitō 泌尿系統 40a

urinate hainyōsuru (v) 排尿する 40a

urologist hinyōkikai 泌尿器科医 40a

us watakushitachi o 私達を 8e

USB yūesubī ユーエスビー 42b

user-friendly yūzā furendorī ユザーフレンドリー 42b

usually itsumo wa (adv) いつもは 4e

utter tsubuyaku (v) つぶやく 17a

V

vacation bakansu バカンス 29a, 36b

vaccination yobōsesshu 予防接種 40a

vacuum cleaner sōjiki 掃除機 23d

vagina chitsu 膣 12a

vain mieppari no (adj) 見栄っ張りの 11e

valley tani 谷 13b

valve (car) barubu バルブ 33e

van ban バン 33a

vapor kitai 気体 13c

variable hendō (no) (adj) 変動（の）26

variable (mathematics) hensū 変数 1f

VCR bideo ビデオ 20b

veal koushi no niku 子牛の肉 24c

vector dōkei 動径 2b

vegetable yasai 野菜 14e, 24e

vegetable garden saien 菜園 14e

vegetable store yasai ya 野菜屋 24n

vegetation kusaki 草木 13b

vein jōmyaku 静脈 40a

venereal disease seibyō 性病 40a

Venezuela Benezuera ベネズエラ 30b

vent (car) benchirētā ベンチレーター 33e

Venus kinsei 金星 13a

verb dōshi 動詞 8a

verdict hyōketsu 評決 41

vernal equinox shunbun 春分 5c

Vernal Equinox Day (March 20 or 21) shunbun no hi 春分の日 5g

versatile tagei na (adj) 多芸な 11e

vertebrate sekitsui dōbutsu 脊椎動物 15a

vertex chōten 頂点 2b

vertical suichoku no *(adj)* 垂直の 3d

vertical line suichokusen 垂直線 2b

Very well! Umaku itte imasu. うまくいっています。 16a

vest besuto/chokki ベスト／チョッキ 25k

victim giseisha 犠牲者 39a

victim higaisha 被害者 39b

video camera bideo kamera ビデオカメラ 25d

video disc bideo disuku ビデオディスク 25d

video game bideo gēmu ビデオゲーム 20b

videocassette bideo kasetto ビデオカセット 20b

videorock bideo rokku ビデオロック 20b

videotape bideo kasetto ビデオカセット 20b

Vienna Uīn ウイーン 30c

view nagame 眺め 35b

village mura 村 11f, 36b

vinegar su 酢 24j

viola biora ビオラ 28c

violence bōryoku 暴力 39b

violet sumire スミレ 14b

violin baiorin バイオリン 28c

violinist baiorin ensōsha バイオリン演奏者 28c

Virgo otomeza 乙女座 5d

virile danseiteki na *(adj)* 男性的な 11a

virus uirusu ウイルス 19f, 40a, 42b

virus check uirusu chekku ウイルスチェック 19f

visa biza ビザ 30a, 31

vise manriki 万力 25b

visit hōmonsuru *(v)* 訪問する 29b, 30a

vitamin bitaminzai ビタミン剤 25h

vivid azayaka na *(adj)* 鮮やかな 7b

vocabulary goi 語彙 17a

vocal cords seitai 声帯 12a

vodka wokka ウォッカ 24k

volcanic ash kazanbai 火山灰 13b

volcano kazan 火山 13b

volleyball barēbōru バレーボール 27b

volume taiseki/yōseki 体積／容積 3a

vomit haku *(v)* 吐く 40a

vote tōhyō 投票 43

vote tōhyōsuru *(v)* 投票する 43

voter tōhyōsha 投票者 43

vowel boin 母音 8a

vulnerable kizutsukiyasui *(adj)* 傷つきやすい 11e

vulture hagetaka 禿鷹 15b

W

wage chingin 賃金 38d

waist koshi 腰 12a

wait matsu *(v)* 待つ 4e

wait for matsu *(v)* 待つ 19e, 34

waiter uētā ウエーター 24m, 38a

waiting room raunji ラウンジ 32a

waitress uētoresu ウエートレス 24m, 38a

wake up me o samasu *(v)*
目を覚ます 12b

wake-up call mōningu koru
モーニングコール 35b

walk aruku *(v)* 歩く 3e, 12b

walk sanpo 散歩 3e

walking wōkingu ウォーキング
27a

walking shoes wōkingu shūzu
ウォーキングシューズ 25n

wall kabe 壁 23a

wall clock kakedokei 掛け時計
4d

walnut kurumi クルミ 14d, 24f

walnut tree kurumi no ki
クルミの木 14c

walrus seiuchi セイウチ 15a, 15c

waltz warutsu ワルツ 28c

ward ku 区 11f, 38b

warehouse sōko 倉庫 38d

warm atatakai *(adj)* 温かい 25l

warm front ondan zensen
温暖前線 6a

warm up atatakakunaru *(v)*
温かくなる 6b

warn keikokusuru *(v)* 警告する
17a

warning keikoku 警告 17a

wash arau *(v)* 洗う 12d, 23f

wash (laundry) sentakusuru *(v)*
洗濯する 25g

wash the clothes sentakusuru *(v)*
洗濯する 23f

wash the dishes sara o arau *(v)*
皿を洗う 23f

washable araeru *(adj)* 洗える
25g

washer sentakuki 洗濯機 25g

washer wasshā ワッシャー 25b

washing machine sentakuki
洗濯機 23d

wasp suzumebachi スズメバチ
15d

waste haikibutsu 廃棄物 13c,
44a

waste disposal haikibutsu shori
廃棄物処理 44a

waste management haikibutsu
kanri 廃棄物管理 44a

wastebasket kuzuire くず入れ
19d

wastebasket kuzukago くずかご
38c

watch battery tokei no denchi
時計の電池 4d

watch, clock tokei 時計 4d, 25i

watchband tokei no bando
時計のバンド 4d, 25i

water mizu 水 13b, 13c, 14a, 24k

water (service) suidō 水道 23e

water color suisaiga 水彩画 28b

water fountain funsui 噴水 36a

water pollution mizu osen
水汚染 44a

water polo suikyū 水球 27b

water skiing wōtā sukī
ウォータースキー 27b

water-heater yuwakashiki
湯沸かし器 23d

watermelon suika スイカ 14d,
24f

watery mizuppoi *(adj)* 水っぽい
24p

wave nami 波 13b

we watakushitachi ga/wa
私達が/は 8c

weak yowai *(adj)* 弱い 13d, 24p

weak yowayowashii *(adj)*
弱々しい 11a, 11e, 40a

weakness yowayowashisa 弱々しさ 11a

weapon kyōki 凶器 39b

wear kiru (v) 着る 25m

weather tenki 天気 6a

weather forecast tenki yohō 天気予報 6c

weather forecaster (radio, TV) tenki yohō gakari 天気予報係 6c

wedding kekkonshiki 結婚式 11c, 29a

wedding invitation kekkonshiki e no shōtai 結婚式への招待 11c

wedding ring kekkon yubiwa 結婚指輪 11c

Wednesday suiyōbi 水曜日 5a

week shū 週 4c

weekend shūmatsu 週末 5a

weekly maishū no (adj) 毎週の 4c

weekly magazine shūkanshi 週刊誌 20a

weekly periodical shūkanshi 週刊紙 20a

weep naku (v) 泣く 21a

weigh mekata o hakaru (v) 目方を量る 3b, 24o

weigh oneself jibun no taijū o hakaru (v) 自分の体重を量る 11a

weight jūryō 重量 3a, 3b

weight mekata 目方 31

weight omosa 重さ 11a

weight omosa/taijū/mekata 重さ／体重／目方 11a

weight lifting jūryōage 重量挙げ 27b

welfare shakai fukushi 社会福祉 43

well-done (steak) yoku yaita (adj) 良く焼けた 24b

well-mannered reigitadashii (adj) 礼儀正しい 11e

west nishi 西 3d

western nishi no (adj) 西の 3d

western seiō no (adj) 西欧の 11d

western-style room yōma 洋間 23b

wet nureta (adj)/shimetta (adj) 濡れた／湿った 6a

whale kujira 鯨 15a, 15c

what nani ga/no/ni 何が／の／に 8h

What? Nani. (inf) 何。 9

What a bore! Unzari. うんざり。 21c

What color is it? Nani iro desu ka. 何色ですか。 7a

What day is it? Kyō wa nani yōbi desu ka. 今日は何曜日ですか。 5a

What does it mean? Sore wa, donna imi desu ka. それは、どんな意味ですか。 9

What month is it? Nangatsu desu ka. 何月ですか。 5b

What time is it? Nanji desu ka. 何時ですか。 4b

What was I talking about? Watakushi wa, nani o hanashitei mashita ka. 私は、何を話していましたか。 17b

What year is it? Kotoshi wa nannen desu ka. 今年は何年ですか。 5e

What's today's date? Kyō wa nannichi desu ka. 今日は何日ですか。 5e

What's your name? Onamae wa, nan desu ka.
お名前は、何ですか。 11f, 16b

wheat komugi 小麦 24i

wheel sharin 車輪 32c, 33e

wheelchair kurumaisu 車椅子 40a

when itsu *(adv)* いつ 4e

When? Itsu. *(inf)* いつ。 9

When were you born? Itsu umaremashita ka.
いつ生まれましたか。 5e

where doko ni *(adv)* どこに 3d

Where? Doko. *(inf)* どこ。 9

Where do you live? Doko ni osumai desu ka.
どこにお住まいですか。 11f

Where is...? ... wa, doko desu ka. ・・・は、どこですか。 36c

which dore ga/dono/dore o どれが／どの／どれを 8h

Which (one)? Dore. *(inf)* どれ。 9

Which tooth hurts? Dono ha ga, itamimasu ka.
どの歯が、痛みますか。 40b

while ~no aida ni ・・・の間に 4e

whine nakigoto o iu *(v)* 泣き言を言う 17a

whiplash muchiuchishō むち打ち症 39c

whiskey uisukī ウイスキー 24k

whisper sasayaku *(v)* 囁く 17a

white shiro 白 7a

white shiroi *(adj)* 白い 7a

white birch shirakaba 白樺 14c

white wine howaito wain ホワイトワイン 24g

who dare ga 誰が 8h

Who? Dare. *(inf)* 誰。 9

Who knows? Dare mo, shirimasen yo. 誰も、知りませんよ。 17b

Who's speaking? (telephone) Donata sama desu ka.
どなた様ですか。 18b

whom dare o 誰を 8h

whooping cough hyakunichizeki 百日咳 40a

whose dare no 誰の 8h

Why? Naze. *(inf)* なぜ。 9

wide hiroi *(adj)* 広い 3b

wide angle lens kōkakurenzu 広角レンズ 25d

widow mibōjin 未亡人 11c

widower yamome やもめ 11c

width hirosa 広さ 3b

wife okusan 奥さん 10a

wife tsuma 妻 10a, 11c

Wi-Fi waifai/musen ran ワイファイ／無線ラン 42b

wild animal yajū 野獣 15a

wild boar inoshishi 猪 15a

wildflower nobana 野花 14b

willow yanagi 柳 14c

wilted flower shioreta hana しおれた花 14b

win katsu *(v)* 勝つ 27b

win a lawsuit shōsosuru *(v)* 勝訴する 41

wind kaze 風 6a

wind neji o maku *(v)* ねじを巻く 4d

wind energy fūryoku enerugī 風力エネルギー 44a

wind instruments mokkan gakki 木管楽器 28c

wind velocity fūryoku 風力 6a

window mado 窓 23a

window seat (plane) madogawa 窓側 32c

windowsill madowaku 窓枠
23a

windshield furontogarasu
フロントガラス 33e

windshield wiper waipā
ワイパー 33e

windsurfing windosāfin
ウィンドサーフィン 27b

wine wain ワイン 24g, 24k

wine glass waingurasu
ワイングラス 24l

wine list wain risuto
ワインリスト 24m

wing tsubasa 翼 15b, 32c

winter fuyu 冬 5c

winter solstice tōji 冬至 5c

winter sports fuyu no supōtsu
冬のスポーツ 27b

wire harigane 針金 25b

wireless waiyaresu ワイヤレス
42b

wireless connection waiyaresu
konekushon ワイヤレスコネ
クション 35c, 42a

wireless headset waiyaresu
heddosetto ワイヤレスヘッ
ドセット 18a

wisdom chie 知恵 22a

wisdom kenmei 賢明 11e

wisdom tooth oyashirazu
親知らず 40b

wise kenmei na (adj) 賢明な 11e

wisteria fuji 藤 14b

with to/de と／で 8j

with a check kogitte de (adv)
小切手で 25a

with a credit card kurejittokādo
de (adv) クレジットカードで
25a

with cash genkin de (adv) 現金で
25a

with ice kōri o irete (adv)
氷を入れて 24p

withdraw (banking) hikidasu (v)
引き出す 26

withdrawal (banking) hikidashi
引き出し 26

withdrawal slip (banking)
hikidashihyō 引き出し票 26

within inai ni 以内に 4e

without ice kōri o irenaide (adv)
氷を入れないで 24p

witness mokugekisuru (v)
目撃する 39b

witness shōnin 証人 41

wolf ōkami オオカミ 15a

woman josei 女性 11a

women's college joshidai 女子大
37a

women's shop fujinfuku ten
婦人服店 25k

wonderful subarashii (adj)
素晴らしい 21a

wooden clogs (Japanese) geta
下駄 35c

woodpecker kitsutsuki キツツキ
15b

woods mori 森 13b

wool ūru ウール 13c, 25g, 25l

Worcestershire sauce sōsu
ソース 24j

word kotoba 言葉 17a, 19c

word processing wāpuro shori
ワープロ処理 42b

work hataraku (v) 働く 11f, 38d

work shigoto 仕事 11f, 38d

work (literary) chosaku 著作
28d

work in a bank ginkō de hataraku 銀行で働く 26

Work in Progress kōjichū 工事中 33d

work out torēningusuru (v) トレーニングする 27b

work overtime zangyōsuru (v) 残業する 38d

workday heijitsu 平日 5a

working hours rōdō jikan 労働時間 38d

world sekai 世界 30a

worm mushi 虫 15d

wound, injury kega 怪我 39c

woven reed mat floor (Japanese) tatami 畳 23b

wrap hōsō 包装 25a

wrench supana スパナ 25b

wrestling resuringu レスリング 27b

wrist tekubi 手首 12a

wristwatch udedokei 腕時計 4d, 25i

write kaku (v) 書く 19e, 20a, 37f

writer chosha/hissha 著者／筆者 20a

writer sakka 作家 28d, 38a

writing desk desuku デスク 23c

writing pad hikki yōshi 筆記用紙 25c

written exam hikki shiken 筆記試験 37f

wrong machigatta (adj) 間違った 37f

Wrong number! Machigai denwa desu. 間違い電話です。 18b

X

X-rays rentogen レントゲン 39c, 40b

Y

yawn akubi あくび 17a

yawn akubisuru (v) あくびする 17a

year toshi 年 4c, 38b

year (e.g., at university) gakunen 学年 37a

Year of the Boar idoshi 亥年 5e

Year of the Cock toridoshi 酉年 5e

Year of the Dog inudoshi 戌年 5e

Year of the Dragon tatsudoshi 辰年 5e

Year of the Hare udoshi 卯年 5e

Year of the Horse umadoshi 午年 5e

Year of the Monkey sarudoshi 申年 5e

Year of the Ox ushidoshi 丑年 5e

Year of the Rat nezumidoshi 子年 5e

Year of the Serpent midoshi 巳年 5e

Year of the Sheep hitsujidoshi 未年 5e

Year of the Tiger toradoshi 寅年 5e

yearly, annually maitoshi no (adj) 毎年の 4c

yell wameku (v) わめく 17a

yellow kiiro 黄色 7a

yellow kiiroi (adj) 黄色い 7a

yellow pages shokugyōbetsu denwa chō 職業別電話帳 18a

yen en 円 26

Yes! Hai. はい。 16c

yesterday kinō 昨日 4a

yesterday afternoon kinō no
   gogo 昨日の午後 4a

yesterday morning kinō no asa
   昨日の朝 4a

yet mada *(adv)* まだ 4e

Yield yūsen 優先 33d

yoga yoga ヨガ 27a

yogurt yōguruto ヨーグルト
   24h

you (plural) anatatachi ga/wa
   あなた達が／は 8c

you (plural) anatatachi o
   あなた達を 8e

you anata ga/wa あなたが／は
   8c

you anata o あなたの 8e

You're welcome! Iie, dō
   itashimashite. いいえ、
   どういたしまして。 16c

young wakai *(adj)* 若い 11b

young man wakamono 若者 11a

younger toshishita no *(adj)*
   年下の 11b

younger brother otōto 弟 10a,
   11b

younger brother otōtosan
   弟さん 10a

younger sister imōto 妹 10a, 11b

younger sister imōtosan 妹さん
   10a

your anata no あなたの 8d

your (plural) anatatachi no
   あなた達の 8d

Yours sincerely keigu 敬具 19a

Yours truly keigu 敬具 19a

yourself anata jishin あなた自身
   8g

yourselves anatatachi jishin
   あなた達自身 8g

youth seinen jidai 青年時代 11b

youth hostel yūsu hosuteru
   ユースホステル 35a

youthful wakawakashii *(adj)*
   若々しい 11a

Z

zebra shimauma 縞馬 15a

Zen Buddhism zenshū 禅宗 11d

zenith tenchō 天頂 13a

zero zero/rei ゼロ／零 1a

zero (temperature) reido/hyōten
   零度／氷点 6c

zinnia hyakunichisō 百日草
   14b

zip code yūbin bangō 郵便番号
   11f, 19e, 38b

zipper jippā ジッパー 25g

zodiac jūnikyūzu 十二宮図 5d

zone chitai/chiiki 地帯／地域
   13e

zoo dōbutsuen 動物園 15a

zoological dōbutsugaku no *(adj)*
   動物学の 15a

zoology dōbutsugaku 動物学
   15a, 37e

zoom zūmu ズーム 25d

zoom lens zūmu renzu
   ズームレンズ 25d

zucchini zukkīni ズッキーニ
   14e, 24e

f. BASIC PERSONAL INFORMATION

> For jobs and professions see Section 38.

address	jūsho	*jōo-shoh*
• avenue	gai	*gah-ee*
• city	shi	*shee*
• country	kuni	*koo-nee*
• metropolis	to	*toh*
• prefecture	ken	*kehn*
• square	hiroba	*hee-roh-bah*
• state	shū	*shōo*
• street	tōri	*toh-ree*
• town	machi	*mah-chee*
• village	mura	*moo-rah*
• ward	ku	*koo*
• live	sumu *(v)*	*soo-moo*
• Where do you live?	Doko ni osumai desu ka.	*DOH-koh nee oh-soo-mah-ee dehs kah*
• I live ...	...ni sunde imasu	*... nee soon-deh ee-mahs*
age	nenrei / toshi	*nehn-reh / toh-shee*
area code	shigaikyokuban	*shee-gah-ee-kyoh-koo-bahn*
be from ...	...kara kimashita	*... kah-rah kee-mah-shtah*
career	keireki	*keh-reh-kee*
date of birth	seinengappi	*seh-nehn-gahp-pee*
divorced	rikon shita *(adj)*	*ree-kohn shtah*
education	kyōiku	*kyoh-ee-koo*
• go to school	gakkō ni iku *(v)*	*gahk-koh nee ee-koo*
• finish school	gakkō o oeru *(v)*	*gahk-koh oh oh-eh-roo*
• elementary school	shōgakkō	*shoh-gahk-koh*
• junior high school	chūgaku	*chōo-gah-koo*
• high school	kōkō	*koh-koh*
• junior college	tandai	*tahn-dah-ee*
• university	daigaku	*dah-ee-gah-koo*
• graduate school	daigakuin	*dah-ee-gah-koo-een*
• university degree	gakushigō	*gahk-shee-goh*
• diploma	sotsugyōshōsho	*soh-tsoo-gyoh-shoh-shoh*
• graduate	sotsugyōsei	*soh-tsoo-gyoh-seh*
• graduate	sotsugyōsuru *(v)*	*soh-tsoo-gyoh-soo-roo*
e-mail address	ī-mēru adoresu	*ēe-meh-roo ah-doh-reh-soo*
employment	koyō	*koh-yoh*
• employer	koyōsha	*koh-yoh-shah*
• employee	jūgyōin	*jōo-gyoh-een*
fax number	fakkusu bangō	*fahk-koos bahn-goh*
identification	mibunshōmei	*mee-boon-shoh-meh*
job	shigoto	*shee-goh-toh*

married	kikon no *(adj)*	*kee-kohn noh*
name	namae	*nah-mah-eh*
• first name	namae	*nah-mah-eh*
• family name	myōji	*myoh-jee*
• surname	myōji	*myoh-jee*
• be called	yobareru *(v)*	*yoh-bah-reh-roo*
• How do you write your name?	Onamae wa, dō kakimasu ka.	*oh-nah-mah-eh wah, DOH kah-kee-mahs kah*
• Print your name.	Onamae o, kaisho de kaite kudasai.	*oh-nah-mah-eh oh, kah-ee-shoh deh kah-ee-teh koo-dah-sah-ee*
• What's your name?	Onamae wa, nan desu ka.	*oh-nah-mah-eh wah NAHN dehs kah*
• My name is ...	Watakushi no namae wa, ... desu.	*wah-tahk-shee noh nah-mah-eh wah, ... dehs*
• sign	shomeisuru *(v)*	*shoh-meh-soo-roo*
• signature	shomei	*shoh-meh*

FOCUS: Names and Titles

Japanese use family names first, first names last.
Yamada Taro is Mr. Yamada. Taro is his first name. When Japanese introduce themselves to each other, they say the family name first.

Japanese prefer family names, not first names.
Japanese adults rarely use first names. Even among close friends, family names are the rule, first names the exception.

Japanese use titles with names.
When speaking to someone or when referring to another person, Japanese use san after the family name. It's like the English Mr., Mrs., Ms., or Miss. Even when using a friend's first name, they add san. For example, if they were using Yamada san's first name, people would say "Taro san," not "Taro." San is never used to refer to oneself. Japanese use young children's first names followed by chan, older children's names followed by san.

Japanese use the word "teacher" for people other than teachers.
Teachers are called sensei, a term of respect. It's also used for people with profound knowledge, exceptional skill, or a certain social status. For example, doctors, dentists, artists, Diet (Congress) members, and celebrities are also addressed as sensei.

nationality	kokuseki	kohk-seh-kee
place of birth	shusseichi	shoos-seh-chee
place of employment	koyōsaki	koh-yoh-sah-kee
profession	shokugyō	shoh-koo-gyoh
• professional	senmonteki na (adj)	sehn-mohn-teh-kee nah
residence	jūsho	jōō-shoh
separated	bekkyoshita (adj)	behk-kyoh-shtah
single	mikon no (adj)	mee-kohn noh
telephone number	denwabangō	dehn-wah-bahn-goh
title	shōgō	shoh-goh
• Dr. (Ph.D. degree)	hakase	hah-kah-seh
• Miss, Ms.	san	sahn
• Mr.	san	sahn
• Mrs., Ms.	san	sahn
• Prof.	kyōju	kyoh-joo
work	shigoto	shee-goh-toh
• work	hataraku (v)	hah-tah-rah-koo
zip code	yūbin bangō	yōō-been bahn-goh

12. THE BODY

a. PARTS OF THE BODY

> See also Section 40.

abdomen	fukubu	foo-koo-boo
ankle	ashikubi	ah-shee-koo-bee
anus	kōmon	koh-mohn
appendix	mōchō	moh-choh
arm	ude	oo-deh

> **capable (lit. with an arm)** | ude no aru | oo-deh noh ah-roo

armpit	wakinoshita	wah-kee-noh-shtah
back	senaka	seh-nah-kah
beard	agohige	ah-goh-hee-geh
belly	onaka	oh-nah-kah
bladder	bōkō	boh-koh
blood	chi/ketsueki	chee/keh-tsoo-eh-kee
body	karada	kah-rah-dah
bone	hone	hoh-neh
brain	nō	noh
breast	chibusa	chee-boo-sah

buttock	oshiri	*oh-shee-ree*
cheek	hoo	*hoh-oh*
chest	mune	*moo-neh*
chin	ago	*ah-goh*

| to order a person about (*lit.* to give orders by pointing with one's chin) | ago de tsukau | *ah-goh deh tskah-oo* |

ear	mimi	*mee-mee*
elbow	hiji	*hee-jee*
esophagus	shokudō	*shoh-koo-doh*
eye	me	*meh*
eyebrow	mayuge	*mah-yoo-geh*
eyelash	matsuge	*mah-tsoo-geh*
eyelid	mabuta	*mah-boo-tah*
face	kao	*kah-oh*
finger	yubi	*yoo-bee*
• fingernail	tsume	*tsoo-meh*
• index finger	hitosashiyubi	*hee-toh-sah-shee-yoo-bee*
• little finger	koyubi	*koh-yoo-bee*
• middle finger	nakayubi	*nah-kah-yoo-bee*
• ring finger	kusuri yubi	*koo-soo-ree yoo-bee*
• thumb	oyayubi	*oh-yah-yoo-bee*
foot	ashi	*ah-shee*
forehead	hitai	*hee-tah-ee*
gallbladder	tannō	*tahn-noh*
genitals	gaiinbu	*gah-ee-een-boo*
gland	sen	*sehn*
hair	kaminoke	*kah-mee-noh-keh*
hand	te	*teh*
head	atama	*ah-tah-mah*
heart	shinzō	*sheen-zoh*

| to be brazen (*lit.* the heart is strong) | shinzō ga tsuyoi | *sheen-zoh gah tsoo-yoh-ee* |

heel	kakato	*kah-kah-toh*
hip	oshiri	*oh-shee-ree*
intestines	chō	*choh*
jaw	ago	*ah-goh*
kidney	jinzō	*jeen-zoh*
knee	hiza	*hee-zah*
knuckles	kobushi	*koh-boo-shee*

leg	ashi	*ah-shee*
lip	kuchibiru	*koo-chee-bee-roo*
liver	kanzō	*kahn-zoh*
lung	hai	*hah-ee*
mouth	kuchi	*koo-chee*
muscle	kinniku	*keen-nee-koo*

FOCUS: Parts of the Body

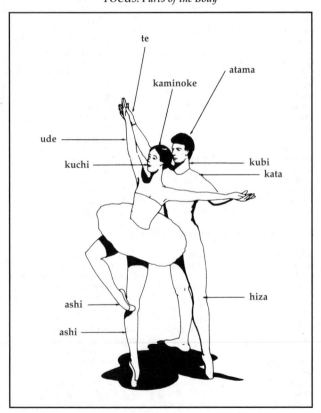

mustache	kuchihige	*koo-chee-hee-geh*
neck	kubi	*koo-bee*
nose	hana	*hah-nah*
nostril	bikō	*bee-koh*
organ	naizō	*nah-ee-zoh*
palm	tenohira	*teh-noh-hee-rah*
pancreas	suizō	*soo-ee-zoh*
penis	penisu	*peh-nees*
prostate	zenritsusen	*zehn-ree-tsoo-sehn*
rectum	kōmon	*koh-mohn*
shoulder	kata	*kah-tah*
skin	hifu	*hee-foo*
skull	zugaikotsu	*zoo-gah-ee-koh-tsoo*
spine, backbone	sebone	*seh-boh-neh*
sole	ashi no ura	*ah-shee noh oo-rah*
stomach	i	*ee*
tendon	ken	*kehn*
testicle	kōgan	*koh-gahn*
thigh	futomomo	*ftoh-moh-moh*
throat	nodo	*noh-doh*
toe	ashiyubi	*ah-shee-yoo-bee*
• toenail	ashi no tsume	*ah-shee noh tsoo-meh*
tongue	shita	*shtah*
tooth	ha	*hah*
vagina	chitsu	*chee-tsoo*
vocal cords	seitai	*seh-tah-ee*
waist	koshi	*koh-shee*
wrist	tekubi	*teh-koo-bee*

b. PHYSICAL STATES AND ACTIVITIES

ache	itamu *(v)*	*ee-tah-moo*
be cold	samui (desu)	*sah-moo-ee (dehs)*
be dizzy	memai ga suru	*meh-mah-ee gah soo-roo*
be fine	genki (desu)	*gehn-kee (dehs)*
be full	onaka ga ippai (desu)	*oh-nah-kah gah eep-pah-ee (dehs)*
be healthy	kenkō (desu)	*kehn-koh (dehs)*
be hot	atsui (desu)	*ah-tsoo-ee (dehs)*
be hungry	onaka ga suite imasu	*oh-nah-kah gah soo-ee-teh ee-mahs*
• hunger	kūfuku	*koo-foo-koo*
be ill	byōki (desu)	*byoh-kee (dehs)*
be painful	itai (desu)	*ee-tah-ee (dehs)*
be sick	byōki (desu)	*byoh-kee (dehs)*
be strong	jōbu (desu)	*joh-boo (dehs)*
be sleepy	nemui (desu)	*neh-moo-ee (dehs)*

• sleep	nemuru *(v)*	neh-moo-roo
be thirsty	nodo ga kawaite imasu	noh-doh gah kah-wah-ee-teh ee-mahs
be tired	tsukarete imasu	tskah-reh-teh ee-mahs
be weak	yowatte (imasu)	yoh-waht-teh (ee-mahs)
breathe	ikizuku *(v)*	ee-kee-zoo-koo
drink	nomu *(v)*	noh-moo
eat	taberu *(v)*	tah-beh-roo
faint	kizetsusuru *(v)*	kee-zeh-tsoo-soo-roo
fall asleep	nekomu *(v)*	neh-koh-moo
feel bad	kibun ga warui	kee-boon gah wah-roo-ee
feel well	kibun ga ii	kee-boon gah ēē
get hurt	kega o suru *(v)*	keh-gah oh soo-roo
get up	okiru *(v)*	oh-kee-roo
go to bed	neru *(v)*	neh-roo
jog	jogingu suru *(v)*	joh-geen-goo soo-roo
nap	hirune	hee-roo-neh
• nap	hirunesuru *(v)*	hee-roo-neh-soo-roo
recover	kaifukusuru *(v)*	kah-ee-foo-koo-soo-roo
relax	kutsurogu *(v)*	ktsoo-roh-goo
rest	yasumu *(v)*	yah-soo-moo
run	hashiru *(v)*	hah-shee-roo
shiver	furueru *(v)*	foo-roo-eh-roo
sweat	ase o kaku *(v)*	ah-seh oh kah-koo
wake up	me o samasu *(v)*	meh oh sah-mahs
walk	aruku *(v)*	ah-roo-koo

c. SENSORY PERCEPTION

blind	me no mienai *(adj)*	meh noh mee-eh-nah-ee
• blindness	mōmoku	moh-moh-koo
deaf	mimi no tōi *(adj)*	mee-mee noh tōh-ee
flavor	aji	ah-jee
• taste	ajiwau *(v)*	ah-jee-wah-oo
hear	kiku *(v)*	kee-koo
• hearing	chōryoku	chōh-ryoh-koo
listen to	kiku *(v)*	kee-koo
look	nagameru *(v)*	nah-gah-meh-roo
mute	gengoshōgai no *(adj)*	gehn-goh-shōh-gah-ee noh
noise	sōon	soh-ohn
• noisy	yakamashii *(adj)*	yah-kah-mah-shēē
perceive	chikakusuru *(v)*	chee-kah-koo-soo-roo
• perception	chikakuryoku	chee-kah-koo-ryoh-koo
	miru *(v)*	mee-roo
• sight	shikaku	shee-kah-koo
sense, feel	kanjiru *(v)*	kahn-jee-roo
• sense	kankaku	kahn-kah-koo

sensitive	binkan na *(adj)*	*been-kahn nah*
sixth sense	dai rokkan	*dah-ee rohk-kahn*
smell	nioi	*nee-oh-ee*
• smell	niou *(vi)*	*nee-oh-oo*
sound	oto	*oh-toh*
touch	shokkan	*shohk-kahn*
• touch	fureru *(v)*	*foo-reh-roo*

d. PERSONAL CARE

barber	rihatsushi	*ree-hah-tsoo-shee*
• barber shop	tokoya	*toh-koh-yah*
bath	ofuro	*oh-foo-roh*
• take a bath	ofuro ni hairu *(v)*	*oh-foo-roh nee hah-ee-roo*
beautician	biyōshi	*bee-yoh-shee*
brush	burashi	*boo-rah-shee*
• brush oneself	burashi o kakeru *(v)*	*boo-rah-shee oh kah-keh-roo*
clean	seiketsu na *(adj)*	*seh-keh-tsoo nah*
comb	kushi	*koo-shee*
• comb	kushi de tokasu *(v)*	*koo-shee deh toh-kah-soo*
cosmetics	keshōhin / kosume	*keh-shoh-heen/koh-soo-meh*
curls	kāru	*kah-roo*
• curlers	kārā	*kah-rah*
cut one's hair	kaminoke o kiru *(v)*	*kah-mee-noh-keh oh kee-roo*
dirty	kitanai *(adj)*	*kee-tah-nah-ee*
drugstore	doraggusutoa	*doh-rahg-goo-stoh-ah*
dry	kawakasu *(v)*	*kah-wah-kah-soo*
esthetician	esute biyōshi	*eh-steh bee-yoh-shee*
esthetics	esute / zenshin biyō	*eh-steh/zehn-sheen bee-yoh*
facial	biganjutsu	*bee-gahn-joo-tsoo*
grooming	midashinami	*mee-dah-shee-nah-mee*
hairdresser	biyōshi	*bee-yoh-shee*
hair dryer	heā doraiyā	*heh-ah doh-rah-ee-yah*
hair spray	heā supurē	*heh-ah spoo-reh*
hygiene	eisei	*eh-seh*
• hygienic	eiseiteki na *(adj)*	*eh-seh-teh-kee nah*
makeup	keshō	*keh-shoh*
• put on makeup	okeshōsuru *(v)*	*oh-keh-shoh-soo-roo*
manicure	manikyua	*mah-nee-kyoo-ah*
mascara	masukara	*mahs-kah-rah*
massage	massāji	*mahs-sah-jee*
nail polish	manikyuaeki	*mah-nee-kyoo-ah-eh-kee*

perfume	kōsui	*koh-soo-ee*
• put on perfume	kōsui o tsukeru *(v)*	*koh-soo-ee oh tskeh-roo*
permanent wave	pāmanento	*pah-mah-nehn-toh*
razor	kamisori	*kah-mee-soh-ree*
• electric razor	denki kamisori	*dehn-kee kah-mee-soh-ree*
• razor blade	kamisori no ha	*kah-mee-soh-ree noh hah*
scissors	hasami	*hah-sah-mee*
shampoo	shanpū	*shahn-poo*
shave	hige o soru *(v)*	*hee-geh oh soh-roo*
shower	shawā	*shah-wah*
• shower	shawā o abiru *(v)*	*shah-wah oh ah-bee-roo*
soap	sekken	*sehk-kehn*
toiletries	senmenyōgu	*sehn-mehn-yoh-goo*
toothbrush	haburashi	*hah-boo-rah-shee*
toothpaste	nerihamigaki	*neh-ree-hah-mee-gah-kee*
towel	taoru	*tah-oh-roo*
wash	arau *(v)*	*ah-rah-oo*

THE PHYSICAL, PLANT, AND ANIMAL WORLDS

13. THE PHYSICAL WORLD

> For Signs of the Zodiac, see Section 5.

a. THE UNIVERSE

asteroid	shōwakusei	*shoh-wahk-seh*
astronomy	tenmongaku	*tehn-mohn-gah-koo*
black hole	burakkuhōru	*boo-rahk-koo-hoh-roo*
comet	suisei	*soo-ee-seh*
corona	korona	*koh-roh-nah*
cosmos	uchū	*oo-choo*
eclipse	shoku	*shoh-koo*
• lunar eclipse	gesshoku	*gehs-shoh-koo*
• partial eclipse	bubunshoku	*boo-boon-shoh-koo*
• solar eclipse	nisshoku	*nees-shoh-koo*
• total eclipse	kaikishoku	*kah-ee-kee-shoh-koo*
galaxy	ginga	*geen-gah*
gravitation	inryoku	*een-ryoh-koo*
• gravity	inryoku	*een-ryoh-koo*
light	hikari/kōsen	*hee-kah-ree/koh-sehn*
• infrared light	sekigaisen	*seh-kee-gah-ee-sehn*
• light year	kōnen	*koh-nehn*
• ultraviolet light	shigaisen	*shee-gah-ee-sehn*
meteor	ryūsei	*ryoo-seh*
meteorite	inseki	*een-seh-kee*
Milky Way	amanogawa	*ah-mah-noh-gah-wah*
moon	tsuki	*tskee*
• full moon	mangetsu	*mahn-geh-tsoo*
• moonbeam, ray	gekkō	*gehk-koh*
• moon phases	tsuki no michikake	*tsoo-kee noh mee-chee-kah-keh*
• new moon	shingetsu	*sheen-geh-tsoo*
orbit	kidō	*kee-doh*
• orbit	kidō ni noru *(vi)*	*kee-doh nee noh-roo*
• orbit	kidō ni noseru *(vt)*	*kee-doh nee noh-seh-roo*
planet	wakusei	*wahk-seh*
• Earth	chikyū	*chee-kyoo*
• Jupiter	mokusei	*mohk-seh*

• Mars	kasei	*kah-seh*
• Mercury	suisei	*soo-ee-seh*
• Neptune	kaiōsei	*kah-ee-oh-seh*
• Pluto	meiōsei	*meh-oh-seh*
• Saturn	dosei	*doh-seh*
• Uranus	tennōsei	*tehn-noh-seh*
• Venus	kinsei	*keen-seh*
Polaris	hokkyokusei	*hohk-kyohk-seh*
satellite	eisei	*eh-seh*
Southern Cross	minamijūjisei	*mee-nah-mee-joo-jee-seh*
space	kūkan	*koo-kahn*
star	kōsei	*koh-seh*
sun	taiyō	*tah-ee-yoh*
• sunlight	nikkō	*neek-koh*
• sunray	taiyō kōsen	*tah-ee-yoh koh-sehn*
• sunspot	taiyō no kokuten	*tah-ee-yoh noh kohk-tehn*
• solar system	taiyōkei	*tah-ee-yoh-keh*
universe	uchū	*oo-choo*
zenith	tenchō	*tehn-choh*

b. THE ENVIRONMENT

> See also Section 44.

air	kūki	*koo-kee*
archipelago	guntō	*goon-toh*
atmosphere	taiki	*tah-ee-kee*
• atmospheric	taiki no *(adj)*	*tah-ee-kee noh*
basin	bonchi	*bohn-chee*
bay	wan	*wahn*
beach	hama	*hah-mah*
bush	yabu	*yah-boo*
canyon	kyōkoku	*kyoh-koh-koo*
cape	misaki	*mee-sah-kee*
cave	dōkutsu	*doh-ktsoo*
channel	suiro	*soo-ee-roh*
cliff	zeppeki	*zehp-peh-kee*
cloud	kumo	*koo-moh*
coast	engan	*ehn-gahn*
• coastal	engan no *(adj)*	*ehn-gahn noh*
continent	tairiku	*tah-ee-ree-koo*
• continental	tairiku no *(adj)*	*tah-ee-ree-koo noh*
cove	irie	*ee-ree-eh*
desert	sabaku	*sah-bah-koo*
dune	sakyū	*sah-kyoo*
earthquake	jishin	*jee-sheen*

environment	kankyō	*kahn-kyoh*
farmland	nōchi	*noh-chee*
fault	dansō	*dahn-soh*
field	nohara	*noh-hah-rah*
forest	shinrin	*sheen-reen*
glacier	hyōga	*kyoh-gah*
gorge	kyōkoku	*kyoh-koh-koo*
grass	sōgen	*soh-gehn*
gulf	wan	*wahn*
hill	oka	*oh-kah*
ice	kōri	*koh-ree*
island	shima	*shee-mah*
jungle	mitsurin	*mee-tsoo-reen*
lake	mizuumi	*mee-zoo-oo-mee*
land	rikuchi	*ree-koo-chee*
landscape	keshiki	*keh-shee-kee*
marsh	shitchi	*sheet-chee*
meadow	sōgen	*soh-gehn*
mountain	yama	*yah-mah*

to take a chance *(lit.* to bet a mountain)	yama o kakeru	*yah-mah oh kah-keh-roo*

• mountain chain	sanmyaku	*sahn-myah-koo*
• mountainous	yama no ōi *(adj)*	*yah-mah noh oh-ee*
• peak	chōjō	*choh-joh*
nature	shizen	*shee-zehn*
• natural	shizen no *(adj)*	*shee-zehn noh*
ocean	taiyō	*tah-ee-yoh*
• Antarctic Ocean	nanpyōyō	*nahn-pyoh-yoh*
• Arctic Ocean	hoppyōyō	*hohp-pyoh-yoh*
• Atlantic Ocean	taiseiyō	*tah-ee seh-yoh*
• Pacific Ocean	taiheiyō	*tah-ee-heh-yoh*
ocean current	kairyū	*kah-ee-ryoo*
peninsula	hantō	*hahn-toh*
plain	heiya	*heh-yah*
plateau	kōgen	*koh-gehn*
rain forest	urin	*oo-reen*
ravine	kyōkoku	*kyoh-koh-koo*
river	kawa	*kah-wah*
• flow	nagareru *(v)*	*nah-gah-reh-roo*
rock	iwa	*ee-wah*
sand	suna	*snah*
sea	umi	*oo-mee*
• Sea of Japan	Nihonkai	*nee-HOHN-kah-ee*

sky	sora	*soh-rah*
soil	dojō	*doh-joh*
stone	ishi	*ee-shee*
swamp	shitchi	*sheet-chee*
tide	chōryū	*choh-ryoo*
• high tide	manchō	*mahn-choh*
• low tide	kanchō	*kahn-choh*
tropical	nettai no *(adj)*	*neht-tah-ee noh*
valley	tani	*tah-nee*
vegetation	kusaki	*ksah-kee*
volcano	kazan	*kah-zahn*
• active volcano	kakkazan	*kahk-kah-zahn*
• dormant volcano	kyūkazan	*kyoo-kah-zahn*
• eruption	funka	*foon-kah*
• extinct volcano	shikazan	*shee-kah-zahn*
• lava	yōgan	*yoh-gahn*
• volcanic ash	kazanbai	*kah-zahn-bah-ee*
water	mizu	*mee-zoo*
wave	nami	*nah-mee*
woods	mori	*moh-ree*

c. MATTER AND THE ENVIRONMENT

See also Section 42.

acid	san	*sahn*
• acid rain	sanseiu	*sahn-seh-oo*
air	kūki	*koo-kee*
aluminum	arumi	*ah-roo-mee*
ammonia	anmonia	*ahn-moh-nee-ah*
asbestos	asubesuto / sekimen	*ahs-beh-stoh/seh-kee-mehn*
atom	genshi	*gehn-shee*
• charge	genshikaku no yōdenka	*gehn-shee-kah-koo noh yoh-dehn-kah*
• electron	denshi	*dehn-shee*
• neutron	chūseishi	*choo-seh-shee*
• nucleus	genshikaku	*gehn-shee-kah-koo*
• proton	yōshi	*yoh-shee*
bronze	seidō	*seh-doh*
carbon	tanso	*tahn-soh*
carbon monoxide	issannka tanso	*ees-sahn-kah tahn-soh*
carbon fiber	tanso sen-i	*tahn-soh sehn-ee*
carbon dioxide	nisanka tanso	*nee-sahn-kah tahn-soh*
chemical	kagaku no *(adj)*	*kah-gah-koo noh*
• chemistry	kagaku	*kah-gah-koo*
chlorine	enso	*ehn-soh*

coal	sekitan	*seh-kee-tahn*
• coal mine	tankō	*tahn-koh*
• coal mining	tankō	*tahn-koh*
compound	kagōbutsu	*kah-goh-boo-tsoo*
copper	dō	*doh*
coral	sango	*sahn-goh*
cotton	men	*mehn*
dioxin	daiokishin	*dah-ee-oh-kee-sheen*
electrical	denki no *(adj)*	*dehn-kee noh*
• electricity	denki	*dehn-kee*
electronic	denshi no *(adj)*	*dehn-shee noh*
• electron	denshi	*dehn-shee*
element	genso	*gehn-soh*
endangered species	zetsumetsu kikenshu	*zeh-tsoo-meh-tsoo kee-kehn-shoo*
energy	enerugī	*eh-neh-roo-gee*
• fossil fuel	kaseki nenryō	*kah-seh-kee nehn-ryoh*
• nuclear energy	kaku enerugī	*kah-koo eh-neh-roo-gee*
• solar energy	taiyō enerugī	*tah-ee-yoh eh-neh-roo-gee*
environmental protection	kankyō hogo	*kahn-kyoh hoh-goh*
fiber	sen-i	*sehn-ee*
fire	kaji	*kah-jee*
fuel	nenryō	*nehn-ryoh*
gas	gasu	*gah-soo*
• natural gas	tennen gasu	*tehn-nehn gah-soo*
gasoline	gasorin	*gah-soh-reen*
global warming	chikyū ondanka	*chee-kyoo ohn-dahn-kah*
gold	kin	*keen*
greenhouse effect	onshitsu kōka	*ohn-shee-tsoo koh-kah*
heat	netsu	*neh-tsoo*
hydrogen	suiso	*soo-ee-soh*
industrial	kōgyō no *(adj)*	*koh-gyoh noh*
• industry	kōgyō	*koh-gyoh*
iodine	yōso	*yoh-soh*
iron	tetsu	*teh-tsoo*
ivory	zōge	*zoh-geh*
laboratory	jikkenshitsu	*jeek-kehn-shee-tsoo*
lead	namari	*nah-mah-ree*
leather	kawa	*kah-wah*
liquid	ekitai	*eh-kee-tah-ee*
material	genryō	*gehn-ryoh*
matter	busshitsu	*boos-shee-tsoo*
mercury	suigin	*soo-ee-geen*
metal	kinzoku	*keen-zoh-koo*
methane	metan	*meh-tahn*
microscope	kenbikyō	*kehn-bee-kyoh*

mineral	kōbutsu	koh-boo-tsoo
molecular	bunshi no *(adj)*	boon-shee noh
• molecular model	bunshi kōzō mokei	boon-shee koh-zoh moh-keh
• molecular formula	bunshishiki	boon-shee-shee-kee
• molecular structure	bunshi kōzō	boon-shee koh-zoh
molecule	bunshi	boon-shee
natural resources	tennenshigen	tehn-nehn-shee-gehn
nitrogen	chisso	chees-soh
oil	sekiyu	seh-kee-yoo
organic	yūki no *(adj)*	yoo-kee noh
• inorganic	muki no *(adj)*	moo-kee noh
oxygen	sanso	sahn-soh
particle	bibunshi	bee-boon-shee
pelt	kegawa	keh-gah-wah
pesticide	satchūzai	saht-choo-zah-ee
petroleum	sekiyu	seh-kee-yoo
phosphate	rinsan-en	reen-sahn-ehn
physical	butsuri no *(adj)*	boo-tsoo-ree noh
• physics	butsuri	boo-tsoo-ree
plankton	purankuton	poo-rahnk-tohn
plastic	purasuchikku	poo-rahs-cheek-koo
platinum	purachina	poo-rah-chee-nah
pollution	osen	oh-sehn
radiation	hōshanō	hoh-shah-noh
• radioactive	hōshasei no *(adj)*	hoh-shah-seh noh
salt	shio	shee-oh
silk	kinu	kee-noo
silver	gin	geen
smoke	kemuri	keh-moo-ree
sodium	natoriumu	nah-toh-ree-oo-moo
solid	kotai no *(adj)*	koh-tah-ee noh
species	shu	shoo
steel	tekkō	tehk-koh
• stainless steel	sutenresu suchīru	stehn-rehs schee-roo
stuff	shizai	shee-zah-ee
styrofoam	happōsuchirōru	hahp-poh-schee-roh-roo
substance	busshitsu	boos-shee-tsoo
sulphur	iō	ee-oh
• sulphuric acid	ryūsan	ryoo-sahn
synthetic	gōsei no *(adj)*	goh-seh noh
textile	orimono	oh-ree-moh-noh
vapor	kitai	kee-tah-ee
waste	haikibutsu	hah-ee-kee-boots
• industrial waste	kōgyō haikibutsu	koh-gyoh hah-ee-kee-boots
• nuclear waste	kaku haikibutsu	kah-koo hah-ee-kee-boots
water	mizu	me-zoo
wool	ūru	oo-roo

d. CHARACTERISTICS OF MATTER

artificial	jinzō no *(adj)*	*jeen-zoh noh*
brittle	moroi *(adj)*	*moh-roh-ee*
authentic	honmono no *(adj)*	*hohn-moh-noh noh*
clear	sukitootta *(adj)*	*skee-toh-oht-tah*
dense	mitsudo ga takai *(adj)*	*MEE-tsoo-doh gah tah-kah-ee*
elastic	danryokusei no aru *(adj)*	*dahn-ryohk-seh noh ah-roo*
fake	nise no *(adj)*	*nee-seh noh*
fragile	kowareyasui *(adj)*	*koh-wah-reh-yah-soo-ee*
hard	katai *(adj)*	*kah-tah-ee*
heavy	omoi *(adj)*	*oh-moh-ee*
large	ōkii *(adj)*	*oh-kee*
light	karui *(adj)*	*kah-roo-ee*
malleable	katansei no aru *(adj)*	*kah-tahn-seh noh ah-roo*
medium	chūgurai no *(adj)*	*choo-goo-rah-ee noh*
natural	tennen no *(adj)*	*tehn-nehn noh*
opaque	futōmei na *(adj)*	*foo-toh-meh nah*
pure	junsui no *(adj)*	*joon-soo-ee noh*
resistant	teikōsei no aru *(adj)*	*teh-koh-seh noh ah-roo*
robust	ganjō na *(adj)*	*gahn-joh nah*
rough	kime ga arai *(adj)*	*kee-meh gah ah-RAH-ee*
small	chiisai *(adj)*	*chee-sah-ee*
smooth	nameraka na *(adj)*	*nah-meh-rah-kah nah*
soft	yawarakai *(adj)*	*yah-wah-rah-kah-ee*
soluble	yōkaisei no aru *(adj)*	*yoh-kah-ee-seh noh ah-roo*
stable	anteishita *(adj)*	*ahn-teh-shtah*
strong	tsuyoi *(adj)*	*tsoo-yoh-ee*
synthetic	gōsei no *(adj)*	*goh-seh noh*
thick	atsui *(adj)*	*ah-tsoo-ee*
thin	usui *(adj)*	*oo-soo-ee*
tough	katai *(adj)*	*kah-tah-ee*
transparent	tōmei na *(adj)*	*toh-meh nah*
weak	yowai *(adj)*	*yoh-wah-ee*

e. GEOGRAPHY

> For names of countries, cities, etc. see Section 30.

altitude	kōdo	*koh-doh*
Antarctic Circle	nankyokuken	*nahn-kyoh-koo-kehn*
Arctic Circle	hokkyokuken	*hohk-kyoh-koo-kehn*
area	chiiki	*chee-ee-kee*

border	kyōkai	*kyoh-kah-ee*
• border	sakaisuru *(v)*	*sah-kah-ee-soo-roo*
city	shi	*shee*
• capital	shuto	*shoo-toh*
climate	kikō	*kee-koh*
cold	kanrei no *(adj)*	*kahn-reh noh*
continent	tairiku	*tah-ee-ree-koo*
• continental	tairiku no *(adj)*	*tah-ee-ree-koo noh*
country	kuni	*koo-nee*
equator	sekidō	*seh-kee-doh*
geographical	chirijō no *(adj)*	*chee-ree-joh noh*
• geography	chiri	*chee-ree*
globe	chikyū	*chee-kyoo*
• global	chikyū zentai no *(adj)*	*chee-kyoo zehn-tah-ee noh*
hemisphere	hankyū	*hahn-kyoo*
• hemispheric	hankyūjō no *(adj)*	*hahn-kyoo-joh noh*
• northern hemisphere	kita hankyū	*kee-tah hahn-kyoo*
• southern hemisphere	minami hankyū	*mee-nah-mee hahn-kyoo*
GPS	zen chikyū sokui shisutemu	*zehn chee-kyoo soh-koo-ee shee-soo-teh-moo*
latitude	ido	*ee-doh*
location	ichi	*ee-chee*
• locate	ichisuru *(v)*	*ee-chee-soo-roo*
longitude	keido	*keh-doh*
map	chizu	*chee-zoo*
meridian	shigosen	*shee-goh-sehn*
• prime meridian	honsho shigosen	*hohn-shoh shee-goh-sehn*
nation	kokka	*kohk-kah*
• national	kokka no *(adj)*	*kohk-kah noh*
pole	kyoku	*kyoh-koo*
• North Pole	hokkyoku	*hohk-kyoh-koo*
• South Pole	nankyoku	*nahn-kyoh-koo*
province	shō	*shoh*
region	chihō	*chee-hoh*
state	shū	*shoo*
temperate	ondan na *(adj)*	*ohn-dahn nah*
territory	ryōdo	*ryoh-doh*
tropic	kaikisen	*kah-ee-kee-sehn*
• Tropic of Cancer	kitakaikisen	*kee-tah-kah-ee-kee-sehn*
• Tropic of Capricorn	minamikaikisen	*mee-nah-mee-kah-ee-kee-sehn*
tropical	nettai no *(adj)*	*neht-tah-ee noh*
zone	chitai / chiiki	*chee-tah-ee/chee-ee-kee*

14. PLANTS

a. GENERAL VOCABULARY

agriculture	nōgyō	noh-gyoh
bloom	hana ga saku (v)	hah-nah gah sah-koo
blossom	hana	hah-nah
botanical	shokubutsu no (adj)	shoh-koo-boo-tsoo noh
• **botany**	shokubutsugaku	shoh-koo-boo-tsoo-gah-koo
branch	eda	eh-dah
bud	tsubomi	tsoo-boh-mee
• **bud**	tsubomi o motsu (v)	tsoo-boh-mee oh moh-tsoo
bulb	kyūkon	kyoo-kohn
calyx	gaku	gah-koo
cell	saibō	sah-ee-boh
• **membrane**	genkeishitsumaku	gehn-keh-shee-tsoo-mah-koo
• **nucleus**	kaku	kah-koo
chlorophyll	yōryokuso	yoh-ryohk-soh
cultivate	saibaisuru (v)	sah-ee-bah-ee-soo-roo
• **cultivation**	saibai	sah-ee-bah-ee
cut	kiru (v)	kee-roo
dig	horu (v)	hoh-roo
fertilize	hiryō o yaru (v)	hee-ryoh oh yah-roo
• **fertilizer**	hiryō	hee-ryoh
flower	hana	hah-nah
foliage	ha no shigeri	hah noh shee-geh-ree
gather, reap	shūkakusuru (v)	shoo-kahk-soo-roo
graft	tsugiki	tsoo-gee-kee
• **graft**	tsugikisuru (v)	tsoo-gee-kee-soo-roo
grain	kokurui	koh-koo-roo-ee
greenhouse	onshitsu	ohn-shee-tsoo
hedge	ikegaki	ee-keh-gah-kee
horticulture	engei	ehn-geh
hybrid	kōhai	koh-hah-ee
insecticide	satchūzai	saht-choo-zah-ee
leaf	ha	hah
organism	yūkibutsu	yoo-kee-boo-tsoo
petal	hanabira/kaben	hah-nah-bee-rah/kah-behn
photosynthesis	kōgōsei	koh-goh-seh
pinch	tsumitoru (v)	tsoo-mee-toh-roo
pistil	meshibe	meh-shee-beh
plant	shokubutsu	shoh-koo-boo-tsoo
• **plant**	ueru (v)	oo-eh-roo
pollen	kafun	kah-foon
prune	senteisuru (v)	sehn-teh-soo-roo
• **pruning**	sentei	sehn-teh

reproduce	saiseisuru *(v)*	*sah-ee-seh-soo-roo*
• reproduction	saisei	*sah-ee-seh*
ripe	jukushita *(adj)*	*joo-koo-shtah*
• ripen	jukusu *(v)*	*joo-koo-soo*
root	ne	*neh*
rotten	kusatta *(adj)*	*ksaht-tah*
saw	nokogiri de kiru *(v)*	*noh-koh-gee-ree deh kee-roo*
seed	tane	*tah-neh*
• seed	tane o maku *(v)*	*tah-neh oh mah-koo*
sow	tane o maku *(v)*	*tah-neh oh mah-koo*
species	hinshu	*heen-shoo*
spore	hōshi	*hoh-shee*
spray	fukikakeru *(v)*	*fkee-kah-keh-roo*
sprig	koeda	*koh-eh-dah*
stamen	oshibe	*oh-shee-beh*
stem	kuki	*koo-kee*
thorn	toge	*toh-geh*
till	tagayasu *(v)*	*tah-gah-yah-soo*
transplant	ishoku	*ee-shoh-koo*
• transplant	ishokusuru *(v)*	*ee-shoh-koo-soo-roo*
trim	karikomu *(v)*	*kah-ree-koh-moo*
trunk	miki	*mee-kee*
twig	koeda	*koh-eh-dah*
water	mizu	*mee-zoo*

b. FLOWERS

amaryllis	amaririsu	*ah-mah-ree-rees*
anemone	anemone	*ah-neh-moh-neh*
azalea	tsutsuji	*tsoo-tsoo-jee*
bellflower	kikyō	*kee-kyoh*
camellia	tsubaki	*tsoo-bah-kee*
carnation	kānēshon	*kah-neh-shohn*
cherry blossom	sakura no hana	*sah-koo-rah noh hah-nah*

Bread is better than the song of birds. (*lit.* A dumpling is better than a cherry blossom.)	Hana yori dango.	*hah-nah yoh-ree dahn-goh*

chrysanthemum	kiku	*kee-koo*
clematis	kuremachisu	*koo-reh-mah-chees*
cornflower	kōnfurawā	*kohn-foo-rah-wah*
cosmos	kosumosu	*kohs-mohs*
cyclamen	shikuramen	*shee-koo-rah-mehn*

daffodil	suisen	soo-ee-sehn
dahlia	daria	dah-ree-ah
daisy	dējī	deh-jee
flower	hana	hah-nah
• bouquet of flowers	hanataba	hah-nah-tah-bah
• cut flower	kiribana	kee-ree-bah-nah
• dead flowers	kareta hana	kah-reh-tah hah-nah
• flower arrangement	ikebana	ee-keh-bah-nah
• flower bed	kadan	kah-dahn
• wildflower	nobana	noh-bah-nah
• wilted flower	shioreta hana	shee-oh-reh-tah hah-nah
geranium	jeranyūmu	jeh-rah-nyoo-moo
gladiolus	gurajiorasu	goo-rah-jee-oh-rahs
hibiscus	haibisukasu	hah-ee-bees-kahs
hyacinth	hiyashinsu	hee-yah-sheen-soo
hydrangea	ajisai	ah-jee-sah-ee
iris	ayame	ah-yah-meh
lily	yuri	yoo-ree
lily of the valley	suzuran	soo-zoo-rahn
marigold	marigōrudo	mah-ree-goh-roo-doh
morning glory	asagao	ah-sah-gah-oh
narcissus	suisen	soo-ee-sehn
orchid	ran	rahn
pansy	panjī	pahn-jee
peony	shakuyaku	shah-koo-yah-koo
petunia	pechunia	peh-choo-nee-ah
(to) pick flowers	hana o tsumu (v)	hah-nah oh tsoo-moo
poppy	keshi	keh-shee
rose	bara	bah-rah
salvia	sarubia	sah-roo-bee-ah
sunflower	himawari	hee-mah-wah-ree
tulip	chūrippu	choo-reep-poo
violet	sumire	soo-mee-reh
wisteria	fuji	foo-jee
zinnia	hyakunichisō	hyah-koo-nee-chee-soh

c. TREES

ash	toneriko	toh-neh-ree-koh
beech tree	buna	boo-nah
birch	kaba no ki	kah-bah noh kee
chestnut tree	kuri no ki	koo-ree noh kee
cypress tree	itosugi	ee-toh-soo-gee
deciduous tree	rakuyōju	rah-koo-yoh-joo
dogwood	hanamizuki	hah-nah-mee-zoo-kee
elm	nire	nee-reh

evergreen	jōryokuju	*jōh-ryoh-koo-joo*
fir	momi	*moh-mee*
fruit tree	kaju	*kah-joo*
• apple tree	ringo no ki	*reen-goh noh kee*
• cherry tree	sakura	*sah-koo-rah*
• fig tree	ichijiku no ki	*ee-chee-jee-koo noh kee*
• mandarin orange tree	mikan no ki	*mee-kahn noh kee*
• olive tree	orību no ki	*oh-rēē-boo noh kee*
• orange tree	orenji no ki	*oh-rehn-jee noh kee*
• peach tree	momo no ki	*moh-moh noh kee*
• pear tree	nashi no ki	*nah-shee noh kee*
• pomegranate tree	zakuro no ki	*zah-koo-roh noh kee*
• walnut tree	kurumi no ki	*koo-roo-mee noh kee*
ginko tree	ichō	*ee-chōh*
Japanese cedar	sugi	*soo-gee*
Japanese cypress	hinoki	*hee-noh-kee*
magnolia	mokuren	*moh-koo-rehn*
maple tree	kaede	*kah-eh-deh*
myrtle	sarusuberi	*sah-roo-soo-beh-ree*
oak tree	kashi	*kah-shee*
palm tree	yashi no ki	*yah-shee noh kee*
paulownia	kiri	*kee-ree*
pine tree	matsu	*mah-tsoo*
poplar tree	popura	*poh-poo-rah*
sapling	wakagi	*wah-kah-gee*
seedling	naegi	*nah-eh-gee*
shrub	kanboku	*kahn-boh-koo*
tree	ki	*kee*
white birch	shirakaba	*shee-rah-kah-bah*
willow	yanagi	*yah-nah-gee*

d. FRUITS

apple	ringo	*reen-goh*
apricot	anzu	*ahn-zoo*
banana	banana	*bah-nah-nah*
blueberry	burūberī	*boo-rōō-beh-rēē*
cherry	sakuranbo	*sah-koo-rahn-boh*
chestnut	kuri	*koo-ree*
citrus	kankitsurui	*kahn-kee-tsoo-roo-ee*
• citric	kankitsurui no *(adj)*	*kahn-kee-tsoo-roo-ee noh*
date	natsume	*nah-tsoo-meh*
fig	ichijiku	*ee-chee-jee-koo*
fruit	kudamono	*koo-dah-moh-noh*
grapefruit	gurēpufurūtsu	*goo-rēh-poo-foo-rōō-tsoo*
grape	budō	*boo-dōh*

lemon	remon	*reh-mohn*
loquat	biwa	*bee-wah*
mandarin orange	mikan	*mee-kahn*
mango	mangō	*mahn-goh*
melon	meron	*meh-rohn*
nectarine	nekutarin	*nehk-tah-reen*
olive	orību	*oh-rēē-boo*
orange	orenji	*oh-rehn-jee*
papaya	papaiya	*pah-pah-ee-yah*
peach	momo	*moh-moh*
pear (Japanese)	nashi	*nah-shee*
pear (western)	yōnashi	*yoh-nah-shee*
persimmon	kaki	*kah-kee*
pineapple	painappuru	*pah-ee-nahp-poo-roo*
plum	sumomo	*soo-moh-moh*
pomegranate	zakuro	*zah-koo-roh*
prune	hoshisumomo	*hoh-shee-soo-moh-moh*
raisin	hoshibudō	*hoh-shee-boo-doh*
raspberry	kiichigo	*kee-ee-chee-goh*
strawberry	ichigo	*ee-chee-goh*
walnut	kurumi	*koo-roo-mee*
watermelon	suika	*soo-ee-kah*

e. VEGETABLES AND HERBS

artichoke	ātichōku	*āh-tee-chōh-koo*
asparagus	asuparagasu	*ahs-pah-rah-gah-soo*
bamboo shoot	takenoko	*tah-keh-noh-koh*
basil	bajiru	*bah-jee-roo*
bean	mame	*mah-meh*
bean sprout	moyashi	*moh-yah-shee*
beet	satōdaikon	*sah-tōh-dah-ee-kohn*
broad bean	soramame	*soh-rah-mah-meh*
broccoli	burokkori	*boo-rohk-koh-ree*
burdock	gobō	*goh-boh*
cabbage	kyabetsu	*kyah-beh-tsoo*
carrot	ninjin	*neen-jeen*
cauliflower	karifurawā	*kah-ree-foo-rah-wāh*
celery	serori	*seh-roh-ree*
chickpea	hiyokomame	*hee-yoh-koh-mah-meh*
corn	tōmorokoshi	*toh-moh-roh-koh-shee*
cucumber	kyūri	*kyōō-ree*
eggplant	nasu	*nah-soo*
fennel	uikyō / fenneru	*oo-ee-kyōh/fehn-neh-roo*
garden	niwa	*nee-wah*
• vegetable garden	saien	*sah-ee-ehn*
garlic	ninniku	*neen-nee-koo*

bug	mushi	*moo-shee*
butterfly	chōchō	*choh-choh*
caterpillar	kemushi	*keh-moo-shee*
cicada	semi	*seh-mee*
centipede	mukade	*moo-kah-deh*
cockroach	gokiburi	*goh-kee-boo-ree*

| a no-good husband (*lit.* a cockroach husband) | gokiburi teishu | *goh-kee-boo-ree teh-shoo* |

cricket	kōrogi	*koh-roh-gee*
crustacean	kōkakurui	*koh-kah-koo-roo-ee*
dragonfly	tonbo	*tohn-boh*
grasshopper	batta	*baht-tah*
firefly	hotaru	*hoh-tah-roo*
flea	nomi	*noh-mee*
fly	hae	*hah-eh*
horsefly	abu	*ah-boo*
insect	konchū	*kohn-choo*
invertebrate	musekitsui dōbutsu	*moo-seh-kee-tsoo-ee doh-boo-tsoo*
ladybug	tentōmushi	*tehn-toh-moo-shee*
larva	yōchū	*yoh-choo*
louse (lice)	shirami	*shee-rah-mee*
maggot	uji	*oo-jee*
mayfly	kagerō	*kah-geh-roh*
metamorphosis	hentai	*hehn-tah-ee*
microbe	biseibutsu	*bee-seh-boo-tsoo*
mosquito	ka	*kah*
moth	ga	*gah*
organism	yūkitai	*yoo-kee-tah-ee*
praying mantis	kamakiri	*kah-mah-kee-ree*
pupa	sanagi	*sah-nah-gee*
rhinoceros beetle	kabutomushi	*kah-boo-toh-moo-shee*
scorpion	sasori	*sah-soh-ree*
silkworm	kaiko	*kah-ee-koh*
slug	namekuji	*nah-meh-koo-jee*
stag beetle	kuwagatamushi	*koo-wah-gah-tah-moo-shee*
snail	katatsumuri	*kah-tah-tsoo-moo-ree*
spider	kumo	*koo-moh*
termite	shiroari	*shee-roh-ah-ree*
tick	dani	*dah-nee*
wasp	suzumebachi	*soo-zoo-meh-bah-chee*
worm	mushi	*moo-shee*

COMMUNICATING, FEELING, AND THINKING

16. BASIC SOCIAL EXPRESSIONS

a. GREETINGS AND FAREWELLS

Farewell!	Gokigenyō.	*goh-kee-gehn-yoh*
Good afternoon! (Hello!)	Konnichiwa.	*kohn-nee-chee-wah*
Good evening! (Hello!)	Konbanwa.	*kohn-bahn-wah*
Good morning! (Hello!)	Ohayō gozaimasu.	*oh-hah-yoh goh-zah-ee-mahs*
Good night!	Oyasuminasai.	*oh-yah-soo-mee-nah-sah-ee*
Good-bye!	Sayōnara.	*sah-yoh-nah-rah*
greet	aisatsusuru *(v)*	*ah-ee-sah-tsoo-soo-roo*
• **greeting**	aisatsu	*ah-ee-sah-tsoo*
Hi!	Yā *(inf)*	*yah*
How have you been?	Ogenki desu ka.	*oh-gehn-kee dehs kah*
How's it going?	Ikaga desu ka.	*ee-kah-gah dehs kah*
• **Badly.**	Anmari yoku arimasen.	*ahn-mah-ree yoh-koo ah-ree-mah-sehn*
• **Fine!**	Junchō desu.	*joon-choh dehs*
• **Not bad!**	Waruku arimasen.	*wah-roo-koo ah-ree-mah-sehn*
• **Quite well!**	Umaku itte imasu.	*oo-mah-koo eet-teh ee-mahs*
• **So, so!**	Māmā desu.	*mah-mah dehs*
• **Very well!**	Umaku itte imasu.	*oo-mah-koo eet-teh ee-mahs*
Please give my regards/greetings to ...	... san ni yoroshiku otsutae kudasai.	*... sahn nee yoh-roh-shee-koo oh-tsoo-tah-ee koo-dah-sah-ee*
See you!	Soredewa, mata.	*soh-reh-deh-wah, mah-tah*
• **See you later!**	Soredewa, nochihodo.	*soh-reh-deh-wah, noh-chee-hoh-doh*
• **See you soon!**	Soredewa, chikaiuchi ni.	*soh-reh-deh-wah, chee-kah-ee-oo-chee nee*
• **See you Sunday!**	Soredewa, nichiyōbi ni.	*soh-reh-deh-wah, nee-chee-yoh-bee nee*
shake hands	akushusuru *(v)*	*ahk-shoo-soo-roo*
• **handshake**	akushu	*ahk-shoo*

b. FORMS OF ADDRESS AND INTRODUCTIONS

A pleasure!	Yorokonde.	yoh-roh-kohn-deh
• The pleasure is mine!	Kochirakoso.	koh-chee-rah-koh-soh
acquaintance	chijin	chee-jeen
Allow me to introduce myself.	Jikoshōkai sasete itadakimasu.	jee-koh-shoh-kah-ee sah-seh-teh ee-tah-dah-kee-mahs
Allow me to introduce you to ...	... san ni, goshōkai itashimasu.	...sahn nee, goh-shoh-kah-ee ee-tah-shee-mahs
be seated	koshikakeru (v)	kohsh-kah-keh-roo
• Be seated, please!	Dōzo okake kudasai.	doh-zoh oh-kah-keh koo-dah-sah-ee
calling card	meishi	meh-shee
Come in!	Ohairi kudasai.	oh-hah-ee-ree koo-dah-sah-ee
• enter	hairu (v)	hah-ee-roo
Delighted!	Ureshii desu.	oo-reh-shee dehs
Happy to make your acquaintance!	Shiriau koto ga dekite ureshii desu.	shee-ree-ah-oo koh-toh gah deh-kee-tee oo-reh-shee dehs
introduce	shōkaisuru (v)	shoh-kah-ee-soo-roo
• introduction	shōkai	shoh-kah-ee
know (someone)	shitteiru (v)	sheet-teh-ee-roo
Let me introduce you to ...	... san ni shōkai sasete kudasai.	... sahn nee shoh-kah-ee sah-seh-teh koo-dah-sah-ee
meet	au (v)	ah-oo
run into (someone)	deau (v)	deh-ah-oo
title	shōgō	shoh-goh
• doctor (M.D. degree)	igaku hakase	ee-gah-koo hah-kah-seh
• doctor (direct address)	sensei	sehn-seh
• Dr. (Ph.D. degree)	hakase	hah-kah-seh
• Miss	san	sahn
• Ms.	san	sahn
• Mr.	san	sahn
• Mrs.	san	sahn
What's your name?	Onamae wa, nan desu ka.	oh-nah-mah-eh wah, NAHN dehs kah
• My name is ...	Watakushi no namae wa, ... desu.	wah-tahk-shee noh nah-mah-ee wah, ... dehs
I'm ...	Watakushi wa, ... desu.	wah-tahk-shee wah, ... dehs

c. COURTESY

Best wishes!	Gokōun o.	*goh-koh-oon oh*
Cheers!	Kanpai.	*kahn-pah-ee*
Congratulations!	Omedetō gozaimasu.	*oh-meh-deh-toh goh-zah-ee-mahs*
Don't mention it!	Iie, dō itashimashite.	*ee-eh, DOH ee-tah-shee-mah-shteh*
Excuse me!	Sumimasen.	*soo-mee-mah-sehn*
Good luck!	Goseikō o.	*goh-seh-koh oh*
Happy birthday!	Tanjōbi omedetō.	*tahn-joh-bee oh-meh-deh-toh*
Happy New Year!	Shinnen omedetō.	*sheen-nehn oh-meh-deh-toh*
Have a good holiday!	Oyasumi o, otanoshimi kudasai.	*oh-yah-soo-mee oh, oh-tah-noh-shee-mee koo-dah-sah-ee*
Have a good time!	Tanoshii toki o, osugoshi kudasai.	*tah-noh-shee toh-kee oh, oh-soo-goh-shee koo-dah-sah-ee*
Have a good trip!	Ryokō o, otanoshimi kudasai.	*ryoh-koh oh, oh-tah-noh-shee-mee koo-dah-sah-ee*
Many thanks!	Kansha shimasu.	*KAHN-shah shee-mahs*
May I come in?	Haittemo yoroshii desu ka.	*hah-eet-teh-moh yoh-roh-shee dehs kah*
May I help you?	Otetsudai shimashō ka.	*oh-teh-tsoo-dah-ee shee-mah-shoh kah*
Merry Christmas!	Kurisumasu omedetō	*koo-ree-soo-mahs oh-meh-deh-toh*
No.	Iie.	*ee-eh*
No!	Dame desu.	*dah-meh dehs*
OK!	Ii desu yo.	*ee dehs yoh*
Please! (go ahead)	Dōzo.	*doh-zoh*
Please! (request)	Onegai shimasu.	*oh-neh-gah-ee shee-mahs*
Thank you!	Arigatō gozaimasu.	*ah-ree-gah-toh goh-zah-ee-mahs*
Yes!	Hai.	*hah-ee*
You're welcome!	Iie, dō itashimashite.	*ee-eh, DOH ee-tah-shee-mah-shteh*

17. SPEAKING AND TALKING

a. SPEECH ACTIVITIES AND TYPES

accuse	hinansuru *(v)*	*hee-nahn-soo-roo*
• accusation	hinan	*hee-nahn*
advice	jogen	*joh-gehn*
• advise	jogensuru *(v)*	*joh-gehn-soo-roo*

affirm	dangensuru (v)	*dahn-gehn-soo-roo*
agree	sanseisuru (v)	*sahn-seh-soo-roo*
allude	honomekasu (v)	*hoh-noh-meh-kah-soo*
analogy	ruihi	*roo-ee-hee*
announce	shiraseru (v)	*shee-rah-seh-roo*
• announcement	happyō	*hahp-pyoh*
answer	kotae	*koh-tah-eh*
• answer	kotaeru (v)	*koh-tah-eh-roo*
argue	gironsuru (v)	*gee-rohn-soo-roo*
• argument	giron	*gee-rohn*
articulate	hakkiri hyōgensuru (v)	*hahk-kee-ree hyoh-gehn-soo-roo*
ask	kiku (v)	*kee-koo*
beg	kongansuru (v)	*kohn-gahn-soo-roo*
blame	togameru (v)	*toh-gah-meh-roo*
call	yobu (v)	*yoh-boo*
change subject	wadai o kaeru (v)	*wah-dah-ee o kah-eh-roo*
chat	zatsudansuru (v)	*zah-tsoo-dahn-soo-roo*
cheer	hagemasu (v)	*hah-geh-mahs*
communicate	tsutaeru (v)	*tsoo-tah-eh-roo*
• communication	dentatsu	*dehn-tah-tsoo*
compare	hikakusuru (v)	*hee-kahk-soo-roo*
• comparison	hikaku	*hee-kah-koo*
complain	kujō o noberu (v)	*koo-joh oh noh-beh-roo*
• complaint	kujō	*koo-joh*
conclude	ketsuron o kudasu (v)	*keh-tsoo-rohn oh koo-dah-soo*
• conclusion	ketsuron	*keh-tsoo-rohn*
confirm	kakuninsuru (v)	*kah-koo-neen-soo-roo*
congratulate	iwau (v)	*ee-wah-oo*
• congratulations!	omedetō!	*oh-meh-deh-toh*
consult	sōdansuru (v)	*soh-dahn-soo-roo*
contradict	hininsuru (v)	*hee-neen-soo-roo*
conversation	kaiwa	*kah-ee-wah*
• converse	katariau (v)	*kah-tah-ree-ah-oo*
curse	akkō o haku (v)	*ahk-koh o hah-koo*
debate	tōronsuru (v)	*toh-rohn-soo-roo*
• debate	toron	*toh-rohn*
declare	sengensuru (v)	*sehn-gehn-soo-roo*
deny	hiteisuru (v)	*hee-teh-soo-roo*
describe	noberu (v)	*noh-beh-roo*
• description	kijutsu	*kee-joo-tsoo*
dictate	kōjutsusuru (v)	*koh-joo-tsoo-soo-roo*
digress	wakimichi ni soreru (v)	*wah-kee-mee-chee nee soh-reh-roo*
disagree	iken o koto ni suru (v)	*ee-kehn oh koh-toh nee soo-roo*
• disagreement	iken no sōi	*ee-kehn noh soh-ee*

discuss	rongisuru *(v)*	rohn-gee-soo-roo
• discussion	rongi	rohn-gee
emphasis	kyōchō	kyoh-choh
• emphasize	kyōchōsuru *(v)*	kyoh-choh-soo-roo
excuse	iiwake	ee-wah-keh
• excuse oneself	iiwakesuru *(v)*	ee-wah-keh-soo-roo
explain	setsumeisuru *(v)*	seh-tsoo-meh-soo-roo
• explanation	setsumei	seh-tsoo-meh
express	noberu *(v)*	noh-beh-roo
• expression	hyōgen	hyoh-gehn
figure of speech	hiyuteki hyōgen	hee-yoo-teh-kee hyoh-gehn
• literal	mojidōri no *(adj)*	moh-jee-doh-ree noh
• metaphor	inyu	een-yoo
• symbol	shōchō	shoh-choh
gossip	uwasabanashi	oo-wah-sah-bah-nah-shee
• gossip	uwasabanashi o suru *(v)*	oo-wah-sah-bah-nah-shee oh soo-roo
guarantee	hoshōsuru *(v)*	hoh-shoh-soo-roo
hesitation	tamerai	tah-meh-rah-ee
• hesitate	tamerau *(v)*	tah-meh-rah-oo
identify	shikibetsusuru *(v)*	shkee-behts-soo-roo
indicate	shisasuru *(v)*	shee-sah-soo-roo
• indication	shisa	shee-sah
inform	tsugeru *(v)*	tsoo-geh-roo
interpret	tsūyakusuru *(v)*	tsoo-yahk-soo-roo
interpretation	tsūyaku	tsoo-yah-koo
interrogate	jinmonsuru *(v)*	jeen-mohn-soo-roo
interrupt	saegiru *(v)*	sah-eh-gee-roo
• interruption	chūdan	choo-dahn
invite	maneku *(v)*	mah-neh-koo
jeer	azakeru *(v)*	ah-zah-keh-roo
jest	karakau *(v)*	kah-rah-kah-oo
joke	jōdan	joh-dahn
• tell a joke	jōdan o iu *(v)*	joh-dahn oh ee-oo
keep quiet	kuchi o hikaeru *(v)*	koo-chee oh hee-kah-eh-roo
lecture	kōgi	koh-gee
• lecture	kōgisuru *(v)*	koh-gee-soo-roo
lie	uso	oo-soh
• lie	uso o tsuku *(v)*	oo-soh oh tsoo-koo
• liar	usotsuki	oo-soh-tsoo-kee
listen to	kiku *(v)*	kee-koo-
malign, speak badly	chūshōsuru *(v)*	choo-shoh-soo-roo
mean	imisuru *(v)*	ee-mee-soo-roo
• meaning	imi	ee-mee
mention	noberu *(v)*	noh-beh-roo

Speak of the devil, and he will appear. (*lit.* When you gossip about someone, the person's shadow will appear.)	Uwasa o sureba kage to yara.	*oo-wah-sah oh soo-reh-bah kah-geh toh yah-rah*
all sorts of lies (*lit.* eight hundred lies)	uso happyaku	*oo-soh hahp-pyah-koo*
The end justifies the means. (*lit.* A lie is sometimes expedient.)	Uso mo hōben	*oo-soh moh hoh-behn*
Silence is golden.	Chinmoku wa kin.	*cheen-moh-koo wah keen*

mumble	bosoboso iu *(v)*	*boh-soh-boh-soh ee-oo*
murmur	tsubuyaku *(v)*	*tsoo-boo-yah-koo*
nag	gamigami iu *(v)*	*gah-mee-gah-mee ee-oo*
object	hantaisuru *(v)*	*hahn-tah-ee-soo-roo*
offend	kanjō o kizutsukeru *(v)*	*kahn-joh oh kee-zoo-tskeh-roo*
offer	mōshideru *(v)*	*moh-shee-deh-roo*
oral	kōtō no *(adj)*	*koh-toh noh*
• orally	kōtō de *(adv)*	*koh- toh deh*
order	meirei	*meh-reh*
• order	meireisuru *(v)*	*meh-reh-soo-roo*
outspokenly	enryonaku *(adv)*	*ehn-ryoh-nah-koo*
praise	homeru *(v)*	*hoh-meh-roo*
pray	inoru *(v)*	*ee-noh-roo*
• prayer	oinori	*oh-ee-noh-ree*
preach	sekkyōsuru *(v)*	*sehk-kyoh-soo-roo*
• sermon	sekkyō	*sehk-kyoh*
point out	shitekisuru *(v)*	*shteh-kee-soo-roo*
promise	yakusokusuru *(v)*	*yahk-sohk-soo-roo*
• promise	yakusoku	*yahk-soh-koo*
pronounce	hatsuonsuru *(v)*	*hah-tsoo-ohn-soo-roo*
• pronunciation	hatsuon	*hah-tsoo-ohn* .
propose	mōshikomu *(v)*	*nohsh-koh-moo*
protest	kōgi	*koh-gee*
• protest	kōgisuru *(v)*	*koh-gee-soo-roo*
recommend	suisensuru *(v)*	*soo-ee-sehn-soo-roo*
relate	kanrenzukeru *(v)*	*kahn-rehn-zoo-keh-roo*
repeat	kurikaesu *(v)*	*koo-ree-kah-eh-soo*
• repetition	kurikaeshi	*koo-ree-kah-eh-shee*

reply	ōtōsuru *(v)*	*oh-toh-soo-roo*
report	hōkoku	*hoh-koh-koo*
• report	hōkokusuru *(v)*	*hoh-koh-koo-soo-roo*
reproach	shikaru *(v)*	*shkah-roo*
request	tanomi	*tah-noh-mee*
• request	tanomu *(v)*	*tah-noh-moo*
rhetoric	shūji	*shoo-jee*
• rhetorical	shūjiteki na *(adj)*	*shoo-jee-teh-kee nah*
• rhetorical question	hango	*hahn-goh*
rumor	uwasa	*oo-wah-sah*
say, tell	iu *(v)*	*ee-oo*
shout, yell	sakebu *(v)*	*sah-keh-boo*
shut up	damaru *(vi)*	*dah-mah-roo*
• Shut up!	Damare!	*dah-mah-reh*
silence	chinmoku	*cheen-moh-koo*
• silent (person)	mukuchi na *(adj)*	*mook-chee nah*
speak, talk	hanasu *(v)*	*hah-nah-soo*
• speech, talk	hanashi	*hah-nah-shee*
state	noberu *(v)*	*noh-beh-roo*
• statement	seimei	*seh-meh*
story	monogatari	*moh-noh-gah-tah-ree*
• tell a story	itsuwa o hanasu *(v)*	*ee-tsoo-wah oh hah-nah-soo*
suggest	teiansuru *(v)*	*teh-ahn-soo-roo*
summarize	yōyakusuru *(v)*	*yoh-yahk-soo-roo*
• summary	yōyaku	*yoh-yah-koo*
swear (in court)	chikau *(v)*	*chee-kah-oo*
swear (profanity)	kitanai kotobazukai o suru *(v)*	*kee-tah-nah-ee koh-toh-bah-zoo-kah-ee oh soo-roo*
talk	hanasu *(v)*	*hah-nah-soo*
tell	tsugeru *(v)*	*tsoo-geh-roo*
testify	shōgensuru *(v)*	*shoh-gehn-soo-roo*
thank	kanshasuru *(v)*	*kahn-shah-soo-roo*
threat	odokashi	*oh-doh-kah-shee*
• threaten	odokasu *(v)*	*oh-doh-kah-roo*
toast	kanpai	*kahn-pah-ee*
• toast	kanpaisuru *(v)*	*kahn-pah-ee-soo-roo*
translate	honyakusuru *(v)*	*hohn-yahk-soo-roo*
• translation	honyaku	*hohn-yah-koo*
utter	tsubuyaku *(v)*	*tsoo-boo-yah-koo*
vocabulary	goi	*goh-ee*
warn	keikokusuru *(v)*	*keh-kohk-soo-roo*
• warning	keikoku	*keh-koh-koo*
whine	nakigoto o iu *(v)*	*nah-kee-goh-toh oh ee-oo*
whisper	sasayaku *(v)*	*sah-sah-yah-koo*
word	kotoba	*koh-toh-bah*
yawn	akubi	*ah-koo-bee*

| • yawn | akubisuru *(v)* | *ah-koo-bee-soo-roo* |
| yell | wameku *(v)* | *wah-meh-koo* |

b. USEFUL EXPRESSIONS

Actually ...	Jitsu wa, ...	*jee-tsoo wah, ...*
As a matter of fact ...	Jissai, ...	*jees-sah-ee, ...*
Briefly, ...	Kantan ni nobereba, ...	*kahn-tahn nee noh-beh-reh-bah, ...*
By the way ...	Tokoro de, ...	*toh-koh-roh deh, ...*
Go ahead!	Dōzo.	*DOH-zoh*
How do you say ... in Japanese?	... wa, Nihongo de dō iimasu ka.	*... wah, nee-hohn-goh deh DOH ee-mahs kah*
I didn't understand.	Wakarimasen deshita.	*wah-kah-ree-mah-sehn deh-shtah*
I don't understand.	Wakarimasen.	*wah-kah-ree-mah-sehn*
I'm sure that ...	Tashika ni, ... to omoimasu.	*TAH-shee-kah nee, ... toh oh-moh-ee-mahs*
Isn't it so?	Sō dewanai desu ka.	*SOH deh-wah-nah-ee dehs KAH*
It seems that ...	... mitai desu	*... mee-tah-ee dehs*
It's necessary that ...	... ga, hitsuyō desu.	*... gah, hee-tsoo-yoh dehs*
It's not true!	Sore wa, hontō dewa arimasen.	*soh-reh wah, hohn-toh deh-wah ah-ree-mah-sehn*
It's obvious that ...	... koto wa, akiraka desu.	*... koh-toh wah, ah-KEE-rah-kah dehs*
It's true!	Sore wa, hontō desu.	*soh-reh wah, hohn-toh dehs*
Listen ...	... o, kiite kudasai.	*... oh, kee-teh koo-dah-sah-ee*
Now ...	Ima, ...	*ee-mah, ...*
To sum up ...	... o yōyakusureba,	*... oh yoh-yahk-soo-reh-bah,*
What was I talking about?	Watakushi wa, nani o hanashite imashita ka.	*wah-tahk-shee wah, NAH-nee oh hah-nah-shteh ee-mah-shtah kah*
Who knows?	Dare, mo, shirimasen yo.	*dah-reh moh, shee-ree-mah-sehn yoh*

18. THE TELEPHONE

a. TELEPHONES AND ACCESSORIES

analog	anarogu	*ah-nah-roh-goo*
answering machine	rusuban denwa	*roo-soo-bahn dehn-wah*
Bluetooth	burūtūsu	*boo-roo-too-soo*
cable	kēburu	*keh-boo-roo*

call waiting	kyatchifon	*kyaht-chee-fohn*
caller ID	chakushin hyōji	*chahk-sheen hyoh-jee*
camera phone	kamera tsuki keitai denwa	*kah-meh-rah tsoo-kee keh-tah-ee dehn-wah*
car telephone	jidōsha denwa	*jee-doh-shah dehn-wah*
cellular phone	keitai denwa	*keh-tah-ee dehn-wah*
cordless phone	kōdoresufon	*koh-doh-rehs-fohn*
digital	dejitaru	*deh-jee-tah-roo*
earphone	iyahōn	*ee-yah-hohn*
fax machine	fakkusu	*fahk-koo-soo*
hands-free	hanzufurī *(adj)*	*hahn-zoo-foo-ree*
headset	heddosetto	*hehd-doh-seht-toh*
IM	insutantomessenjā	*een-stahn-toh-mehs-sehn-jah*
intercom	tsūwa sōchi	*tsoo-wah soh-chee*
Internet function	intānetto kinō	*een-tah-neht-toh kee-noh*
Internet telephone	intānetto denwa	*een-tah-neht-toh dehn-wah*
modem	modemu	*moh-deh-moo*
music function	ongaku kinō	*ohn-gahk kee-noh*
optical fiber	hikari faibā	*hee-kah-ree fah-ee-bah*
outlet	sashikomi	*sah-shee-koh-mee*
pay phone	kōshū denwa	*koh-shoo dehn-wah*
PDA	keitai jōhō tanmatsu	*keh-tah-ee joh-hoh tahn-mah-tsoo*
phone book	denwachō	*dehn-wah-choh*
phone booth	denwa bokkusu	*dehn-wah bohk-koo-soo*
phone outlet	denwa no sashikomi-guchi	*dehn-wah noh sahsh-koh-mee-goo-chee*
PIN	anshō bangō	*ahn-shoh bahn-goh*
plug	sashikomi	*sahsh-koh-mee*
receiver	juwaki	*joo-wah-kee*
smart phone	sumātofon	*soo-mah-toh-fohn*
telecommunication	enkyori tsūshin	*ehn-kyoh-ree tsoo-sheen*
• telecommunications satellite	tsūshin eisei	*tsoo-sheen eh-seh*
telephone	denwa	*dehn-wah*
telephone card	terefon kādo	*teh-reh-fohn kah-doh*
text messaging	tekisuto messēji	*teh-kee-stoh mehs-seh-jee*
wireless headset	waiyaresu heddosetto	*wah-ee-yah-reh-soo hehd-doh-seht-toh*
yellow pages	shokugyōbetsu denwa chō	*shoh-koo-gyoh-beh-tsoo dehn-wah choh*

b. USING THE TELEPHONE

answer	denwa ni deru *(v)*	*dehn-wah nee deh-roo*
• pick up (the phone)	juwaki o toriageru *(v)*	*joo-wah-kee oh toh-ree-ah-geh-roo*
area code	shigaikyokuban	*shee-gah-ee-kyoh-koo-bahn*
busy	hanashichū	*hah-nah-shee-chōō*
collect call	jushinninbarai no denwa	*joo-sheen-neen-bah-rah-ee noh dehn-wah*
cut off	kiru *(v)*	*kee-roo*
dial	daiaru	*dah-ee-ah-roo*
• dial	daiaru o mawasu *(v)*	*dah-ee-ah-roo oh mah-wah-soo*
• direct dialing	daiaru chokutsū	*dah-ee-ah-roo chohk-tsōō*
extension	naisen	*nah-ee-sehn*
fax	fakkusu	*fahk-koo-soo*
hang up	kiru *(v)*	*kee-roo*
information	jōhō	*joh-hoh*
international call	kokusai denwa	*kohk-sah-ee dehn-wah*
local call	shinai denwa	*shee-nah-ee dehn-wah*
long-distance call	chōkyori denwa	*choh-kyoh-ree dehn-wah*
make a call	denwa o kakeru *(v)*	*dehn-wah oh kah-keh-roo*
• Hello!	Moshi moshi.	*MOH-shee moh-shee*
• Is ... in?	... wa, irasshaimasu ka.	*... wah, ee-rahs-shah-ee-mahs kah*
• This is ...	Watakushi wa, ... desu ga.	*wah-tahk-shee wah, ... dehs gah*
• Who's speaking?	Donata sama desu ka.	*DOH-nah-tah sah-mah dehs kah*
• Wrong number!	Machigai denwa desu.	*mah-chee-gah-ee dehn-wah dehs*
message	dengon	*dehn-gohn*
• Can I leave a message?	Dengon o nokoshitemo ii desu ka.	*dehn-gohn oh noh-koh-shteh-moh ēē dehs kah*
• Can I take a message?	Nanika, dengon ga arimasu ka.	*NAH-nee-kah, dehn-gohn gah ah-ree-mahs kah*
operator	kōkanshu	*koh-kahn-shoo*
person-to-person call	pāsonaru kōru	*pah-soh-nah-roo kōh-roo*
telephone	denwa	*dehn-wah*
telephone bill	denwa ryōkin no seikyūsho	*dehn-wah ryōh-keen noh seh-kyōō-shoh*
telephone call	denwa	*dehn-wah*
• Hold the line!	Kiranaide kudasai.	*kee-rah-nah-ee-deh koo-dah-sah-ee*
• This line is busy.	Hanashichū desu.	*hah-nah-shee-chōō dehs*
telephone number	denwa bangō	*dehn-wah bahn-gōh*

toll-free	torufurī no *(adj)* / muryō no *(adj)*	*toh-roo-foo-rēē noh/moo-ryoh noh*
ring (phone)	naru *(vi)*	*nah-roo*

19. LETTER WRITING

a. FORMAL SALUTATIONS/CLOSINGS

Dear Sir	haikei	*hah-ee-keh*
Dear Madam	haikei	*hah-ee-keh*
To Whom It May Concern	kankeisha kakui dono	*kahn-keh-shah kah-koo-ee doh-noh*
Gentlemen	haikei	*hah-ee-keh*
Yours truly	keigu	*keh-goo*
Yours sincerely	keigu	*keh-goo*

b. FAMILIAR SALUTATIONS/CLOSINGS

Dear ...	... sama	*... sah-mah*
Dearest ...	shinai naru ... sama	*sheen-ah-ee nah-roo ... sah-mah*
Affectionately	kokoro o komete	*koh-koh-roh oh koh-meh-teh*
Give my regards to ...	... san ni yoroshiku	*... sahn nee yoh-roh-shkoo*

c. PARTS OF A LETTER/PUNCTUATION

block letter	katsujitai ōmoji	*kah-tsoo-jee-tah-ee ōh-moh-jee*
body	honbun	*hohn-boon*
boldface	nikubutokatsuji	*nee-koo-boo-toh-kah-tsoo-jee*
capital letter	ōmoji	*oh-moh-jee*
closing	musubi no kotoba	*moo-soo-bee noh koh-toh-bah*
cursive-style letter	hikkitai	*heek-kee-tah-ee*
date	hizuke	*hee-zoo-keh*
heading	midashi	*mee-dah-shee*
lowercase	komoji	*koh-moh-jee*
page	pēji	*peh-jee*
punctuation	kutōten	*ktoh-tehn*
• accent	akusento	*ahk-sehn-toh*
• apostrophe	aposutorofi	*ah-pohs-toh-roh-fee*
• asterisk	hoshijirushi	*hoh-shee-jee-roo-shee*
• bracket, parenthesis	kakko	*kahk-koh*
• capital letter	ōmoji	*ōh-moh-jee*
• colon	koron	*koh-rohn*

• comma	konma	*kohn-mah*
• dash	dasshu	*dahs-shoo*
• exclamation mark	kantanfu	*kahn-tahn-foo*
• hyphen	haifun	*hah-ee-foon*
• italics	itarikkutai	*ee-tah-reek-koo-tah-ee*
• period	shūshiten	*shōō-shtehn*
• question mark	gimonfu	*gee-mohn-foo*
• quotation mark	inyōfu	*een-yoh-foo*
• semicolon	semikoron	*seh-mee-koh-rohn*
• slash	shasen/surasshu	*shah-sehn/soo-rahs-shoo*
• small letter	komoji	*koh-moh-jee*
• square bracket	kaku kakko	*kah-koo kahk-koh*
• underlining	andārain	*ahn-dah-rah-een*
salutation	aisatsu no kotoba	*ah-ee-sah-tsoo noh koh-toh-bah*
sentence	bun	*boon*
signature	shomei	*shoh-mēh*
• sign	shomeisuru (v)	*shoh-meh-soo-roo*
spelling	tsuzuri	*tsoo-zoo-ree*
style	buntai	*boon-tah-ee*
text	honbun	*hohn-boon*
• abbreviation	shōryakukei	*shoh-ryahk-kēh*
• clause	setsu	*seh-tsoo*
• letter (of the alphabet)	arufabetto no moji	*ah-roo-fah-beht-toh noh moh-jee*
• line	gyō	*gyoh*
• margin	yohaku	*yoh-hah-koo*
• P.S.	tsuishin	*tsoo-ee-sheen*
• paragraph	danraku	*dahn-rah-koo*
• phrase	ku	*koo*
uppercase	ōmoji	*oh-moh-jee*
word	kotoba	*koh-toh-bah*

d. WRITING MATERIALS AND ACCESSORIES

brush	fude	*foo-deh*
card	kādo	*kāh-doh*
clip	kurippu	*koo-reep-poo*
computer	konpyūta	*kohn-pyōo-tah*
copy	kopī/utsushi	*koh-pēē/oo-tsoo-shee*
correction fluid/ correction tape	shūsei eki/shūsei tēpu	*shōō-seh eh-kee/shōō-seh teh-poo*
draft	shitagaki/sōkō	*shtah-gah-kee/sōh-kōh*
envelope	fūtō	*fōō-toh*
eraser	keshigomu	*keh-shee-goh-moo*
glue	setchakuzai	*seht-chah-koo-zah-ee*
greeting card	gurītingu kādo	*goo-rēē-teen-goo kah-doh*

ink	inku	*een-koo*
ink stick (calligraphy)	sumi	*soo-mee*
inkstone (calligraphy)	suzuri	*soo-zoo-ree*
label	raberu / retteru	*rah-beh-roo/reht-teh-roo*
letter	tegami	*teh-gah-mee*
letterhead	binsen tōbu no jōhō insatsu	*been-sehn toh-boo noh joh-hoh een-sah-tsoo*
magnifying glass	kakudaikyō	*kahk-dah-ee-kyoh*
marker	majikku mākā	*mah-jeek-koo mah-kah*
notebook	nōto	*noh-toh*
page	pēji	*peh-jee*
paper	kami	*kah-mee*
paper clip	kurippu	*koo-reep-poo*
shredder	shureddā	*shoo-rehd-dah*
pen	pen	*pehn*
• ballpoint pen	bōru pen	*boh-roo pehn*
• felt-tip pen	feruto pen	*feh-roo-toh pehn*
• fountain pen	mannenhitsu	*mahn-nehn-hee-tsoo*
pencil	enpitsu	*ehn-pee-tsoo*
• mechanical pencil	shāpu penshiru	*shah-poo pehn-shee-roo*
printer	purinta	*poo-reen-tah*
punch	panchi	*pahn-chee*
ruler	jōgi	*joh-gee*
scanner	sukyana	*skyah-nah*
scissors	hasami	*hah-sah-mee*
Scotch tape	serotēpu	*seh-roh-teh-poo*
staple	hotchikisu no hari	*hoht-chee-kees noh hah-ree*
• stapler	hotchikisu	*hoht-chee-kees*
string	himo	*hee-moh*
typewriter	taipuraitā	*tah-ee-poo-rah-ee-tah*
wastebasket	kuzuire	*koo-zoo-ee-reh*

e. AT THE POST OFFICE

abroad	gaikoku	*gah-ee-koh-koo*
address	jūsho	*joo-shoh*
• return address	sashidashinin jūsho	*sah-shee-dah-shee-neen joo-shoh*
addressee	naatenin	*nah-ah-teh-neen*
airmail	kōkūbin	*koh-koo-been*
business letter	bijinesu retā	*bee-jee-nehs reh-tah*
book rate	shoseki ryōkin	*shoh-seh-kee ryoh-keen*
certified	naiyō shōmei no *(adj)*	*nah-ee-yoh shoh-meh noh*
clerk	kyokuin	*kyoh-koo-een*
clerk's window	madoguchi	*mah-doh-goo-chee*
confidential	shinten	*sheen-tehn*
correspondence	tsūshin	*tsoo-sheen*
delivery confirmation	haitatsu shōmei	*hah-ee-tah-tsoo shoh-meh*

envelope	fūtō	*foo-toh*
express mail	shin tokkyū yūbin	*sheen tohk-kyoo yoo-been*
insurance	hoken	*hoh-kehn*
international express mail	kokusai supīdo bin	*kohk-sah-ee spee-doh been*
letter carrier	yūbin haitatsu	*yoo been hah-ee-tah-tsoo*
mail	yūbin	*yoo-been*
• mail (letters)	dasu *(v)*	*dasu*
• mail (packages)	okuru *(v)*	*oh-koo-roo*
mail delivery	yūbin haitatsu	*yoo-been hah-ee-tah-tsoo*
mailbox	posuto	*pohs-toh*
money order	yūbin kawase	*yoo-been kah-wah-seh*
note	mijikai tegami	*mee-jee-kah-ee teh-gah-mee*
package	kozutsumi	*koh-zoo-tsoo-mee*
parcel	konimotsu	*koh-nee-moh-tsoo*
post office box	shishobako	*shee-shoh-bah-koh*
postage	yūbin ryōkin	*yoo-been ryoh-keen*
postal rate	yūbin ryōkin	*yoo-been ryoh-keen*
postcard	hagaki	*hah-gah-kee*
post office	yūbinkyoku	*yoo-been-kyoh-koo*
printed matter	insatsubutsu	*een-sah-tsoo-boo-tsoo*
registered letter	kakitome yūbin	*kah-kee-toh-meh yoo-been*
receive	uketoru *(v)*	*oo-keh-toh-roo*
reply	henji	*hehn-jee*
• reply	henji o dasu *(v)*	*hehn-jee oh dahs*
send	okuru *(v)*	*oh-koo-roo*
sender	sashidashinin	*sah-shee-dah-shee-neen*
special delivery	sokutatsu	*sohk-tah-tsoo*
stamp	kitte	*keet-teh*
surface mail	funabin	*foo-nah-been*
tracking number	tsuiseki bangō	*tsoo-ee-seh-kee bahn-goh*
wait for	matsu *(v)*	*mah-tsoo*
write	kaku *(v)*	*kah-koo*
zip code	yūbin bangō	*yoo-been bahn-goh*

f. E-MAIL

@	atto māku	*aht-toh mah-koo*
address book	adoresubukku	*ah-doh-reh-soo-book-koo*
attachment	tenpu	*tehn-poo*
• attach	tenpusuru *(v)*	*tehn-poo-soo-roo*
cancel	torikeshi	*toh-ree-keh-shee*
delete	sakujo	*sah-koo-joh*
dot com	dotto komu	*doht-toh koh-moo*
draft	shitagaki	*shee-tah-gah-kee*
e-mail	īmēru	*ee-meh-roo*

e-mail address	īmēru adoresu	ēe-mēh-roo ah-doh-reh-soo
erase	shōkyo	shoh-kyoh
file	bunsho	boon-shoh
folder	forudā	foh-roo-dāh
forward	tensō	tehn-soh
inbox	jushinbako	joo-sheen-bah-koh
junk mail	meiwaku mēru	meh-wah-koo meh-roo
move to	idōsuru (v)	ee-dōh-soo-roo
movie	dōga	dōh-gah
photo	shashin	shah-sheen
recipient	jushinnin	joo-sheen-neen
reply	henshin	hehn-sheen
reply all	zenin ni henshin	zehn-een nee hehn-sheen
save	hozon	hoh-zohn
sender	sashidashinin	sah-shee-dah-shee-neen
sent	sōshinzumi	soh-sheen-zoo-mee
text	honbun	hohn-boon
trash	gomibako	goh-mee-bah-koh
virus	uirusu	oo-ee-roo-soo
virus check	uirusu chekku	oo-ee-roo-soo chehk-koo

20. THE MEDIA

a. PRINT MEDIA

advertising	kōkoku	kōh-koh-koo
appendix	furoku	foo-roh-koo
atlas	chizuchō	chee-zoo-chōh
author	chosha	choh-shah
best seller	besuto serā	behs-toh seh-rāh
book	hon	hohn
circulation	hakkō busū	hahk-koh boo-sōo
column	koramu	koh-rah-moo
columnist	koramunisuto	koh-rah-moo-nee-stoh
comics	manga	mahn-gah
contributor	kikōsha	kee-kōh-shah
cover	hyōshi	hyōh-shee
critic	hyōronka	hyōh-rohn-kah
editor-in-chief	henshūchō	hehn-shōo-chōh
essay	essei	ehs-sēh
fiction	shōsetsu	shoh-seh-tsoo
• nonfiction	nonfikushon	nohn-feek-shohn
• science fiction	saiensu fikushon	sah-ee-ehn-soo feek-shohn
index	sakuin	sah-koo-een
magazine	zasshi	zahs-shee
• weekly magazine	shūkanshi	shōo-kahn-shee
• monthly magazine	gekkanshi	gehk-kahn-shee

newspaper	shinbun	*sheen-boon*
• article	kiji	*kee-jee__*
• criticism	hihyō	*hee-hyoh*
• daily newspaper	nikkanshi	*neek-kahn-shee*
• editor	henshūsha	*hehn-shōō-shah*
• editorial	shasetsu	*shah-seh-tsoo*
• evening paper	yūkan	*yōō-kahn*
• front page	ichimen	*ee-chee-mehn*
• headline	midashi	*mee-dah-shee*
• illustration	irasuto	*ee-rah-stoh*
• interview	intabyū	*een-tah-byōō*
• journalist	jānarisuto	*jāh-nah-ree-stoh*
• news	nyūsu	*nyōō-soo*
• obituary	shibōkiji	*shee-bōh-kee-jee*
• photo	shashin	*shah-sheen*
• reader	dokusha	*dohk-shah*
• reporter	repōtā	*reh-poh-tah*
• review	hyōron	*hyoh-rohn*
• weekly periodical	shūkanshi	*shōō-kahn-shee*
note	chūshaku	*chōō-shah-koo*
• footnote	kyakuchū	*kyahk-chōō*
novel	shōsetsu	*shoh-seh-tsoo*
• adventure	bōken	*boh-kehn*
• mystery	misuterī	*mee-steh-rēē*
• plot	suji	*soo-jee*
• romance	renai	*rehn-ah-ee*
page	pēji	*peh-jee*
pamphlet, brochure	panfuretto	*pahn-foo-reht-toh*
paperback	pēpābakku	*peh-pah-bahk-koo*
periodical	teiki kankōbutsu	*teh-kee kahn-koh-boo-tsoo*
play	geki	*geh-kee*
• comedy	kigeki	*kee-geh-kee*
• drama	dorama	*doh-rah-mah*
• tragedy	higeki	*hee-geh-kee*
pocket book	bunkohon	*boon-koh-hohn*
poem	shi	*shee*
poetry	shi	*shee*
print	insatsusuru (v)	*een-sah-tsoo-soo-roo*
printing, typography	insatsujutsu	*een-sah-tsoo-joo-tsoo*
print run	insatsu busū	*een-sah-tsoo boo-sōō*
proof	kōseizuri	*kōh-seh-zoo-ree*
proofreader	kōseisha	*koh-seh-shah*
publish	shuppansuru (v)	*shoop-pahn-soo-roo*
• publisher	shuppansha	*shoop-pahn-shah*
read	yomu (v)	*yoh-moo*
reference book	sankōsho	*sahn-kōh-shoh*
• definition	gogi	*goh-gee*

• videotape	bideo kasetto	*bee-deh-oh kah-seht-toh*
turn off	kesu *(v)*	*keh-soo*
turn on	tsukeru *(v)*	*tskeh-roo*

21. FEELINGS

a. MOODS/ATTITUDES/EMOTIONS

active	kappatsu na *(adj)*	*kahp-pah-tsoo nah*
affection	aijō	*ah-ee-joh*
• affectionate	aijō no fukai *(adj)*	*ah-ee-joh noh fkah-ee*
agree	sanseisuru *(v)*	*sahn-seh-soo-roo*
• agreeable	kokoroyoi *(adj)*	*koh-koh-roh-yoh-ee*
aggressive	kōgekiteki na *(adj)*	*koh-geh-kee-teh-kee nah*
anger	ikari	*ee-kah-ree*
• angry	okotta *(adj)*	*oh-koht-tah*
anxiety, anxiousness	fuan	*foo-ahn*
• anxious	fuan na *(adj)*	*foo-ahn nah*
argumentative	rikutsuppoi *(adj)*	*ree-koo-tsoop-poh-ee*
assure	ukeau *(v)*	*oo-keh-ah-oo*
attitude	taido	*tah-ee-doh*
be down	ki ga meitte iru	*kee gah meh-eet-teh ee-roo*
be up	ki ga takamatte iru	*kee gah tah-kah-maht-teh ee-roo*
bold	daitan na *(adj)*	*dah-ee-tahn nah*
bore	unzarisaseru *(vt)*	*oon-zah-ree-sah-seh-roo*
• become bored	taikutsusuru *(vi)*	*tah-ee-ktsoo-soo-roo*
• bored	taikutsushita *(adj)*	*tah-ee-ktsoo-shtah*
• boredom	taikutsu	*tah-ee-ktsoo*
brag	jimansuru *(v)*	*jee-mahn-soo-roo*
cautious	shinchō na *(v)*	*sheen-choh nah*
cheerful	yōki na *(adj)*	*yoh-kee nah*
complain	kujō o noberu *(v)*	*koo-joh oh noh-beh-roo*
• complaint	kujō	*koo-joh*
cordial	kokoro no komotta *(adj)*	*koh-koh-roh noh koh-moht-tah*
cruel	zankoku na *(adj)*	*zahn-koh-koo nah*
cry	naku *(v)*	*nah-koo*
• tears	namida	*nah-mee-dah*
decent	kichin to shita *(adj)*	*kee-cheen toh shtah*
depressed	yūutsu na *(adj)*	*yoo-oo-tsoo nah*
• depression	yūutsu	*yoo-oo-tsoo*
desperate	hisshi no *(adj)*	*hees-shee noh*
disagree	sansei shinai	*sahn-seh shee-nah-ee*
• disagreement	fusansei	*foo-sahn-seh*
• be against	hantaisuru *(v)*	*hahn-tah-ee-soo-roo*
disappoint	shitsubōsaseru *(vt)*	*shee-tsoo-boh-sah-seh-roo*

• disappointed	gakkarishita *(adj)*	gahk-kah-ree-shtah
• disappointment	shitsubō	shtsoo-boh
disgusting	mukamuka suru *(adj)*	moo-kah-moo-kah soo-roo
dissatisfaction	fuman	foo-mahn
• dissatisfied	fuman no aru *(adj)*	foo-mahn noh ah-roo
eager	nesshin na *(adj)*	nehs-sheen nah
efficient	yūnō na *(adj)*	yoo-noh nah
egoistic	jibun katte na *(adj)*	jee-boon kaht-teh nah
emotion	kanjō	kahn-joh
• emotional	kanjōteki na *(adj)*	kahn-joh-teh-kee nah
encourage	hagemasu *(v)*	hah-geh-mahs
• encouragement	gekirei	geh-kee-reh
enthusiastic	nesshin na *(adj)*	nehs-sheen nah
faith, trust	shinrai	sheen-rah-ee
• trust	shinraisuru *(v)*	sheen-rah-ee-soo-roo
fantastic	subarashii *(adj)*	soo-bah-rah-shee
fear	osore	oh-soh-reh
• be afraid	osoreru *(v)*	oh-soh-reh-roo
feel	kanjiru *(v)*	kahn-jee-roo
• feeling	kanji	kahn-jee
fierce	hageshii *(adj)*	hah-geh-shee
flatter	oseji o iu *(v)*	oh-seh-jee oh ee-oo
• flattery	oseji	oh-seh-jee
friendly	shitashimiyasui *(adj)*	shtah-shee-mee-yah-soo-ee
fun, enjoyment	tanoshimi	tah-noh-shee-mee
• have fun, enjoy oneself	tanoshimu *(v)*	tah-noh-shee-moo
gentle	yasashii *(adj)*	yah-sah-shee
gloomy	inki na *(adj)*	een-kee nah
happiness	shiawase	shee-ah-wah-seh
• happy	shiawase na *(adj)*	shee-ah-wah-seh nah
hesitant	tameraigachi na *(adj)*	tah-meh-rah-ee-gah-chee nah
hope	nozomi	noh-zoh-mee
• hope	nozomu *(v)*	noh-zoh-moo
humble	hikaeme na *(adj)*	hee-kah-eh-meh nah
humorous	yūmoa no aru *(adj)*	yoo-moh-ah noh ah-roo
indifference	mukanshin	moo-kahn-sheen
• indifferent	mukanshin na *(adj)*	moo-kahn-sheen nah
joy	yorokobi	yoh-roh-koh-bee
kind	shinsetsu na *(adj)*	sheen-seh-tsoo nah
laugh	warau *(v)*	wah-rah-oo
• laughter	warai	wah-rah-ee
mean	iji no warui *(adj)*	ee-jee noh wah-roo-ee
merciful	nasakebukai *(adj)*	nah-sah-keh-boo-kah-ee
merciless	zankoku na *(adj)*	zahn-koh-koo nah
modest	tsutsushimibukai *(adj)*	tsoo-tsoo-shee-mee-boo-kah-ee

21a MOODS/ATTITUDES/EMOTIONS

mood	kibun	kee-boon
• bad mood	warui kibun	wah-roo-ee kee-boon
• good mood	ii kibun	ee kee-boon
moody	kimagure na (adj)	kee-mah-goo-reh nah
need	hitsuyō	hee-tsoo-yoh
• need	iru (v)	ee-roo
negative	hiteiteki na (adj)	hee-teh-teh-kee nah
nosy	sensakuzuki na (adj)	sehn-sah-koo-zoo-kee nah
oppose	hantaisuru (v)	hahn-tah-ee-soo-roo
passionate	netsuretsu na (adj)	neh-tsoo-reh-tsoo nah
passive	shōkyokuteki na (adj)	shoh-kyoh-koo-teh-kee nah
patience	nintai	neen-tah-ee
• patient	nintaizuyoi (adj)	neen-tah-ee-zoo-yoh-ee
positive	sekkyokuteki na (adj)	sehk-kyoh-koo-teh-kee nah
provocative	chōhatsuteki na (adj)	choh-hah-tsoo-teh-kee nah
relief	anshin	ahn-sheen
• sigh of relief	ando no tameiki	ahn-doh noh tah-meh-ee-kee
sad	kanashii (adj)	kah-nah-shee
• sadness	kanashimi	kah-nah-shee-mee
satisfaction	manzoku	mahn-zoh-koo
• satisfied	manzokushita (adj)	mahn-zoh-koo-shtah
sensitive	kanjiyasui (adj)	kahn-jee-yah-soo-ee
serious	shinken na (adj)	sheen-kehn nah
shame	haji	hah-jee
• be ashamed	hajiru (v)	hah-jee-roo
shameless	hajishirazu no (adj)	hah-jee-shee-rah-zoo noh
silly	oroka na (adj)	oh-ro-kah nah
sincere	seijitsu na (adj)	seh-jee-tsoo nah
smile	hohoemi	hoh-hoh-eh-mee
• smile	hohoemu (v)	hoh-hoh-eh-moo
sociable	shakōteki na (adj)	shah-koh-teh-kee nah
sorrow	kanashimi	kah-nah-shee-mee
strict	genkaku na (adj)	gehn-kah-koo nah
surprise	odoroki	oh-doh-roh-kee
• surprise	odorokasu (vt)	oh-doh-roh-kah-soo
sympathy	dōjō	doh-joh
• sympathetic	dōjōteki na (adj)	doh-joh-teh-kee nah
tender	yasashii (adj)	yah-sah-shee
tense	kinchōshita (adj)	keen-choh-shtah
thankfulness	kansha	kahn-shah
• thankful	kansha no (adj)	kahn-shah noh
• thank	kanshasuru (v)	kahn-shah-soo-roo
timid	okubyō na (adj)	oh-koo-byoh nah
tolerance	kanyō	kahn-yoh
• tolerant	kanyō na (adj)	kahn-yoh nah
trustworthy	shinrai dekiru (adj)	sheen-rah-ee deh-kee-roo

unbearable	taegatai *(adj)*	tah-ee-gah-tah-ee
weep	naku *(v)*	nah-koo
wonderful	subarashii *(adj)*	soo-bah-rah-shēē

b. LIKES AND DISLIKES

accept	ukeireru *(v)*	oo-keh-ee-reh-roo
• acceptable	ukeirerareru *(adj)*	oo-keh-ee-reh-rah-reh-roo
• unacceptable	ukeiregatai *(adj)*	oo-keh-ee-reh-gah-tah-ee
approval	zenin	zeh-neen
• approve	mitomeru *(v)*	mee-toh-meh-roo
be fond of, like	konomu *(v)*	koh-noh-moo
detest	kirau *(v)*	kee-rah-oo
disgust	mukamukasaseru *(v)*	moo-kah-moo-kah-sah-seh-roo
disgusted	unzarishita *(adj)*	oon-zah-ree-shtah
hate	nikumu *(v)*	nee-koo-moo
• hatred	ken-o	kehn-oh
kiss	kisu	kee-soo
• kiss	kisusuru *(v)*	kee-soo-soo-roo
like	konomu *(v)*	koh-noh-moo
• liking	konomi	KOH-noh-mee
• dislike	kirau *(v)*	kee-rah-oo
love	ai	ah-ee
• love	aisuru *(v)*	ah-ee-soo-roo
pleasant	tanoshii *(adj)*	tah-noh-shēē
• unpleasant	fuyukai na *(adj)*	foo-yoo-kah-ee nah
prefer	konomu *(v)*	koh-noh-moo
• preference	konomi	KOH-noh-mee
reject	kyozetsusuru *(v)*	kyoh-zeh-tsoo-soo-roo
• rejection	kyozetsu	kyoh-zeh-tsoo

c. EXPRESSING EMOTIONS

Are you joking?	Jōdan desho.	jōh-dahn deh-shoh
Be careful!	Ki o tsukete.	kee oh tskeh-teh
Enough! (No more!)	Mō yoshinasai.	moh yoh-shee-nah-sah-ee
Fortunately!	Un yoku.	oon yoh-koo
Good heavens!/Oh my!	Oya.	oh-YAH
I don't believe it!	Shinjiraremasen.	sheen-jee-rah-reh-mah-sehn
I don't feel like ...	... ki ni naremasen.	... kee nee nah-reh-mah-sehn
I wish!	Sō da to iindesu ga.	SŌH dah toh ēēn-dehs gah
I'm serious!	Honki desu yo.	hohn-kee dehs yoh
I'm sorry!	Sumimasen.	soo-mee-mah-sehn

Impossible!	Masakā.	*mah-sah-KAH*
It doesn't matter!	Kamaimasen.	*kah-mah-ee-mah-sehn*
My God!	Komatta. *(inf)*	*koh-maht-tah*
Oh, my!	Oya, mā.	*OH-yah, mah*
Poor man!	Kawaisō ni.	*kah-wah-ee-soh nee*
Poor woman!	Kawaisō ni.	*kah-wah-ee-soh nee*
Quiet!	Shizuka ni. *(inf)*	*shee-zoo-kah nee*
Really?	Hontō. *(inf)*	*hohn-TOH*
Shutup!	Damare. *(inf)*	*dah-mah-reh*
Thank goodness!	Arigatai. *(inf)*	*ah-ree-gah-tah-ee*
Too bad!	Zannen.	*zahn-nehn*
Ugh!	Wā, yada.	*WAH, yah-dah*
Unbelievable!	Shinjirarenai. *(inf)*	*sheen-jee-rah-reh-nah-ee*
Unfortunately!	Un waruku.	*oon wah-roo-koo*
What a bore!	Unzari.	*OON-zah-ree*

22. THINKING

a. DESCRIBING THOUGHT

abstract	chūshōteki na *(adj)*	*choo-shoh-teh-kee nah*
belief	shinnen	*sheen-nehn*
complicated	fukuzatsu na *(adj)*	*fkoo-zah-tsoo nah*
concept	gainen	*gah-ee-nehn*
concrete	gutaiteki na *(adj)*	*goo-tah-ee-teh-kee nah*
conscience	ryōshin	*ryoh-sheen*
conscientious	ryōshinteki na *(adj)*	*ryoh-sheen-teh-kee nah*
creative	sōzōteki na *(adj)*	*soh-zoh-teh-kee nah*
difficult	muzukashii *(adj)*	*moo-zoo-kah-shee*
doubt	utagai	*oo-tah-gah-ee*
easy	yasashii *(adj)*	*yah-sah-shee*
existence	sonzai	*sohn-zah-ee*
hypothesis	kasetsu	*kah-seh_tsoo*
idea	aidia	*ah-ee-dee-ah*
ignorant	muchi no *(adj)*	*moo-chee noh*
imagination	sōzōryoku	*soh-zoh-ryoh-koo*
ingenious	dokusōteki na *(adj)*	*dohk-soh-teh-kee nah*
interest	kyōmi	*kyoh-mee*
interesting	omoshiroi *(adj)*	*oh-moh-shee-roh-ee*
judgment	handan	*hahn-dahn*
justice	seigi	*seh-gee*
knowledge	chishiki	*chee-shee-kee*
knowledgeable	yoku shitteiru *(adj)*	*yoh-koo sheet-teh-ee-roo*
logic	ronri	*rohn-ree*
memory	kioku	*kee-oh-koo*
mind	kokoro	*koh-koh-roh*
opinion	iken	*ee-kehn*

• in my opinion	watakushi no iken dewa	*wah-tahk-shee noh ee-kehn deh-wah*
problem	mondai	*mohn-dah-ee*
• No problem!	Mondai arimasen.	*mohn-dah-ee ah-ree-mah-sehn*
reason	riyū	*ree-yōō*
simple	tanjun na *(adj)*	*tahn-joon nah*
thought	kangae	*kahn-gah-eh*
wisdom	chie	*chee-eh*

b. BASIC THOUGHT PROCESSES

agree	sanseisuru *(v)*	*sahn-seh-soo-roo*
be interested in	kyōmi ga aru *(v)*	*kyoh-mee gah ah-roo*
be right	tadashii *(desu)*	*tah-dah-shee (dehs)*
be wrong	machigai *(desu)*	*mah-chee-gah-ee (dehs)*
believe	shinjiru *(v)*	*sheen-jee-roo*
convince	nattokusaseru *(v)*	*naht-tohk-sah-seh-roo*
demonstrate	hyōmeisuru *(v)*	*kyoh-meh-soo-roo*
doubt	utagau *(v)*	*oo-tah-gah-oo*
dream	yume ni egaku *(v)*	*yoo-meh nee eh-gah-koo*
forget	wasureru *(v)*	*wah-soo-reh-roo*
imagine	sōzōsuru *(v)*	*soh-zoh-soo-roo*
judge	handansuru *(v)*	*hahn-dahn-soo-roo*
know	shiru *(v)*	*shee-roo*
learn	narau *(v)*	*nah-rah-oo*
memorize	kiokusuru *(v)*	*kee-oh-koo-soo-roo*
persuade	settokusuru *(v)*	*seht-tohk-soo-roo*
reason	ronshōsuru *(v)*	*rohn-shoh-soo-roo*
reflect	shiansuru *(v)*	*SHEE-ahn-soo-roo*
remember	omoidasu *(v)*	*oh-moh-ee-dahs*
study	manabu *(v)*	*mah-nah-boo*
think	kangaeru *(v)*	*kahn-gah-eh-roo*
understand	rikaisuru *(v)*	*ree-kah-ee-soo-roo*

DAILY LIFE

23. AT HOME

a. PARTS OF THE HOUSE

attic	yaneurabeya	*yah-neh-oo-rah-beh-yah*
balcony	barukonī	*bah-roo-koh-nēe*
banister	kaidan no tesuri	*kah-ee-dahn no teh-soo-ree*
basement	chikashitsu	*chee-kah-shtsoo*
bathtub	yokusō	*yohk-soh*
ceiling	tenjō	*tehn-joh*
chimney	entotsu	*ehn-toh-tsoo*
corridor	rōka	*roh-kah*
door	to	*toh*
doorbell	yobirin	*yoh-bee-reen*
entrance	iriguchi	*ee-ree-goo-chee*
faucet	jaguchi	*jah-goo-chee*
fireplace	danro	*dahn-roh*
floor	yuka	*yoo-kah*
floor (level)	kai	*kah-ee*
garage	shako	*shah-koh*
garden	niwa	*nee-wah*
gate	mon	*mohn*
ground floor	ikkai	*eek-kah-ee*
handrail	tesuri	*teh-soo-ree*
house	ie	*ee-eh*
kitchen sink	nagashi	*nah-gah-shee*
mailbox	yūbinuke	*yōo-been-oo-keh*
patio	nakaniwa	*nah-kah-nee-wah*
porch	beranda	*beh-rahn-dah*
roof	yane	*yah-neh*
shelf	tana	*tah-nah*
shower	shawā	*shah-wah*
sink	senmendai	*sehn-mehn-dah-ee*
stairs	kaidan	*kah-ee-dahn*
switch	suitchi	*soo-eet-chee*
terrace	terasu	*teh-rah-soo*
toilet	otearai	*oh-teh-ah-rah-ee*
wall	kabe	*kah-beh*

The walls have ears.	Kabe ni mimi ari.	*kah-beh nee mee-mee ah-ree*

| window | mado | *mah-doh* |
| windowsill | madowaku | *ntah-doh-wah-koo* |

b. ROOMS

FOCUS: Features Unique to the Japanese House

entrance hall (where shoes are removed and kept)	genkan	*gehn-kahn*
woven reed mat floor in a Japanese-style room	tatami	*tah-tah-mee*

The most important Japanese-style room in a house often has an alcove with a scroll and a flower arrangement.

| alcove | tokonoma | *toh-koh-noh-mah* |

In a Japanese house, the toilet and the bathroom are usually separate.

| toilet | otearai | *oh-teh-ah-rah-ee* |
| bathroom | furoba | *foo-roh-bah* |

alcove	tokonoma	*toh-koh-noh-mah*
bathroom (western style)	basurūmu	*bah-soo-rōō-moo*
bathroom (Japanese style)	furoba	*foo-roh-bah*
bedroom	shinshitsu	*sheen-shee-tsoo*
closet	oshiire	*oh-shee-ee-reh*
dining room	shokudō	*shoh-koo-doh*
entrance hall	genkan	*gehn-kahn*
kitchen	daidokoro	*dah-ee-doh-koh-roh*
living room	ima	*ee-mah*
room	heya	*heh-yah*
• Japanese-style room	washitsu	*wah-shee-tsoo*
• western-style room	yōma	*yōh-mah*

c. FURNITURE AND DECORATION

Japanese rooms may have two kinds of sliding partitions:

screen made of paper and a wooden grid	shōji	shoh-jee
heavier screen made of paper or fabric	fusuma	foo-soo-mah

Many Japanese homes have a household Buddhist altar, a household Shinto shrine, or both.

household Buddhist altar	butsudan	boo-tsoo-dahn
household Shinto shrine	kamidana	kah-mee-dah-nah

armchair	hijikakeisu	hee-jee-kah-keh-ee-soo
bed	beddo	behd-doh
bedding (Japanese mattress for the floor)	futon	ftohn
bedside table	saidotēburu	sah-ee-doh-teh-boo-roo
bookcase	hondana	hohn-dah-nah
cabinet	kyabinetto	kyah-bee-neht-toh
carpet, rug	jūtan	joo-tahn
chair	isu	ee-soo
chest of drawers (Japanese style)	tansu	tahn-soo
chest of drawers (western style)	yōdansu	yoh-dahn-soo
curtains	kāten	kah-tehn
drawer	hikidashi	hee-kee-dah-shee
furniture	kagu	KAH-goo
household Buddhist altar	butsudan	boo-tsoo-dahn
household Shinto shrine	kamidana	kah-mee-dah-nah
lamp	ranpu	rahn-poo
mirror	kagami	kah-gah-mee
painting	e	eh
screen with paper and wooden grid	shōji	shoh-jee
• heavier screen with paper or fabric	fusuma	fsoo-mah
shelf	tana	tah-nah
sideboard	shokki todana	shohk-kee toh-dah-nah

sofa	sofā	soh-fah
table	tēburu	teh-boo-roo
writing desk	desuku	dehs-koo

d. APPLIANCES AND COMMON HOUSEHOLD ITEMS

bag	fukuro	fkoo-roh
• shopping bag	kaimonobukuro	kah-ee-moh-noh-boo-koo-roh
basket	kago	kah-goh
bathroom scale	taijūkei	tah-ee-joo-keh
bedspread	beddokabā	behd-doh-kah-bah
blanket	mōfu	moh-foo
bottle	bin	been
box	hako	hah-koh
broom	hōki	hoh-kee
chopstick	hashi	hah-shee
• chopstick rest	hashioki	hah-shee-oh-kee
clothes hanger	hangā	hahn-gah
coffee machine	kōhīmēkā	koh-hee-meh-kah
coffee pot	kōhīpotto	koh-hee-poht-toh
cup	kōhījawan	koh-hee-jah-wahn
• teacup (Japanese)	yunomijawan	yoo-noh-mee-jah-wahn
dishwasher	shokkiaraiki	shohk-kee-ah-rah-ee-kee
dryer	kansōki	kahn-soh-kee
fork	fōku	foh-koo
dust pan	chiritori	chee-ree-toh-ree
duster	hataki	hah-tah-kee
freezer	reitōko	reh-toh-koh
glass (drinking)	koppu	kohp-poo
heater	hītā	hee-tah
iron	airon	ah-ee-rohn
juicer	jūsā	joo-sah
kettle	yakan	yah-kahn
key	kagi	kah-gee
knife	hōchō	hoh-choh
• blade	ha	hah
• handle	totte	toht-teh
ladle	hishaku	hee-shah-koo
lid	futa	foo-tah
microwave oven	denshirenji	dehn-shee-rehn-jee
mixer	mikisā	mee-kee-sah
mop	moppu	mohp-poo
napkin	napukin	nah-poo-keen
oven	ōbun	oh-boon
pail	teoke	teh-oh-keh
pan	hiranabe	hee-rah-nah-beh
pillow	makura	mah-koo-rah

pillowcase	makurakabā	mah-koo-rah-kah-bah̄
plastic container	purasuchikku yōki	poo-rahs-cheek-koo yoh̄-kee
plate	sara	sah-rah
pot	fukanabe	fkah-nah-beh
radio	rajio	rah-jee-oh
rice bowl (Japanese)	gohanjawan	goh-hahn-jah-wahn
rice cooker	suihanki	soo-ee-hahn-kee
refrigerator	reizōko	reh-zōh-koh
saucer	ukezara	oo-keh-zah-rah
sewing machine	mishin	mee-sheen
sheet (bed)	shītsu	shē̄-tsoo
soup bowl (Japanese)	owan	oh-wahn
spoon	supūn	soo-pōōn
• tablespoon	ōsaji	ōh-sah-jee
• teaspoon	kosaji	koh-sah-jee
stove	renji	rehn-jee
• electric stove	denki sutōbu	dehn-kee soo-tōh-boo
• gas stove	gasu sutōbu	gah-soo soo-tōh-boo
tablecloth	tēburukurosu	teh-boo-roo-koo-roh-soo
tableware	shokutakuyō shokkigu	shohk-tah-koo-yōh shohk-kee-goo
teapot	tīpotto	tē̄-poht-toh
• small teapot (Japanese)	kyūsu	kyōō-soo
• large teapot (Japanese)	dobin	doh-been
television set	terebi	teh-reh-bee
toaster	tōsutā	tōh-stah
tools	daikudōgu	dah-ee-koo-dōh-goo
towel	taoru	tah-oh-roo
tray	obon	oh-bohn
vacuum cleaner	sōjiki	sōh-jee-kee
washing machine	sentakuki	sehn-tahk-kee
water-heater	yuwakashiki	yoo-wah-kah-shee-kee

e. SERVICES

air conditioning	reibō	rēh-bōh
• air conditioner	eakon	eh-ah-kohn
broadband	burōdobando	boo-rōh-doh-bahn-doh
cable	kēburu	keh-boo-roo
electricity	denki	dehn-keē
furnace	danbōro	dahn-bōh-roh
gas	gasu	gah-soo̲
heating	danbō	dahn-bōh̄
plumbing	suidō setsubi	soo-ee-dōh̄ seh-tsoo-bee

| telephone | denwa | *dehn-wah* |
| water | suidō | *soo-ee-doh* |

f. ADDITIONAL HOUSEHOLD VOCABULARY

at home	uchi de	*oo-chee-deh*
build	tateru (v)	*tah-teh-roo*
buy	kau (v)	*kah-oo*
clean	sōjisuru (v)	*soh-jee-soo-roo*
clear the table	atokatazukesuru (v)	*ah-toh-kah-tah-zoo-keh-soo-roo*
live in	sumikomu (v)	*soo-mee-koh-moo*
make the bed	beddo o totonoeru (v)	*behd-doh oh toh-toh-noh-eh-roo*
move	hikkosu (v)	*heek-koh-soo*
paint	penki o nuru (v)	*pehn-kee oh noo-roo*
put a room in order	heya o katazukeru (v)	*heh-yah oh kah-tah-zoo-keh-roo*
restore	shūfukusuru (v)	*shoo-fkoo-soo-roo*
set the table	tēburu o totonoeru (v)	*teh-boo-roo oh toh-toh-noh-eh-roo*
wash	arau (v)	*ah-rah-oo*
• wash the clothes	sentakusuru (v)	*sehn-tahk-soo-roo*
• wash the dishes	sara o arau (v)	*sah-rah oh ah-rah-oo*

g. LIVING IN AN APARTMENT

In Japan, an inexpensive, small, and not-so-modern apartment is called apāto (apartment). In contrast with apāto, a modern, larger, and upscale apartment is distinguished by the name manshon (mansion).

apartment (an inexpensive one)	apāto	*ah-pah-toh*
apartment (an upscale one)	manshon	*mahn-shohn*
building	biru	*bee-roo*
condominium	bunjō manshon	*boon-joh mahn-shohn*
elevator	erebētā	*eh-reh-beh-tah*
ground floor	ikkai	*eek-kah-ee*
indoor garage	okunai chūshajō	*oh-koo-nah-ee choo-shah-joh*
intercom	intāhon	*een-tah-hohn*
landlord	yanushi	*yah-noo-shee*
lease	rīsu	*ree-soo*
parking lot	chūshajō	*choo-shah-joh*

rent	yachin	*yah-cheen*
• rent	kariru *(v)*	*kah-ree-roo*
security system	keibi shisutemu	*keh-bee shees-teh-moo*
superintendent	kanrinin	*kahn-ree-neen*
tenant	kyojūsha	*kyoh-jōō-shah*

24. EATING AND DRINKING

a. MEALS

breakfast	asagohan	*ah-sah-goh-hahn*
	chōshoku	*choh-shoh-koo*
dinner	bangohan	*bahn-goh-hahn*
	yūshoku	*yōō-shoh-koo*
food	tabemono	*tah-beh-moh-noh*
lunch	hirugohan	*hee-roo-goh-hahn*
	chūshoku	*chōō-shoh-koo*
meal	shokuji	*shoh-koo-jee*
snack	kanshoku	*kahn-shoh-koo*
	oyatsu	*oh-yah-tsoo*
	sunakku	*soo-nahk-koo*

b. PREPARATION OF FOOD

baked	tenpi de yaita *(adj)*	*tehn-pee deh yah-ee-tah*
boiled	yudeta *(adj)*	*yoo-deh-tah*
broiled	jikabi de yaita *(adj)*	*jee-kah-bee deh yah-ee-tah*
cooking, cuisine	ryōri	*ryoh-ree*
fried	ageta *(adj)*	*ah-geh-tah*
grilled	amiyaki no *(adj)*	*ah-mee-yah-kee noh*
marinated	marine shita *(adj)*	*mah-ree-neh shtah*
medium	midiamu no *(adj)*	*mee-dee-ah-moo noh*
rare	rea no *(adj)*	*reh-ah noh*
roast	rōsuto	*roh-stoh*
sautéed	sotē ni shita *(adj)*	*soh-teh nee shtah*
steamed	mushita *(adj)*	*moo-shtah*
well-done	yoku yaita *(adj)*	*yoh-koo yah-ee-tah*

c. MEAT AND POULTRY

bacon	bēkon	*beh-kohn*
beef	gyūniku	*gyōō-nee-koo*
	bīfu	*bee-foo*
chicken	toriniku	*toh-ree-nee-koo*
	chikin	*chee-keen*
cold cuts	reiniku no moriawase	*reh-nee-koo noh moh-ree-ah-wah-seh*

duck	ahiru	*ah-hee-roo*
	dakku	*dahk-koo*
ham	hamu	*hah-moo*
kidney	jinzō	*jeen-zoh*
lamb	kohitsuji no niku	*koh-hee-tsoo-jee noh nee-koo*
	ramu	*rah-moo*
liver	kanzō	*kahn-zoh*
	rebā	*reh-bah*
meat	niku	*nee-koo*
mutton	yōniku	*yoh-nee-koo*
	maton	*mah-tohn*
oxtail	okkusutēru	*ohk-ksoo-teh-roo*
pork	butaniku	*boo-tah-nee-koo*
	pōku	*poh-koo*
salami	sarami sōsēji	*sah-rah-mee SOH-seh-jee*
sausage	sōsēji	*SOH-seh-jee*
tongue	tan	*tahn*
turkey	shichimenchō	*shee-chee-mehn-choh*
veal	koushi no niku	*koh-oo-shee noh nee-koo*

d. FISH, SEAFOOD, AND SHELLFISH

abalone	awabi	*ah-wah-bee*
anchovy	anchobi	*ahn-choh-bee*
clam	hamaguri	*hah-mah-goo-ree*
crab	kani	*kah-nee*
cod	tara	*tah-rah*
eel	unagi	*oo-nah-gee*
fish	sakana	*sah-kah-nah*
flounder	hirame	*hee-rah-meh*
halibut	ohyō	*oh-hyoh*
herring	nishin	*nee-sheen*
lobster	robusutā	*roh-boo-stah*
mackerel	saba	*sah-bah*
mussel	mūrugai	*moo-roo-gah-ee*
octopus	tako	*tah-koh*
oyster	kaki	*KAH-kee*
porgy	tai	*tah-ee*
prawn	kurumaebi	*koo-roo-mah-eh-bee*
salmon	sake	*SAH-keh*
sardine	iwashi	*ee-wah-shee*
scallops	kaibashira	*kah-ee-bah-shee-rah*
seafood	gyokairui	*gyoh-kah-ee-roo-ee*
sea bass	suzuki	*soo-zoo-kee*
shellfish	ebi, kani, kairui	*eh-bee, kah-nee, kah-ee-roo-ee*

shrimp	ebi	*eh-bee*
smelt	wakasagi	*wah-kah-sah-gee*
squid	ika	*ee-kah*
sole	shitabirame	*shee-tah-bee-rah-meh*
swordfish	kajiki	*kah-jee-kee*
trout	masu	*mah-soo*
tuna	maguro	*mah-goo-roh*

e. VEGETABLES

artichoke	ātichōku	*āh-tee-chōh-koo*
asparagus	asuparagasu	*ahs-pah-rah-gah-soo*
bamboo shoot	takenoko	*tah-keh-noh-koh*
bean	mame	*mah-meh*
bean sprout	moyashi	*moh-yah-shee*
beet	satōdaikon	*sah-toh-dah-ee-kohn*
broccoli	burokkori	*boo-rohk-koh-ree*
burdock	gobō	*goh-bōh*
cabbage	kyabetsu	*kyah-beh-tsoo*
carrot	ninjin	*neen-jeen*
cauliflower	karifurawā	*kah-ree-foo-rah-wāh*
celery	serori	*seh-roh-ree*
chickpea	hiyoko mame	*hee-yoh-koh mah-meh*
corn	tōmorokoshi	*toh-moh-roh-koh-shee*
cucumber	kyūri	*kyōō-ree*
eggplant	nasu	*nah-soo*
garlic	ninniku	*neen-nee-koo*
green pepper	pīman	*pēe-mahn*
leek	naganegi	*nah-gah-neh-gee*
lentil	renzu mame	*rehn-zoo mah-meh*
lettuce	retasu	*reh-tahs*
lotus root	renkon	*rehn-kohn*
mushroom	kinoko	*kee-noh-koh*
onion	tamanegi	*tah-mah-neh-gee*
peas	endōmame	*ehn-dōh-mah-meh*
potato	jagaimo	*jah-gah-ee-moh*
pumpkin	kabocha	*kah-boh-chah*
radish (Japanese)	daikon	*dah-ee-kohn*
radish (western)	hatsuka daikon	*hah-tsoo-kah dah-ee-kohn*
soy bean	daizu	*dah-ee-zoo __*
spinach	hōrensō	*hōh-rehn-sōh*
spring onion, scallion	hosonegi	*hoh-soh-neh-gee*
string bean	sayaingen	*sah-yah-een-gehn*
sweet potato	satsumaimo	*sah-tsoo-mah-ee-moh*
taro	satoimo	*sah-toh-ee-moh*
tomato	tomato	*toh-mah-toh*
turnip	kabu	*kah-boo*

| vegetables | yasai | *yah-sah-ee* |
| zucchini | zukkīni | *zook-kēē-nee* |

f. FRUITS

apple	ringo	*reen-goh*
apricot	anzu	*ahn-zoo*
banana	banana	*bah-nah-nah*
blueberry	burūberī	*boo-rōo-beh-rēē*
cherry	sakuranbo	*sah-koo-rahn-boh*
chestnut	kuri	*koo-ree*
date	natsume	*nah-tsoo-meh*
fig	ichijiku	*ee-chee-jee-koo*
fruit	kudamono	*koo-dah-moh-noh*
grape	budō	*boo-dōh*
grapefruit	gurēpufurūtsu	*goo-reh-poo-foo-rōo-tsoo*
lemon	remon	*reh-mohn*
kiwi	kīwī	*kēē-wēē*
mandarin orange	mikan	*mee-kahn*
mango	mangō	*mahn-goh*
melon	meron	*meh-rohn*
nectarine	nekutarin	*nehk-tah-reen*
orange	orenji	*oh-rehn-jee*
papaya	papaiya	*pah-pah-ee-yah*
peach	momo	*moh-moh*
pear (Japanese)	nashi	*nah-shee*
pear (western)	yōnashi	*yōh-nah-shee*
persimmon	kaki	*kah-kee*
pineapple	painappuru	*pah-ee-nahp-poo-roo*
plum	sumomo	*soo-moh-moh*
pomegranate	zakuro	*zah-koo-roh*
prune	hoshisumomo	*hoh-shee-soo-moh-moh*
raisin	hoshibudō	*hoh-shee-boo-dōh*
raspberry	kiichigo	*kee-ee-chee-goh*
strawberry	ichigo	*ee-chee-goh*
walnut	kurumi	*koo-roo-mee*
watermelon	suika	*soo-ee-kah*

g. MEAL AND MENU COMPONENTS

aperitif	shokuzenshu	*shoh-koo-zehn-shoo*
appetizer	zensai	*zehn-sah-ee*
bread	pan	*pahn*
cheese	chīzu	*chēē-zoo*
course	kōsu	*koh-soo*
dessert	dezāto	*deh-zah-toh*
fruit	kudamono	*koo-dah-moh-noh*
ice cream	aisukurīmu	*ah-ees-koo-rēē-moo*

main course	meinkōsu	*meh-een-koh-soo*
menu	menyū	*meh-nyoo*
pasta	pasuta	*pah-stah*
pie	pai	*pah-ee*
pudding	purin	*poo-reen*
rice	raisu	*rah-ee-soo*
roll	rōrupan	*roh-roo-pahn*
salad	sarada	*sah-rah-dah*
• salad dressing	doresshingu	*doh-rehs-sheen-goo*
sandwich	sandoitchi	*sahn-doh-eet-chee*
sherbet	shābetto	*shah-beht-toh*
soup	sūpu	*soo-poo*
spaghetti	supagetti	*soo-pah-geht-tee*
wine	wain	*wah-een*
• red wine	reddo wain	*rehd-doh wah-een*
• white wine	howaito wain	*hoh-wah-ee-toh wah-een*

h. DAIRY PRODUCTS, EGGS, AND RELATED FOODS

butter	batā	*bah-tah*
cheese	chīzu	*chee-zoo*
cottage cheese	kotēji chīzu	*koh-TEH-jee chee-zoo*
cream	kurīmu	*koo-ree-moo*
dairy product	nyūseihin	*nyoo-seh-heen*
egg	tamago	*tah-mah-goh*
• fried egg	medamayaki	*meh-dah-mah-yah-kee*
• hard-boiled egg	yudetamago	*yoo-deh-tah-mah-goh*
• omelette	omuretsu	*oh-moo-reh-tsoo*
• poached egg	pōchido eggu	*poh-chee-doh ehg-goo*
• soft-boiled egg	hanjuku	*hahn-joo-koo*
ice cream	aisukurīmu	*ah-ees-koo-ree-moo*
milk	gyūnyū	*gyoo-nyoo*
	miruku	*mee-roo-koo*
• lowfat milk	rōfatto miruku	*roh-faht-toh mee-roo-koo*
• nonfat milk	mushibō gyūnyū	*moo-shee-boh gyoo-nyoo*
• skim milk	sukimu miruku	*skee-moo mee-roo-koo*
yogurt	yōguruto	*yoh-goo-roo-toh*

i. GRAINS AND GRAIN PRODUCTS

barley	ōmugi	*oh-moo-gee*
biscuit	bisuketto	*bees-keht-toh*
bread	pan	*pahn*
buckwheat	sobako	*soh-bah-koh*
cereal	shiriaru	*shee-ree-ah-roo*
• cornflakes	kōnfurēku	*kohn-foo-reh-koo*
• oatmeal	ōtomīru	*oh-toh-mee-roo*

cracker	kurakkā	*koo-rahk-kah*
cookie	kukkī	*kook-kee*
corn	tōmorokoshi	*toh-moh-roh-koh-shee*
• corn chip	kōnchippu	*kohn-cheep-poo*
• popcorn	poppukōn	*pohp-poo-kohn*
flour	komugiko	*koh-moo-gee-koh*
oat	ōtomugi	*oh-toh-moo-gee*
pastry	pesutorī	*pehs-toh-ree*
rice (cooked)	gohan	*goh-hahn*
rice (uncooked)	kome	*koh-meh*
• rice cake (Japanese)	mochi	*moh-chee*
• rice cracker (Japanese)	senbei	*sehn-beh*
rye	raimugi	*rah-ee-moo-gee*
wheat	komugi	*koh-moo-gee*

j. CONDIMENTS AND SPICES

basil	bajiriko / bajiru	*bah-jee-ree-koh/bah-jee-roo*
butter	batā	*bah-tah*
cinnamon	shinamon	*shee-nah-mohn*
cream	kurīmu	*koo-ree-moo*
garlic	ninniku	*neen-nee-koo*
ginger	shōga	*shoh-gah*
grated ginger (Japanese)	oroshi shōga	*oh-roh-shee shoh-gah*
grated radish (Japanese)	daikon oroshi	*dah-ee-kohn oh-roh-shee*
herb	hābu	*hah-boo*
honey	hachimitsu	*hah-chee-mee-tsoo*
horseradish (Japanese)	wasabi	*wah-sah-bee*
horseradish (western)	hōsuradisshu	*hoh-soo-rah-dees-shoo*
jam	jamu	*jah-moo*
jelly	zerī	*zeh-ree*
ketchup	kechappu	*keh-chahp-poo*
lemon	remon	*reh-mohn*
margarine	māgarin	*mah-gah-reen*
marmalade	māmarēdo	*mah-mah-reh-doh*
mayonnaise	mayonēzu	*mah-yoh-neh-zoo*
mint	minto	*meen-toh*
mustard	karashi	*kah-rah-shee*
	masutādo	*mahs-tah-doh*
oil	oiru	*oh-ee-roo*
paprika	papurika	*pah-poo-ree-kah*
parsley	paseri	*pah-seh-ree*
pepper	koshō	*koh-shoh*
rosemary	rōzumarī	*roh-zoo-mah-ree*

salt	shio	*shee-oh*
saffron	safuran	*sah-foo-rahn*
soy sauce	shōyu	*shoh-yoo*
spice	yakumi	*yah-koo-mee*
sugar	satō	*sah-toh*
syrup	shiroppu	*shee-rohp-poo*
Tabasco	tabasuko	*tah-bah-skoh*
vinegar	su	*soo*
Worcestershire sauce	sōsu	*soh-soo*

k. DRINKS

alcoholic beverage	arukōru inryō	*ah-roo-koh-roo een-ryoh*
aperitif	shokuzenshu	*shoh-koo-zehn-shoo*
beer	bīru	*bee roo*
bourbon whiskey	bābon	*bah-bohn*
brandy	burandē	*boo-rahn-deh*
champagne	shanpen	*shahn-pehn*
club soda	tansan (sui)	*tahn-sahn (soo-ee)*
Coca-Cola	Kokakōra	*koh-kah-koh-rah*
coffee	kōhī	*koh-hee*
cognac	konyakku	*koh-nyahk-koo*
diet soda	daietto no nomimono	*dah-ee-eht-toh noh noh-mee-moh-noh*
drink	nomimono	*noh-mee-moh-noh*
espresso	esupuresso	*ehs-poo-rehs-soh*
gin	jin	*jeen*
ginger ale	jinjaēru	*jeen-jah-eh-roo*
herbal tea	hābutī	*hah-boo-tee*
juice	jūsu	*joo-soo*
lemonade	remonēdo	*reh-moh-neh-doh*
liqueur	rikyūru	*ree-kyoo-roo*
mineral water	mineraru wōtā	*mee-neh-rah-roo woh-tah*
Pepsi-Cola	pepushikōra	*peh-poo-shee-koh-rah*
rice wine (Japanese)	sake	*sah-keh*
rum	ramu	*rah-moo*
scotch whiskey	sukotchi	*skoht-chee*
soft drink	sofuto dorinku	*soh-foo-toh doh-reen-koo*
Sprite	supuraito	*spoo-rah-ee-toh*
tea (Japanese)	ocha	*oh-chah*
tea (western)	kōcha	*koh-chah*
vodka	wokka	*wohk-kah*
water	mizu	*mee-zoo*
whiskey	uisukī	*oo-ee-skee*
wine	wain	*wah-een*

I. AT THE TABLE

Tableware for a Japanese meal may include the following items:

chopsticks	hashi	*hah-shee*
chopstick rest	hashioki	*hah-shee-oh-kee*
large teapot	dobin	*doh-been*
pickle dish	okozara	*oh-koh-zah-rah*
rice bowl	ochawan	*oh-chah-wahn*
	gohanjawan	*goh-hahn-jah-wahn*
sake cup	sakazuki	*sah-kah-zoo-kee*
sake jug	tokkuri	*tohk-koo-ree*
small teapot	kyūsu	*kyōō-soo*
soup bowl	owan	*oh-wahn*
soy sauce	shōyu	*shoh-yoo*
soy sauce dish	okozara	*oh-koh-zah-rah*
soy sauce pitcher	shōyusashi	*shoh-yoo-sah-shee*
teacup	yunomijawan	*yoo-noh-mee-jah-wahn*
teacup saucer	chataku	*chah-tah-koo*

bottle	bin	*been*
bowl	bōru	*boh-roo*
cup	kōhījawan	*koh-hee-jah-wahn*
cutlery, tableware	shokutakuyō	*shohk-tah-koo-yoh*
	shokkigu	*shohk-kee-goo*
fork	fōku	*foh-koo*
glass	koppu	*kohp-poo*
knife	naifu	*nah-ee-foo*
napkin	napukin	*nah-poo-keen*
plate	sara	*sah-rah*
saucer	ukezara	*oo-keh-zah-rah*

FOCUS: Phrases for Drinking and Eating

Cheers!	Kanpai.	*kahn-pah-ee*
I hope you like it.	Okuchi ni au to ii no desu ga.	*ohk-chee nee AH-oo toh ēē noh dehs gah.*

The following ritual expressions are used at mealtimes:

Before beginning the meal:	Itadakimasu.	*ee-tah-dah-kee-mahs*
After finishing the meal:	Gochisōsama deshita.	*goh-chee-sōh-sah-mah deh-shtah*

spoon	supūn	*soo-pōōn*
table	tēburu	*teh-boo-roo*
tablecloth	tēburukurosu	*teh-boo-roo-koo-roh-soo*
teaspoon	kosaji	*koh-sah-jee*
toothpick	yōji	*yoh-jee*
tray	obon	*oh-bohn*
wine glass	waingurasu	*wah-een-goo-rah-soo*

m. DINING OUT

bartender	bāten	*bāh-tehn*
bill, check	kanjō	*kahn-joh*
cafeteria	kafeteria	*kah-feh-teh-ree-ah*
cover charge	kabā chāji	*kah-bah chah-jee*
fast food	fāsuto fūdo	*fah-stoh fōō-doh*
fixed price	kimatta nedan	*kee-maht-tah neh-dahn*
price	nedan	*neh-dahn*
reservation	yoyaku	*yoh-yah-koo*
• reserved	yoyakushitearu *(adj)*	*yoh-yah-koo-shteh-ah-roo*
restaurant	resutoran	*reh-stoh-rahn*
• informal	keishikibaranai	*keh-shee-kee-bah-rah-*
restaurant	resutoran	*nah-ee reh-stoh-rahn*
service	sābisu	*sah-bee-soo*
• self-service	serufu sābisu	*seh-roo-foo sah-bee-soo*
service charge	sābisu ryō	*sah-bee-soo ryoh*
snack bar	sunakku	*soo-nahk-koo*
take out	mochikaeru *(v)*	*moh-chee-kah-eh-roo*
tax	zeikin	*zeh-keen*
tip	chippu	*cheep-poo*
• tip	chippu o ageru *(v)*	*cheep-poo oh ah-geh-roo*
waiter	uēta	*oo-eh-tah*
waitress	uētoresu	*oo-eh-toh-reh-soo*
wine list	wain risuto	*wah-een ree-stoh*

n. BUYING FOOD AND DRINK

bakery	pan ya	*pahn yah*
butcher shop	niku ya	*nee-koo yah*
convenience store	konbini sutoā	*kohn-bee-nee stoh-āh*
dairy	gyūnyū ya	*gyōō-nyōō yah*
delicatessen	derikatessen	*deh-ree-kah-tehs-sehn*
fish store	sakana ya	*sah-kah-nah yah*
fruit store	kudamono ya	*koo-dah-moh-noh yah*
grocery store	shokuryōhin ten	*shoh-koo-ryoh-heen tehn*
health food store	kenkōshokuhinten	*kehn-koh-shohk-heen-tehn*
ice cream parlor	aisukurīmu ya	*ah-ees-koo-rēē-moo yah*
liquor store	sakaya	*sah-kah-yah*
market	ichiba	*ee-chee-bah*

pastry shop	kēki ya	*kēh-kee yah*
produce market	yasai ichiba	*yah-sah-ee ee-chee-bah*
rice store	okome ya	*oh-koh-meh ya*
supermarket	sūpā	*sōō-pāh*
tea store	ocha ya	*oh-chah yah*
vegetable store	yasai ya	*yah-sah-ee yah*

o. FOOD AND DRINK: ACTIVITIES

add up the bill	kaikeisuru (v)	*kah-ee-kēh-soo-roo*
bake	tenpi de yaku (v)	*tehn-pee deh yah-koo*
beat	kakuhansuru (v)	*kah-koo-hahn-soo-roo*
be hungry	onaka ga suite imasu	*oh-nah-kah gah soo-ee-teh ee-mahs*
be thirsty	nodo ga kawaite imasu	*noh-doh gah kah-wah-ee-teh ee-mahs*
boil	yuderu (v)	*yoo-deh-roo*
broil	jikabi de yaku (v)	*jee-kah-bee deh yah-koo*
carve	kiriwakeru (v)	*kee-ree-wah-keh-roo*
chop	kizamu (v)	*kee-zah-moo*
clear the table	atokatazukesuru (v)	*ah-toh-kah-tah-zoo-keh-soo-roo*
cook	ryōrisuru (v)	*ryōh-ree-soo-roo*
cost	kakaru (v)	*kah-kah-roo*
cut	kiru (v)	*KEE-roo*
drink	nomu (v)	*noh-moo*
eat	taberu (v)	*tah-beh-roo*
grate	orosu (v)	*oh-roh-soo*
grill	amiyaki ni suru (v)	*ah-mee-yah-kee nee soo-roo*
have a snack	kanshokusuru (v)	*kahn-shoh-koo-soo-roo*
have breakfast	asagohan o taberu (v)	*ah-sah-goh-hahn oh tah-beh-roo*
have dinner	bangohan o taberu (v)	*bahn-goh-hahn oh tah-beh-roo*
have lunch	hirugohan o taberu (v)	*hee-roo-goh-hahn oh tah-beh-roo*
mix	mazeru (v)	*mah-zeh-roo*
order	chūmonsuru (v)	*chōō-mohn-soo-roo*
peel	kawa o muku (v)	*kah-wah oh moo-koo*
pour	tsugu (v)	*tsoo-goo*
serve (food or drink)	dasu (v)	*dah-soo*
set the table	tēburu o totonoeru (v)	*teh-boo-roo oh toh-toh-noh-eh-roo*
shop for food	shokuryōhin o kau (v)	*shoh-koo-ryōh-heen oh kah-oo*
slice	usugiri ni suru (v)	*oo-soo-gee-ree nee soo-roo*

steam	musu *(v)*	moo-soo
stir	kakimawasu *(v)*	kah-kee-mah-wah-soo
take out (food to go)	mochikaeru *(v)*	moh-chee-kah-eh-roo
toast	kongari yaku *(v)*	kohn-gah-ree yah-koo
weigh	mekata o hakaru *(v)*	meh-kah-tah oh hah-kah-roo

p. DESCRIBING FOOD AND DRINK

appetizing	oishisō na *(adj)*	oh-ee-shee-sōh nah
bad	mazui *(adj)*	mah-zoo-ee
bitter	nigai *(adj)*	nee-gah-ee
cheap	yasui *(adj)*	yah-soo-ee
chilled	hiyashita *(adj)*	hee-yah-shtah
cold	tsumetai *(adj)*	tsoo-meh-tah-ee
crunchy	pariparishita *(adj)*	pah-ree-pah-ree-shee-tah
double	daburu no *(adj)*	dah-boo-roo noh
expensive	takai *(adj)*	tah-kah-ee
fatty	abura ga ōi *(adj)*	ah-boo-rah gah ōh-ee
good	oishii *(adj)*	oh-ee-shēē
hot (spice)	karai *(adj)*	kah-rah-ee
hot (temperature)	atsui *(adj)*	ah-tsoo-ee
lukewarm	namanurui *(adj)*	nah-mah-noo-roo-ee
mild	karakunai *(adj)*	kah-rah-koo-nah-ee
raw	nama no *(adj)*	nah-mah noh
salty	shiokarai *(adj)*	shee-oh-kah-rah-ee
single	shinguru no *(adj)*	sheen-goo-roo noh
smooth	nameraka na *(adj)*	nah-meh-rah-kah nah
sour	suppai *(adj)*	soop-pah-ee
spicy	piritto shita *(adj)*	pee-reet-toh shtah
strong	tsuyoi *(adj)*	tsoo-yoh-ee
tough	katai *(adj)*	kah-tah-ee
sweet	amai *(adj)*	ah-mah-ee
tasty	oishii *(adj)*	oh-ee-shēē
watery	mizuppoi *(adj)*	mee-zoop-poh-ee
weak	yowai *(adj)*	yoh-wah-ee

Sake (Japanese rice wine) is pronounced *sah-keh*, not *SAH-kee*. There are several ways of serving it.

chilled sake	reishu	rēh-shoo
hot sake	atsukan	ahts-kahn
sake on the rocks	sake no on za rokku	sah-keh noh ohn zah rokku
straight sake	hiya	hee-yah

| with ice | kōri o irete (adv) | koh-ree oh ee-reh-teh |
| without ice | kōri o irenaide (adv) | koh-ree oh ee-reh-nah-ee-deh |

25. SHOPPING AND ERRANDS

a. GENERAL VOCABULARY

bag (shopping)	kaimonobukuro	kah-ee-moh-noh-boo-koo-roo
bill	seikyūsho	seh-kyoo-shoh
brand	burando/meigara	boo-rahn-doh/meh-gah-rah
buy	kau (v)	kah-oo
cash register	shiharai basho	shee-hah-rah-ee bah-shoh
• cashier	shiharaigakari	shee-hah-rah-ee-gah-kah-ree
change (money)	otsuri	oh-tsoo-ree
change	kuzusu (v)	koo-zoo-soo
cost	nedan	neh-dahn
• cost	kakaru (v)	kah-kah-roo
• How much does it cost?	Ikura desu ka.	EE-koo-rah dehs kah
counter	kauntā	kah-oon-tah
customer	okyaku	oh-kyah-koo
department (of a store)	uriba	oo-ree-bah
delivery	haitatsu	hah-ee-tah-tsoo
entrance	iriguchi	ee-ree-goo-chee
exchange	kōkansuru (v)	koh-kahn-soo-roo
exit	deguchi	deh-goo-chee
gift	gifuto	gee-foo-toh
look for something	sagasu (v)	sah-gah-soo
outlet	autoretto	ah-oo-toh-reht-toh
package	tsutsumi	tsoo-tsoo-mee
pay	harau (v)	hah-rah-oo
• with cash	genkin de (adv)	gehn-keen deh
• with a check	kogitte de (adv)	koh-geet-teh deh
• with a credit card	kurejittokādo de (adv)	koo-reh-jeet-toh-kah-doh deh
price	nedan	neh-dahn
• discount	waribiki no (adj)	wah-ree-bee-kee noh
• expensive	takai (adj)	tah-kah-ee
• fixed price	teika	teh-kah
• inexpensive	yasui (adj)	yah-soo-ee
• price tag	nedanhyō	neh-dahn-hyoh
• reduced price	waribiki nedan	wah-ree-bee-kee neh-dahn
product	seihin	seh-heen
purchase	kaimono	kah-ee-moh-noh

• purchase	kau *(v)*	*kah-oo*
receipt	reshīto	*reh-shēē-toh*
• Receipt, please!	Reshīto o onegai shimasu.	*reh-SHĒĒ-toh oh oh-neh-gah-ee shee-mohs*
refund	haraimodoshi	*hah-rah-ee-moh-doh-shee*
• refund	haraimodosu *(v)*	*hah-rah-ee-moh-doh-soo*
sale	hanbai	*hahn-bah-ee*
• for sale	uridashichū	*oo-ree-dah-shee-chōō*
• on sale	sēru	*seh-roo*
• sell	uru *(v)*	*oo-roo*
shop	mise	*mee-seh*
• shop	kaimonosuru *(v)*	*kah-ee-moh-noh-soo-roo*
shopping mall	shoppingu mōru	*shohp-peen-goo moh-roo*
size	saizu	*sah-ee-zoo*
spend	tsukau *(v)*	*tsoo-kah-oo*
store	mise	*mee-seh*
• closed	heiten	*heh-tehn*
• closing time	heiten jikan	*heh-tehn jee-kahn*
• department store	depāto	*deh-pah-toh*
• open	kaitensuru *(v)*	*kah-ee-tehn-soo-roo*
• opening hours	eigyō jikan	*eh-gyoh jee-kahn*
• store clerk	ten-in	*tehn-een*
• store/shop window	shōwindō	*shoh-ween-doh*
• store hours	eigyō jikan	*eh-gyoh jee-kahn*
take (purchase)	kau *(v)*	*kah-oo*
• take back	kaesu *(v)*	*kah-eh-soo*
wrap	hōsō	*hoh-soh*
• gift wrap	gifuto hōsō	*gee-ftoh hoh-soh*

b. HARDWARE

battery	denchi	*dehn-chee*
	batterī	*baht-teh-rēē*
bolt	boruto	*boh-roo-toh*
brush	burashi	*boo-rah-shee*
cable	hifuku densen	*hee-foo-koo dehn-sehn*
chisel	nomi	*NOH-mee*
clamp	shimegu	*shee-meh-goo*
drill	doriru	*doh-ree-roo*
electrical	denki (no) *(adj)*	*dehn-kee (noh)*
file	yasuri	*yah-soo-ree*
flashlight	kaichūdentō	*kah-ee-chōō-dehn-toh*
fuse	hyūzu	*hyōō-zoo*
glue	setchakuzai	*seht-chah-koo-zah-ee*
hammer	kanazuchi	*kah-nah-zoo-chee*
hardware store	daikudōgu ten	*dah-ee-koo-doh-goo tehn*
insulation (wire)	zetsuen	*zeh-tsoo-ehn*

a hard-headed person (*lit.* a hammer head)	kanazuchi atama	*kah-nah-zoo-chee ah-tah-mah*

ladder	hashigo	*hah-shee-goh*
light (bulb)	denkyū	*dehn-kyoo*
• fluorescent light	keikōtō	*keh-koh-toh*
masking tape	masukingu tēpu	*mahs-keen-goo teh-poo*
mechanical	shudō no (*adj*)	*shoo-doh noh*
monkey wrench	jizai supana	*jee-zah-ee spah-nah*
nail	kugi	*koo-gee*
nut	natto	*naht-toh*
outlet	konsento	*kohn-sehn-toh*
plane	kanna	*kahn-nah*
pliers	penchi	*pehn-chee*
plug	puragu	*POO-rah-goo*
plumbing	haikan	*hah-ee-kahn*
punch	panchi	*pahn-chee*
rake	kumade	*koo-mah-deh*
roller	rōrā	*roh-rah*
sandpaper	kamiyasuri	*kah-mee-yah-soo-ree*
saw	nokogiri	*noh-koh-gee-ree*
screw	neji	*neh-jee*
screwdriver	nejimawashi	*neh-jee-mah-wah-shee*
shovel	shaberu	*shah-beh-roo*
tool	daikudōgu	*dah-ee-koo-doh-goo*
transformer	henatsuki	*hehn-ah-tsoo-kee*
vise	manriki	*mahn-ree-kee*
washer	wasshā	*wahs-shah*
wire	harigane	*hah-ree-gah-neh*
wrench	supana	*spah-nah*

c. STATIONERY

adhesive tape	setchaku tēpu	*seht-chah-koo teh-poo*
ballpoint pen	bōrupen	*boh-roo-pehn*
correction fluid/ correction tape	shūsei eki / shūsei tēpu	*shoo-seh eh-kee/shoo-seh teh-poo*
eraser	keshigomu	*keh-shee-goh-moo*
envelope	fūtō	*foo-toh*
felt-tip pen	feruto pen	*feh-roo-toh pehn*
file folder	shoruibasami	*shoh-roo-ee-bah-sah-mee*
fountain pen	mannenhitsu	*mahn-nehn-hee-tsoo*
glue	setchakuzai	*seht-chah-koo-zah-ee*
ink	inku	*een-koo*
label	retteru	*reht-teh-roo*
notebook	nōto	*noh-toh*

office supplies	jimuyōhin	*jee-moo-yoh-heen*
paper	kami	*kah-mee*
paper clip	kurippu	*koo-reep-poo*
pen	pen	*pehn*
pencil	enpitsu	*ehn-pee-tsoo*
pencil sharpener	enpitsu kezuri	*ehn-pee-tsoo keh-zoo-ree*
rubber band	wagomu	*wah-goh-moo*
ruler	jōgi	*joh-gee*
scissors	hasami	*hah-sah-mee*
staple	hotchikisu no hari	*hoht-chee-kee-soo noh hah-ree*
stapler	hotchikisu	*hoht-chee-kee-soo*
stationery	binsen	*been-sehn*
stationery store	bunbōgu ten	*boon-boh-goo tehn*
string	himo	*hee-moh*
thumbtack	gabyō	*gah-byoh*
writing pad	hikki yōshi	*heek-kee joh-shee*

d. PHOTO/CAMERA

aperture	shibori	*shee-boh-ree*
camera	kamera	*kah-meh-rah*
• camcorder	kamukōdā	*kah-moo-koh-dah*
• digital camera	dejitaru kamera	*deh-jee-tah-roo kah-meh-rah*
• digital SLR camera	dejitaru ichiganrefu	*deh-jee-tah-roo ee-chee-gahn-reh-foo*
• disposable camera	tsukaisute kamera	*tsoo-kah-ee-steh kah-meh-rah*
• video camera	bideo kamera	*bee-deh-oh kah-meh-rah*
camera shop	kamera ya	*kah-meh-rah yah*
develop	genzōsuru *(v)*	*gehn-zoh-soo-roo*
• development	genzō	*gehn-zoh*
enlarge	hikinobasu *(v)*	*hee-kee-noh-bah-soo*
• enlargement	hikinobashi	*hee-kee-noh-bah-shee*
exposure	roshutsu	*roh-shoo-tsoo*
extra copy	yakimashi	*yah-kee-mah-shee*
film	fuirumu	*foo-ee-roo-moo*
• black and white film	shiro kuro no fuirumu	*shee- roh koo-roh noh foo-ee-roo-moo*
• color film	karā fuirumu	*kah-rah foo-ee-roo-moo*
filter	firutā	*fee-roo-tah*
finish	shiagari	*shee-ah-gah-ree*
• glossy	kōtaku no aru *(adj)*	*koh-tah-koo noh ah-roo*
• matte	tsuyakeshi no *(adj)*	*tsoo-yah-keh-shee noh*
flash	furasshu	*foo-rahs-shoo*
GB (gigabyte)	gigabaito	*gee-gah-bah-ee-toh*

image stabilization	tebure bōshi	teh-boo-reh bōh-shee
LCD monitor	ekishō monitā	eh-kee-shōh moh-nee-tah
lens	renzu	rehn-zoo
• telescopic lens	bōen renzu	bōh-ehn rehn-zoo
• wide angle lens	kōkaku renzu	kōh-kah-koo rehn-zoo
• zoom lens	zūmu renzu	zoo-moo rehn-zoo
macro	sessha (no) (adj)	sehs-shah (noh)
MB (megabyte)	megabaito	meh-gah-bah-ee-toh
memory card	memorī kādo	meh-moh-rēe kah-doh
panoramic	panorama (no) (adj)	pah-noh-rah-mah (noh)
photo, picture	shashin	shah-sheen
• clear	semnei na (adj)	sehn-meh nah
• out of focus	pinboke no (adj)	peen-boh-keh noh
• color picture	karā shashin	kah-rāh shah-sheen
• focus	shōten o awaseru (v)	shōh-tehn oh ah-wah-seh-roo
• in black and white	shiro kuro de	shee-roh koo-roh deh
• take a picture	shashin o toru (v)	shah-sheen oh toh-roo
• The picture turned out badly.	Shashin wa, yoku utsutte imasen deshita.	shah-sheen wah, YOH-koo oo-tsoot-teh ee-mah-sehn deh-shtah
• The picture turned out well.	Shashin wa, yoku utsutte imashita.	shah-sheen wah, YOH-koo oo-tsoot-teh ee-mah-shtah
photo printer	fotopurinta	foh-toh-poo-reen-tah
pixel	gaso	gah-soh
print	purinto	poo-rēen-toh
rechargeable battery	saijūden kanō denchi	sah-ee-jōo-dehn kah-nōh dehn-chee
red-eye fix	akame shūsei	ah-kah-meh shōo-sēh
screen	sukurīn	skoo-reen
slide	suraido	soo-rah-ee-doh
tripod	sankyaku	sahn-kyah-koo
video disc	bideo disuku	bee-deh-oh dees-koo
zoom	zūmu	zōo-moo

e. TOBACCO

cigar	hamaki	hah-mah-kee
cigarette	tabako	tah-bah-koh
lighter	raitā	rah-ee-tāh
matches	matchi	maht-chee
pipe	paipu	pah-ee-poo
tobacco	kizami tabako	kee-zah-mee tah-bah-koh
tobacco shop	tabako senmonten	tah-bah-koh sehn-mohn-tehn

f. COSMETICS/TOILETRIES

anti-aging cream	rōka bōshi kurīmu	roh-kah boh-shee koo-rēē-moo
anti-wrinkle cream	shiwatori kurīmu	shee-wah-toh-ree koo-rēē-moo
bath oil	basu oiru	bah-soo oh-ee-roo
body lotion	bodī rōshon	boh-dēē roh-shohn
cologne	ōdekoron	oh-deh-koh-rohn
comb	kushi	koo-shee
cosmetics shop	keshōhin ten	keh-shoh-heen tehn
curler	kārā	kah-rah
deodorant	deodoranto	deh-oh-doh-rahn-toh
electric razor	denki kamisori	dehn-kee kah-mee-soh-ree
emery board	tsume yasuri	tsoo-meh yah-soo-ree
eyeliner	airainā	ah-ee-rah-ee-nah
eye shadow	aishadō	ah-ee-shah-doh
face powder	oshiroi	oh-shee-roh-ee
foundation	fandēshon	fahn-deh-shohn
hairbrush	heā burashi	heh-ah boo-rah-shee
hair conditioner	rinsu	reen-soo
hair dryer	heā doraiyā	heh-ah doh-rah-ee-yah
hair color	heā karā	heh-ah kah-rah
hair remover	jomōzai	joh-moh-zah-ee
hairpin	heāpin	he-ah-peen
hair spray	heā supurē	heh-ah spoo-reh
hand cream	hando kurīmu	hahn-doh koo-rēē-moo
hand lotion	hando rōshon	hahn-doh roh-shohn
lipstick	kuchibeni	koo-chee-beh-nee
makeup	okeshō	oh-keh-shoh
mascara	masukara	mahs-kah-rah
mirror	kagami	kah-gah-mee
moisturizer	moisucharaizā	moh-ees-chah-rah-ee-zah
nail clippers	tsume kiri	tsoo-meh kee-ree
nail file	tsume yasuri	tsoo-meh yah-soo-ree
nail polish	manikyua eki	mah-nee-kyoo-ah eh-kee
nail polish remover	jokōeki	joh-koh-eh-kee
perfume	kōsui	koh-soo-ee
razor	kamisori	kah-mee-soh-ree
razor blade	kamisori no ha	kah-mee-soh-ree noh hah
shampoo	shanpū	shahn-pōō
shaving cream	shēbingu kurīmu	sheh-been-goo koo-ree-moo
shower cap	shawā kyappu	shah-wah kyahp-poo
soap	sekken	sehk-kehn
talcum powder	shikkarōru	sheek-kah-roh-roo
tissues	tisshū	tees-shōō
toiletries	senmenyōgu	sehn-meh yoh-goo

toothbrush	haburashi	*hah-boo-rah-shee*
toothpaste	nerihamigaki	*neh-ree-hah-mee-gah-kee*
tweezers	kenuki	*keh-noo-kee*

g. LAUNDRY

bleach	hyōhakuzai	*kyoh-hah-koo-zah-ee*
button	botan	*boh-tahn*
clean	kirei na *(adj)*	*kee-reh nah*
clothes	sentakumono	*sehn-tah-koo-moh-noh*
• clothes basket	sentaku kago	*sehn-tah-koo kah-goh*
• clothespin	sentakubasami	*sehn-tah-koo-bah-sah-mee*
cotton	men/momen	*mehn/moh-mehn*
dirty	yogoreta *(adj)*	*yoh-goh-reh-tah*
dry cleaner	doraikurīningu ya	*doh-rah-ee-koo-rēē-neen-goo yah*
dryer	doraiyā	*doh-rah-ee-yah*
fabric softener	sofuto shiagezai	*soh-foo-toh shee-ah-geh-zah-ee*
hole	ana	*ah-nah*
iron	airon	*ah-ee-rohn*
• iron	airon o kakeru *(v)*	*ah-ee-rohn oh kah-keh-roo*
laundromat	koin randorī	*koh-een rahn-doh-rēē*
laundry	sentakumono	*sehn-tah-koo-moh-noh*
linen	rinneru/asa	*reen-neh-roo/ah-sah*
mend	tsukurou *(v)*	*tsoo-koo-roh-oo*
pocket	poketto	*poh-keht-toh*
polyester	poriesuteru	*poh-ree-ehs-teh-roo*
sew	nuu *(v)*	*noo-oo*
silk	shiruku/kinu	*shee-roo-koo/kee-noo*
sleeve	sode	*soh-deh*
soap powder	konasekken	*koh-nah-sehk-kehn*
spot, stain	shimi	*shee-mee*
starch	sentaku nori	*sehn-tah-koo noh-ree*
stitch	nuime	*noo-ee-meh*
wash	sentakusuru *(v)*	*sehn-tahk-soo-roo*
• washable	araeru *(adj)*	*ah-rah-eh-roo*
washer	sentakuki	*sehn-tahk-kee*
wool	ūru	*ōō-roo*
zipper	jippā	*jeep-pah*

h. PHARMACY/DRUGSTORE

antacid	isan	*ee-sahn*
anti-diarrheal medicine	geridome	*geh-ree-doh-meh*
antibiotic	kōseibusshitsu	*kōh-sēh-boos-shee-tsoo*
antiseptic	shōdokuyaku	*shoh-doh-koo-yah-koo*

aspirin	asupirin	*ahs-pee-reen*
bandage	hōtai	*hoh-tah-ee*
Band-Aid	bandoeido	*bahn-doh-eh-ee-doh*
cold medicine	kazegusuri	*kah-zeh-goo-soo-ree*
cortisone	kōchizon	*koh-chee-zohn*
cotton	dasshimen	*dahs-shee-mehn*
cotton swab	menbō	*mehn-boh*
cough syrup	sekidome shiroppu	*seh-kee-doh-meh shee-rohp-poo*
dosage	yōryō	*yoh-ryoh*
drugstore	doraggusutoā	*doh-rahg-goo-stoh-ah*
eye drops	megusuri	*meh-goo-soo-ree*
first aid	kyūkyūbako	*kyoo-kyoo-bah-koh*
gauze	gāze	*gah-zeh*
injection	chūsha	*choo-shah*
insulin	inshurin	*een-shoo-reen*
laxative	gezai	*geh-zah-ee*
medicine	kusuri	*ksoo-ree*
ointment	nankō	*nahn-koh*
painkiller	chintsūzai	*cheen-tsoo-zah-ee*
penicillin	penishirin	*peh-nee-shee-reen*
pharmacist	yakuzaishi	*yah-koo-zah-ee-shee*
pharmacy	yakkyoku	*yahk-kyoh-koo*
pill	ganyaku	*gahn-yah-koo*
powder	konagusuri	*koh-nah-goo-soo-ree*
prescription	shohōsen	*shoh-hoh-sehn*
sanitary napkin	seiri napukin	*seh-ree nah-poo-keen*
suppository	zayaku	*zah-yah-koo*
syrup	shiroppu	*shee-rohp-poo*
tablet	jōzai	*joh-zah-ee*
tampon	tanpon	*tahn-pohn*
thermometer	taionkei	*tah-ee-ohn-keh*
vitamin	bitaminzai	*bee-tah-meen-zah-ee*

i. JEWELRY

artificial	jinkō no *(adj)*	*jeen-koh noh*
bracelet	buresuretto	*boo-reh-soo-reht-toh*
brooch	burōchi	*boo-roh-chee*
carat	karatto	*kah-raht-toh*
chain	chēn	*chehn*
diamond	daiamondo	*dah-ee-ah-mohn-doh*
earring	iaringu	*ee-ah-reen-goo*
emerald	emerarudo	*eh-meh-rah-roo-doh*
false	imitēshon no *(adj)*	*ee-mee-teh-shohn noh*
fix, repair	shūrisuru *(v)*	*shoo-ree-soo-roo*
gold	kin	*keen*

imitation	imitēshon	*ee-mee-teh-shon*
jewel	hōseki	*hoh-seh-kee*
jeweler	hōshokuten	*hoh-shoh-koo-tehn*
necklace	nekkuresu	*nehk-koo-reh-soo*
opal	opāru	*oh-pah-roo*
pearl	shinju	*sheen-joo*
	pāru	*pah-roo*

Pearls (cast) before swine.	Buta ni shinju.	*boo-tah nee sheen-joo*

platinum	purachina	*poo-rah-chee-nah*
precious stone	kiseki	*kee-seh-kee*
ring	yubiwa	*yoo-bee-wah*
ruby	rubī	*roo-bee*
sapphire	safaia	*sah-fah-ee-ah*
silver	gin	*geen*
topaz	topāzu	*TOH-pah-zoo*
true	honmono no *(adj)*	*hohn-moh-noh noh*
watch, clock	tokei	*toh-keh*
• watchband	tokei no bando	*toh-keh noh bahn-doh*
• wristwatch	udedokei	*oo-deh-doh-keh*

j. MUSIC

band	bando	*bahn-doh*
	gakudan	*gah-koo-dahn*
blues	burūsu	*boo-roo-soo*
CD	shīdī	*shee-dee*
chamber music	shitsunaigaku	*sheets-nah-ee-gah-koo*
classical music	kurashikku myūjikku	*koo-rah-sheek-koo myoo-jeek-koo*
composer	sakkyoku ka	*sahk-kyoh-koo kah*
conductor	shikisha	*shkee-shah*
country music	kantorī mūjikku	*kahn-toh-ree myoo-jeek-koo*
dance music	dansu ongaku	*dahn-soo ohn-gah-koo*
DVD	dībuidī	*dee-boo-ee-dee*
folk music	minzoku ongaku	*meen-zoh-koo ohn-gah-koo*
group	gurūpu	*goo-roo-poo*
instrument	gakki	*gahk-kee*
jazz	jazu	*jah-zoo*
music	ongaku	*ohn-gah-koo*
musical	myūjikaru	*myoo-jee-kah-roo*
opera	opera	*oh-peh-rah*

orchestra	ōkesutora	*ōh-kehs-toh-rah*
popular music	popyurā myūjikku	*poh-pyoo-rah myōō-jeek-koo*
rock music	rokku	*rohk-koo*
singer	kashu	*kah-shoo*
	shingā	*sheen-gah*
song	uta	*oo-tah*
symphony	shinfonī	*sheen-foh-nēē*

k. CLOTHING

articles of clothing	irui	*ee-roo-ee*
bathing suit	mizugi	*mee-zoo-gee*
bathrobe	basurōbu	*bah-soo-rōh-boo*
blazer	burēzā	*boo-rēh-zah*
blue jeans	jīnzu	*jēēn-zoo*
belt	beruto	*beh-roo-toh*
blouse	burausu	*boo-rah-oo-soo*
bra	burajā	*boo-rah-jah*
cap	bōshi	*bōh-shee*
cardigan	kādigan	*kah-dee-gahn*
clothing store	yōfuku ya	*yōh-fkoo yah*
coat	kōto	*koh-toh*
dress	doresu	*DOH-reh-soo*
dressing room	shichakushitsu	*shchah-koo-shtsoo*
fashion	fasshon	*fahs-shohn*
fit	au (v)	*ah-oo*
fur coat	kegawa no kōto	*keh-gah-wah noh kōh-toh*
garment	ifuku	*ee-fkoo*
glove	tebukuro	*teh-boo-koo-roo*
handkerchief	hankachi	*hahn-kah-chee*
hat	bōshi	*bōh-shee*
jacket	jaketto	*jah-keht-toh*
lingerie	ranjerī	*RAHN-jeh-rēē*
men's shop	shinshifuku ten	*sheen-shee-fkoo tehn*
nightgown	nemaki	*neh-mah-kee*
pajamas	pajama	*pah-jah-mah*
panties	pantī	*pahn-tēē*
pants	zubon	*zoo-bohn*
pantyhose	pantīsutokkingu	*pahn-tēē-stohk-keen-goo*
raincoat	reinkōto	*reh-een-kōh-toh*
scarf	sukāfu	*skah-foo*
shawl	shōru	*shoh-roo*
shirt	shatsu	*shah-tsoo*
shorts	shōtsu	*shoh-tsoo*
	hanzubon	*hahn-zoo-bohn*
size	saizu	*sah-ee-zoo*

skirt	sukāto	*skah-toh*
slacks	surakkusu	*soo-rahk-koo-soo*
slip	surippu	*soo-reep-poo*
suit	sūtsu	*soo-tsoo*
sweater	sētā	*seh-tah*
sweatshirt	torēnā	*toh-reh-nah*
tailor	shitateya	*shee-tah-teh-yah*
tee-shirt	tīshatsu	*tee-shah-tsoo*
three-piece suit	mitsuzoroi	*mee-tsoo-zoh-roh-ee*
tie	nekutai	*nehk-tah-ee*
tights	taitsu	*tah-ee-tsoo*
trenchcoat	torenchikōto	*toh-rehn-chee-koh-toh*
trousers	zubon	*zoo-bohn*
underwear	shitagi	*shtah-gee*
vest	besuto / chokki	*behs-toh/chohk-kee*
women's shop	fujinfuku ten	*foo-jeen-fkoo tehn*

1. DESCRIBING CLOTHING

For colors, see Section 7.

beautiful	utsukushii *(adj)*	*oots-kshee*
big	ōkii *(adj)*	*oh-kee*
cotton	men / momen	*mehn/moh-mehn*
elegant	ereganto na *(adj)*	*eh-reh-gahn-toh nah*
fabric	kiji	*kee-jee*
in the latest style/fashion	ima hayatte iru	*ee-mah hah-yaht-teh ee-roo*
leather	kawa	*kah-wah*
linen	asa	*ah-sah*
long	nagai *(adj)*	*nah-gah-ee*
loose	yuttarishita *(adj)*	*yoot-tah-ree-shtah*
nylon	nairon	*nah-ee-rohn*
polyester	poriesuteru	*poh-ree-ehs-teh-roo*
short	mijikai *(adj)*	*mee-jee-kah-ee*
silk	shiruku	*shee-roo-koo*
small	chiisai *(adj)*	*chee-sah-ee*
suede	suēdo	*soo-eh-doh*
tight	kitsui *(adj)*	*kee-tsoo-ee*
ugly	minikui *(adj)*	*mee-nee-koo-ee*
warm	atatakai *(adj)*	*ah-tah-tah-kah-ee*
wool	ūru	*oo-roo*

m. CLOTHING: ACTIVITIES

alteration	shitatenaoshi	shee-tah-teh-nah-oh-shee
change clothes	kigaeru (v)	kee-gah-eh-roo
enlarge	ōkikusuru (v)	oh-keek-soo-roo
fold	tatamu (v)	tah-tah-moo
get dressed	kiru (v)	kee-roo
hang	kakeru (v)	kah-keh-roo
iron	airon o kakeru (v)	ah-ee-rohn oh kah-keh-roo
lengthen	nagakusuru(v)	nah-gahk-soo-roo
loosen	yurumeru (v)	yoo-roo-meh-roo
put on	kiru (v)	kee-roo
shorten	mijikakusuru (v)	mee-jee-kahk-soo-roo
take off	nugu (v)	noo-goo
tighten	pittarisaseru (v)	peet-tah-ree-sah-seh-roo
try on	tamesu (v)	tah-meh-soo
undress	nugu (v)	noo-goo
wear	kiru (v)	kee-roo

n. SHOES

boot	būtsu	bōo-tsoo
footwear	hakimono	hah-kee-moh-noh
heel	kakato	kah-kah-toh
high-heeled shoe	haihīru	hah-ee-hēe-roo
pair	issoku	ees-soh-koo
put on (shoes)	haku (v)	hah-koo
sandal	sandaru	sahn-dah-roo
shoe	kutsu	ktsoo
shoe department	kutsu uriba	ktsoo oo-ree-bah
shoe polish	kutsuzumi	ktsoo-zoo-mee
shoe repair shop	kutsu no shūriya	koo-tsoo noh shōo-ree-yah
shoe store	kutsu ya	ktsoo yah
shoehorn	kutsubera	koo-tsoo-beh-rah
shoelace	kutsu himo	ktsoo hee-moh
size	saizu	sah-ee-zoo
slipper	surippa	soo-reep-pah
sneaker	sunīkā	soo-nēe-kah
sole	kutsu zoko	ktsoo zoh-koh
sock	sokkusu	sohk-ksoo
stocking	sutokkingu	stohk-keen-goo
take off (shoes)	nugu (v)	noo-goo
walking shoes	wōkingu shūzu	wōh-keen-goo shōo-zoo

o. BOOKS

atlas	chizuchō	*chee-zoo-choh*
author	chosha / sakka / hissha	*choh-shah / sahk-kah / hees-shah*
autobiography	jiden	*jee-dehn*
biography	denki	*dehn-kee*
book	hon	*hohn*
• **best seller**	besuto serā	*beh-stoh seh-rah*
bookstore	hon ya	*hohn yah*
comics	manga	*mahn-gah*
cookbook	ryōri no hon	*ryoh-ree noh hohn*
dictionary	jisho	*jee-shoh*
encyclopedia	hyakkajiten	*hyahk-kah-jee-tehn*
essay	essei	*ehs-seh*
guidebook	gaidobukku	*gah-ee-doh-book-koo*
index	sakuin	*sah-koo-een*
literature	bungaku	*boon-gah-koo*
magazine	zasshi	*zahs-shee*
memoir	kaikoroku	*kah-ee-koh-roh-koo*
mystery	misuterī	*mees-teh-ree*
newspaper	shinbun	*sheen-boon*
novel	shōsetsu	*shoh-seh-tsoo*
poem	shi	*shee*
poetry	shi	*shee*
publisher	shuppansha	*shoop-pahn-shah*
reference book	sankōsho	*sahn-koh-shoh*
romance	renaishōsetsu	*rehn-ah-ee-shoh-seh-tsoo*
science fiction	saiensu fikushon	*sah-ee-ehn-soo feek-shohn*
short story	tanpen shōsetsu	*tahn-pehn shoh-seh-tsoo*
table of contents	mokuji	*moh-koo-jee*
technical book	senmonsho	*sehn-mohn-shoh*
textbook	kyōkasho	*kyoh-kah-shoh*

26. BANKING AND COMMERCE

> For numerical concepts, see Section 1.

account	kōza	*koh-zah*
• **close an account**	kōza o tojiru	*koh-zah oh toh-jee-roo*
• **open an account**	kōza o hiraku	*koh-zah oh hee-rah-koo*
bank	ginkō	*geen-koh*
• **branch office**	shiten	*shee-tehn*
• **head office**	honten	*hohn-tehn*
• **work in a bank**	ginkō de hataraku	*geen-koh deh hah-tah-rah-koo*

bankbook	ginkō tsūchō	*geen-koh tsoo-choh*
bank rate	kōteibuai	*koh-teh-boo-ah-ee*
• fixed	kotei (no) *(adj)*	*koh-teh (noh)*
• variable	hendo (no) *(adj)*	*hehn-doh (noh)*
bill, bank note	osatsu	*oh-sah-tsoo*
• dollar	doru	*doh-roo*
• large bill	ōkii osatsu	*oh-kee oh-sah-tsoo*
• small bill	chiisai osatsu	*chee-sah-ee oh-sah-tsoo*
• yen	en	*ehn*
bond	saiken	*sah-ee-kehn*
budget	yosan	*yoh-sahn*
cash	genkin	*gehn-keen*
• cash	genkinkasuru *(v)*	*gehn-keen-kah-soo-roo*
cashier, teller	madoguchigakari	*mah-doh-goo-chee-gah-kah-ree*
check	kogitte	*koh-geet-teh*
• checkbook	kogitte chō	*koh-geet-teh choh*
credit	shinyō	*sheen-yoh*
• credit card	kurejitto kādo	*koo-reh-jeet-toh kah-doh*
• credit limit	riyō gendogaku	*ree-yoh gehn-doh-gah-koo*
currency	tsūka	*tsoo-kah*
current account	tōza kanjō	*toh-zah kahn-joh*
customer	kokyaku	*koh-kyah-koo*
debit	kashikata	*kah-shee-kah-tah*
debt	fusai	*foo-sah-ee*
deposit	yokin	*yoh-keen*
• deposit	yokinsuru *(v)*	*yoh-keen-soo-roo*
• deposit slip	yokinhyō	*yoh-keen-kyoh*
discount	waribiki	*wah-ree-bee-kee*
draft	tegata furidashi	*teh-gah-tah foo-ree-dah-shee*
employee (bank)	ginkōin	*geen-koh-een*
endorse	uragakisuru *(v)*	*oo-rah-gah-kee-soo-roo*
• endorsement	uragaki	*oo-rah-gah-kee*
exchange	kōkan	*koh-kahn*
• exchange	kōkansuru *(v)*	*koh-kahn-soo-roo*
• exchange rates	kōkan ritsu	*koh-kahn ree-tsoo*
income	shūnyū	*shoo-nyoo*
insurance	hoken	*hoh-kehn*
interest	rishi	*ree-shee*
• annual interest	nenri	*nehn-ree*
• compound interest	fukuri	*foo-koo-ree*
• interest rate	riritsu	*ree-ree-tsoo*
• simple interest	tanri	*tahn-ree*
invest	tōshisuru *(v)*	*toh-shee-soo-roo*
• investment	tōshi	*toh-shee*
liability	saimu	*sah-ee-moo*

line	retsu	reh-tsoo
• line up	narabu (v)	nah-rah-boo
loan	rōn	rohn
• get a loan	yūshi o ukeru (v)	yoo-shee oh oo-keh-roo
loose change	kozeni	koh-zeh-nee
manager	manējā	mah-neh-jah
money	okane	oh-kah-neh
money order	kawase	kah-wah-seh
mortgage	jūtaku rōn	joo-tah-koo rohn
	teitōken	teh-toh-kehn
mutual fund	tōshi shintaku	toh-shee sheen-tah-koo
pay	harau (v)	hah-rah-oo
• pay off	zengaku shiharau (v)	zehn-gah-koo shee-hah-rah-oo
• payment	shiharai	shee-hah-rah-ee
postdate	jigohizuke ni suru (v)	jee-goh-hee-zoo-keh nee soo-roo
promissory note	yakusoku tegata	yahk-soh-koo teh-gah-tah
receipt	uketorishō	oo-keh-toh-ree-shoh
safe	kinko	keen-koh
• safe deposit box	kashikinko	kah-shee-keen-koh
salary	sararī	sah-rah-ree
save	chokinsuru (v)	choh-keen-soo-roo
savings	chokin	choh-keen
sign	shomeisuru (v)	shoh-meh-soo-roo
• signature	shomei	shoh-meh
stock, share	kabuken	kah-boo-kehn
• stock market	kabushikishijō	kah-boo-shee-kee-shee-joh
teller's window	madoguchi	mah-doh-goo-chee
traveler's check	toraberā chekku	toh-rah-beh-rah chehk-koo
withdraw	hikidasu (v)	hee-kee-dah-soo
• withdrawal	hikidashi	hee-kee-dah-shee
• withdrawal slip	hikidashihyō	hee-kee-dah-shee-hyoh

27. GAMES AND SPORTS

a. GAMES, HOBBIES, AND PHYSICAL FITNESS

billiards	tamatsuki	tah-mah-tskee
• billiard ball	tamatsuki no tama	tah-mah-tskee noh tah-mah
• billiard table	tamatsuki no tēburu	tah-mah-tskee noh teh-boo-roo
• cue	tamatsuki no kyū	tah-mah-tskee noh kyoo
• cushion	kusshon	koos-shohn
• pocket	poketto	poh-keht-toh
bingo	bingo	been-goh

• bingo card	bingo no kādo	been-goh noh kah-doh
blogging	burogu	boo-roh-goo
checkers	chekkā	chehk-kah
• checkerboard	chekkā ban	chehk-kah bahn
• checker piece	chekkā no koma	chehk-kah noh koh-mah
chess	chesu	cheh-soo
• bishop	bishoppu	bee-shohp-poo
• chessboard	chesu ban	cheh-soo bahn
• king	kingu	keen-goo
• knight	naito	nah-ee-toh
• pawn	pōn	pohn
• queen	kuīn	koo-een
• rook	rūku	roo-koo
coin	kōka	koh-kah
• coin collecting	kōka shūshū	koh-kah shoo-shoo
collection	shūshū	shoo-shoo
• collector	shūshūka	shoo-shoo-kah
computer game	konpyūta gēmu	kohn-pyoo-tah geh-moo
cooking	ryōri	ryoh-ree
embroidery	shishū	shee-shoo
fishing	tsuri	tsoo-ree
game	gēmu	geh-moo
gardening	engei	ehn-geh
gym	jimu	jee-moo
hobby	shumi	shoo-mee
horse race	keiba	keh-bah
hunting	shuryō	shoo-ryoh
instrument	gakki	gahk-kee
• play (an instrument)	ensōsuru (v)	ehn-soh-soo-roo
jog	jogingusuru (v)	joh-geen-goo-soo-roo
• jogging	jogingu	joh-geen-goo
karaoke	karaoke	kah-rah-oh-keh
knitting	amimono	ah-mee-mon-noh
movie(s)	eiga kanshō	eh-gah kahn-shoh
painting	kaiga	kah-ee-gah
play (a game)	suru (v)	soo-roo
playing cards	toranpu	toh-rahn-poo
pottery	tōgei	toh-geh
puzzle	pazuru	pah-zoo-roo
• crossword puzzle	kurosuwādo pazuru	koo-roh-soo-wah-doh pah-zoo-roo
• sudoku	sudoku	soo-doh-koo
reading	dokusho	dohk-shoh
sports	supōtsu	spoh-tsoo
stamp	kitte	keet-teh
• stamp collecting	kitte shūshū	keet-teh shoo-shoo

theater	kangeki	*kahn-geh-kee*
walking	wōkingu	*woh-keen-goo*
yoga	yoga	*yoh-gah*

Several games are popular leisure-time activities, especially among men. Go, Japan's national board game, is a highly sophisticated territorial version of checkers.

Japanese checkers	go	*goh*
Japanese chess	shōgi	*shoh-gee*
Japanese pinball	pachinko	*pah-cheen-koh*
mah-jongg	mājan	*mah-jahn*

b. SPORTS

aerobics	earobikusu	*eh-ah-roh-beek-soo*
amateur	amachua	*ah-mah-choo-ah*
archery	ācherī	*ah-cheh-rēē*
athlete	undō no senshu	*oon-doh noh sehn-shoo*
badminton	badominton	*bah-doh-meen-tohn*
ball	bōru	*boh-roo*
• catch	toru *(v)*	*toh-roo*
• hit	utsu *(v)*	*oo-tsoo*
• kick	keru *(v)*	*keh-roo*
• pass	pasusuru *(v)*	*pahs-soo-roo*
• throw	nageru *(v)*	*nah-geh-roo*
ballroom dance	shakō dansu	*shah-koh dahn-soo*
baseball	yakyū	*yah-kyōō*
• base	bēsu	*beh-soo*
• bat	batto	*baht-toh*
• batter	battā	*baht-tah*
• catcher's mask	kyatchā no masuku	*kyaht-chah noh mahs-koo*
• foul line	fāru rain	*fah-roo rah-een*
• glove	gurōbu	*goo-roh-boo*
• home (base)	hōmu	*hoh-moo*
• pitcher	pitchā	*peet-chah*
basketball	basukettobōru	*bahs-keht-toh-boh-roo*
bicycling	saikuringu	*sah-ee-koo-reen-goo*
body building	bodī biru	*boh-dēē bee-roo*
• weight lifting	jūryōage	*jōō-ryoh-ah-geh*
bowling	bōringu	*boh-reen-goo*
• bowling alley	bōringujō	*boh-reen-goo-joh*
• bowling ball	bōringu no bōru	*boh-reen-goo noh boh-roo*
• bowling pin	pin	*peen*
boxing	bokushingu	*bohk-sheen-goo*

• boxing gloves	gurabu	*goo-rah-boo*
• boxing ring	ringu	*reen-goo*
bungee-jumping	banjījanpingu	*bahn-jēē-jahn-peen-goo*
canoeing	kanū	*kah-nōō*
coach	kōchi	*koh-chee*
competition	kyōgi	*kyoh-gee*
fencing	fenshingu	*fehn-sheen-goo*
• fencing outfit	fenshingu no yunifōmu	*fehn-sheen-goo noh yoo-nee-foh-moo*
• mask	masuku	*mahs-koo*
field	kyōgijō	*kyoh-gee-jōh*
football	futtobōru	*foot-toh-boh-roo*
game, match	shiai	*shee-ah-ee*
goal	gōru	*goh-roo*
golf	gorufu	*goh-roo-foo*
gymnasium	jimu	*jee-moo*
• work out	torēningusuru (v)	*toh-reh-neen-goo-soo-roo*
hang gliding	hangu guraidingu	*hahn-goo goo-rah-ee-deen-goo*
helmet	herumetto	*heh-roo-meht-toh*
ice hockey	aisu hokkē	*ah-ee-soo hohk-keh*
• hockey rink	hokkējō	*hohk-keh-jōh*
• hockey stick	sutikku	*steek-koo*
• puck	pakku	*pahk-koo*
kayaking	kayakku	*KAH-yahk-koo*
motorcycling	ōtobai	*oh-toh-bah-ee*
mountain climbing	tozan	*TOH-zahn*
• mountain boot	tozangutsu	*toh-zahn-goo-tsoo*
• rope	zairu	*zah-ee-roo*
• snow goggles	gōguru	*goh-goo-roo*
net	netto	*neht-toh*
penalty	penarutī	*peh-nah-roo-tēē*
Ping-Pong	pinpon	*peen-pohn*
play	shiaisuru (v)	*shee-ah-ee-soo-roo*
• player	senshu	*sehn-shoo*
• playoff	yūshō kettei shirīzu	*yōō-shoh keht-teh shee-rēē-zoo*
point	tokuten	*tohk-tehn*
professional	puro	*poo-roh*
race	rēsu	*reh-soo*
referee	refurī	*reh-foo-rēē*
rock climbing	rokku kuraimingu	*rohk-koo koo-rah-ee-meen-goo*
• free climbing	furī kuraimingu	*foo-rēē koo-rah-ee-meen-goo*
rollerblading	rōrāburēdo	*roh-rah-boo-rēh-doh*
rowing	sōtei	*soh-teh*

English	Japanese	Pronunciation
run	hashiru (v)	hah-shee-roo
sailing	sēringu	seh-reen-goo
score	tokuten	toh-k-tehn
• draw	hikiwake	hee-kee-wah-keh
• draw	hikiwakeru (v)	hee-kee-wah-keh-roo
• lose	makeru (v)	mah-keh-roo
• loss	haiboku	hah-ee-boh-koo
• tie	dōten	doh-tehn
• win	katsu (v)	kah-tsoo
skate	sukēto de suberu (v)	skeh-toh deh soo-beh-roo
• skating	sukēto	skeh-toh
skateboarding	sukētobōdo	skeh-toh-boh-doh
ski	sukī o suru (v)	skee oh soo-roo
• skiing	sukī	skee
• water skiing	wōtā sukī	woh-tah skee
snowboarding	sunōbōdo	soo-noh-boh-doh
soccer	sakkā	sahk-kah
• corner	kōnā	koh-nah
• goalkeeper	gōrukīpā	goh-roo-kee-pah
• goal kick	gōru kikku	goh-roo-keek-koo
sport	supōtsu	spoh-tsoo
• sports fan	supōtsu fan	spoh-tsoo fahn
• winter sports	fuyu no supōtsu	foo-yoo noh spoh tsoo
squash	sukasshu	skahs-shoo
stadium	sutajiamu	stah-jee-ah-moo
surfing	sāfin	sah-feen
swim	oyogu (v)	oh-yoh-goo
• swimming	suiei	soo-ee-eh
• swimming pool	pūru	poo-roo
team	chīmu	chee-moo
tennis	tenisu	teh-nee-soo
• racket	raketto	rah-keht-toh

FOCUS: Traditional Japanese Sports

Sumo is centuries-old Japanese wrestling. Professional sumo is Japan's national sport.

sumo	sumō	soo-moh

The Japanese martial arts are also practiced as sports. The most popular kinds are judo, karate, and kendo (Japanese fencing).

	judō	joo-doh
	karate	kah-rah-teh
	kendō	kehn-doh

28b ART/SCULPTURE/ARCHITECTURE

ticket	ken	kehn
tournament	tōnamento	toh-nah-mehn-toh
track	torakku	toh-rahk-koo
track and field	rikujōkyōgi	ree-koo-joh-kyoh-gee
training	torēningu	toh-rēh-neen-goo
• trainer	torēnā	toh-rēh-nah
volleyball	barēbōru	bah-rēh-boh-roo
water polo	suikyū	soo-ee-kyoo
windsurfing	windosāfin	ween-doh-sah-feen
wrestling	resuringu	reh-soo-reen-goo

28. THE ARTS

a. CINEMA

actor	danyū	dahn-yōo
actress	joyū	joh-yōo
aisle	tsūro	tsoo-roh
box office	kippu uriba	keep-poo oo-ree-bah
charge	ryōkin	ryoh-keen
concession	baiten	bah-ee-tehn
dubbing	fukikae	fkee-kah-eh
first-run film	fūkiri eiga	fōo-kee-ree ēh-gah
foreign movie	gaikoku eiga	gah-ee-koh-koo ēh-gah
lobby	robī	roh-bēē
movie, film	eiga	ēh-gah
• make a movie	eiga o seisakusuru (v)	ēh-gah oh sēh-sahk-soo-roo
• premiere showing	puremia shō	poo-reh-mee-ah shoh
movie director	eiga kantoku	ēh-gah kahn-toh-koo
movie star	eiga sutā	ēh-gah stah
movie theater	eiga gekijō	ēh-gah geh-kee-jōh
producer	seisakusha	sēh-sahk-shah
production	seisakugaisha	sēh-sahk-koo-gah-ee-shah
row	retsu	reh-tsoo
screen	sukurīn	skoo-rēēn
seat	seki	seh-kee
senior discount	shinia waribiki	shee-nee-ah wah-ree-bee-kee
soundtrack	saundotorakku	sah-oon-doh-toh-rahk-koo
student discount	gakusei waribiki	gahk-seh wah-ree-bee-kee
subtitles	jimaku	jee-mah-koo

b. ART/SCULPTURE/ARCHITECTURE

architect	kenchikuka	kehn-cheek-kah
• architecture	kenchiku	kehn-chee-koo
• blueprint	aojashin	ah-oh-jah-sheen

art	geijutsu	*gēh-joo-tsoo*
• art gallery	āto gyararī	*ah-toh gyah-rah-rēē*
artist	geijutsuka	*gēh-joo-tsoo-kah*
bronze sculpture	buronzu no chōkoku	*boo-rohn-zoo noh chōh-koh-koo*
brush	burashi	*boo-rah-shee*
canvas	kyanbasu	*kyahn-bah-soo*
chisel	nomi	*NOH-mee*
drawing	sobyō	*soh-byōh*
easel, tripod	īzeru	*ēe-zeh-roo*
etching	etchingu	*eht-cheen-goo*
exhibition	tenjikai	*tehn-jee-kah-ee*
fresco painting	hekiga	*heh-kee-gah*
marble sculpture	dairiseki no chōkoku	*dah-ēe-ree-seh-kee noh chōh-koh-koo*
masterpiece	meisaku	*mēh-sah-koo*
museum	bijutsukan	*bee-joo-tsoo-kahn*
paint	e o kaku (v)	*eh oh kah-koo*
• oil paint	aburaenogu	*ah-boo-rah-eh-noh-goo*
• painter	gaka	*gah-kah*
• painting	kaiga	*kah-ee-gah*
palette	paretto	*pah-reht-toh*
pastel	pasuteru	*pahs-teh-roo*
portrait	pōtorēto	*poh-toh-rēh-toh*
relief	ukibori	*oo-kee-boh-ree*
sculpt	chōkokusuru (v)	*chōh-kohk-soo-roo*
• sculptor	chōkokuka	*chōh-koh-koo-kah*
• sculpture	chōkoku	*chōh-koh-koo*
show	shō	*shoh*
sketch	sukecchi	*skeht-chee*
statue	zō	*zoh*
watercolor	suisaiga	*soo-ee-sah-ee-gah*

c. MUSIC/DANCE

accordion	akōdion	*ah-kōh-dee-ohn*
ball..	barē	*bah-rēh*
band	bando	*bahn-doh*
brass ...ments	kinkan gakki	*keen-kahn gahk-kee*
horn	horun	*hoh-roon*
trombo..	toronbōn	*toh-rohn-bōhn*
trumpet	toranpetto	*toh-rahn-peht-toh*
tuba	chūba	*chōō-bah*
classical n..	kurashikku myūjikku	*koo-rah-sheek-koo myōō-jeek-koo*
composer	sakkyoku ka	*sahk-kyoh-koo kah*
• composi..	sakkyoku	*sahk-kyoh-koo*
co.cert	..nsāto	*kohn-sah-toh*

dance	dansu	*dahn-soo*
• dance	odoru *(v)*	*oh-doh-roo*
• dancer	dansā	*dahn-sah*
	butō ka	*boo-toh kah*
disco	disuko	*dees-koh*
duet	nijūshō	*nee-joo-shoh*
folk dance	fōku dansu	*foh-koo dahn-soo*
folk music	fōku myūjikku	*foh-koo myoo-jeek-koo*
guitar	gitā	*gee-tah*
• guitarist	gitarisuto	*gee-tah-ree-stoh*
harmony	hāmonī	*hah-moh-nee*
harp	hāpu	*hah-poo*
hip-hop	hippuhoppu	*heep-poo-hohp-poo*
instrument	gakki	*gahk-kee*
• play an instrument	gakki o ensōsuru *(v)*	*gahk-kee oh ehn-soh-soo-roo*
jazz	jazu	*jah-zoo*
keyboard instruments	kenban gakki	*kehn-bahn gahk-kee*
• grand piano	gurando piano	*goo-rahn-doh pee-ah-noh*
• harpsichord	hāpushikōdo	*hah-pshee-koh-doh*
• keyboard	kenban	*kehn-bahn*
• organ	orugan	*oh-roo-gahn*
• piano	piano	*pee-ah-noh*
• synthesizer	shinsesaizā	*sheen-seh-sah-ee-zah*
• upright piano	tategata piano	*tah-teh-gah-tah pee-ah-noh*
light music	kei ongaku	*keh ohn-gah-koo*
mambo	manbo	*mahn-boh*
mandolin	mandorin	*mahn-doh-reen*
melody	merodī	*meh-roh-dee*
modern dance	modan dansu	*moh-dahn dahn-soo*
music	ongaku	*ohn-gah-koo*
• musician	ongakuka	*ohn-gahk-kah*
note	onpu	*ohn-poo*
opera	opera	*oh-peh-rah*
orchestra	ōkesutora	*oh-kehs-toh-rah*
orchestra conductor	ōkesutora no shikisha	*oh-kehs-toh-rah noh shee-kee-shah*
percussion instruments	dagakki	*dah-gahk-kee*
• bass drum	ōdaiko	*oh-dah-ee-koh*
• cymbals	shinbaru	*sheen-bah-roo*
• drum	taiko	*tah-ee-koh koh*
• set of drums	taiko no setto	*tah-ee-koh*
• tambourine	tanbarin	*tahn-bah-r*
• timpani	tinpanī	*teen-pah-*
pianist	pianisuto	*pee-ah-*
play	ensōsuru *(v)*	*ehn-so*
player	ensōka	*ehn-*

popular music	popyurā myūjikku	*poh-pyoo-rah myoo-jeek-koo*
quartet	karutetto	*kah-roo-teht-toh*
rap	rappu	*rahp-poo*
rhythm	rizumu	*ree-zoo-moo*
rock	rokku	*rohk-koo*
samba	sanba	*sahn-bah*
score	gakufu	*gahk-foo*
show	shō	*shoh*
solo	dokushō (singing)/ dokusō (instrumental)	*dohk-shoh/dohk-soh*
song	uta	*oo-tah*
• **sing**	utau *(v)*	*oo-tah-oo*
• **singer**	kashu	*kah-shoo*
stringed instruments	gengakki	*gehn-gahk-kee*
• **banjo**	banjō	*bahn-yoh*
• **bow**	yumi	*yoo-mee*
• **cello**	chero	*cheh-roh*
• **double bass**	kontorabasu	*kohn-toh-rah-bah-soo*
• **string**	gen	*gehn*
• **ukulele**	ukurere	*oo-koo-reh-reh*
• **viola**	biora	*bee-oh-rah*
• **violin**	baiorin	*bah-ee-oh-reen*
symphony	shinfonī	*sheen-foh-nee*
tango	tango	*tahn-goh*
trio	torio	*TOH-ree-oh*
violinist	baiorin ensōsha	*bah-ee-oh-reen ehn-soh-shah*
waltz	warutsu	*wah-roo-tsoo*
wind instruments	mokkan gakki	*mohk-kahn gahk-kee*
• **bagpipes**	baggupaipu	*bahg-goo-pah-ee-poo*
• **bassoon**	fagotto	*fah-goht-toh*
• **clarinet**	kurarinetto	*koo-rah-ree-neht-toh*
• **flute**	furūto	*foo-roo-toh*
• **oboe**	ōboe	*oh-boh-eh*
• **saxophone**	sakisofōn	*sah-kee-soh-fohn*

FOCUS: Traditional Japanese Dance, Music, and Musical Instruments

folk dance	bon odori	*bohn oh-doh-ree*
formal dance	Nihon buyō	*nee-hon boo-yoh*
court music	gagaku	*gah-gah-koo*
bamboo clarinet	shakuhachi	*shah-koo-hah-chee*
Japanese harp	koto	*koh-toh*
Japanese mandolin	shamisen	*shah-mee-sehn*

d. LITERATURE

appendix	furoku	*foo-roh-koo*
author	chosha/sakka	*choh-shah/sahk-kah*
autobiography	jiden	*jee-dehn*
biography	denki	*dehn-kee*
chapter	shō	*shoh*
character (novel, play)	tōjō jinbutsu	*toh-joh jeen-boo-tsoo*
criticism	hyōron	*hyoh-rohn*
essay	essei	*ehs-seh*
fable	gūwa	*goo-wah*
fairy tale	dōwa	*doh-wah*
fiction	fikushon	*feek-shohn*
genre	yōshiki	*yoh-shee-kee*
index	sakuin	*sah-koo-een*
literature	bungaku	*boon-gah-koo*
myth	shinwa	*sheen-wah*
mythology	shinwa	*sheen-wah*
novel	shōsetsu	*shoh-seh-tsoo*
plot	suji	*soo-jee*
poet	shijin	*shee-jeen*
poetry	shi	*shee*
preface	maeoki	*mah-eh-oh-kee*
prose	sanbun	*sahn-boon*
publisher	shuppansha	*shoop-pahn-shah*
review	hyōron	*hyoh-rohn*
short story	tanpen shōsetsu	*tahn-pehn shoh-seh-tsoo*
style	buntai	*boon-tah-ee*
table of contents	mokuji	*moh-koo-jee*
theme	tēma	*teh-mah*
work (literary)	chosaku	*choh-sah-koo*
writer	sakka	*sahk-kah*

e. THEATER

act	maku	*mah-koo*
• **act**	enjiru *(v)*	*ehn-jee-roo*
applause	hakushu	*hahk-shoo*
• **applaud**	hakushusuru *(v)*	*hahk-shoo-soo-roo*
audience	kankyaku	*kahn-kyah-koo*
comedian	kigeki yakusha	*kee-geh-kee yahk-shah*
comedy	kigeki	*kee-geh-kee*
costume	ishō	*ee-shoh*
curtain	maku	*mah-koo*
drama	dorama	*doh-rah-mah*
hero	shujinkō	*shoo-jeen-koh*
heroine	onna shujinkō	*ohn-nah shoo-jeen-koh*
intermission	makuai	*mah-koo-ah-ee*

makeup	mēkyappu	*meh-kyahp-poo*
mime	mugon geki	*moo-gohn geh-kee*
pantomime	pantomaimu	*pahn-toh-mah-ee-moo*
play	engeki	*ehn-geh-kee*
playwright	geki sakka	*geh-kee sahk-kah*
plot	suji	*soo-jee*
program	puroguramu	*poo-roh-goo-rah-moo*
scene	bamen	*bah-mehn*
scenery	haikei	*hah-ee-keh*
stage	butai	*boo-tah-ee*
theater	gekijō	*geh-kee-joh*
tragedy	higeki	*hee-geh-kee*

FOCUS: Three Major Forms of Traditional Japanese Theater

dance-drama	Kabuki	*kah-boo-kee*
masked play	Noh	*noh*
puppet theater	Bunraku	*boon-rah-koo*

29. HOLIDAYS AND GOING OUT

a. HOLIDAYS/SPECIAL OCCASIONS

For more national holidays and important dates, see Section 5g.

anniversary	kinenbi	*kee-nehn-bee*
birthday	tanjōbi	*tahn-joh-bee*
Christmas	Kurisumasu	*koo-ree-soo-mah-soo*
engagement	konyaku	*kohn-yah-koo*
holiday	shukujitsu	*shoo-koo-jee-tsoo*
New Year's Day	ganjitsu	*gahn-jee-tsoo*
New Year's Eve	ōmisoka no ban	*oh-mee-soh-kah noh bahn*
picnic	pikunikku	*pee-koo-neek-koo*
vacation	bakansu	*BAH-kahn-soo*
wedding	kekkonshiki	*kehk-kohn-shkee*

b. GOING OUT

dance	dansu	*dahn-soo*
• dance	odoru *(v)*	*oh-doh-roo*
date	dēto	*deh-toh*
disco	disuko	*dees-koh*
go out	dekakeru *(v)*	*deh-kah-keh-roo*

have fun	tanoshimu *(v)*	*tah-noh-shee-moo*
movies	eiga	*eh-gah*
party	pātī	*pah-tee*
remain	nokoru *(v)*	*noh-koh-roo*
return	kaeru *(v)*	*kah-eh-roo*
shopping	shoppingu	*shohp-peen-goo*
visit	hōmonsuru *(v)*	*hoh-mohn-soo-roo*

c. SPECIAL GREETINGS

Best wishes!	Gokōun o.	*goh-koh-oon oh*
Congratulations!	Omedetō gozaimasu.	*oh-meh-deh-toh goh-zah-ee-mahs*
Happy Birthday!	Tanjōbi omedetō.	*tahn-joh-bee oh-meh-deh-toh*
Happy New Year!	Shinnen omedetō.	*sheen-nehn oh-meh-deh-toh*
Have a good holiday!	Oyasumi o, otanoshimi kudasai.	*oh-yah-soo-mee oh, oh-TAH-noh-shee-mee koo-dah-sah-ee*
Have fun!	Tanoshinde kite kudasai.	*tah-noh-sheen-deh kee-teh koo-dah-sah-ee*
Merry Christmas!	Kurisumasu omedetō.	*koo-ree-soo-mah-soo oh-meh-deh-toh*

TRAVEL

30. CHOOSING A DESTINATION

For more related vocabulary, see Section 13e.

a. AT THE TRAVEL AGENCY

abroad	kaigai ni *(adv)*	*kah-ee-gah-ee nee*
brochure	panfuretto	*pahn-foo-reht-toh*
bus tour	basu tsuā	*bahs tsoo-ah*
charter flight	chātā bin	*chah-tah been*
city	toshi	*toh-shee*
• capital city	shuto	*shoo-toh*
class	kurasu	*koo-rah-soo*
• business class	bijinesu kurasu	*bee-jee-nehs koo-rah-soo*
• economy class	ekonomī kurasu	*eh-koh-noh-mee koo-rah-soo*
• first class (plane)	fāsuto kurasu	*fah-stoh koo-rah-soo*
• first class (train)	gurīn sha	*goo-reen shah*
connection	konekushon	*koh-nehk-shohn*
country	kuni	*koo-nee*
discount	waribiki	*wah-ree-bee-kee*
• group discount	dantai waribiki	*dahn-tah-ee wah-ree-bee-kee*
• senior discount	kōreisha waribiki	*koh-reh-shah wah-ree-bee-kee*
• student discount	gakusei waribiki	*gahk-seh wah-ree-bee-kee*
downtown	toshin	*toh-sheen*
excursion	gurūpu tsuā	*goo-roo-poo tsoo-ah*
group tour	dantai ryokō/ gurūpu tsuā	*dahn-tah-ee ryoh-koh/ goo-roo-poo tsoo-ah*
guided tour	gaido tsuki tsuā	*gah-ee-doh tsoo-kee tsoo-ah*
insurance	hoken	*hoh-kehn*
outskirts, suburbs	kōgai	*koh-gah-ee*
package tour	pakkēji tsuā	*pahk-keh-jee tsoo-ah*
passport	pasupōto	*pahs-poh-toh*
reservation	yoyaku	*yoh-yah-koo*
• reserve	yoyakusuru *(v)*	*yoh-yahk-soo-roo*
see	miru *(v)*	*mee-roo*
ticket	ken	*kehn*
• advance ticket	maeuri ken	*mah-eh-oo-ree kehn*
• boat ticket	fune no ken	*foo-neh noh kehn*

• buy a ticket	ken o kau *(v)*	*kehn oh kah-oo*
• one-way ticket	katamichi ken	*kah-tah-mee-chee kehn*
• plane ticket	kōkū ken	*koh-koo kehn*
• round-trip ticket	ōfuku ken	*oh-fkoo kehn*
• train ticket	kisha no kippu	*kee-shah noh keep-poo*
tour	kankō ryokō	*kahn-koh ryoh-koh*
tour bus	kankō basu	*kahn-koh bah-soo*
tour guide	kankō gaido	*kahn-koh gah-ee-doh*
tourist	kankō kyaku	*kahn-koh kyah-koo*
travel	ryokō	*ryoh-koh*
• travel	ryokōsuru *(v)*	*ryoh-koh-soo-roo*
• travel agency	ryokō dairiten	*ryoh-koh dah-ee-ree-tehn*
trip, journey	ryokō	*ryoh-koh*
• Have a nice trip!	Ryokō o, otanoshimi kudasai.	*ryoh-koh oh oh-tah-noh-shee-mee koo-dah-sah-ee*
• take a trip	ryokō ni iku	*ryoh-koh nee ee-koo*
visa	biza	*bee-zah*
visit	hōmonsuru *(v)*	*hoh-mohn-soo-roo*
world	sekai	*seh-kah-ee*

b. COUNTRIES AND CONTINENTS

Africa	Afurika	*ah-foo-ree-kah*
America	Amerika	*ah-meh-ree-kah*
• Central America	Chūō Amerika	*choo-oh ah-meh-ree-kah*
• Latin America	Raten Amerika	*rah-tehn ah-meh-ree-kah*
• North America	Kita Amerika	*kee-tah ah-meh-ree-kah*
• South America	Minami Amerika	*mee-nah-mee ah-meh-ree-kah*
Argentina	Aruzenchin	*ah-roo-zehn-cheen*
Asia	Ajia	*ah-jee-ah*
Australia	Ōsutoraria	*oh-stoh-rah-ree-ah*
Austria	Ōsutoria	*oh-stoh-ree-ah*
Belgium	Berugī	*beh-roo-gee*
Brazil	Burajiru	*boo-rah-jee-roo*
Canada	Kanada	*kah-nah-dah*
China	Chūgoku	*choo-goh-koo*
Denmark	Denmāku	*dehn-mah-koo*
Egypt	Ejiputo	*eh-jee-poo-toh*
England	Igirisu	*ee-gee-ree-soo*
Europe	Yōroppa	*yoh-rohp-pah*
Finland	Finrando	*feen-rahn-doh*
France	Furansu	*foo-rahn-soo*
Germany	Doitsu	*doh-ee-tsoo*
Greece	Girisha	*gee-ree-shah*
Holland	Oranda	*oh-rahn-dah*
India	Indo	*een-doh*
Indonesia	Indoneshia	*een-doh-neh-shee-ah*

Iran	Iran	*ee-rahn*
Iraq	Iraku	*ee-rah-koo*
Ireland	Airurando	*ah-ee-roo-rahn-doh*
Israel	Isuraeru	*ee-soo-rah-eh-roo*
Italy	Itaria	*ee-tah-ree-ah*
Japan	Nihon/Nippon	*nee-hohn/neep-pohn*
Jordan	Yorudan	*yoh-roo-dahn*
Kenya	Kenia	*keh-nee-ah*
Korea	Kankoku	*kahn-koh-koo*
Kuwait	Kuwēto	*koo-weh-toh*
Lebanon	Rebanon	*reh-bah-nohn*
Malaysia	Marēshia	*mah-reh-shee-ah*
Mexico	Mekishiko	*meh-kee-shee-koh*
Middle and Near East	Chūkintō	*choo-keen-toh*
New Zealand	Nyūjīrando	*nyoo-jee-rahn-doh*
Norway	Noruwē	*noh-roo-weh*
Pakistan	Pakisutan	*pah-kees-tahn*
Philippines	Firippin	*fee-reep-peen*
Poland	Pōrando	*poh-rahn-doh*
Portugal	Porutogaru	*poh-roo-toh-gah-roo*
Russia	Roshia	*roh-shee-ah*
Saudi Arabia	Saujiarabia	*sah-oo-jee-ah-rah-bee-ah*
Singapore	Shingapōru	*sheen-gah-poh-roo*
South Africa	Minami Afurika	*mee-nah-mee ah-foo-ree-kah*
Spain	Supein	*soo-peh-een*
Sweden	Suwēden	*soo-weh-dehn*
Switzerland	Suisu	*SOO-ee-soo*
Thailand	Taikoku	*tah-ee-koh-koo*
Turkey	Toruko	*toh-roo-koh*
United States of America	Amerika	*ah-meh-ree-kah*
Venezuela	Benezuera	*beh-neh-zoo-eh-rah*

c. A FEW CITIES

Bangkok	Bankokku	*bahn-kohk-koo*
Beijing	Bējin	*beh-jeen*
Berlin	Berurin	*beh-roo-reen*
Chicago	Shikago	*shee-kah-goh*
Frankfurt	Furankufuruto	*foo-rahn-koo-foo-roo-toh*
Geneva	Junēbu	*joo-neh-boo*
Hong Kong	Honkon	*hohn-kohn*
Honolulu	Honoruru	*hoh-noh-roo-roo*
Jakarta	Jakaruta	*jah-kah-roo-tah*
Kuala Lumpur	Kuararunpūru	*koo-ah-rah-roon-poo-roo*
Kyoto	Kyōto	*kyoh-toh*
London	Rondon	*rohn-dohn*

Los Angeles	Rosanjerusu	*roh-sahn-jeh-roo-soo*
Manila	Manira	*mah-nee-rah*
Milan	Mirano	*mee-rah-noh*
Montreal	Montoriōru	*mohn-toh-ree-oh-roo*
Moscow	Mosukuwa	*mohs-koo-wah*
New York	Nyūyōku	*nyoo-yoh-koo*
Osaka	Ōsaka	*oh-sah-kah*
Paris	Pari	*pah-ree*
Rome	Rōma	*roh-mah*
San Francisco	Sanfuranshisuko	*sahn-foo-rahn-shees-koh*
Seoul	Souru	*soh-oo-roo*
Taipei	Taipei	*tah-ee-peh*
Tokyo	Tōkyō	*toh-kyoh*
Vienna	Uīn	*oo-een*

d. NATIONALITIES AND LANGUAGES

American	Amerikajin	*ah-meh-ree-kah-jeen*
• English	eigo	*eh-goh*
Arab	Arabujin	*ah-rah-boo-jeen*
• Arabic	Arabiago	*ah-rah-bee-ah-goh*
Australian	Ōsutorariajin	*oh-stoh-rah-ree-ah-jeen*
• English	eigo	*eh-goh*
Austrian	Ōsutoriajin	*oh-stoh-ree-ah-jeen*
• German	Doitsugo	*doh-ee-tsoo-goh*
Belgian	Berugijin	*beh-roo-gee-jeen*
• French	Furansugo	*foo-rahn-soo-goh*
• Flemish	Furandāsugo	*foo-rahn-dah-soo-goh*
Brazilian	Burajirujin	*boo-rah-jee-roo-jeen*
• Portuguese	Porutogarugo	*poh-roo-toh-gah-roo-goh*
Canadian	Kanadajin	*kah-nah-dah-jeen*
• English	eigo	*eh-goh*
• French	Furansugo	*foo-rahn-soo-goh*
Chinese	Chūgokujin	*choo-goh-koo-jeen*
• Chinese	Chūgokugo	*choo-goh-koo-goh*
Dane	Denmākujin	*dehn-mah-koo-jeen*
• Danish	Denmākugo	*dehn-mah-koo-goh*
Dutch	Orandajin	*oh-rahn-dah-jeen*
• Dutch	Orandago	*oh-rahn-dah-goh*
English	Igirisujin	*ee-gee-ree-soo-jeen*
• English	eigo	*eh-goh*
Finn	Finrandojin	*feen-rahn-doh-jeen*
• Finnish	Finrandogo	*feen-rahn-doh-goh*
French	Furansujin	*foo-rahn-soo-jeen*
• French	Furansugo	*foo-rahn-soo-goh*
German	Doitsujin	*doh-ee-tsoo-jeen*
• German	Doitsugo	*doh-ee-tsoo-goh*

Greek	Girishajin	*gee-ree-shah-jeen*
• Greek	Girishago	*gee-ree-shah-goh*
Israeli	Isuraerujin	*ee-soo-rah-eh-roo-jeen*
• Hebrew	Heburaigo	*heh-boo-rah-ee-goh*
Italian	Itariajin	*ee-tah-ree-ah-jeen*
• Italian	Itariago	*ee-tah-ree-ah-goh*
Japanese	Nihonjin	*nee-hohn-jeen*
• Japanese	Nihongo	*nee-hohn-goh*
Korean	Kankokujin	*kahn-koh-koo-jeen*
• Korean	Kankokugo	*kahn-koh-koo-goh*
Malaysian	Marējin	*mah-reh-jeen*
• Malay	Marēgo	*mah-reh-goh*
Norwegian	Noruwējin	*noh-roo-weh-jeen*
• Norwegian	Noruwēgo	*noh-roo-weh-goh*
Pole	Pōrandojin	*poh-rahn-doh-jeen*
• Polish	Pōrandogo	*poh-rahn-doh-goh*
Portuguese	Porutogarujin	*poh-roo-toh-gah-roo-jeen*
• Portuguese	Porutogarugo	*poh-roo-toh-gah-roo-goh*
Russian	Roshiajin	*roh-shee-ah-jeen*
• Russian	Roshiago	*roh-shee-ah-goh*
Spaniard	Supeinjin	*soo-peh-een-jeen*
• Spanish	Supeingo	*soo-peh-een-goh*
Swede	Suwēdenjin	*soo-weh-dehn-jeen*
• Swedish	Suwēdengo	*soo-weh-dehn-goh*
Thai	Taijin	*tah-ee-jeen*
• Thai	Taigo	*tah-ee-goh*
Turk	Torukojin	*toh-roo-koh-jeen*
• Turkish	Torukogo	*toh-roo-koh-goh*

31. PACKING AND GOING THROUGH CUSTOMS

baggage, luggage	nimotsu	*nee-moh-tsoo*
• hand luggage	tenimotsu	*teh-nee-moh-tsoo*
border	kokkyō	*kohk-kyoh*
carry	hakobu (v)	*hah-koh-boo*
carry-on	kinai mochikomi hin	*kee-nah-ee moh-chee-koh-mee heen*
customs	zeikan	*zeh-kahn*
• customs officer	zeikan no kakariin	*zeh-kahn noh kah-kah-ree-een*
customs declaration form	zeikan shinkokusho	*zeh-kahn sheen-kohk-shoh*
declare	shinkokusuru (v)	*sheen-kohk-soo-roo*
• There's nothing to declare.	Nani mo, shinkokusuru mono ga arimasen.	*nah-nee moh, sheen-kohk-soo-roo moh-noh gah ah-ree-mah-sehn*
• There's something to declare.	Shinkokusuru mono ga arimasu.	*sheen-kohk-soo-roo moh-noh gah ah-ree-mahs*

documents	shorui	*shoh-roo-ee*
duty	kanzei	*kahn-zeh*
• pay customs/duty	kanzei o harau *(v)*	*kahn-zeh oh hah-rah-oo*
foreign currency	gaikoku tsūka	*gah-ee-koh-koo tsoo-kah*
foreigner	gaikokujin	*gah-ee-koh-koo-jeen*
form (to fill out)	shoshiki	*shoh-shee-kee*
identification (paper)	mibun shōmeisho	*mee-boon shoh-meh-shoh*
import	yunyūsuru *(v)*	*yoo-nyoo-soo-roo*
measurement	sunpō	*soon-poh*
nationality	kokuseki	*kohk-seh-kee*
pack (one's bags/ luggage)	nizukurisuru *(v)*	*nee-zoo-koo-ree-soo-roo*
passport	pasupōto	*pahs-poh-toh*
passport control	ryoken shinsa	*ryoh-kehn sheen-sah*
suitcase, piece of luggage	sūtsukēsu	*soo-tsoo-keh-soo*
tariff	kanzei	*kahn-zeh*
visa	biza	*bee-zah*
weight	mekata	*meh-kah-tah*
• heavy	omoi *(adj)*	*oh-moh-ee*
• light	karui *(adj)*	*kah-roo-ee*
• maximum	saidai no *(adj)*	*sah-ee-dah-ee noh*

32. TRAVELING BY AIR

a. IN THE TERMINAL

airline	kōkūgaisha	*koh-koo-gah-ee-shah*
airport	kūkō	*koo-koh*
arrival	tōchaku	*toh-chah-koo*
baggage claim	tenimotsu uketorijo	*teh-nee-moh-tsoo oo-keh-toh-ree-joh*
boarding	tōjō	*toh-joh*
• boarding pass	tōjō ken	*toh-joh kehn*
business class	bijinesu kurasu	*bee-jee-neh-soo koo-rah-soo*
carry-on	kinai mochikomi hin	*kee-nah-ee moh-chee-koh-mee heen*
check in (baggage)	azukeru *(v)*	*ah-zoo-keh-roo*
check-in	chekkuin	*chehk-koo-een*
connection	konekushon	*koh-neh-koo-shohn*
departure	shuppatsu	*shoop-pah-tsoo*
economy class	ekonomī kurasu	*eh-koh-noh-mee koo-rah-soo*
e-ticket	īchiketto	*ee-chee-keht-toh*
first class	fāsuto kurasu	*fah-soo-toh koo-rah-soo*
flight	bin	*been*
gate	gēto	*geh-toh*

information desk	annaisho	*ahn-nah-ee-shoh*
no smoking	kin-en	*keen-ehn*
porter	pōtā	*poh-tah*
reservation	yoyaku	*yoh-yah-koo*
terminal	tāminaru	*tah-mee-nah-roo*
ticket	ken	*kehn*
waiting room	raunji	*rah-oon-jee*

b. FLIGHT INFORMATION

canceled	kyanseru sareta	*kyan-seh-roo sah-reh-tah*
early	hayai *(adj)*	*hah-yah-ee*
	hayaku *(adv)*	*hah-yah-koo*
late	osoi *(adj)*	*oh-soh-ee*
	okurete *(adv)*	*oh-koo-reh-teh*
on time	teikoku ni *(adv)*	*teh-koh-koo nee*

c. ON THE PLANE

airplane	hikōki	*hee-koh-kee*
aisle	tsūro	*tsoo-roh*
cabin	kyabin	*kyah-been*
captain	kichō	*kee-choh*
co-pilot	fuku sōjūshi	*foo-koo soh-joo-shee*
crew	tōjoin	*toh-joh-een*
emergency exit	hijōguchi	*hee-joh-goo-chee*
flight attendant	kyakushitsu jōmuin	*kyah-koo-shtsoo joh-moo-een*
headphones	heddohōn	*hehd-doh-hohn*
land	chakurikusuru *(v)*	*chah-koo-reek-soo-roo*
landing gear	chakuriku sōchi	*chah-koo-ree-koo soh-chee*
life jacket	kyūmeidōgi	*kyoo-meh-doh-gee*
local time	genchi jikan	*gehn-chee jee-kahn*
luggage compartment	tenimotsu dana	*teh-nee-moh-tsoo dah-nah*
passenger	jōkyaku	*joh-kyah-koo*
pilot	sōjūshi	*soh-joo-shee*
runway	kassōro	*kahs-soh-roh*
seat	seki	*seh-kee*
• aisle	tsūrogawa	*tsoo-roh-gah-wah*
• window	madogawa	*mah-doh-gah-wah*
seat belt	shītoberuto	*shee-toh-beh-roo-toh*
• fasten	shimeru *(v)*	*shee-meh-roo*
sit down	suwaru *(v)*	*soo-wah-roo*
takeoff	ririku	*ree-ree-koo*
• take off	ririkusuru *(v)*	*ree-ree-koo-soo-roo*
time difference	jisa	*jee-sah*
toilet	toire	*toh-ee-reh*

tray	tēburu	*teh-boo-roo*
turbulence	rankiryū	*rahn-kee-ryoo*
wheel	sharin	*shah-reen*
wing	tsubasa	*tsoo-bah-sah*

33. ON THE ROAD

a. VEHICLES

ambulance	kyūkyūsha	*kyoo-kyoo-shah*
automobile	jidōsha	*jee-doh-shah*
bicycle	jitensha	*jee-tehn-shah*
• brake	burēki	*boo-reh-kee*
• chain guard	chēn gādo	*chehn gah-doh*
• handlebar	handoru	*hahn-doh-roo*
• pedal	pedaru	*peh-dah-roo*
• seat	sadoru	*sah-doh-roo*
• spoke	supōku	*spoh-koo*
• tire	taiya	*tah-ee-yah*
bus	basu	*bah-soo*
• trolley	torōrīkā	*toh-roh-ree-kah*
car	jidōsha	*jee-doh-shah*
cement mixer	konkurīto mikisā	*kohn-koo-ree-toh mee-kee-sah*
compact car	konpakutokā	*kohn-pahk-toh-kah*
convertible	konbāchiburu	*kohn-bah-chee-boo-roo*
fire engine	shōbōsha	*shoh-boh-shah*
hybrid car	haiburiddo kā	*hah-ee-boo-reed-doh kah*
jeep	jīpu	*jee-poo*
limousine	rimujīn	*ree-moo-jeen*
minivan	miniban	*mee-nee-bahn*
motorcycle	ōtobai	*oh-toh-bah-ee*
• scooter	sukūtā	*skoo-tah*
passenger car	jōyōsha	*joh-yoh-shah*
rental car	rentakā	*rehn-tah-kah*
sports car	supōtsukā	*spoh-tsoo kah*
station wagon	wagonsha	*wah-gohn-shah*
streetcar	romendensha	*roh-mehn-dehn-shah*
SUV	tamokuteki supōtsusha	*tah-mohk-teh-kee tsoo-shah*
taxi	takushi	*tah-koo-shee*
trailer	torērā	*toh-reh-rah*
transporter	jidōsha unpansha	*jee-doh-shah oon-pahn-shah*
truck	torakku	*toh-rahk-koo*
• dump truck	danpukā	*dahn-poo-kah*
• garbage truck	gomi shūshūsha	*goh-mee shoo-shoo-shah*

• tow truck	rekkāsha	*rehk-kāh-shah*
van	ban	*bahn*

b. DRIVING: PEOPLE AND DOCUMENTS

driver	untenshu	*oon-tehn-shoo*
• to drive	untensuru *(v)*	*oon-tehn-soo-roo*
driver's license	unten menkyosho	*oon-tehn mehn-kyoh-shoh*
insurance card	hoken sho	*hoh-kehn-shoh*
passenger	dōjōsha	*doh-joh-shah*
pedestrian	hokōsha	*hoh-koh-shah*
police	keisatsu	*keh-sah-tsoo*
• highway police	haiwē patorōru	*hah-ee-weh pah-toh-roh-roo*
• policeman	keikan	*keh-kahn*
• policewoman	fujin keikan	*foo-jeen keh-kahn*
• traffic police	kōtsū junsa	*koh-tsoo joon-sah*
registration papers	tōrokusho	*toh-roh-koo-shoh*
road map	dōro chizu	*doh-roh chee-zoo*

c. DRIVING: ADDITIONAL VOCABULARY

accident	jiko	*jee-koh*
back up	bakkusuru *(v)*	*bahk-koo-soo-roo*
brake	burēki	*boo-reh-kee*
breakdown	koshō	*koh-shoh*
bridge	hashi	*hah-shee*
corner (street)	kado	*kah-doh*
curve	kābu	*kah-boo*
distance	kyori	*kyoh-ree*
drive	untensuru *(v)*	*oon-tehn-soo-roo*
fine, ticket	ihan no ken	*ee-hahn noh kehn*
gas station	gasorin sutando	*gah-soh-reen stahn-doh*
• check the oil	oiru o chekkusuru *(v)*	*oh-ee-roo oh chehk-koo-soo-roo*
• fill up	mantan ni suru *(v)*	*mahn-tahn nee soo-roo*
• fix	naosu *(v)*	*nah-oh-soo*
• gas	gasorin	*gah-soh-reen*
• leaded gas	regyurā	*reh-gyoo-rah*
• mechanic	shūrikō	*shoo-ree-koh*
• self-service	serufu sābisu	*seh-roo-foo sah-bee-soo*
• tools	dōgu	*doh-goo*
• unleaded gas	muen gasorin	*moo-ehn gah-soh-reen*
gearshift	gia shifuto	*gee-ah shee-foo-toh*
go forward	zenshinsuru *(v)*	*zehn-sheen-soo-roo*
going through a red light	shingō mushi	*sheen-goh moo-shee*
highway	kōsokudōro	*koh-soh-koo-doh-roh*

intersection	kōsaten	*kōh-sah-tehn*
lane (traffic)	shasen	*shah-sehn*
park	chūshasuru *(v)*	*chōo-shah-soo-roo*
• parking	chūsha	*chōo-shah*
• public parking	chūshajō	*chōo-shah-joh*
pass	oikosu *(v)*	*oh-ee-koh-soo*
pedestrian crossing	ōdanhodō	*oh-dahn-hoh-dōh*
ramp	intāchenji	*een-tāh-chehn-jee*
road	michi	*mee-chee*
rush hour	rasshu awā	*rahs-shoo ah-wāh*
signal	shigunaru	*shee-goo-nah-roo*
slow down	gensokusuru *(v)*	*gehn-soh-koo-soo-roo*
speed	sokudo	*soh-koo-doh*
• speed limit	sokudo seigen	*soh-koo-doh sēh-gehn*
• speed up	kasokusuru *(v)*	*kah-sohk-soo-roo*
start (car)	enjin o kakeru *(v)*	*ehn-jeen oh kah-keh-roo*
toll booth	ryōkinsho	*ryoh-keen-shoh*
toll road	yūryō dōro	*yōo-ryoh doh-roh*
traffic	kōtsū	*kōh-tsōo*
• traffic jam	kōtsū jūtai	*kōh-tsoo jōo-tah-ee*
traffic light	shingō	*sheen-goh*
tunnel	tonneru	*tohn-neh-roo*
turn	magaru *(v)*	*mah-gah-roo*
• turn to the left	hidari ni magaru *(v)*	*hee-dah-ree nee mah-gah-roo*
• turn to the right	migi ni magaru *(v)*	*mee-gee nee mah-gah-roo*

d. ROAD SIGNS

Bicycle Path	jitenshadō	*jee-tehn-shah-dōh*
Emergency Lane	kinkyū shasen	*keen-kyōo shah-sehn*
Entrance	iriguchi	*ee-ree-goo-chee*
Exit	deguchi	*deh-goo-chee*
Intersection	kōsaten	*koh-sah-tehn*
Level Crossing	fumikiri	*foo-mee-kee-ree*
Merge	gōryū	*goh-ryōo*
No Entry	shinnyū kinshi	*sheen-nyōo keen-shee*
No Left Turn	sasetsu kinshi	*sah-seh-tsoo keen-shee*
No Parking	chūsha kinshi	*choo-shah keen-shee*
No Passing	oikoshi kinshi	*oh-ee-koh-shee keen-shee*
No Right Turn	usetsu kinshi	*oo-seh-tsoo keen-shee*
No Stopping	teisha kinshi	*tēh-shah keen-shee*
No Thoroughfare	tsūkōdome	*tsōo-kōh-doh-meh*
No U-Turn	yūtān kinshi	*yōo-tāhn keen-shee*
One Way	ippōtsūkō	*eep-poh-tsōo-kōh*
Passing Lane	oikoshisen	*oh-ee-koh-shee-sehn*
Speed Limit	sokudo seigen	*soh-koo-doh sēh-gehn*

Emergency
Telephone

Caution

Stop

Slow
Down

Minimum
Speed

Maximum Parking
60 Minutes
(8 AM–8 PM)

No
Passing

Sound
Horn

Parking

No Parking
(8 AM–8 PM)

No Parking,
No Standing
(8 AM–8 PM)

Standing
Permitted

Pedestrians
Only

Cars Only

Bicycles
Only

Service
Area

Detour

Exit

No
Entrance

Entrance to
Expressway

Road
Closed

National
Highway

No Right
Turn

No U-Turn

Traffic
Island

Two Way
Traffic
Dividing Line

One Way

This Lane for
Motorcycles and
Lightweight Cars

Stop	teishi	*teh-shee*
Toll	ryōkinsho	*ryoh-keen-shoh*
Tow-Away Zone	ken-in chiiki	*kehn-een chee-ee-kee*
Work in Progress	kōjichū	*koh-jee-chōo*
Yield	yūsen	*yōo-sehn*

e. THE CAR

air bag	eā baggu	*eh-āh bahg-goo*
air conditioner	eakon	*eh-ah-kohn*
battery	batterī	*baht-teh-rēe*
brake	burēki	*boo-reh-kee*
bumper	banpā	*bahn-pāh*
car body	bodī	*boh-dēe*
car window	windō	*ween-dōh*
carburetor	kyaburetā	*kyah-boo-reh-tāh*
clutch (pedal)	kuratchi	*koo-raht-chee*
dashboard	dasshubōdo	*dahs-shoo-boh-doh*
door	doa	*doh-ah*
fender	fendā	*fehn-dāh*
filter	firutā	*fee-roo-tah*
gas pedal	akuseru	*ah-koo-seh-roo*
gas tank	gasorin tanku	*gah-soh-reen tahn-koo*
gearshift	shifuto rebā	*shee-foo-toh reh-bāh*
glove compartment	gurōbu bokkusu	*goo-rōh-boo bohk-ksoo*
hazard flash	hazādo ranpu	*hah-zāh-doh rahn-poo*
heater	hītā	*hēe-tah*
hood	bonnetto	*bohn-neht-toh*
horn	keiteki	*keh-teh-kee*
horsepower	bariki	*bah-ree-kee*
license plate	nanbā purēto	*nahn-bāh poo-reh-toh*
lights	raito	*rah-ee-toh*
motor	enjin	*ehn-jeen*
• fan	fan	*fahn*
• gas pump	ponpu	*pohn-poo*
• generator	jenerētā	*jeh-neh-rēh-tāh*
• spark plug	supāku puragu	*soo-pāh-koo poo-rah-goo*
• valve	barubu	*bah-roo-boo*
muffler	mafurā	*mah-foo-rāh*
oil	oiru	*oh-ee-roo*
oil filter	oiru firutā	*oh-ee-roo fee-roo-tah*
power brake	pawā burēki	*pah-wāh boo-reh-kee*
power steering	pawā handoru	*pah-wāh hahn-doh-roo*
power window	pawā windō	*pah-wāh ween-dōh*
radiator	rajiētā	*rah-jee-eh-tah*
rearview mirror	bakkumirā	*bahk-koo mee-rāh*
roof	rūfu	*rōo-foo*

seat	shīto	shēē-toh
seat belt	shīto beruto	shēē-toh beh-roo-toh
side mirror	saido mirā	sah-ee-doh mee-rah
speedometer	sokudokei	soh-koo-doh-keh
steering wheel	handoru	hahn-doh-roo
tire	taiya	tah-ee-yah
• spare tire	supea taiya	speh-ah tah-ee-yah
trunk	toranku	toh-rahn-koo
turn signal	hōkō shijiki	hoh-koh shee-jee-kee
vent	benchirētā	behn-chee-reh-tah
wheel	sharin	shah-reen
windshield	furontogarasu	foo-rohn-toh-gah-rah-soo
• windshield wiper	waipā	wah-ee-pah

34. TRAIN, BUS, AND SUBWAY

bus	basu	bah-soo
bus driver	basu no untenshu	bah-soo noh oon-tehn-shoo
bus station, depot	basu no hatchakusho	bah-soo noh haht-chah-koo-shoh
bus stop	basu no teiryūsho	bah-soo noh tēh-ryōō-shoh
change	norikaeru (v)	noh-ree-kah-eh-roo
coach	futsū	foo-tsoo
conductor	shashō	shah-shoh
commuter train	densha	dehn-shah
compartment	koshitsu	koh-shtsoo
• nonsmoking	kin-en no (adj)	keen-ehn noh
• smoking	kitsuen no (adj)	kee-tsoo-ehn noh
connection	noritsugi	noh-ree-tsoo-gee
dining car	shokudōsha	shoh-koo-doh-shah
direct train	chokutsū ressha	chohk-tsoo rehs-shah
express train	kyūkō	kyoo-koh
fare box	ryōkinbako	ryoh-keen-bah-koh
leave, depart	hasshasuru (v)	hahs-shah-soo-roo
limited express train	tokkyū	tohk-kyoo
local train	kakueki teisha (no kisha)	kah-koo-eh-kee tēh-shah (noh kee-shah)
miss (the train)	norisokonau (v)	noh-ree-soh-koh-nah-oo
newsstand	shinbun uriba	sheen-boon oo-ree-bah
platform	purattohōmu	poo-raht-toh-hoh-moo
porter	akabō	ah-kah-boh
railroad	tetsudō	teh-tsoo-doh
• station	eki	eh-kee
schedule	jikokuhyō	jee-koh-koo-hyoh
• early	hayai (adj)	hah-yah-ee
• late	osoi (adj)	oh-soh-ee
• on time	jikandōri ni (adv)	jee-kahn-doh-ree nee

seat	seki	*seh-kee*
• economy seat	futsū seki	*foo-tsōō seh-kee*
• first class	gurīnsha no seki	*goo-rēēn-shah noh seh-kee*
• reserved seat	shitei seki	*shtēh seh-kee*
• unreserved seat	jiyū seki	*jee-yōō seh-kee*
sleeping car	shindaisha	*sheen-dah-ee-shah*
stop	tomaru *(v)*	*toh-mah-roo*
subway	chikatetsu	*chee-kah-teh-tsoo*
• subway station	chikatetsu no eki	*chee-kah-teh-tsoo noh eh-kee*
take/catch the train, bus, taxi, etc.	noru *(v)*	*noh-roo*
ticket	ken	*kehn*
• buy a ticket	ken o kau *(v)*	*kehn o kah-oo*
• ticket counter	kippu uriba	*keep-poo oo-ree-bah*
timetable	jikokuhyō	*jee-koh-koo-hyoh*
track	sen	*sehn*
train	kisha	*kee-shah*
• All aboard!	Gojōsha kudasai.	*goh-JOH-shah koo-dah-sah-ee*
• train station	eki	*eh-kee*
wait for	matsu *(v)*	*mah-tsoo*

35. HOTELS

a. LODGING

hotel	hoteru	*hoh-teh-roo*
• luxury hotel	kōkyū hoteru	*kōh-kyōō hoh-teh-roo*
motel	moteru	*moh-teh-roo*
youth hostel	yūsu hosuteru	*yōō-soo hohs-teh-roo*

b. STAYING IN HOTELS

bill	kanjō	*kahn-jōh*
• ask for the bill	kanjō o tanomu	*kahn-jōh oh tah-noh-moo*
• Charge it to my bill.	Watakushi no kanjō ni, tsukete oite kudasai.	*wah-tahk-shee noh kahn-jōh nee, tsoo-keh-teh oh-ee-teh koo-dah-sah-ee*
bellhop	bōi	*boh-ee*
breakfast	asa gohan	*ah-sah goh-hahn*
• breakfast included	chōshoku komi	*chōh-shoh-koo koh-mee*
complain	kujō o noberu *(v)*	*koo-jōh oh noh-beh-roo*
• complaint	kujō	*koo-jōh*
doorman	doaman	*doh-ah-mahn*

FOCUS: Other Kinds of Lodging in Japan

Major hotels are similar in quality and service to those in western cities. Another category is the business hotel, also western-style, but inexpensive, with small rooms and no-frills service. Business hotels are clean and are conveniently located near train stations or in the business districts.

| business hotel | bijinesu hoteru | bee-jee-neh-soo hoh-teh-roo |

Japanese inns, or **ryokan**, have traditional Japanese-style accommodations and service. As with western-style hotels, they range in quality and price from luxurious to simple. Breakfast and dinner are included in the price.

| Japanese inn | ryokan | ryoh-kahn |

Minshuku are guest houses where travelers can stay. Many are located in resort and vacation areas, and their rates are much lower than at hotels or **ryokan**. Because most are family-run operations, regular hotel services (maid, laundry, etc.) are not provided. Breakfast and dinner are included in the rate, and guests eat with the family.

| family guest house | minshuku | meen-shoo-koo |

elevator	erebētā	eh-reh-bēh-tāh
entrance	iriguchi	ee-ree-goo-chee
exit	deguchi	deh-goo-chee
floor (level)	kai	kah-ee
garage	chūshajō	chōo-shah-jōh
hotel clerk	hoteru no kakariin	hoh-teh-rōo noh kah-kah-ree-een
identification card	mibun shōmeisho	mee-boon shōh-mēh-shoh
key	kagi	kah-gee
• give back the room key	kagi o kaesu	kah-gee oh kah-eh-soo
lobby	robī	roh-bēe
luggage	nimotsu	nee-moh-tsoo
maid	mēdo	mēh-doh
manager	manējā	mah-nēh-jāh
message	dengon	dehn-gohn
passport	pasupōto	pahs-pōh-toh
pay	harau (v)	hah-rah-oo
• cash	genkin	gehn-keen

• credit card	kurejitto kādo	koo-reh-jeet-toh kāh-doh
• traveler's check	toraberā chekku	toh-rah-beh-rāh chehk-koo
price, rate	ryokin	ryoh-keen
• low season	isogashikunai toki	ee-soh-gah-shee-koo-nah-ee toh-kee
• peak season	isogashii toki	ee-soh-gah-shēē toh-kee
porter	pōtā	poh-tah
receipt	reshīto	reh-shēē-toh
request a taxi	takushī o tanomu	tahk-shēē oh tah-noh-moo
reservation	yoyaku	yoh-yah-koo
• reserve	yoyakusuru (v)	yoh-yah-koo-soo-roo
room	heya	heh-yah
• Do you have a vacant room?	Heya ga arimasu ka.	heh-yah gah ah-ree-mahs kah
• double room	daburu no heya	dah-boo-roo noh heh-yah
• have baggage taken to one's room	nimotsu o heya e motte itte morau	nee-moh-tsoo oh heh-yah eh moht-teh eet-teh moh-rah-oo
• nonsmoking room	kin-en no heya	keen-ehn noh heh-yah
• room with two beds	tsuin no heya	tsoo-een noh heh-yah
• single room	shinguru no heya	sheen-goo-roo noh heh-yah
• smoking room	kitsuen dekiru heya	kee-tsoo-ehn deh-kee-roo heh-yah
services	sābisu	sāh-bee-soo
stairs	kaidan	kah-ee-dahn
swimming pool	pūru	pōō-roo
view	nagame	nah-gah-meh
wake-up call	mōningu kōru	moh-neen-goo kōh-roo

c. THE HOTEL ROOM

balcony	barukonī	bah-roo-koh-nēē
• sliding door	hikido	hee-kee-doh
bathrobe	basurōbu	bah-soo-roh-boo
bathroom	basurūmu	bah-soo-rōō-moo
bathtub	yokusō	yohk-sōh
bed	beddo	behd-doh
• crib	bebībeddo	beh-bēē-behd-doh
• double bed	daburu beddo	dah-boo-roo behd-doh
bedside table	saido tēburu	sah-ee-doh teh-boo-roo
blanket	mōfu	moh-foo
chest of drawers	yōdansu	yoh-dahn-soo
closet	oshiire	oh-shee-ee-reh
clothes hanger	hangā	hahn-gāh
curtains	kāten	kah-tehn
dresser	kyōdai	kyoh-dah-ee

FOCUS: At a Japanese Inn

Besides the vocabulary for the hotel room, some special vocabulary may be needed for staying at a Japanese inn or **ryokan**.

armrest	hijikake	*hee-jee-kah-keh*
backrest	semotare	*seh-moh-tah-reh*
bathroom	furoba	*foo-roh-bah*
floor cushion	zabuton	*zah-boo-tohn*
Japanese bedding	futon	*ftohn*
light cotton kimono	yukata	*yoo-kah-tah*
sash (for kimono)	obi	*oh-bee*
time for taking bath	ofuro no jikan	*oh-foo-roh noh jee-kahn*
time for breakfast	chōshoku no jikan	*chōh-shoh-koo noh jee-kahn*
time for dinner	yūshoku no jikan	*yōo-shoh-koo noh jee-kahn*
thermos	mahōbin	*mah-hōh-been*
wooden clogs	geta	*geh-tah*

Ethernet connection	Īsanetto konekushon	*ēe-sah-neht-toh koh-nehk-shohn*
faucet	jaguchi	*jah-goo-chee*
refrigerator	reizōko	*reh-zōh-koh*
Internet	intānetto	*een-tāh-neht-toh*
lamp	ranpu	*rahn-poo*
lights	akari	*ah-kah-ree*
• current	denryū	*dehn-ryōo*
• switch	suitchi	*soo-eet-chee*
• turn off	kesu *(v)*	*keh-soo*
• turn on	tsukeru *(v)*	*tsoo-keh-roo*
mirror	kagami	*kah-gah-mee*
pillow	makura	*mah-koo-rah*
radio	rajio	*rah-jee-oh*
soap	sekken	*sehk-kehn*
shampoo	shanpū	*shahn-pōo*
sheets	shītsu	*shēe-tsoo*
shower	shawā	*shah-wāh*
sink, wash basin	senmendai	*sehn-mehn-dah-ee*
• cold water	mizu	*mee-zoo*
• hot water	oyu	*oh-yoo*
table	tēburu	*tēe-boo-roo*
telephone	denwa	*dehn-wah*
television set	terebi	*teh-reh-bee*

thermostat	jidō chōon sōchi	*jee-dōh-chōh-ohn sōh-chee*
toilet	toire	*toh-ee-reh*
• toilet paper	toiretto pēpā	*toh-ee-reht-toh pēh-pah*
towel	taoru	*tah-oh-roo*
wireless connection	waiyaresu konekushon	*wah-ee-yah-rehs koh-nehk-shohn*

36. ON VACATION

a. SIGHTSEEING

art gallery	garō	*gah-rōh*
avenue	tōri	*toh-ree*
bell tower	shōrō	*shoh-roh*
botanical garden	shokubutsuen	*shoh-koo-boo-tsoo-ehn*
bridge	hashi	*hah-shee*
castle	shiro	*shee-roh*
cathedral	daiseidō	*dah-ee-seh-dōh*
church	kyōkai	*kyoh-kah-ee*
city	toshi	*toh-shee*
city map	toshi chizu	*toh-shee chee-zoo*
corner	kado	*kah-doh*
downtown	toshin	*toh-sheen*
garden	niwa	*nee-wah*
guide	gaido	*gah-ee-doh*
interpreter	tsūyaku	*tsōō-yah-koo*
intersection	kōsaten	*koh-sah-tehn*
kiosk	kiosuku	*kee-oh-skoo*
market	ichiba	*ee-chee-bah*
monument	kinentō	*kee-nehn-tōh*
museum	bijutsukan	*bee-joo-tsoo-kahn*
park	kōen	*koh-ehn*
parking meter	chūsha mētā	*chōō-shah meh-tah*
parliament building	gijidō	*gee-jee-dōh*
public notices	kōji	*koh-jee*
public phone	kōshū denwa	*koh-shōō dehn-wah*
public washroom	kōshū benjo	*koh-shōō behn-joh*
railway crossing	fumikiri	*foo-mee-kee-ree*
shrine	jinja	*jeen-jah*
souvenir shop	omiyageya	*oh-mee-yah-geh-yah*
square	hiroba	*hee-roh-bah*
street	michi	*mee-chee*
• street sign	dōro hyōshiki	*doh-roh hyoh-shee-kee*
take an excursion	gurūpu tsuā ni sankasuru *(v)*	*goo-rōō-poo tsoo-ah nee sahn-kah-soo-roo*
temple	otera	*oh-teh-rah*
tower	tō	*toh*

| traffic light | shingō | *sheen-gōh* |
| water fountain | funsui | *foon-soo-ee* |

b. GETTING OUT OF THE CITY

beach	kaigan	*kah-ee-gahn*
• at the beach	kaigan de	*kah-ee-gahn deh*
boat	bōto	*boh-toh*
brook	ogawa	*oh-gah-wah __*
camping area	kyanpujō	*kyahn-poo-jōh*
canoe	kanū	*kah-nōō*
cruise	kurūzu	*koo-rōō-zoo*
fishing	tsuri	*tsoo-ree*
hiking	haikingu	*hah-ee-keen-goo*
hot-springs resort	onsenchi	*ohn-sehn-chee*
in the country	inaka de	*ee-nah-kah deh*
in the mountains	yama de	*yah-mah deh*
lake	mizuumi	*mee-zoo-oo-mee*
mountain boots	tozangutsu	*toh-zahn-goo-tsoo*
mountain climbing	tozan	*toh-zahn*
river	kawa	*kah-wah __*
scenic route	nagame no ii kōsu	*nah-gah-meh noh ēē kōh-soo*
sea	umi	*oo-mee*
skiing	sukī	*soo-kēē*
ski resort	sukījō	*soo-kēē-jōh*
sleeping bag	surīpingubaggu	*soo-rēē-peen-goo-bahg-goo*
suburb	kōgai	*koh-gah-ee*
tent	tento	*tehn-toh*
trip	ryokō	*ryoh-kōh*
vacation	bakansu	*BAH-kahn-soo*
village	mura	*moo-rah*

c. ASKING FOR DIRECTIONS

across ...	... o yokogitte	*... oh yoh-koh-geet-teh*
ahead ...	... no saki ni	*... noh sah-kee nee*
at the end of ...	... no owari ni	*... noh oh-wah-ree nee*
at the top of ...	... no ue ni	*... noh oo-eh nee*
back ...	... no ushiro ni	*... noh oo-shee-roh nee*
behind ...	... no kage ni	*... noh kah-geh nee*
cross (over) ...	... o yokogiru *(v)*	*... oh yoh-koh-gee-roo*
• cross the street	michi o yokogiru *(v)*	*mee-chee oh yoh-koh-gee-roo*
direction	hōkō	*hoh-kōh*

down ...	... o kudatta tokoro ni	... oh koo-daht-tah toh-koh-roh nee
enter	hairu (v)	hah-ee-roo
everywhere	doko demo (adv)	doh-koh deh-moh
exit, go out	deru (v)	deh-roo
far (from)	tōi (adj)	toh-ee
follow	tadotte iku (v)	tah-doht-teh ee-koo
go	iku (v)	ee-koo
go down	kudaru (v)	koo-dah-roo
go up	noboru (v)	noh-boh-roo
here	koko ni	koh-koh nee
in front of ...	... no mae ni	... noh mah-eh nee
inside ...	... no naka ni	... noh nah-kah-nee
near ...	... no chikaku ni	... noh chee-kah-koo nee
outside ...	... no soto ni	... noh soh-toh nee
straight ahead	kono mama massugu	koh-noh mah-mah mahs-soo-goo
there	soko ni	soh-koh nee
through ...	... o tootte	... o toh-oht-teh
to the east	higashi ni	hee-gah-shee nee
to the left	hidari ni	hee-dah-ree nee
to the north	kita ni	kee-tah nee
to the right	migi ni	mee-gee nee
to the south	minami ni	mee-nah-mee nee
to the west	nishi ni	nee-shee nee
toward ...	... no hō e	... noh hoh eh
turn	magaru (v)	mah-gah-roo

Can you tell me where...?	... ga doko ni aru ka oshiete kudasai.	... gah doh-koh nee ah-roo kah oh-shee-eh-teh koo-dah-sah-ee
How do you get to...?	... niwa, dō yatte ikimasu ka.	... nee-wah, DOH yaht-teh ee-kee-mahs kah
Where is...?	wa, doko desu ka.	... wah, DOH-koh dehs kah

SCHOOL AND WORK

37. SCHOOL

a. TYPES OF SCHOOLS AND GRADES

coed school	danjo kyōgaku no gakkō	*dahn-joh kyōh-gah-koo noh gahk-kōh*
conservatory	ongaku gakkō	*ohn-gah-koo gahk-kōh*
day care	takujisho	*tah-koo-jee-shoh*
elementary school	shōgakkō	*shoh-gahk-koh*
evening school	yagaku	*yah-gah-koo*
grade	gakunen	*gah-koo-nehn*
• grade one	ichīnen	*ee-chee-nehn*
• grade two	ninen	*nee-nehn*
graduate school	daigakuin	*dah-ee-gah-koo-een*
high school	kōkō	*koh-koh*
junior college	tandai	*tahn-dah-ee*
junior high school	chūgaku	*chōo-gah-koo*
kindergarten	yōchien	*yoh-chee-ehn*
nursery school	hoikuen	*hoh-ee-koo-ehn*
private school	shiritsu gakkō	*shee-ree-tsoo gahk-kōh*
technical/vocational school	shokugyō gakkō	*shoh-koo-gyoh gahk-kōh*
university	daigaku	*dah-ee-gah-koo*
women's college	joshidai	*joh-shee-dah-ee*
year (e.g., at university)	gakunen	*gah-koo-nehn*
• first year	ichinen	*ee-chee-nehn*
• second year	ninen	*nee-nehn*

b. THE CLASSROOM

assignment	shukudai	*shoo-koo-dah-ee*
assignment book	shukudai chō	*shoo-koo-dah-ee chōh*
atlas	chizu chō	*chee-zoo chōh*
ballpoint pen	bōrupen	*bōh-roo-pehn*
blackboard	kokuban	*koh-koo-bahn*
blackboard eraser	kokubankeshi	*koh-koo-bahn-keh-shee*
book	hon	*hohn*
bookcase	hondana	*hohn-dah-nah*
chalk	chōku	*chōh-koo*
compass	konpasu	*kohn-pah-soo*
computer	konpyūta	*kohn-pyōo-tah*
desk	tsukue	*tskoo-eh*
dictionary	jisho	*jee-shoh*
encyclopedia	hyakkajiten	*hyahk-kah-jee-tehn*

eraser	keshigomu	*keh-shee-goh-moo*
glue	nori	*noh-ree*
magazine	zasshi	*zahs-shee*
map	chizu	*chee-zoo*
notebook	chōmen	*choh-mehn*
overhead projector	ōbāheddo purojekutā	*oh-bah-hehd-doh poo-roh-jehk-tah*
paper	kami	*kah-mee*
pen	pen	*pehn*
pencil	enpitsu	*ehn-pee-tsoo*
pencil sharpener	enpitsukezuri	*ehn-pee-tsoo-keh-zoo-ree*
ruler	jōgi	*joh-gee*
school bag	tsūgaku kaban	*tsoo-gah-koo kah-bahn*
slide projector	suraido eishaki	*soo-rah-ee-doh eh-shah-kee*
textbook	kyōkasho	*kyoh-kah-shoh*
thumbtack	gabyō	*gah-byoh*

c. AREAS OF A SCHOOL

cafeteria	kafeteria	*kah-feh-teh-ree-ah*
campus	kōnai	*koh-nah-ee*
classroom	kyōshitsu	*kyoh-shee-tsoo*
dormitory	ryō/kishukusha	*ryoh/kee-shoo-koo-shah*
gymnasium	taiikukan	*tah-ee-ee-koo-kahn*
hallway	rōka	*roh-kah*
laboratory	jikkenshitsu	*jeek-kehn-shee-tsoo*
language laboratory	gaikokugo rabo	*gah-ee-koh-koo-goh rah-boh*
library	toshokan	*toh-shoh-kahn*
main office	jimushitsu	*jee-moo-shee-tsoo*
professor's office	kenkyūshitsu	*kehn-kyoo-shtsoo*
school yard	kōtei	*koh teh*
toilet	toire	*toh-ee-reh*

d. SCHOOL: PEOPLE

assistant	joshu	*joh-shoo*
class (of students)	gakkyū	*gahk-kyoo*
classmate	kyūyū	*kyoo-yoo*
dean	gakubuchō	*gah-koo-boo-choh*
janitor	yōmuin	*yoh-moo-een*
librarian	toshokan-in	*toh-shoh-kah-een*
president of a university	gakuchō	*gahk-choh*
principal	kōchō	*koh-choh*
professor	kyōju	*kyoh-joo*

pupil	seito	*seh-toh*
schoolmate	gakuyū	*gah-koo-yoo*
secretary	hisho	*hee-shoh*
student	gakusei	*gahk-seh*
teacher	kyōshi	*kyoh-shee*

e. SCHOOL: SUBJECTS

accounting	kaikeigaku	*kah-ee-keh-gah-koo*
anatomy	kaibōgaku	*kah-ee-boh-gah-koo*
anthropology	jinruigaku	*jeen-roo-ee-gah-koo*
archeology	kōkogaku	*koh-koh-gah-koo*
architecture	kenchikugaku	*kehn-chee-koo-gah-koo*
area studies	chiiki kenkyū	*chee-ee-kee kehn-kyoo*
art	bijutsu	*bee-joo-tsoo*
arts	kyōyō kamoku	*kyoh-yoh kah-moh-koo*
astronomy	tenmongaku	*tehn-mohn-gah-koo*
biology	seibutsugaku	*seh-boo-tsoo-gah-koo*
botany	shokubutsugaku	*shoh-koo-boo-tsoo-gah-koo*
calculus	bisekibungaku	*bee-seh-kee-boon-gah-koo*
chemistry	kagaku	*kah-gah-koo*
commerce	shōgyō	*shoh-gyoh*
computer science	konpyūta saiensu	*kohn-pyoo-tah sah-ee-ehn-soo*
economics	keizai	*keh-zah-ee*
engineering	kōgaku	*koh-gah-koo*
foreign languages	gaikokugo	*gah-ee-koh-koo-goh*
fine arts	bijutsu	*bee-joo-tsoo*
geography	chiri	*chee-ree*
geometry	kikagaku	*kee-kah-gah-koo*
history	rekishi	*reh-kee-shee*
humanities	jinbunkagaku	*jeen-boon-kah-gah-koo*
international relations	kokusai kankei	*kohk-sah-ee kahn-keh*
journalism	jānarizumu	*jah-nah-ree-zoo-moo*
law	hōgaku	*hoh-gah-koo*
linguistics	gengogaku	*gehn-goh-gah-koo*
literature	bungaku	*boon-gah-koo*
mathematics	sūgaku	*soo-gah-koo*
medicine	igaku	*ee-gah-koo*
music	ongaku	*ohn-gah-koo*
natural science	shizen kagaku	*shee-zehn kah-gah-koo*
philosophy	tetsugaku	*teh-tsoo-gah-koo*
physical education	taiiku	*tah-ee-ee-koo*
physics	butsurigaku	*boo-tsoo-ree-gah-koo*
physiology	seirigaku	*seh-ree-gah-koo*
political science	seijigaku	*seh-jee-gah-koo*
psychology	shinrigaku	*sheen-ree-gah-koo*

sciences	kagaku	*kah-gah-koo*
sociology	shakaigaku	*shah-kah-ee-gah-koo*
statistics	tōkeigaku	*toh-keh-gah-koo*
subject	gakka	*gahk-kah*
trigonometry	sankakuhō	*sahn-kahk-hoh*
zoology	dōbutsugaku	*doh-boo-tsoo-gah-koo*

f. ADDITIONAL SCHOOL VOCABULARY

> For concepts of thought, see Section 22.

answer	kotae	*koh-tah-eh*
• answer	kotaeru *(v)*	*koh-tah-eh-roo*
• brief	kantan na *(adj)*	*kahn-tahn nah*
• long	nagai *(adj)*	*nah-gah-ee*
• right	tadashii *(adj)*	*tah-dah-shee*
• short	mijikai *(adj)*	*mee-jee-kah-ee*
• wrong	machigatta *(adj)*	*mah-chee-gaht-tah*
assignments, homework	shukudai	*shoo-koo-dah-ee*
attend school	gakkō ni iku *(v)*	*gahk-koh nee ee-koo*
audit	chōkōsuru *(v)*	*choh-koh-soo-roo*
be absent	kesseki (desu)	*kehs-seh-kee (dehs)*
be present	shusseki (desu)	*shoos-seh-kee (dehs)*
be promoted	shinkyūsuru *(v)*	*sheen-kyoo-soo-roo*
class (of students)	gakkyū	*gahk-kyoo*
• lesson	jugyō	*joo-gyoh*
• skip a class	jugyō o saboru *(v)*	*joo-gyoh oh sah-boh-roo*
• skip school, play hooky	gakkō o saboru *(v)*	*gahk-koh oh sah-boh-roo*
• There is no class today.	Kyō wa, gakkō ga arimasen.	*kyoh wah, gahk-koh gah ah-ree-mah-sehn*
composition	sakubun	*sah-koo-boon*
copy	kakikata	*kah-kee-kah-tah*
• good, final copy	seisho	*seh-shoh*
• rough copy, draft	shitagaki	*shee-tah-gah-kee*
course	kamoku	*kah-moh-koo*
• take a course/ subject	kamoku o toru *(v)*	*kah-moh-koo oh toh-roo*
curriculum	karikyuramu	*kah-ree-kyoo-rah-moo*
degree (university)	gakui	*gah-koo-ee*
• master's degree	shūshigō	*shoo-shee-goh*
• doctorate	hakasekō	*hah-kah-seh-goh*
• get a degree	gakui o toru *(v)*	*gah-koo-ee oh toh-roo*
dictation	kakitori	*kah-kee-toh-ree*

diploma	sotsugyō shōsho	soh-tsoo-gyoh shoh-shoh
• get a diploma	sotsugyō shōsho o morau (v)	soh-tsoo-gyoh shoh-shoh oh moh-rah-oo
• high school diploma	kōkō no sotsugyō shōsho	koh-koh noh soh-tsoo-gyoh shoh-shoh
drop out	chūtaisuru (v)	choo-tah-ee-soo-roo
education	kyōiku	kyoh-ee-koo
error	machigai	mah-chee-gah-ee
essay	essei	ehs-seh
exam	shiken	shee-kehn
• entrance exam	nyūgaku shiken	nyoo-gah-koo shee-kehn
• fail an exam	shiken ni ochiru (v)	shee-kehn nee oh-chee-roo
• oral exam	mensetsu shiken	mehn-seh-tsoo shee-kehn
• pass an exam	shiken ni ukaru (v)	shee-kehn nee oo-kah-roo
• take an exam	shiken o ukeru (v)	shee-kehn oh oo-keh-roo
• written exam	hikki shiken	heek-kee shee-kehn
exercise	renshū mondai	rehn-shoo mohn-dah-ee
explanation	setsumei	seh-tsoo-meh
• explain	setsumeisuru (v)	seh-tsoo-meh-soo-roo
field of study	kenkyū bunya	kehn-kyoo boon-yah
give/hand back	kaesu (v)	kah-eh-soo
grade/mark	seiseki	seh-seh-kee
graduate	sotsugyōsuru (v)	soh-tsoo-gyoh-soo-roo
grammar	bunpō	boon-poh
learn	narau (v)	nah-rah-oo
lecture	kōgi	koh-gee
• lecture	kōgisuru (v)	koh-gee-soo-roo
listen to	kiku (v)	kee-koo
memorize	ankisuru (v)	ahn-kee-soo-roo
mistake	machigai	mah-chee-gah-ee
• make mistakes	machigaeru (v)	mah-chee-gah-eh-roo
note	nōto	noh-toh
• take notes	nōto o toru (v)	noh-toh oh toh-roo
problem	mondai	mohn-dah-ee
• solve a problem	mondai o toku (v)	mohn-dah-ee oh toh-koo
question	shitsumon	shee-tsoo-mohn
• ask a question	shitsumonsuru (v)	shee-tsoo-mohn-soo-roo
read	yomu (v)	yoh-moo
• reading passage	yomikata	yoh-mee-kah-tah
registration	tetsuzuki	teh-tsoo-zoo-kee
• registration fee	tetsuzuki ryō	teh-tsoo-zoo-kee ryoh
repeat	kurikaesu (v)	koo-ree-kah-eh-soo
report card	seisekihyō	seh-seh-kee-hyoh
review	fukushū	fkoo-shoo
• review	fukushūsuru (v)	fkoo-shoo-soo-roo
school	gakkō	gahk-koh

• finish school	gakkō o oeru (v)	gahk-kōh oh oh-eh-roo
• go to school	gakkō ni iku (v)	gahk-kōh nee ee-koo
study	benkyōsuru (v)	behn-kyoh-soo-roo
submit	teishutsusuru (v)	teh-shoo-tsoo-soo-roo
take attendance	shusseki o toru (v)	shoos-seh-kee oh toh-roo
teach	oshieru (v)	oh-shee-eh-roo
test	tesuto	tehs-toh
thesis	ronbun	rohn-boon
understand	rikaisuru (v)	ree-kah-ee-soo-roo
write	kaku (v)	kah-koo

38. WORK

a. JOBS AND PROFESSIONS

accountant	kaikeishi	kah-ee-kēh-shee
actor	dan-yū	dahn-yōō
actress	joyū	joh-yōō
architect	kenchikuka	kehn-chee-koo-kah
baker	panyaki no shokunin	pahn-yah-kee noh shoh-koo-neen
banker	ginkōka	geen-koh-kah
barber	rihatsushi	ree-hah-tsoo-shee
bookseller	hon-ya	hohn-yah
builder	kenchikugyōsha	kehn-chee-koo-gyoh-shah
bus driver	basu no untenshu	bah-soo noh oon-tehn-shoo
businessman	bijinesuman	bee-jee-neh-soo-mahn
businesswoman	bijinesuūman	bee-jee-neh-soo-ōō-mahn
butcher	nikuya	nee-koo-yah
cabin attendant	kyakushitsu jōmuin	kyahk-shee-tsoo jōh-moo-een
carpenter	daiku	dah-ee-koo
chemist	kagakusha	kah-gahk-shah
construction worker	kenchikugenba no sagyōin	kehn-chee-koo-gehn-bah noh sah-gyoh-een
consultant	konsarutanto	kohn-sah-roo-tahn-toh
cook	chōrishi	choh-ree-shee
dentist	haisha	hah-ee-shah
doctor	isha	ee-shah
editor	henshūsha	hehn-shōō-shah
electrician	denkikō	dehn-kee-kōh
engineer	gishi	gee-shee
eye doctor	meisha	meh-ee-shah
factory worker	kōin	kōh-een
farmer	nōgyō jūjisha	nōh-gyoh jōō-jee-shah
firefighter	shōbōshi	shoh-boh-shee
fishmonger	sakanaya	sah-kah-nah-yah

florist	hanaya	*hah-nah-yah*
government worker	kōmuin	*koh-moo-een*
• national government worker	kokka kōmuin	*kohk-kah koh-moo-een*
• local government worker	chihō kōmuin	*chee-hoh koh-moo-een*
hairdresser	biyōshi	*bee-yoh-shee*
jeweler	hōsekishō	*hoh-seh-kee-shoh*
job	shigoto	*shee-goh-toh*
journalist	jānarisuto	*jah-nah-ree-stoh*
lawyer	bengoshi	*behn-goh-shee*
librarian	toshokan-in	*toh-shoh-kahn-een*
mechanic	jidōsha shūrikō	*jee-doh-shah shoo-ree-koh*
movie director	eiga kantoku	*eh-gah kahn-toh-koo*
musician	ongakuka	*ohn-gahk-kah*
nurse	kangoshī	*kahn-goh-shee*
occupation	shokugyō	*shoh-koo-gyoh*
office worker (male)	sararīman	*sah-rah-ree-mahn*
office worker (female)	ōeru	*oh-eh-roo*
painter (artist)	gaka	*gah-kah*
painter (of buildings, rooms)	penkiya	*pehn-kee-yah*
pharmacist	yakuzaishi	*yah-koo-zah-ee-shee*
photographer	shashinka	*shah-sheen-kah*
pilot	pairotto	*pah-ee-roht-toh*
plumber	haikankō	*hah-ee-kahn-koh*
police officer (female)	fujinkeikan	*foo-jeen-keh-kahn*
police officer (male)	keikan	*keh-kahn*
politician	seijika	*seh-jee-kah*
professor	kyōju	*kyoh-joo*
profession	shokugyō	*shoh-koo-gyoh*
professional	puro no *(adj)*	*poo-roh noh*
programmer	puroguramā	*poo-roh-goo-rah-mah*
psychiatrist	seishinkai	*seh-sheen-kah-ee*
psychologist	shinrigakusha	*sheen-ree-gahk-shah*
real estate agent	fudōsan assennin	*foo-doh-sahn ahs-sehn-neen*
researcher	kenkyūin	*kehn-kyoo-een*
sailor	sen-in	*sehn-een*
sales representative	hanbaiin / ten-in	*hahn-bah-ee-een/tehn-een*
scientist	kagakusha	*kah-gah-koo-shah*
secretary	hisho	*hee-shoh*
singer	kashu	*kah-shoo*
social worker	sōsharu wākā	*soh-shah-roo wah-kah*
soldier	heishi	*heh-shee*
stockbroker	kabu no burōkā	*kah-boo noh boo-roh-kah*

store clerk	ten-in	*tehn-een*
storekeeper	tenshu	*tehn-shoo*
surgeon	gekai	*geh-kah-ee__*
surveyor	sokuryōshi	*soh-koo-ryoh-shee*
tailor	shitateya	*shee-tah-teh-yah*
taxi driver	takushī no untenshu	*tahk-shēē noh oon-tehn-shoo*
teacher	kyōshi	*kyoh-shee*
tour guide	tsuā gaido	*tsoo-ah gah-ee-doh*
truck driver	torakku no untenshu	*toh-rahk-koo noh oon-tehn-shoo*
waiter	uētā	*oo-eh-tah*
waitress	uētoresu	*oo-eh-toh-rehs*
writer	sakka	*sahk-kah*

b. INTERVIEWING FOR A JOB

See also Section 11f, Basic Personal Information.

<u>Name</u>	namae	*nah-mah-eh*
first name	namae	*nah-mah-eh*
	mei	*meh*
surname, family name	myōji	*myoh-jee*
	sei	*seh__*
signature	shomei	*shoh-meh*
<u>Address</u>	jūsho	*joo-shoh*
number	banchi	*bahn-chee*
street	tōri / gai	*toh-ree/gah-ee*
city	shi	*shee*
prefecture	ken	*kehn*
state	shū	*shoo*
ward	ku	*koo*
zip code	yūbin bangō	*yoo-been bahn-goh__*
<u>Telephone Number</u>	denwa bangō	*dehn-wah bahn-goh*
area code	shigai kyokuban	*shee-gah-ee kyoh-koo-bahn*
extension	naisen	*nah-ee-sehn*
fax number	fakkusu bangō	*fahk-koo-soo bahn-goh__*
<u>E-mail</u>	īmēru	*ee-meh-roo*
<u>Date and Place of Birth</u>	seinengappi to shusseichi	*seh-nehn-gahp-pee toh shoos-seh-chee*
date	seinengappi	*seh-nehn-gahp-pee*
day	hi	*hee*
month	tsuki	*tsoo-kee__*
place	shusseichi	*shoos-seh-chee*

year	toshi	*toh-shee*
<u>Age</u>	nenrei	*nehn-reh*
<u>Sex</u>	seibetsu	*seh-beh-tsoo*
male	otoko	*oh-toh-koh*
female	onna	*ohn-nah*
<u>Marital Status</u>	kekkon shikaku	*kehk-kohn shee-kah-koo*
divorced	rikon	*ree-kohn*
married	kikon	*kee-kohn*
single	dokushin	*doh-koo-sheen*
<u>Nationality</u>	kokuseki	*kohk-seh-kee*

See also Section 30d—Nationalities and Languages.

<u>Education</u>	gakureki	*gah-koo-reh-kee*
elementary school	shōgakkō	*shoh-gahk-koh*
junior high school	chūgaku	*choo-gah-koo*
high school	kōkō	*koh-koh*
junior college	tandai	*tahn-dah-ee*
university	daigaku	*dah-ee-gah-koo*
graduate school	daigakuin	*dah-ee-gah-koo-een*
major	senkō	*sehn-koh*
<u>Profession</u>	shokureki	*shoh-koo-reh-kee*
<u>Résumé</u>	rirekisho	*ree-reh-kee-shoh*
<u>References</u>	shin-yō shōkaisaki	*sheen-yoh shoh-kah-ee-sah-kee*
<u>Special Skills</u>	tokugi	*toh-koo-gee*

c. THE OFFICE

See also Sections 20 and 25.

adhesive tape	setchaku tēpu	*seht-chah-koo teh-poo*
appointment book	yotei hyō	*yoh-teh hyoh*
briefcase	atasshe kēsu	*ah-tahs-sheh keh-soo*
calendar	karendā	*kah-rehn-dah*
chair	isu	*ee-soo*
computer	konpyūta	*kohn-pyoo-tah*
fax	fakkusu	*fahk-koos*
file	bunsho fairu	*boon-shoh fah-ee-roo*
file card	fairu yō kādo	*fah-ee-roo yoh kah-doh*
shredder	shureddā	*shoo-rehd-dah*
pen	pen	*pehn*
pencil	enpitsu	*ehn-pee-tsoo*

photocopier	fukushaki	*fkoo-shah-kee*
printer	purinta	*poo-reen-tah*
projector	purojekuta	*poo-roh-jehk-tah*
ruler	jōgi	*joh-gee*
scanner	sukyana	*skyah-nah*
scissors	hasami	*hah-sah-mee*
staple	hotchikisu no hari	*hoht-chee-kee-soo noh hah-ree*
stapler	hotchikisu	*hoht-chee-kee-soo*
telephone	denwa	*dehn-wah*
thumbtack	gabyō	*gah-byoh*
wastebasket	kuzukago	*koo-zoo-kah-goh*

d. ADDITIONAL WORK VOCABULARY

advertising	kōkoku	*koh-koh-koo*
annual leave	nenji yūkyū kyūka	*nehn-jee yoo-kyoo kyoo-kah*
bankruptcy	hasan	*hah-sahn*
• go bankrupt	hasansuru *(v)*	*hah-sahn-soo-roo*
benefit	onkei	*ohn-keh*
be transferred	tenkinsuru *(v)*	*tehn-keen-soo-roo*
boss (in an office)	jōshi	*joh-shee*
branch	shiten	*shee-tehn*
break	kyūkei	*kyoo-keh*
career	keireki	*keh-reh-kee*
classified ad	kōmokubetsu kōkoku	*koh-moh-koo-beh-tsoo koh-koh-koo*
colleague	dōryō	*doh-ryoh*
commerce	shōgyō	*shoh-gyoh*
company	kaisha	*kah-ee-shah*
company policy	shasoku	*shah-soh-koo*
contract	keiyaku	*keh-yah-koo*
earn	kasegu *(v)*	*kah-seh-goo*
employ	yatou *(v)*	*yah-toh-oo*
employee	shain	*shah-een*
	jūgyōin	*joo-gyoh-een*
employer	koyōsha	*koh-yoh-shah*
employment agency	shokugyō shōkaisho	*shoh-koo-gyoh shoh-kah-ee-shoh*
factory	kōjō	*koh-joh*
fire (dismiss)	kaikosuru *(v)*	*kah-ee-koh-soo-roo*
hire	yatou *(v)*	*yah-toh-oo*
job description	shokumu naiyō	*shoh-koo-moo nah-ee-yoh*
labor union	rōdō kumiai	*roh-doh koo-mee-ah-ee*
• union member	kumiaiin	*koo-mee-ah-ee-een*
layoff	ichiji kaiko	*ee-chee-jee kah-ee-koh*

lifetime job security	shūshin koyō seido	*shōō-sheen koh-yōh seh-doh*
lunch break	ranchi no kyūkei	*rahn-chee noh kyōō-keh*
manager	manējā	*mah-neh-jah*
market	shijō	*shee-joh*
maternity leave	shussan kyūka/ sankyū	*shoos-sahn kyōō-kah/ sahn-kyōō*
meeting room	kaigishitsu	*kah-ee-gee-shee-tsoo*
negotiation(s)	kōshō	*koh-shoh*
office	ofisu	*oh-fee-soo*
overtime work	zangyō	*zahn-gyōh*
• work overtime	zangyōsuru *(v)*	*zahn-gyōh-soo-roo*
payday	kyūryōbi	*kyōō-ryoh-bee*
pension	nenkin	*nehn-keen*
plant	kōjō	*koh-joh*
promotion	shōshin	*shoh-sheen*
retirement	taishoku	*tah-ee-shoh-koo*
• retire	taishokusuru *(v)*	*tah-ee-shoh-koo-soo-roo*
• retirement money	taishoku kin	*tah-ee-shoh-koo keen*
salary	kyūryō	*kyōō-ryōh*
seniority system	nenkōjoretsu sei	*nehn-koh-joh-reh-tsoo seh*
sick leave	byōki kyūka	*byoh-kee kyōō-kah*
starting salary	shoninkyū	*shoh-neen-kyōō*
subordinate	buka	*boo-kah*
take-home pay	tedori no kyūryō	*teh-doh-ree noh kyōō-ryōh*
temporary	rinji yatoi	*reen-jee yah-toh-ee*
unemployment	shitsugyō	*shee-tsoo-gyōh*
unemployment compensation	shitsugyō teate	*shee-tsoo-gyōh teh-ah-teh*
wage	chingin	*cheen-geen*
warehouse	sōko	*soh-koh*
work	shigoto	*shee-goh-toh*
• work	hataraku *(v)*	*hah-tah-rah-koo*
working hours	rōdō jikan	*roh-doh jee-kahn*

EMERGENCIES

39. REPORTING AN EMERGENCY

a. FIRE

ambulance	kyūyūsha	kyōo-kyōo-shah
arson	hōka	hoh-kah
building	biru	bee-roo
burn (injury)	yakedo	yah-keh-doh
burn (on fire)	moeru *(vi)*	moh-eh-roo
call	denwasuru *(v)*	dehn-wah-soo-roo
catch fire	hi ga tsuku	HEE gah tsoo-koo
danger	kiken	kee-kehn
destroy	hakaisuru *(v)*	hah-kah-ee-soo-roo
emergency exit	hijōguchi	hee-jōh-goo-chee
escape, get out	nogareru *(v)*	noh-gah-reh-roo
extinguish, put out	kesu *(v)*	keh-soo
fire	kaji	kah-jee
• be on fire	moete iru	moh-eh-teh ee-roo
• Fire!	Kaji da.	KAH-jee dah
• fire alarm	kasai hōchiki	kah-sah-ee hōh-chee-kee
• fire department	shōbōsho	shoh-boh-shoh
• fire engine	shōbōsha	shoh-boh-shah
• fire extinguisher	shōkaki	shoh-kah-kee
• firefighter	shōbōshi	shoh-boh-shee
• fire hose	shōka yō hōsu	shoh-kah yoh hoh-soo
• fire hydrant	shōkasen	shoh-kah-sehn
fireproof	taikasei no *(adj)*	tah-ee-kah-seh noh
first aid	ōkyū teate	oh-kyōo teh-ah-teh
flame	honoo	hoh-noh-oh
help	tasuke	tahs-keh
• help	tasukeru *(v)*	tahs-keh-roo
• Help!	Tasukete.	tahs-KEH-teh
• give help	tasukete ageru	tahs-keh-teh ah-geh-roo
ladder	hashigo	hah-shee-goh
out	soto e *(adv)*	soh-toh eh
• Everybody out!	Soto e dete kudasai.	soh-toh eh DEH-teh koo-dah-sah-ee
protect	fusegu *(v)*	foo-seh-goo
rescue	kyūjo	kyōo-joh
shout	sakebi	sah-keh-bee
• shout	sakebu *(v)*	sah-keh-boo
siren	sairen	sah-ee-rehn
smoke	kemuri	keh-moo-ree

| spark | hinoko | *hee-noh-koh* |
| victim | giseisha | *gee-seh-shah* |

b. ROBBERY AND ASSAULT

accomplice	kyōhan	*kyoh-hahn*
argue	iiarasou (v)	*ee-ah-rah-soh-oo*
arrest	taiho	*tah-ee-hoh*
• arrest	taihosuru (v)	*tah-ee-hoh-soo-roo*
assault	osou (v)	*oh-soh-oo*
catch	tsukamaeru (v)	*tskah-mah-eh-roo*
chase	oikakeru (v)	*oh-ee-kah-keh-roo*
Come quickly!	Isoide kite.	*ee-SOH-ee-deh kee-teh*
crime	hanzai	*hahn-zah-ee*
• criminal	hanzaisha	*hahn-zah-ee-shah*
description	ninsōgaki	*neen-soh-gah-kee*
escape	tōbōsuru (v)	*toh-boh-soo-roo*
eyewitness	mokugekisha	*moh-koo-geh-kee-shah*
fight	kakutō	*kahk-toh*
firearm	kaki	*KAH-kee*
getaway car	tobō yō no kuruma	*toh-boh yoh noh koo-roo-mah*
gun	jū	*joo*
handcuffs	tejō	*teh-joh*
hurry	isogu (v)	*ee-soh-goo*
injure, wound	kegasaseru (vt)	*keh-gah-sah-seh-roo*
• injury, wound	kega	*keh-gah*
kill	korosu (v)	*koh-roh-soo*
• killer	satsujinsha	*sah-tsoo-jeen-shah*
knife	naifu	*nah-ee-foo*
murder	satsujin	*sah-tsoo-jeen*
• murder	korosu (v)	*koh-roh-soo*
murderer	satsujinsha	*sah-tsoo-jeen-shah*
pickpocket	suri	*soo-ree*
police	keisatsu	*keh-sah-tsoo*
• policeman	keikan	*keh-kahn*
• policewoman	fujinkeikan	*foo-jeen-keh-kahn*
• call the police	keisatsu o yobu (v)	*keh-sah-tsoo oh yoh-boo*
rape	gōkan	*goh-kahn*
• rape	gōkansuru (v)	*goh-kahn-soo-roo*
rifle	raifuru	*rah-ee-foo-roo*
rob	ubau (v)	*oo-bah-oo*
• robber	gōtō	*goh-toh*
• armed robbery	busō gōtō	*boo-soh-goh-toh*
• robbery	gōtō	*goh-toh*
• Stop thief!	Dorobō.	*doh-roh-boh*
steal	nusumu (v)	*noo-soo-moo*

suspect	yōgisha	yōh-gee-shah
thief	dorobō	doh-roh-bōh
victim	higaisha	hee-gah-ee-shah
violence	bōryoku	bōh-ryoh-koo
weapon	kyōki	kyōh-kee
• shoot	utsu (v)	oo-tsoo
witness	mokugekisuru (v)	moh-koo-geh-kee-soo-roo

c. TRAFFIC ACCIDENTS

accident	jiko	jee-koh
• serious accident	daijiko	dah-ee-jee-koh
• traffic accident	kōtsū jiko	kōh-tsōo jee-koh
ambulance	kyūkyūsha	kyōo-kyōo-shah
• call an ambulance	kyūkyūsha o yobu (v)	kyōo-kyōo-shah oh yoh-boo
be run over	hikareru (v)	hee-kah-reh-roo
bleed	shukketsusuru (v)	shook-keh-tsoo-soo-roo
• blood	chi	chee
broken bone	kossetsu	kohs-seh-tsoo
bump	kobu	koh-boo
collision	shōtotsu	shōh-toh-tsoo
• collide	shōtotsusuru (v)	shōh-tohts-soo-roo
crash	shōtotsu	shōh-toh-tsoo
• crash	shōtotsusuru (v)	shōh-tohts-soo-roo
doctor	isha	ee-shah
• get a doctor	isha o yobu (v)	ee-shah oh yoh-boo
first aid	ōkyū teate	ōh-kyōo teh-ah-teh
• antiseptic	shōdokuyaku	shōh-doh-koo-yah-koo
• bandage	hōtai	hōh-tah-ee
• gauze	gāze	gāh-zeh
• splint	fukuboku	fkoo-boh-koo
Help!	Tasuketē.	tahs-KEH-teh
hospital	byōin	byōh-een
• emergency hospital	kyūkyū byōin	kyōo-kyōo byōh-een
• X-rays	rentogen	rehn-toh-gehn
insurance	hoken	hoh-kehn
• auto insurance	jidōsha hoken	jee-dōh-shah hoh-kehn
• health insurance	kenkō hoken	kehn-kōh hoh-kehn
police	keisatsu	kēh-sah-tsoo
• call the police	keisatsu o yobu (v)	kēh-sah-tsoo oh yoh-boo
shock	shokku	shohk-koo
whiplash	muchiuchishō	moo-chee-oo-chee-shōh
wound, injury	kega	keh-gah

40. MEDICAL CARE

a. THE DOCTOR

See also Section 12 — The Body.

AIDS	eizu	*eh-ee-zoo*
abortion	chūzetsu	*chōō-zeh-tsoo*
acne	nikibi	*nee-kee-bee*
addiction	chūdoku	*chōō-doh-koo*
allergy	arerugī	*ah-reh-roo-gēē*
anemia	hinketsu	*heen-keh-tsoo*
appendicitis	mōchōen	*moh-choh-ehn*
• **appendix**	mōchō	*moh-choh*
appointment	yoyaku	*yoh-yah-koo*
arrhythmia	fuseimyaku	*foo-seh-myah-koo*
arteriosclerosis	dōmyakukōkashō	*doh-myah-koo-kōh-kah-shōh*
artery	dōmyaku	*doh-myah-koo*
arthritis	kansetsuen	*kahn-seh-tsoo-ehn*
aspirin	asupirin	*ahs-pee-reen*
asthma	zensoku	*zehn-soh-koo*
bacteria	bakuteria	*bah-koo-teh-ree-ah*
backache	yōtsū	*yoh-tsōō*
bandage	hōtai	*hoh-tah-ee*
• **bandage**	hōtai o maku *(v)*	*hoh-tah-ee oh mah-koo*
benign	ryōsei *(adj)*	*ryoh-seh*
blood	ketsueki	*keh-tsoo-eh-kee*
• **blood pressure**	ketsuatsu	*keh-tsoo-ah-tsoo*
• **blood test**	ketsueki kensa	*keh-tsoo-eh-kee kehn-sah*
bone	hone	*hoh-neh*
brain	nō	*nōh*
bronchitis	kikanshien	*kee-kahn-shee-ehn*
bruise	dabokushō	*dah-boh-koo-shōh*
cancer	gan	*gahn*
capsule	kapuseru	*kah-poo-seh-roo*
cataract	hakunaishō	*hah-koo-nah-ee-shōh*
chicken pox	mizubōsō	*mee-zoo-bōh-soh*
chill	okan	*oh-kahn*
cold	kaze	*kah-zeh*
colitis	daichōen	*dah-ee-chōh-ehn*
concussion	nōshintō	*noh-sheen-toh*
constipation	benpi	*behn-pee*
convalescence	kaifuku	*kah-ee-foo-koo*
cough	seki	*seh-kee*

• cough	seki o suru *(v)*	seh-kee oh soo-roo __
CPR	shinpaisoseihō	sheen-pah-ee-soh-seh-hoh
cure	ryōhō	ryoh-hoh
• cure	naosu *(vt)*	nah-oh-soo
• get cured	yokunaru *(v)*	yoh-koo-nah-roo
cyst	nōshu	noh-shoo
defibrillator	jo saidō ki	joh sah-ee-doh kee __
dehydration	dassui shōjō	dahs-soo-ee shoh-joh
depression	utsubyō	oo-tsoo-byoh
dermatitis	hifuen	hee-foo-ehn __
diabetes	tōnyōbyō	toh-nyoh-byoh
diagnosis	shindan	sheen-dahn
diarrhea	geri	geh-ree
digestive system	shōka keitō	shoh-kah keh-toh __ __
• anus	kōmon	koh-mohn
• defecate	haibensuru *(v)*	hah-ee-behn-soo-roo
• intestine	chō	choh
• large intestine	daichō	dah-ee-choh
• rectum	chokuchō	chohk-choh
• small intestine	shōchō	shoh-choh
• stomach	i	ee
• have a stomachache	i ga itai	ee gah ee-tah-ee
dislocation	dakkyū	dahk-kyoo
dizziness	memai	meh-mah-ee
doctor	isha	ee-shah __
doctor's instruments	shinryō kigu	sheen-ryoh kee-goo
• electrocardiograph	shindenkei	sheen-dehn-kei
• stethoscope	chōshinki	choh-sheen-kee
• syringe	chūshaki	choo-shah-kee __
• thermometer	taionkei	tah-ee-ohn-keh
doctor's visit	ōshin	oh-sheen
drowsiness	nemuke	neh-moo-keh
drug addiction	mayaku chūdoku	mah-yah-koo choo-doh-koo
EMT	kyūkyū kyūmei shi	kyoo-kyoo kyoo-meh shee
examine (medically)	shinsatsusuru *(v)*	sheen-sahts-soo-roo
• get examined	shinsatsu o ukeru *(v)*	sheen-sah-tsoo oh oo-keh-roo
eye doctor	me isha	meh ee-shah
• contact lenses	kontakuto renzu	kohn-tahk-toh rehn-zoo
• eyeglasses	megane	meh-gah-neh
• eyesight	shiryoku	shee-ryoh-koo
faint	shisshin	shees-sheen
feel	kanji ga suru	kahn-jee gah soo-roo
• feel bad	kibun ga warui	kee-boon gah wah-roo-ee
• feel well	kibun ga ii	kee-boon gah ee
• strong	genki na *(adj)*	gehn-kee nah

• weak	yowayowashii *(adj)*	*yoh-wah-yoh-wah-shee*
• How do you feel?	Kibun wa, dō desu ka.	*kee-boon wah, DOH dehs kah*
fever	netsu	*neh-tsoo*
flu	ryūkan	*ryoo-kahn*
food poisoning	shokuchūdoku	*shoh-koo-choo-doh-koo*
fracture	kossetsu	*kohs-seh-tsoo*
gallstones	tanseki	*TAHN-seh-kee*
glaucoma	ryokunaishō	*ryoh-koo-nah-ee-shoh*
gynecologist	fujinnkai	*foo-jeen-kah-ee*
headache	zutsū	*zoo-tsoo*
• have a headache	zutsū ga suru	*zoo-tsoo gah soo-roo*
heal	naoru *(v)*	*nah-oh-roo*
health	kenkō	*kehn-koh*
• healthy	kenkō na *(adj)*	*kehn-koh nah*
heart	shinzō	*sheen-zoh*
• heart attack	shinzō mahi	*sheen-zoh mah-hee*
heartburn	muneyake	*moo-neh-yah-keh*
hemorrhage	shukketsu	*shook-keh-tsoo*
hemorrhoids	ji	*jee*
herpes	herupesu	*heh-roo-pehs*
high blood pressure	kōketsuatsu	*koh-keh-tsoo-ah-tsoo*
HIV	eizu uirusu	*eh-ee-zoo oo-ee-roo-soo*
HIV-positive	eizu uirusu ga yōsei no *(adj)*	*eh-ee-zoo oo-ee-roo-soo gah yoh-seh noh*
hurt	itamu *(v)*	*ee-tah-moo*
incontinence	shikkin	*sheek-keen*
indigestion	shōka furyō	*shoh-kah foo-ryoh*
infection	kanō	*kah-noh*
inflammation	enshō	*ehn-shoh*
injection	chūsha	*choo-shah*
insomnia	fuminshō	*foo-meen-shoh*
insulin	inshurin	*een-shoo-reen*
itch	kayumi	*kah-yoo-mee*
kidney stone	jinzō kesseki	*jeen-zoh kehs-seh-kee*
laryngitis	kōtōen	*koh-toh-ehn*
leukemia	hakketsubyō	*hahk-keh-tsoo-byoh*
lymphatic system	rinpasen	*reen-pah-sehn*
malignant	akusei *(adj)*	*ah-koo-seh*
measles	hashika	*hah-shee-kah*
medicine (one takes)	kusuri	*koo-soo-ree*
mumps	otafukukaze	*oh-tah-foo-koo-kah-zeh*
muscle	kinniku	*keen-nee-koo*
nausea	hakike	*hah-kee-keh*
nerves	shinkei	*sheen-keh*
nurse	kangoshi	*kahn-goh-shee*
obstetrician	sankai	*sahn-kah-ee*

operation	shujutsu	shoo-joo-tsoo
• operating room	shujutsushitsu	shoo-joo-tsoo-shee-tsoo
optician	megane ya	meh-gah-neh yah
optometrist	kengan-i	kehn-gahn-ee
orthopedic surgeon	seikeigekai	seh-keh-geh-kah-ee
oxygen	sanso	sahn-soh
pain	itami	ee-tah-mee
• painful	itai (adj)	ee-tah-ee
• painkiller	chintsūzai	cheen-tsoo-zah-ee
pale	aozameta (adj)	ah-oh-zah-meh-tah
patient	kanja	kahn-jah
pediatrician	shōnikai	shoh-nee-kah-ee
pill	ganyaku	gahn-yah-koo
pimple	nikibi	nee-kee-bee
pneumonia	haien	hah-ee-ehn
pregnant	ninshinchū no (adj)	neen-sheen-choo noh
prognosis	yogoshindan	yoh-goh-sheen-dahn
prescription	shohōsen	shoh-hoh-sehn
psychiatrist	seishinkai	seh-sheen-kah-ee
pulse	myaku	myah-koo
pus	umi	oo-mee
radiologist	hōshasen-ishi	hoh-shah-sehn-ee-shee
rash	hasshin	hahs-sheen
recover	kaifukusuru (v)	kah-ee-foo-koo-soo-roo
respiratory system	kokyū keitō	koh-kyoo keh-toh
• breath	kokyū	koh-kyoo
• breathe	kokyūsuru (v)	koh-kyoo-soo-roo
• be out of breath	iki ga kireru	ee-kee gah kee-reh-roo
• lung	hai	hah-ee
• nostril	bikō	bee-koh
rheumatism	ryūmachi	ryoo-mah-chee
sedative	chinseizai	cheen-seh-zah-ee
shingles	taijōhōshin	tah-ee-joh-hoh-sheen
sick	byōki no (adj)	byoh-kee noh
• get sick	byōki ni naru (v)	byoh-kee nee nah-roo
• sickness, disease	byōki	byoh-kee
sneeze	kushami	koo-shah-mee
• sneeze	kushami o suru (v)	koo-shah-mee oh soo-roo
sore back	kata no kori	kah-tah noh koh-ree
sore/stiff neck	kubi no kori	koo-bee noh koh-ree
sore throat	inkōen	een-koh-ehn
spasm	keiren	keh-rehn
specialist	senmonka	sehn-mohn-kah
sprain	nenza	nehn-zah
stitch	nuu (v)	noo-oo
stomachache	fukutsū	fook-tsoo
stress	sutoresu	stoh-rehs

stroke	nōsotchū	noh-soht-choo
suffer	kurushimu (v)	koo-roo-shee-moo
sunstroke	nisshabyō	nees-shah-byoh
suppository	zayaku	zah-yah-koo
surgeon	gekai	geh-kah-ee
• surgery	shujutsu	shoo-joo-tsoo
swollen	hareta (adj)	hah-reh-tah
symptom	shōjō	shoh-joh
syphilis	baidoku	bah-ee-doh-koo
tablet	jōzai	joh-zah-ee
temperature (fever)	netsu	neh-tsoo
• take one's		
• temperature	netsu o hakaru (v)	neh-tsoo oh hah-kah-roo
throat	nodo	noh-doh
• have a sore throat	nodo ga itamu	noh-doh gah ee-tah-moo
throw up	haku (v)	HAH-koo
tonsils	hentōsen	hehn-toh-sehn
tumor	shuyō	shoo-yoh
ulcer	ikaiyō	ee-kah-ee-yoh
urinary system	hinyō keitō	hee-nyoh keh-toh
• kidney	jinzō	jeen-zoh
• urinate	hainyōsuru (v)	hah-ee-nyoh-soo-roo
urologist	hinyōkikai	hee-nyoh-kee-kah-ee
vaccination	yobōsesshu	yoh-boh-sehs-shoo
vein	jōmyaku	joh-myah-koo
venereal disease	seibyō	seh-byoh
virus	uirusu	oo-ee-roo-soo
vomit	haku (v)	HAH-koo
wheelchair	kurumaisu	koo-roo-mah-ee-soo
whooping cough	hyakunichizeki	hyah-koo-nee-chee-zeh-kee

b. THE DENTIST

anesthetic	masui	mah-soo-ee
appointment	yoyaku	yoh-yah-koo
brace	shiretsu kyōseiki	shee-reh-tsoo kyoh-seh-kee
cavity, tooth decay	mushiba	moo-shee-bah
clean, brush (teeth)	ha o migaku (v)	hah oh mee-gah-koo
crown	shikan	shee-kahn
dental hygiene	shika eisei	shee-kah eh-seh
dentist	haisha	hah-ee-shah
• at the dentist's	haisha de	hah-ee-shah deh
• dentist's office	haisha no shinryōsho	hah-ee-shah noh sheen-ryoh-shoh
denture, false teeth	ireba	ee-reh-bah
drill	doriru	doh-ree-roo
examine	shiraberu (v)	shee-rah-beh-roo

extract, pull	nuku (v)	noo-koo
• extraction	basshi	bahs-shee
filling	tsumemono	tsoo-meh-moh-noh
mouth	kuchi	koo-chee
• gums	haguki	hah-goo-kee
• jaw	ago	ah-goh
• lip	kuchibiru	kchee-bee-roo
• Open your mouth!	Kuchi o, akete kudasai.	koo-chee oh, ah-keh-teh koo-dah-sah-ee
• palate	kōgai	koh-gah-ee
• tongue	shita	shtah
office hours	shinryō jikan	sheen-ryoh jee-kahn
plaque	shikō	shee-koh
rinse	kuchi o susugu (v)	koo-chee oh soo-soo-goo
tartar	shiseki	shee-seh-kee
tooth	ha	hah
• canine	kenshi	kehn-shee
• incisor	monba	mohn-bah
• molar	kyūshi	kyoo-shee
• root	shikon	shee-kohn
• wisdom tooth	oyashirazu	oh-yah-shee-rah-zoo
toothache	shitsū	shee-tsoo
• have a toothache	ha ga itamu	hah gah ee-tah-moo
• My tooth hurts!	Ha ga, itai desu.	hah gah, ee-tah-ee dehs
• Which tooth hurts?	Dono ha ga, itamimasu ka.	DOH-noh hah gah, ee-tah-mee-mahs kah
toothbrush	haburashi	hah-boo-rah-shee
toothpaste	nerihamigaki	neh-ree-hah-mee-gah-kee
X-rays	rentogen	rehn-toh-gehn

41. LEGAL MATTERS

accusation	kokuhatsu	koh-koo-hah-tsoo
• accuse	kokuhatsusuru (v)	koh-koo-hah-tsoo-soo-roo
• accused person	hikoku	hee-koh-koo
• accuser	kokuhatsunin	koh-koo-hah-tsoo-neen
acquit	muzai o hanketsusuru (v)	moo-zah-ee oh hahn-keh-tsoo-soo-roo
admit	mitomeru (v)	mee-toh-meh-roo
agree	gōisuru (v)	goh-ee-soo-roo
appeal	jōkokusuru (v)	joh-kohk-soo-roo
arbitration	chōtei	choh-teh
attorney	bengoshi	behn-goh-shee
bail	hoshaku	hoh-shah-koo
capital punishment	shikei	shee-keh
charge	kokuhatsusuru (v)	koh-koo-hah-tsoo-soo-roo
chief of police	keisatsu shochō	keh-sah-tsoo shoh-choh
client	irainin	ee-rah-ee-neen

confess	jihakusuru *(v)*	*jee-hahk-soo-roo*
• confession	jihaku	*jee-hah-koo*
convince	kakushinsaseru *(v)*	*kahk-sheen-sah-seh-roo*
court	saibansho	*sah-ee-bahn-shoh*
• court of appeal	kōsoin	*koh-soh-een*
• supreme court	saikō saibansho	*sah-ee-koh sah-ee-bahn-shoh*
courtroom	hōtei	*hoh-teh*
debate	tōron	*toh-rohn*
• debate	tōronsuru *(v)*	*toh-rohn-soo-roo*
decision	hanketsu	*hahn-keh-tsoo*
• final decision	saishū kettei	*sah-ee-shoo keht-teh*
• interim decision	kari kettei	*kah-ree keht-teh*
defend oneself	jikobengosuru *(v)*	*jee-koh-behn-goh-soo-roo*
deposition	kyōjutsu	*kyoh-joo-tsoo*
detain	kōryūsuru *(v)*	*koh-ryoo-soo-roo*
disagree	hantaisuru *(v)*	*hahn-tah-ee-soo-roo*
discuss	sōdansuru *(v)*	*soh-dahn-soo-roo*
evidence	shōko	*shoh-koh*
guilt	tsumi	*tsoo-mee*
• guilty	yūzai no *(adj)*	*yoo-zah-ee noh*
indict	kisosuru *(v)*	*kee-soh-soo-roo*
innocence	muzai	*moo-zah-ee*
• innocent	muzai no *(adj)*	*moo-zah-ee noh*
judge	saibankan	*sah-ee-bahn-kahn*
• judge	hanketsu o kudasu *(v)*	*hahn-keh-tsoo oh koo-dah-soo*
jury	baishin	*bah-ee-sheen*
justice	seigi	*seh-gee*
law	hōritsu	*hoh-ree-tsoo*
• lawful, legal	gōhō no *(adj)*	*goh-hoh noh*
• unlawful, illegal	ihō no *(adj)*	*ee-hoh noh*
• civil law	minpō	*meen-poh*
• criminal law	keihō	*keh-hoh*
lawsuit, charge	soshō	*soh-shoh*
• lose a lawsuit	haisosuru *(v)*	*hah-ee-soh-soo-roo*
• win a lawsuit	shōsosuru *(v)*	*shoh-soh-soo-roo*
lawyer	bengoshi	*behn-goh-shee*
• trial lawyer	hōtei bengoshi	*hoh-teh behn-goh-shee*
litigate	soshō o okosu *(v)*	*soh-shoh oh oh-koh-soo*
• litigation	soshō	*soh-shoh*
magistrate	keihanzai no hanji	*keh-hahn-zah-ee noh hahn-jee*
object	igi o tonaeru *(v)*	*ee-gee oh toh-nah-eh-roo*
• objection	igi	*ee-gee*
persuade	settokusuru *(v)*	*seht-tohk-soo-roo*
plaintiff	genkoku	*gehn-koh-koo*

plea	tangan	*tahn-gahn*
• plea for mercy	jihi no tangan	*jee-hee noh tahn-gahn*
• plead	tangansuru (v)	*tahn-gahn-soo-roo*
police station	keisatsusho	*keh-sah-tsoo-shoh*
prison, jail	keimusho	*keh-moo-shoh*
• imprison	tōgokusuru (v)	*toh-gohk-soo-roo*
• life imprisonment	muki chōeki	*moo-kee choh-eh-kee*
probation	shikkō yūyo	*sheek-koh yoo-yoh*
proof	shōko	*shoh-koh*
public prosecutor	kensatsukan	*kehn-sahts-kahn*
represent	daihyōsuru (v)	*dah-ee-hyoh-soo-roo*
right, privilege	kenri	*kehn-ree*
sentence	hanketsu	*hahn-keh-tsoo*
• life sentence	shūshinkei	*shoo-sheen-keh*
• prison sentence	yūkikei	*yoo-kee-keh*
• pass a sentence	hanketsu o iiwatasu (v)	*hahn-keh-tsoo oh ee-wah-tah-soo*
• serve a sentence	keiki ni fukusuru (v)	*keh-kee nee foo-koo-soo-roo*
settlement	wakai	*wah-kah-ee*
• out of court settlement	jidan	*jee-dahn*
sue	uttaeru (v)	*oot-tah-eh-roo*
summons	shōkanjō	*shoh-kahn-joh*
testify	shōgensuru (v)	*shoh-gehn-soo-roo*
• testimony	shōgen	*shoh-gehn*
trial	saiban	*sah-ee-bahn*
• be on trial	saiban ni tatsu (v)	*sah-ee-bahn nee tah-tsoo*
verdict	hyōketsu	*hyoh-keh-tsoo*
• guilty	yūzai	*yoo-zah-ee*
	kuro	*koo-roh*
• not guilty	muzai	*moo-zah-ee*
	shiro	*shee-roh*
witness	shōnin	*shoh-neen*
• eyewitness	mokugekisha	*moh-koo-geh-kee-shah*
• for the defense	bengogawa no (adj)	*behn-goh-gah-wah noh*
• for the prosecution	kensatsugawa no (adj)	*kehn-sah-tsoo-gah-wah noh*

THE CONTEMPORARY WORLD

42. SCIENCE AND TECHNOLOGY

a. THE CHANGING WORLD

antenna	antena	*ahn-teh-nah*
• **dish antenna**	parabora antena	*pah-rah-boh-rah ahn-teh-nah*
astronaut	uchū hikōshi	*oo-chōō hee-koh-shee*
atom	genshi	*gehn-shee*
• **electron**	denshi	*dehn-shee*
• **molecule**	bunshi	*boon-shee*
• **neutron**	chūseishi	*chōō-seh-shee*
• **proton**	yōshi	*yoh-shee*
cellular phone	keitai denwa	*keh-tah-ee dehn-wah*
clone	kurōn	*koo-rohn*
compact disc	konpakuto disuku	*kohn-pahk-toh dees-koo*
fax machine	fakkusu	*fahk-koo-soo*
laser	rēzā	*reh zah*
• **laser beam**	rēzā kōsen	*reh-zah koh-sehn*
microtechnology	maikuro gijutsu	*mah-ee-koo-roh gee-joo-tsoo*
microwave	chōtanpa	*choh-tahn-pah*
missile	misairu	*mee-sah-ee-roo*
monorail vehicle	monorēru	*moh-noh-reh-roo*
nuclear industry	genshiryoku sangyō	*gehn-shee-ryoh-koo sahn-gyoh*
• **fission reactor**	kakubunretsuro	*kah-koo-boon-reh-tsoo-roh*
• **fusion reactor**	kakuyūgōro	*kah-koo-yōō-goh-roh*
• **nuclear energy**	kaku enerugī	*kah-koo eh-neh-roo-gēē*
• **nuclear fuel**	kakunenryō	*kah-koo-nehn-ryoh*
• **nuclear reactor**	genshiro	*gehn-shee-roh*
robot	robotto	*roh-boht-toh*
satellite	jinkōeisei	*jeen-koh-eh-seh*
scientific research	kagaku kenkyū	*kah-gah-koo kehn-kyōō*
spacecraft	uchūsen	*oo-chōō-sehn*
• **lunar module**	tsuki chakurikusen	*tskee chah-koo-reek-sehn*
• **space shuttle**	supēsushatoru	*speh-soo-shah-toh-roo*
technology	gijutsu	*gee-joo-tsoo*
• **advanced technology**	sentan gijutsu	*sehn-tahn gee-joo-tsoo*
telecommunications	enkyori tsūshin	*ehn-kyoh-ree tsōō-sheen*
• **teleconferencing**	terekonfarensu	*teh-reh-kohn-fah-rehn-soo*

| theory of relativity | sōtaisei genri | *sōh-tah-ee-seh gehn-ree* |
| wireless connection | waiyaresu konekushon | *wah-ee-yah-rehs koh-nehk-shohn* |

b. COMPUTERS

attachment	tenpu	*tehn-poo*
broadband	burōdobando	*boo-rōh-doh-bahn-doh*
byte	baito	*bah-ee-toh*
• gigabyte	gigabaito	*gee-gah-bah-ee-toh*
• megabyte	megabaito	*meh-gah-bah-ee-toh*
CD	shīdī	*shēē-dēē*
chat	chatto	*chaht-toh*
compatible	konpachi (no) *(adj)*	*kohn-pah-chee (noh)*
computer	konpyūta	*kohn-pyōō-tah*
• computer language	konpyūta gengo	*kohn-pyōō-tah gehn-goh*
• computer science	konpyūta saiensu	*kohn-pyōō-tah sah-ee-ehn-soo*
crash	kurasshu	*koo-rahs-shoo*
data	dēta	*dēh-tah*
• database	dētabēsu	*dēh-tah-beh-soo*
• data processing	dēta shori	*deh-tah shoh-ree*
disk	disuku	*dees-koo*
download	daunrōdo	*dah-oon-rōh-doh*
DVD	dībuidī	*dēē-boo-ee-dēē*
e-mail	īmēru	*ēē-meh-roo*
e-mail address	īmēru adoresu	*ēē-meh-roo AH-doh-reh-soo*
Ethernet	Īsanetto	*EE-sah-neht-toh*
file	fairu	*fah-ee-roo*
function	kinō	*keen-noh*
hard disk	hādo disuku	*hah-doh-dees-koo*
hardware	hādowea	*hah-doh-weh-ah*
graphic	gurafikku	*goo-rah-feek-koo*
icon	aikon	*ah-ee-kohn*
interactive	intāakutibu	*een-tah-ah-koo-tee-boo*
interface	intāfēsu	*een-tah-feh-soo*
Internet	intānetto	*een-tah-neht-toh*
• hotspot	hottosupotto	*hoht-toh-spoht-toh*
• Internet café	intānetto kafe	*een-tah-neht-toh kah-feh*
• ISP	intānetto sābisu purobaida	*een-tah-neht-toh sah-bee-soo poo-roh-bah-ee-dah*
• Wi-Fi	waifai / musen ran	*wah-ee-fah-ee/moo-sehn rah*
keyboard	kībōdo	*kēē-boh-doh*
memory	memorī	*meh-moh-rēē*
• memory card	memorī kādo	*meh-moh-rēē kah-doh*
• memory stick	memorī sutikku	*meh-moh-rēē steek-koo*

menu	menyū	*meh-nyōō*
modem	modemu	*moh-deh-moo*
monitor	monitā	*moh-nee-tah*
mouse	mausu	*mah-oo-soo*
network	nettowāku	*neht-toh-wah-koo*
notebook computer	nōtopasokon	*noh-toh-pah-soh-kohn*
office automation	ofisu ōtomēshon	*oh-fee-soo oh-toh-meh-shohn*
online	onrain	*ohn-rah-een*
peripherals	shūhen sōchi	*shoo-hehn soh-chee*
personal computer	pasokon	*pah-soh-kohn*
printer	purinta	*poo-reen-tah*
program	puroguramu	*poo-roh-goo-rah-moo*
• programmer	puroguramā	*poo-roh-goo-rah-mah*
programming	puroguramingu	*poo-roh-goo-rah-meen-goo*
scanner	sukyana	*skyah-nah*
screen	sukurīn	*skoo-rēēn*
software	sofutowea	*soh-ftoh-weh-ah*
trackpad	torakkupaddo	*toh-rahk-koo-pahd-doh*
terminal	tāminaru	*tah-mee-nah-roo*
USB	yūesubī	*yōō-eh-soo-bēē*
user-friendly	yūzā furendorī	*yōō-zah foo-rehn-doh-rēē*
virus	uirusu	*oo-ee-roo-soo*
wireless	waiyaresu	*wah-ee-yah-reh-soo*
word processing	wāpuro shori	*wah-poo-roh shoh-ree*

43. POLITICS

See also Sections 16, 17, 21, and 22.

administration	seiken	*sēh-kehn*
advanced country	senshinkoku	*sehn-sheen-koh-koo*
arms race	gunbi kyōsō	*goon-bee kyoh-soh*
arms reduction	gunbi sakugen	*goon-bee sah-koo-gehn*
assembly	shūkai	*shōō-kah-ee*
cabinet	naikaku	*nah-ee-kah-koo*
• cabinet member	kakuryō	*kah-koo-ryoh*
coalition	rengō/renritsu	*rehn-goh/rehn-ree-tsoo*
committee	iinkai	*ee-een-kah-ee*
communism	kyōsanshugi	*kyoh-sahn-shoo-gee*
• communist	kyōsanshugisha	*kyoh-sahn-shoo-gee-shah*
congress	gikai	*gee-kah-ee*

• congressman/ congresswoman	giin	*gee-een*
conservative	hoshuteki na *(adj)*	*hoh-shoo-teh-kee nah*
• conservative party	hoshutō	*hoh-shoo-toh*
council	chihōgikai	*chee-hoh-gee-kah-ee*
democracy	minshushugi	*meen-shoo-shoo-gee*
• democrat	minshushugisha	*meen-shoo-shoo-gee-shah*
• democratic	minshushugi no *(adj)*	*meen-shoo-shoo-gee noh*
demonstration	demo	*deh-moh*
developing country	hatten tojōkoku	*haht-tehn toh-joh-koh-koo*
Diet (Japanese congress)	kokkai	*kohk-kah-ee*
• Diet member	kokkai giin	*kohk-kah-ee gee-een*
disarmament	gunbi teppai	*goon-bee tehp-pah-ee*
dissolve	kaisansuru *(v)*	*kah-ee-sahn-soo-roo*
economy	keizai	*keh-zah-ee*
elect	erabu *(v)*	*eh-rah-boo*
• election	senkyo	*sehn-kyoh*
faction	habatsu	*hah-bah-tsoo*
govern	tōjisuru *(v)*	*toh-jee-soo-roo*
• government	seifu	*seh-foo*
governor	chiji	*chee-jee*
ideology	ideorogī	*ee-deh-oh-roh-gee*
inflation	infure	*een-foo-reh*
labor/trade union	rōdōkumiai	*roh-doh-koo-mee-ah-ee*
left wing	sayoku	*sah-yoh-koo*
legislation	rippō	*reep-poh*
liberal	kakushinteki na *(adj)*	*kahk-sheen-teh-kee nah*
• liberal party	kakushintō	*kahk-sheen-toh*
mayor	shichō	*shee-choh*
minister	daijin	*dah-ee-jeen*
monarchy	kunshusei	*koon-shoo-seh*
• emperor	tennō	*tehn-noh*
• empress	kōgō	*koh-goh*
• king	kokuō	*koh-koo-oh*
• queen	jo-ō	*joh-oh*
• prince	ōji	*oh-jee*
• princess	ōjo	*oh-joh*
municipal	chihō jichitai no *(adj)*	*chee-hoh jee-chee-tah-ee noh*
mutual	sōgoteki na *(adj)*	*soh-goh-teh-kee nah*
national	kuni no *(adj)*	*koo-nee noh*
parliament	gikai	*gee-kah-ee*
• elected politician, representative	giin	*gee-een*

• House of Representatives (U.S.)	kain	*kah-een*
• House of Councilors (Japanese)	sangiin	*sahn-gee-een*
• House of Representatives (Japanese)	shūgiin	*shōō-gee-een*
• Senate (U.S.)	jōin	*jōh-heen*
senator	jōin giin	*joh-een gee-een*
• universal suffrage/ right to vote	futsū senkyoken	*foo-tsōō sehn-kyoh-kehn*
peace	heiwa	*hēh-wah*
platform	kōryō	*kōh-ryoh*
policy	seisaku	*sēh-sah-koo*
politician	seijika	*sēh-jee-kah*
politics	seiji	*sēh-jee*
• political party	seitō	*sēh-toh*
• political power	seijiryoku	*seh-jee-ryoh-koo*
president	daitōryō	*dah-ee-tōh-ryoh*
prime minister	shushō	*shoo-shoh*
protest	kōgi	*kōh-gee*
• protest	kōgisuru *(v)*	*koh-gee-soo-roo*
provincial	chihō no *(adj)*	*chee-hōh noh*
ratify	hijunsuru *(v)*	*hee-joon-soo-roo*
reform	kaikaku	*kah-ee-kah-koo*
• reform	kaikakusuru *(v)*	*kah-ee-kahk-soo-roo*
republic	kyōwakoku	*kyōh-wah-koh-koo*
revolt	hanran	*hahn-rahn*
• revolt	hanransuru *(v)*	*hahn-rahn-soo-roo*
• revolution	kakumei	*kah-koo-mēh*
right wing	uyoku	*oo-yoh-koo*
riot	bōdō	*boh-dōh*
socialism	shakaishugi	*shah-kah-ee-shoo-gee*
• socialist	shakaishugisha	*shah-kah-ee-shoo-gee-shah*
state	kokka	*kohk-kah*
• head of state	genshu	*gehn-shoo*
Third World	daisansekai	*dah-ee-sahn-seh-kah-ee*
unilateral	ippōteki na *(adj)*	*eep-poh-teh-kee nah*
vote	tōhyō	*tōh-hyōh*
• vote	tōhyōsuru *(v)*	*toh-hyoh-soo-roo*
• voter	tōhyōsha	*toh-hyoh-shah*
welfare	shakai fukushi	*shah-kah-ee foo-koo-shee*

44. CONTROVERSIAL ISSUES

a. THE ENVIRONMENT

> For more vocabulary, see Sections 13 and 42.

air pollution	taiki osen	*tah-ee-kee oh-sehn*
conservation	shizen hogo	*shee-zehn hoh-goh*
consumption	shōhi	*shoh-hee*
ecology	seitaigaku	*seh-tah-ee-gah-koo*
ecosystem	seitaikei	*seh-tah-ee-keh*
energy	enerugī	*eh-neh-roo-gēē*
• **energy crisis**	enerugī kiki	*eh-neh-roo-gēē kee-kee*
• **energy needs**	enerugī juyō	*eh-neh-roo-gēē joo-yoh*
• **energy source**	enerugī shigen	*eh-neh-roo-gēē shee-gehn*
• **energy waste**	enerugī rōhi	*eh-neh-roo-gēē roh-hee*
environment	kankyō	*kahn-kyoh*
fossil fuel	kaseki nenryō	*kah-seh-kee nehn-ryoh*
geothermal energy	chinetsu enerugī	*chee-neh-tsoo eh-neh-roo-gēē*
global warming	chikyū ondanka	*chee-kyoo ohn-dahn-kah*
green	kankyō ni yasashii	*kahn-kyoh nee yah-sah-shēē*
greenhouse effect	onshitsu kōka	*ohn-shtsoo koh-kah*
natural resources	tennen shigen	*tehn-nehn shee-gehn*
ozone	ozon	*oh-zohn*
petroleum	sekiyu	*seh-kee-yoo*
pollution	kōgai	*koh-gah-ee*
radiation	hōshasen	*hoh-shah-sehn*
• **radioactive waste**	hōshasei haikibutsu	*hoh-shah-seh hah-ee-kee-boo-tsoo*
sewage	osui	*oh-soo-ee*
solar cell	taiyō denchi	*tah-ee-yoh dehn-chee*
solar energy	taiyō enerugī	*tah-ee-yoh eh-neh-roo-gēē*
thermal energy	netsu enerugī	*neh-tsoo eh-neh-roo-gēē*
toxic	dokusei no *(adj)*	*doh-koo-seh noh*
waste	haikibutsu	*hah-ee-kee-boo-tsoo*
• **waste disposal**	haikibutsu shori	*hah-ee-kee-boo-tsoo shoh-ree*
• **waste management**	haikibutsu kanri	*hah-ee-kee-boo-tsoo kahn-ree*
water pollution	mizu osen	*mee-zoo oh-sehn*
wind energy	fūryoku enerugī	*foo-ryoh-koo eh-neh-roo-gēē*

b. SOCIETY

abortion	datai	*dah-tah-ee*
• fetus	taiji	*tah-ee-jee*
AIDS	eizu	*eh-ee-zoo*
alcoholism	arukōru chūdoku	*ah-roo-koh-roo chōo-doh-koo*
biological weapon	seibutsu heiki	*seh-boo-tsoo hēh-kee*
capital punishment	shikei	*shee-keh*
censorship	ken-etsu	*kehn-eh-tsoo*
chemical weapon	kagaku heiki	*kah-gah-koo hēh-kee*
contraception	hinin	*hee-neen*
discrimination	sabetsu	*sah-beh-tsoo*
drugs	mayaku	*mah-yah-koo*
• drug addiction	mayaku chūdoku	*mah-yah-koo chōo-doh-koo*
• drug pusher	mayaku mitsubainin	*mah-yah-koo mee-tsoo-bah-ee-neen*
• drug trafficking	mayaku baibai	*mah-yah-koo bah-ee-bah-ee*
• rehab	rehabiri sentā	*reh-hab-ee-ree sehn-tāh*
• take drugs	mayaku o tsukau *(v)*	*mah-yah-koo oh tsoo-kah-oo*
feminism	feminizumu	*feh-mee-nee-zoo-moo*
• feminist	feminisuto	*feh-mee-nee-stoh*
health insurance	kenkō hoken	*kehn-koh hoh-kehn*
HIV	eizu uirusu ga yōsei no *(adj)*	*eh-ee-zoo oo-ee-roo-soo gah yoh-seh noh*
homeless	hōmuresu	*hoh-moo-reh-soo*
homosexual	dōseiai no *(adj)*	*dōh-seh-ah-ee noh*
• gay	dōseiai no *(adj)*	*dōh-seh-ah-ee noh*
	dōseiai no dansei	*dōh-seh-ah-ee noh dahn-seh*
• homosexuality	dōseiai	*dōh-seh-ah-ee*
• lesbian	dōseiai no josei	*dōh-seh-ah-ee noh joh-seh*
land mine	jirai	*jee-rah-ee*
morality	dōtoku	*dōh-toh-koo*
nuclear war	kaku sensō	*kah-koo sehn-sōh*
nuclear weapon	kaku heiki	*kah-koo hēh-kee*
• antinuclear protest	hankaku demo	*hahn-kah-koo deh-moh*
• atomic bomb	genshi bakudan	*gehn-shee bah-koo-dahn*
• hydrogen bomb	suiso bakudan	*soo-ee-soh bah-koo-dahn*
overpopulation	jinkō kajō	*jeen-kōh kah-jōh*
pornography	poruno	*poh-roo-noh*
poverty	hinkon	*heen-kohn*
prostitute	baishunfu	*bah-ee-shoon-foo*
• prostitution	baishun	*bah-ee-shoon*

racism	jinshu sabetsu	*jeen-shoo sah-beh-tsoo*
suicide bombing	bakudan jisatsu	*bah-koo-dahn jee-sah-tsoo*
terrorism	tero / tero kōi	*teh-roh/teh-roh koh-ee*
torture	gōmon	*goh-mohn*

c. EXPRESSING YOUR OPINION

according to me	watakushi ni yoreba	*wah-tahk-shee nee yoh-reh-bah*
as a matter of fact	jissai	*jees-sah-ee*
by the way	tokorode	*toh-koh-roh-deh*
for example	tatoeba	*tah-toh-eh-bah*
from my point of view	watakushi no mikata dewa	*wah-tahk-shee noh mee-kah-tah deh-wah*
I believe that ...	... to omoimasu	*... toh oh-moh-ee-mahs*
I don't know if ...	... ka dō ka shirimasen	*... kah doh kah shee-ree-mah-sehn*
I doubt that ...	... ka dō ka gimon desu	*... kah doh kah gee-mohn dehs*
I think that ...	... to omoimasu	*... toh oh-moh-ee-mahs*
I'd like to say ...	... to iitai no desu ga	*... toh ee-tah-ee noh dehs gah*
I'm not sure that ...	... ka dō ka tashika dewa arimasen	*... kah doh kah tah-shkah deh-wah ah-ree-mah-sehn*
I'm sure that ...	... wah, tashika desu	*...wah, tah-shkah dehs*
in conclusion	ketsuron to shitewa	*keh-tsoo-rohn toh shteh-wah*
in my opinion	watakushi no iken dewa	*wah-tahk-shee noh ee-kehn deh-wah*
in my view	watakushi no kangae dewa	*wah-tahk-shee noh kahn-gah-eh deh-wah*
It seems that ...	... yō desu	*... yoh dehs*
It's clear that ...	... wa, akiraka desu	*... wah, ah-kee-rah-kah dehs*
that is to say	sunawachi	*soo-nah-wah-chee*
There's no doubt that ...	... wa, utagai no yochi mo arimasen	*... wah, oo-tah-gah-ee noh yoh-chee moh ah-ree-mah-sehn*
therefore	soreyue	*soh-reh-yoo-eh*

ENGLISH-JAPANESE WORDFINDER

This alphabetical listing of all of the English words in *Japanese Vocabulary* will enable you to find the information you need quickly and efficiently. If all you want is the Japanese equivalent of an entry word, you will find it here. If you also want pronunciation and usage aids, or closely associated words and phrases, use the reference number(s) and letter(s) to locate the section(s) in which the entry appears. This is especially important for English words that have multiple meanings or for multiple Japanese entries of the same English word.

A

@ atto māku アットマーク 19f

a little sukoshi *(adv)* 少し 3c

a lot, much takusan たくさん 3c

A pleasure! Yorokonde.
喜んで。 16b

abalone awabi あわび 15c, 24d

abbreviation shōryakukei
省略形 19c

abdomen fukubu 腹部 12a

abort (pregnancy) chūzetsusuru
(v)/dataisuru *(v)*
中絶する／堕胎する 11c

abortion chūzetsu 中絶 40a

abortion chūzetsu/datai
中絶／堕胎 11c

abortion datai 堕胎 44b

above ue ni *(adv)* 上に 3d

above ue no *(adj)* 上の 3d

above zero reido ijō no
零度以上の 6c

abroad gaikoku 外国 19e

abroad kaigai ni *(adv)* 海外に
30a

abscissa coordinate yoko zahyō
横座標 2b

abstract chūshōteki na *(adj)*
抽象的な 22a

accelerate kasokusuru *(v)*
加速する 3e

accent akusento アクセント 8a,
19c

accept ukeireru *(v)* 受け入れる
21b

acceptable ukeirerareru *(adj)*
受け入れられる 21b

accident jiko 事故 33c

accomplice kyōhan 共犯 39b

according to me watakushi ni
yoreba 私によれば 44c

accordion akōdion
アコーディオン 28c

account kōza 口座 26

accountant kaikeishi 会計士 38a

accounting kaikeigaku 会計学
37e

accusation hinan 非難 17a

accusation kokuhatsu 告発 41

accuse hinansuru *(v)* 非難する
17a

accuse kokuhatsusuru *(v)*
告発する 41

accused person hikoku 被告 41

accuser kokuhatsunin 告発人 41

ache itamu *(v)* 痛む 12b

acid san 酸 13c

acid rain sanseiu 酸性雨 6a, 13c

acne nikibi にきび 40a

acquaintance chijin 知人 10b, 16b

acquit muzai o hanketsusuru (v) 無罪を判決する 41

acre ēkā エーカー 3a

across mukōgawa no (adj) 向こう側の 3d

across ... ... o yokogitte ・・・を横切って 36c

act enjiru (v) 演じる 28e

act maku 幕 28e

active kappatsu na (adj) 活発な 21a

active katsudōteki na (adj) 活動的な 11e

active nōdōtai no (adj) 能動態の 8a

active volcano kakkazan 活火山 13b

activity katsudō 活動 11e

actor danyū 男優 28a

actress joyū 女優 28a

actually ... Jitsu wa, ... 実は、・・・ 17b

acute angle eikaku 鋭角 2b

acute-angled eikaku (adj) 鋭角 2a

adapt tekigōsaseru (vt) 適合させる 11e

adaptable tekigōsei ga aru (adj) 適合性がある 11e

add kuwaeru/tasu (v) 加える／たす 1e

add up the bill kaikeisuru (v) 会計する 24o

addiction chūdoku 中毒 40a

addition tashizan 足し算 1e

address jūsho 住所 11f, 19e, 38b

address book adoresubukku アドレスブック 19f

addressee naatenin 名宛人 19e

adhesive tape setchaku tēpu 接着テープ 25c, 38c

adjacent angle rinsetsukaku 隣接角 2b

adjective keiyōshi 形容詞 8a

administration seiken 政権 43

admit mitomeru (v) 認める 41

adolescent shishunki no (adj) 思春期の 11b

adult otona 大人 11b

Adulthood Day (second Monday in January) seijin no hi 成人の日 5g

advance ticket maeuri ken 前売り券 30a

advanced country senshinkoku 先進国 43

advanced technology sentan gijutsu 先端技術 42a

adventure bōken 冒険 20a

adverb fukushi 副詞 8a

advertising kōkoku 広告 20a, 38d

advice jogen 助言 17a

advise jogensuru (v) 助言する 17a

aerobics earobikusu エアロビクス 27b

affection aijō 愛情 11e, 21a

affectionate aijō no fukai (adj) 愛情の深い 11e, 21a

affectionately kokoro o komete 心を込めて 19b

affirm dangensuru (v) 断言する 17a

affirmative kōtei (adj) 肯定 8a

Africa Afurika アフリカ 30b

after ato de *(adv)* 後で 4e

afternoon gogo 午後 4a

again mata *(adv)* また 4e

age nenrei/toshi 年齢／年 11b, 11f

age toshitoru *(v)* 年取る 11b

aged kōreisha 高齢者 11b

aggressive kōgekiteki na *(adj)* 攻撃的な 11e, 21a

aggressiveness kōgekisei 攻撃性 11e

ago mae ni *(adv)* 前に 4e

agree gōisuru *(v)* 合意する 41

agree sanseisuru *(v)* 賛成する 17a, 21a

agreeable kokoroyoi *(adj)* こころよい 21a

agriculture nōgyō 農業 14a

ahead ... ... no saki ni ···の先に 36c

ahead, forward mukōgawa ni *(adv)* 向こう側に 3d

ahead, forward saki ni *(adv)*/mae ni *(adv)* 先に／前に 3d

ahead, forward saki no *(adj)*/mae no *(adj)* 先の／前の 3d

AIDS eizu エイズ 40a, 44b

air hōsōsuru *(v)* 放送する 20b

air kūki 空気 6a, 13b, c

air bag eā baggu エアーバッグ 33e

air conditioner eakon エアコン 23e, 33e

air conditioning reibō 冷房 23e

air pollution taiki osen 大気汚染 44a

airline kōkūgaisha 航空会社 32a

airmail kōkūbin 航空便 19e

airplane hikōki 飛行機 32c

airport kūkō 空港 32a

aisle tsūro 通路 28a

aisle tsūrogawa 通路側 32c

alarm clock mezamashi 目覚まし 4d

alcoholic beverage arukōru inryō アルコール飲料 24k

alcoholism arukōru chūdoku アルコール中毒 44b

alcove tokonoma 床の間 23b

algebra daisū 代数 1f

algebraic daisū no *(adj)* 代数の 1f

all zenbu 全部 8i

All aboard! Gojōsha kudasai. 御乗車ください。 34

all, everything subete *(adv)* 全て 3c

all, everything zenbu 全部 3c

all day ichinichijū 一日中 4a

allergy arerugī アレルギー 40a

alligator arigētā アリゲーター 15c

allude honomekasu *(v)* ほのめかす 17a

almost always daitai itsumo 大体いつも 4e

almost, nearly hotondo *(adv)* 殆ど 3c

almost, never hotondo ~ shinai *(adv)* 殆ど～しない 4e

alphabet arufabetto アルファベット 8a

already sude ni/mō *(adv)* 既に／もう 4e

also soshite/mata *(conj)* そして／また 8k

alteration shitatenaoshi 仕立て直し 25m

altitude kōdo 高度 13e

aluminum arumi アルミ 13c

always itsumo (adv) いつも 4e

amaryllis amaririsu アマリリス 14b

amateur amachua アマチュア 27b

ambition taibō 大望 11e

ambitious nozomi ga takai (adj) 望みが高い 11e

ambulance kyūkyūsha 救急車 33a

America Amerika アメリカ 30b

American Amerikajin アメリカ人 30d

ammonia anmonia アンモニア 13c

among naka ni (adv) 中に 3d

amphibian ryōseirui 両棲類 15c

amplifier anpu アンプ 20b

analog anarogu アナログ 18a

analogy ruihi 類比 17a

anatomy kaibōgaku 解剖学 37e

anchovy anchobi アンチョビ 24d

and (at the beginning of a sentence) soshite そして 8k

and (between nouns) to と 8j

anemia hinketsu 貧血 40a

anemone anemone アネモネ 14b

anesthetic masui 麻酔 40b

anger ikari 怒り 11e, 21a

angle kakudo 角度 2b

anglerfish ankō アンコウ 15c

angry okotta (adj) 怒った 11e, 21a

animal dōbutsu 動物 15a

animism seirei shinkō 精霊信仰 11d

ankle ashikubi 足首 12a

anniversary kekkon kinenbi 結婚記念日 11c

anniversary kinenbi 記念日 29a

announce shiraseru (v) 知らせる 17a

announcement happyō 発表 17a

annual interest nenri 年利 26

annual leave nenji yūkyū kyūka 年次有給休暇 38d

answer denwa ni deru (v) 電話に出る 18b

answer kotae 答 9, 17a, 37f

answer kotaeru (v) 答える 9, 17a, 37f

answering machine rusuban denwa 留守番電話 18a

ant ari 蟻 15d

antacid isan 胃散 25h

Antarctic Circle nankyokuken 南極圏 13e

Antarctic Ocean nanpyōyō 南氷洋 13b

antenna antena アンテナ 20b, 42a

anthropology jinruigaku 人類学 37e

anti-aging cream rōka bōshi kurīmu 老化防止クリーム 25f

antibiotic kōseibusshitsu 抗生物質 25h

anti-diarrheal medicine geridome 下痢止め 25h

antiseptic shōdokuyaku 消毒薬 25h

anti-wrinkle cream shiwatori kurīmu しわ取りクリーム 25f

anus kōmon 肛門 12a, 40a

anxiety fuankan 不安感 11e

anxiety, anxiousness fuan 不安 21a

anxious fuan na *(adj)* 不安な 21a

anxious shinpai na *(adj)* 心配な 11e

apartment (inexpensive) apāto アパート 23g

apartment (upscale) manshon マンション 23g

ape ruijin-en 類人猿 15a

aperitif shokuzenshu 食前酒 24g, 24k

aperture shibori 絞り 25d

aphid aburamushi アブラムシ 15d

apostrophe aposutorofi アポストロフィ 19c

appeal jōkokusuru *(v)* 上告する 41

appendicitis mōchōen 盲腸炎 40a

appendix furoku 付録 20a, 28d

appendix mōchō 盲腸 12a, 40a

appetizer zensai 前菜 24g

appetizing oishisō na *(adj)* 美味しそうな 24p

applaud hakushusuru *(v)* 拍手する 28e

applause hakushu 拍手 28e

apple ringo リンゴ 14d

apple tree ringo no ki リンゴの木 14c

appointment yoyaku 予約 40a, b

appointment book yotei hyō 予定表 38c

approach sekkinsuru *(v)* 接近する 3e

approval zenin 是認 21b

approve mitomeru *(v)* 認める 21b

approximately ōyoso *(adv)* おおよそ 3c

apricot anzu アンズ 14d

April shigatsu 四月 5b

Aquarius mizugameza 水瓶座 5d

Arab Arabujin アラブ人 30d

Arabic Arabiago アラビア語 30d

Arabic numeral Arabia sūji アラビア数字 1d

arbitration chōtei 調停 41

archbishop daishikyō 大司教 11d

archeology kōkogaku 考古学 37e

archery ācherī アーチェリー 27b

archipelago guntō 群島 13b

architect kenchikuka 建築家 28b

architecture kenchiku 建築 28b

architecture kenchikugaku 建築学 37e

Arctic Circle hokkyokuken 北極圏 13e

Arctic Ocean hoppyōyō 北氷洋 13b

Are you joking? Jōdan desho. 冗談でしょ。 21c

area chiiki 地域 13e

area menseki 面積 3a

area code shigaikyokuban 市外局番 11f, 18b, 38b

area studies chiiki kenkyū 地域研究 37e

Argentina Aruzenchin アルゼンチン 30b

argue gironsuru *(v)* 議論する 17a

argue iiarasou *(v)* 言い争う 39b

argument giron 議論 17a

argumentative rikutsuppoi *(adj)*
理屈っぽい 21a

Aries ohitsujiza 牡羊座 5d

arithmetical sansū no *(adj)*
算数の 1f

arithmetical operations enzan
演算 1e

arm ude 腕 12a

armchair hijikakeisu 肘掛け椅子
23c

armed robbery busō gōtō
武装強盗 39b

armpit wakinoshita 脇の下 12a

armrest hijikake 肘掛け 35c

arms race gunbi kyōsō 軍備競争
43

arms reduction gunbi sakugen
軍備削減 43

around mawari ni 回りに 3d

arrest taiho 逮捕 39b

arrest taihosuru *(v)* 逮捕する
39b

arrhythmia fuseimyaku 不整脈
40a

arrival tōchaku 到着 32a

arrive tsuku *(v)* 着く 3e

arrogance gōman 傲慢 11e

arrogant gōman na *(adj)* 傲慢な
11e

arson hōka 放火 39a

art geijutsu 芸術 28b

art gallery āto gyararī
アートギャラリー 28b

art gallery garō 画廊 36a

arteriosclerosis
dōmyakukōkashō 動脈硬化症
40a

artery dōmyaku 動脈 40a

arthritis kansetsuen 関節炎 40a

artichoke ātichōku
アーティチョーク 14e

article kanshi 冠詞 8a

article kiji 記事 20a

articulate hakkiri hyōgensuru *(v)*
はっきり表現する 17a

artificial jinkō no *(adj)* 人工の
25i

artificial jinzō no *(adj)* 人造の
13d

artist geijutsuka 芸術家 11e, 28b

artistic geijutsuteki na *(adj)*
芸術的な 11e

arts kyōyō kamoku 教養科目
37e

as a matter of fact jissai 実際
17b, 44c

as much as dake だけ 3c

as soon as sugu ni 直ぐに 4e

asbestos asubesuto/sekimen
アスベスト／石綿 13c

ash toneriko トネリコ 14c

Asia Ajia アジア 30b

ask kiku *(v)* 聞く 17a

ask a question shitsumonsuru
(v) 質問する 37f

ask for tanomu *(v)* 頼む 9

ask for something nanika o
tanomu 何かを頼む 9

ask for the bill kanjō o tanomu
勘定を頼む 35b

ask someone dareka ni kiku
誰かに聞く 9

asparagus asuparagasu
アスパラガス 14e

aspirin asupirin アスピリン 25h

assault osou *(v)* 襲う 39b

assembly shūkai 集会 43

assignment book shukudai chō
宿題帳 37b

assignments, homework
shukudai 宿題 37f

assistant joshu 助手 37d

assure ukeau (v) 請け合う 21a

asterisk hoshijirushi 星印 19c

asteroid shōwakusei 小惑星 13a

asthma zensoku 喘息 40a

astronaut uchū hikōshi
宇宙飛行士 42a

astronomy tenmongaku 天文学
13a, 37f

astute kibin na (adj) 機敏な 11e

at ni/de に／で 8j

at home uchi de うちで 23f

at midnight mayonaka ni
真夜中に 4a

at night yoru ni 夜に 4a

at noon shōgo ni 正午に 4a

at the beach kaigan de 海岸で
36b

at the bottom soko ni (adv) 底に
3d

at the center chūō ni (adv)
中央に 3d

at the dentist's haisha de
歯医者で 40b

at the edge of hashi ni 端に 3d

at the end of... ...no owari ni
・・・の終わりに 36c

at the same time dōji ni 同時に
4e

at the top ichiban ue de
一番上で 3d

at the top of ... no ue ni
・・・の上に 36c

At what time? Nanji ni.
何時に。 4b

atheism mushinron 無神論 11d

atheist mushinronsha 無神論者
11d

athlete undō no senshu
運動の選手 27b

Atlantic Ocean taiseiyō 大西洋
13b

atlas chizu chō 地図帳 20a, 25o,
37b

atmosphere taiki 大気 6a, 13b

atmospheric taiki no (adj) 大気の
13b

atmospheric conditions kiatsu
気圧 6a

atom genshi 原子 13c, 42a

atomic bomb genshi bakudan
原子爆弾 44b

attach tenpusuru (v) 添付する
19f

attachment tenpu 添付 19f, 42b

attend school gakkō ni iku (v)
学校に行く 37f

attic yaneurabeya 屋根裏部屋
23a

attitude taido 態度 21a

attorney bengoshi 弁護士 41

attractive miryokuteki na (adj)
魅力的な 11a, 11e

audience kankyaku 観客 28e

audio equipment ōdio sōchi
オーディオ装置 20b

audit chōkōsuru (v) 聴講する 37f

August hachigatsu 八月 5b

aunt oba 叔母 10a

aunt obasan 叔母さん 10a

Australia Ōsutoraria
オーストラリア 30b

Australian Ōsutorariajin
オーストラリア人 30d

Austria Ōsutoria オーストリア
30b

Austrian Ōsutoriajin
オーストリア人 30d

authentic honmono no *(adj)*
本物の 13d

author chosha 著者 20a

author chosha/sakka
著者／作家 28d

author chosha/sakka/hissha
著者／作家／筆者 25o

auto insurance jidōsha hoken
自動車保険 39c

autobiography jiden 自伝 25o,
28b

automobile jidōsha 自動車 33a

autumnal equinox shūbun 秋分
5c

**Autumnal Equinox Day
(September 23 or 24)** shūbun
no hi 秋分の日 5g

avarice, greed donyoku 貪欲
11e

avaricious, greedy yoku no fukai
(adj) 欲の深い 11e

avenue gai 街 11f

average heikin 平均 1f

away hedatatta *(adj)* 隔たった
3d

away hedatatte *(adv)* 隔たって
3d

awful hidoi *(adj)* 酷い 6a

axis jiku 軸 2b

B

baboon hihi ヒヒ 15a

baby akachan 赤ちゃん 11b

bachelor dokushin 独身 11c

back ... ... no ushiro ni
···の後に 36c

back senaka 背中 12a

back up bakkusuru *(v)*
バックする 33c

back, backward ushiro ni *(adv)*
後に 3d

back, backward ushiro no *(adj)*
後の 3d

backache yōtsū 腰痛 40a

backrest semotare 背もたれ 35c

bacon bēkon ベーコン 24c

bacteria bakuteria バクテリア
40a

bad mazui *(adj)* まずい 24p

bad warui *(adj)* 悪い 11e

bad mood warui kibun 悪い気分
21a

bad weather warui tenki
悪い天気 6a

Badly. Anmari yoku arimasen.
あんまりよくありません。 16a

badminton badominton
バドミントン 27b

bag fukuro 袋 23d

bag (shopping) kaimonobukuro
買い物袋 25a

baggage claim tenimotsu
uketorijo 手荷物受取所 32a

baggage, luggage nimotsu 荷物
31

bagpipes baggupaipu
バッグパイプ 28c

bail hoshaku 保釈 41

bake tenpi de yaku *(v)*
天火で焼く 24o

baked tenpi de yaita *(adj)*
天火で焼いた 24b

baker panyaki no shokunin
パン焼きの職人 38a

bakery pan ya パン屋 24n

balcony barukonī バルコニー
23a, 35c

ball bōru ボール 27b

ballet barē バレー 28c

ballpoint pen bōru pen
ボールペン 19d, 25c, 37b

ballroom dance shakō dansu
社交ダンス 27b

bamboo clarinet shakuhachi
尺八 28c

bamboo shoot takenoko
タケノコ 14e, 24e

banana banana バナナ 14d, 24f

band bando バンド 25j, 28c

band gakudan 楽団 25j

bandage hōtai 包帯 25h, 39c,
40a

bandage hōtai o maku (v)
包帯を巻く 40a

Band-Aid bandoeido
バンドエイド 25h

Bangkok Bankokku バンコック
30c

banister kaidan no tesuri
階段の手すり 23a

banjo banjō バンジョー 28c

bank ginkō 銀行 26

bankbook ginkō tsūchō
銀行通帳 26

bank rate kōteibuai 公定歩合 26

banker ginkōka 銀行家 38a

bankruptcy hasan 破産 38d

baptism senrei 洗礼 11d

barber rihatsushi 理髪師 38a,
12d

barber shop tokoya 床屋 12d

bark hoeru (v) 吠える 15a

barley ōmugi 大麦 24i

barn naya 納屋 15a

barometer kiatsukei 気圧計 6c

barometric pressure kiatsu 気圧
6c

bartender bāten バーテン 24m

base bēsu ベース 27b

baseball yakyū 野球 27b

basement chikashitsu 地下室
23a

basil bajiriko/bajiru
バジリコ／バジル 24j

basil bajiru バジル 14e

basin bonchi 盆地 13b

basket kago 篭 23d

basketball basukettobōru
バスケットボール 27b

bass drum ōdaiko 大太鼓 28c

bassoon fagotto ファゴット 28c

bat batto バット 27b

bat kōmori コウモリ 15a

bath ofuro お風呂 12d

bath oil basu oiru バスオイル
25f

bathing suit mizugi 水着 25k

bathrobe basurōbu バスローブ
25k, 35c

bathroom (Japanese style)
furoba 風呂場 23b, 35c

bathroom (western style)
basurūmu バスルーム 23b,
35c

bathroom scale taijūkei 体重計
23d

bathtub yokusō 浴槽 23a, 35c

batter battā バター 27b

battery batterī バッテリー 25b,
33c

battery denchi 電池 25b

bay wan 湾 13b

be about to ~kaketeiru
～かけている 4e

be absent kesseki (desu)
欠席（です） 37f

be afraid osoreru (v) 恐れる 21a

be against hantaisuru (v)
反対する 21a

be ashamed hajiru (v) 恥じる
21a

be born umareru (v) 生まれる
11c

be called yobareru (v) 呼ばれる
11f

Be careful! Ki o tsukete.
気をつけて。 21c

be cold samui desu 寒いです
12b

be dizzy memai ga suru
目眩がする 12b

be down ki ga meitte iru
気が滅入っている 21a

be fine genki (desu)
元気（です） 12b

be fond of, like konomu (v)
好む 21b

be from... ...kara kimashita
・・・から来ました 11f

be full onaka ga ippai (desu)
お腹が一杯（です） 12b

be healthy kenkō (desu)
健康（です） 12b

be hot atsui desu 暑いです 12b

be hungry onaka ga suite imasu
お腹がすいています 12b, 24o

be ill byōki (desu) 病気（です）
12b

be in a bad mood kigen ga warui
機嫌が悪い 11e

be in a good mood kigen ga ii
機嫌がいい 11e

be interested in kyōmi ga aru (v)
興味がある 22b

be late osokunaru 遅くなる 4e

be on fire moete iru 燃えている
39a

be on the point/verge of
~kaketeiru ～かけている 4e

be on time jikandōri ni
時間通りに 4e

be on trial saiban ni tatsu (v)
裁判に立つ 41

be out of breath iki ga kireru
息が切れる 40a

be painful itai (desu)
痛い（です） 12b

be pregnant ninshin chū desu
妊娠中です 11c

be present shusseki (desu)
出席（です） 37f

be promoted shinkyūsuru (v)
進級する 37f

be right tadashii (desu)
正しい（です） 22b

be run over hikareru (v)
ひかれる 39c

be seated koshikakeru (v)
腰掛ける 16b

Be seated, please! Dōzo okake
kudasai.
どうぞお掛けください。 16b

be sick byōki (desu)
病気（です） 12b

be sleepy nemui desu 眠いです
12b

be strong jōbu (desu)
丈夫（です） 12b

be thirsty nodo ga kawaite
imasu 喉が渇いています 12b,
24o

be tired tsukarete imasu
疲れています 12b

be transferred tenkinsuru (v)
転勤する 38d

be up ki ga takamatte iru
気が高まっている 21a

be weak yowatte (imasu)
弱って（います） 12b

be windy kaze ga tsuyoi
風が強い 6a

be wrong machigai (desu)
間違い（です）22b

beach hama 浜 13b

beach kaigan 海岸 36b

beak kuchibashi くちばし 15b

bean mame 豆 14e, 24e

bean sprout moyashi もやし
14e, 24e

bear kuma 熊 15a

beard agohige あごひげ 12a

beast kemono けもの 15a

beat kakuhansuru (v) 撹拌する
24o

beautician biyōshi 美容師 12d

beautiful subarashii (adj)
素晴らしい 6a

beautiful utsukushii (adj) 美しい
11a, 25l

beautiful weather subarashii
tenki 素晴らしい天気 6a

beauty bijin 美人 11a

beaver bībā ビーバー 15a

because nazenara なぜなら 8k

become ~ ni naru (v) ～になる
4e

become angry okoru (v) 怒る
11e

become big ōkiku naru (v)
大きくなる 3c, 11a

become bored taikutsusuru (vi)
退屈する 21a

become engaged konyakusuru
(v) 婚約する 11c

become fat futoru (v) 太る 11a

become friends tomodachi ni
naru (v) 友達になる 10b

become old toshitoru (v) 年取る
11b

become sick byōki ni naru (v)
病気になる 11a

become small chiisakunaru (v)
小さくなる 3c

become thin yaseru (vi) 痩せる
11a

become weak yowakunaru (v)
弱くなる 11a

bed beddo ベッド 23c, 35c

bed bug nankinmushi 南京虫
15d

**bedding (Japanese mattress for
the floor)** futon 布団 23c

bedroom shinshitsu 寝室 23b

bedside table saidotēburu
サイドテーブル 23c, 35c

bedspread beddokabā
ベッドカバー 23d

bee hachi 蜂 15d

beech tree buna ブナ 14c

beef bīfu ビーフ 24c

beef gyūniku 牛肉 24c

beer bīru ビール 24k

beet satōdaikon 砂糖大根 14e,
24e

beetle kōchū 甲虫 15d

before mae ni (adv) 前に 4e

beg kongansuru (v) 懇願する
17a

begin hajimaru (vi) 始まる 4e

begin hajimeru (vt) 始める 4e

beginning hajimari 始まり 4e

behind... ...no kage ni
・・・の陰に 36c

beige bēju iro no (adj)
ベージュ色の 6a

Beijing Bējin ベージン 30c

Belgian Berugijin ベルギー人
30d

Belgium Berugī ベルギー 30b

belief shinnen 信念 11d, 22a

believe shinjiru (v) 信じる 11d, 22b

believe in shinjiru (v) 信じる 11d

believer shinja 信者 11d

bell tower shōrō 鐘楼 36a

bellflower kikyō 桔梗 14b

bellhop bōi ボーイ 35b

belly onaka お腹 12a

below freezing hyōtenka no (adj) 氷点下の 6a

below zero hyōtenka 氷点下 6c

belt beruto ベルト 25k

benefit onkei 恩恵 38d

benign ryōsei (adj) 良性 40a

Berlin Berurin ベルリン 30c

beside, next to tonari ni (adv) 隣に 3d

beside, next to tonari no (adj) 隣の 3d

best friend dai no shinyū 大の親友 10b

best seller besutoserā ベストセラー 20a, 25o

Best wishes! Gokōun o. ご幸運を。 16c, 29c

between aida ni (adv) 間に 3d

between aida no (adj) 間の 3d

between friends tomodachi no aida no/ni/de 友達の間の／に／で 10b

beyond koeta (adj) 越えた 3d

beyond koete (adv) 越えて 3d

bicycle jitensha 自転車 33a

Bicycle Path jitenshadō 自転車道 33d

bicycling saikuringu サイクリング 27b

big ōkii (adj) 大きい 11a, 25l

big, large ōkii (adj) 大きい 3c

bill kanjō 勘定 35b

bill seikyūsho 請求書 25a

bill, bank note osatsu お札 26

bill, check kanjō 勘定 24m

billiard ball tamatsuki no tama 玉突きの玉 27a

billiard table tamatsuki no tēburu 玉突きのテーブル 27a

billiards tamatsuki 玉突き 27a

billionth jūokubanme 十億番目 1b

bingo bingo ビンゴ 27a

bingo card bingo no kādo ビンゴのカード 27a

biography denki 伝記 25o, 28d

biological weapon seibutsu heiki 生物兵器 44b

biology seibutsugaku 生物学 37e

birch kanba no ki かんばの木 14c

bird tori 鳥 15b

bird of prey mōkin 猛禽 15b

birth tanjō 誕生 11c

birthday tanjōbi 誕生日 11c, 29c

biscuit bisuketto ビスケット 24i

bisector nitōbunsen 二等分線 2b

bishop bishoppu ビショップ 27a

bishop shikyō 司教 11d

bitter nigai (adj) 苦い 24p

black kokujin 黒人 11d

black kuro 黒 7a

black kuroi (adj) 黒い 7a

black and white film shiro kuro no fuirumu 白黒のフイルム 25d

black hole burakkuhōru ブラックホール 13a

blackboard kokuban 黒板 37b

blackboard eraser kokubankeshi 黒板消し 37b

bladder bōkō 膀胱 12a

blade ha 刃 23d

blame togameru (v) 咎める 17a

blanket mōfu 毛布 23d, 35c

blazer burēzā ブレーザー 25k

bleach hyōhakuzai 漂白剤 25g

bleed shukketsusuru (v) 出血する 39c

blind me no mienai (adj) 目の見えない 12c

blindness mōmoku 盲目 12c

block letter katsujitai ōmoji 活字体大文字 19c

blogging burogu ブログ 27a

blond kinpatsu no (adj) 金髪の 11a

blond kinpatsu no hito 金髪の人 11a

blood chi 血 39c

blood chi/ketsueki 血／血液 12a

blood ketsueki 血液 40a

blood pressure ketsuatsu 血圧 40a

blood test ketsueki kensa 血液検査 40a

bloom hana ga saku (v) 花が咲く 14a

blossom hana 花 14a

blouse burausu ブラウス 25k

blue ao 青 7a

blue aoi (adj) 青い 7a

blue jeans jīnzu ジーンズ 25k

blueberry burūberī ブルーベリー 14d, 24f

bluejay aokakesu 青カケス 15b

blueprint aojashin 青写真 28b

blues burūsu ブルース 25j

Bluetooth burūtūsu ブルートゥース 18a

Blu-ray DVD recorder burūrei disuku rekōdā ブルーレイディスクレコーダー 20b

boarding tōjō 搭乗 32a

boarding pass tōjō ken 搭乗券 32a

boastful jiman shitagaru (adj) 自慢したがる 21a

boat bōto ボート 36b

boat ticket fune no ken 船の券 30a

bodily physique taikaku 体格 11a

body honbun 本文 19c

body karada 身体 11a, 12a

body building bodī biru ボディービル 27b

body lotion bodī rōshon ボディーローション 25f

boil yuderu (v) 茹でる 24o

boiled yudeta (adj) 茹でた 24b

boiling point futtōten 沸騰点 6c

bold daitan na (adj) 大胆な 21a

boldface nikubutokatsuji 肉太活字 19c

bolt boruto ボルト 25b

Bon Festival (August 12–16) obon お盆 5g

bond saiken 債券 26

bone hone 骨 12a, 40a

book hon 本 20a, 25o, 37b

book rate shoseki ryōkin 書籍料金 19e

bookcase hondana 本棚 23c, 37b

bookseller hon ya 本屋 38a

bookstore hon ya 本屋 25o

boot būtsu ブーツ 25n

border kokkyō 国境 31

border kyōkai 境界 13e

border sakaisuru (v) 境する 13e

bore unzarisaseru (vt)
うんざりさせる 21a

bored taikutsushita (adj)
退屈した 21a

boredom taikutsu 退屈 21a

boss (in an office) jōshi 上司
38d

botanical shokubutsu no (adj)
植物の 14a

botanical garden shokubutsuen
植物園 36a

botany shokubutsugaku 植物学
14a, 37e

both ryōhō 両方 3c

bottle bin ビン 23d, 24l

bottom soko 底 3d

bouquet of flowers hanataba
花束 14b

bourbon whiskey bābon
バーボン 24k

bow yumi 弓 28c

bowl bōru ボール 24l

bowling bōringu ボーリング
27b

bowling alley bōringujō
ボーリング場 27b

bowling ball bōringu no bōru
ボーリングのボール 27b

bowling pin pin ピン 27b

box hako 箱 23d

box office kippu uriba
切符売り場 28a

boxing gloves gurabu グラブ
27b

boxing ring ringu リング 27b

boxing bokushingu ボクシング
27b

boy otoko no ko 男の子 11a

boyfriend otoko tomodachi/bōi
furendo
男友達／ボーイフレンド 10b

boyish shōnen no yō na (adj)
少年のような 11a

bra burajā ブラジャー 25k

brace shiretsu kyōseiki 歯列矯正
40b

bracelet buresuretto
ブレスレット 25i

bracket, parenthesis kakko 括弧
19c

brag jimansuru (v) 自慢する 21a

brain nō 脳 12a, 40a

brake burēki ブレーキ 33a, 33c,
33e

branch eda 枝 14a

branch shiten 支店 38d

branch office shiten 支店 26

brand burando/meigara
ブランド／銘柄 25a

brandy burandē ブランデー 24k

brash sekkachi na (adj)
せっかちな 11e

brass instruments kinkan gakki
金管楽器 28c

Brazil Burajiru ブラジル 30b

Brazilian Burajirujin ブラジル人
30d

bread pan パン 24g, 24i

break kyūkei 休憩 38d

break off a friendship
zekkōsuru (v) 絶交する 10b

breakdown koshō 故障 33c

breakfast asagohan 朝ご飯 24a,
35b

breakfast chōshoku 朝食 24a

breakfast included chōshoku
komi 朝食込み 35b

breast chibusa 乳房 12a

breath kokyū 呼吸 40a

breathe ikizuku *(v)* 息づく 12b

breathe kokyūsuru *(v)* 呼吸する 40a

bride hanayome 花嫁 11c

bridge hashi 橋 33c, 36a

brief kantan na *(adj)* 簡単な 4e, 37f

briefcase atasshe kēsu アタッシェケース 38c

briefly kantan ni *(adv)* 簡単に 4e

Briefly,... Kantan ni nobercba,... 簡単に述べれば、 … 17b

bright hanayaka na *(adj)* 華やかな 7b

brilliant sainō ni michita *(adj)* 才能に満ちた 11e

brittle moroi *(adj)* もろい 13d

broad bean soramame そら豆 14e

broadband burōdobando ブロードバンド 23e, 42b

broadcast hōsō 放送 20b

broadcast hōsōsuru *(v)* 放送局 20b

broccoli burokkori ブロッコリ 14e, 24e

brochure panfuretto パンフレット 30a

broil jikabi de yaku *(v)* 直火で焼く 24o

broiled jikabi de yaita *(adj)* 直火で焼いた 24b

broken bone kossetsu 骨折 39c

broken line hasen 破線 2b

bronchitis kikanshien 気管支炎 40a

bronze sculpture buronzu no chōkoku ブロンズの彫刻 28b

bronze seidō 青銅 13c

brooch burōchi ブローチ 25i

brook ogawa 小川 36b

broom hōki ほうき 23d

brother-in-law (spouse's elder brother, or elder sister's husband) gikei 義兄 10a

brother-in-law (spouse's elder brother, or elder sister's husband) giri no oniisan 義理のお兄さん 10a

brother-in-law (spouse's younger brother, or younger sister's husband) gitei 義弟 10a

brother-in-law (spouse's younger brother, or younger sister's husband) giri no otōtosan 義理の弟さん 10a

brothers gokyōdai ご兄弟 10a

brothers kyōdai 兄弟 10a

brothers and sisters kyōdai to shimai 兄弟と姉妹 10a

brown chairo 茶色 7a

brown chairoi *(adj)* 茶色い 7a

bruise dabokushō 打撲傷 40a

brush burashi ブラシ 12d, 25b, 28b

brush fude 筆 19d

brush oneself burashi o kakeru *(v)* ブラシをかける 12d

buckwheat sobako そば粉 24i

bud tsubomi o motsu *(v)* つぼみを持つ 14a

bud tsubomi つぼみ 14a

Buddhism bukkyō 仏教 11d

Buddhist bukkyō no *(adj)* 仏教の 11d

Buddhist bukkyō no shinja 仏教の信者 11d

Buddhist priest obōsan
お坊さん 11d

Buddhist temple otera お寺 11d

budget yosan 予算 26

buffalo baffarō バッファロー 15a

bug mushi 虫 15d

build tateru (v) 建てる 23f

builder kenchikugyōsha
建築業者 38a

building biru ビル 23g, 39a

bulb kyūkon 球根 14a

bull oushi 牡牛 15a

bump kobu こぶ 39c

bumper banpā バンパー 33e

bungee-jumping banjījanpingu
バンジージャンピング 27b

burdock gobō ごぼう 14e, 24e

burn (injury) yakedo 火傷 39a

burn (on fire) moeru (vi) 燃える
39a

bus basu バス 33a, 34

bus driver basu no untenshu
バスの運転手 34, 38a

bus station, depot basu no
hatchakusho バスの発着所 34

bus stop basu no teiryūsho
バスの停留所 34

bus tour basu tsuā バスツアー
30a

bush yabu 薮 13b

business class bijinesu kurasu
ビジネスクラス 30a, 32a

business hotel bijinesu hoteru
ビジネスホテル 35a

business letter bijinesu retā
ビジネスレター 19e

businessman bijinesuman
ビジネスマン 38a

businesswoman bijinesuūman
ビジネスウーマン 38a

busy (telephone) hanashichū
話し中 18b

but dakedo (conj) だけど 8k

demo (conj) でも 8k

keredomo (conj) けれども 8k

shikashi (conj) しかし 8k

butcher nikuya 肉屋 38a

butcher shop niku ya 肉屋 24n

butter batā バター 24h, 24j

butterfly chōchō 蝶々 15d

buttock oshiri お尻 12a

button botan ボタン 25g

buy kau (v) 買う 23f, 25a

buy a ticket ken o kau (v)
券を買う 30a, 34

by de で 8j

by means of de で 8j

by now imagoro wa 今頃は 4e

by the way tokorode ところで
44c

By the way... Tokoro de,...
ところで、… 17b

byte baito バイト 42b

C

cabbage kyabetsu キャベツ 14e,
24e

cabin kyabin キャビン 32c

cabin attendant kyakushitsu
jōmuin 客室乗務員 38a

cabinet kyabinetto キャビネット
23c

cabinet naikaku 内閣 43

cabinet member kakuryō 閣僚
43

cable hifuku densen 被覆電線
25b

cable kēburu ケーブル 18a, 23e

cafeteria kafeteria カフェテリア
24m, 37c

calculate keisansuru *(v)*
計算する 1f

calculating keisandakai *(adj)*
計算高い 11e

calculation keisan 計算 1f

calculus bisekibungaku
微積分学 37e

calendar karendā カレンダー
5b, 38c

call denwasuru *(v)* 電話する 39a

call yobu *(v)* 呼ぶ 17a

call an ambulance kyūkyūsha o
yobu *(v)* 救急車を呼ぶ 39c

call the police keisatsu o yobu
(v) 警察を呼ぶ 39b, 39c

call waiting kyatchifon
キャッチフォン 18a

caller ID chakushin hyōji
着信表示 18a

calling card meishi 名刺 16b

calm odayaka na *(adj)* 穏やかな
11e

calmness odayakasa 穏やかさ 11e

calyx gaku がく 14a

camcorder kamukōdā
カムコーダー 25d

camel rakuda ラクダ 15a

camellia tsubaki 椿 14b

camera kamera カメラ 25d

camera phone kamera tsuki
keitai denwa
カメラ付き携帯電話 18a

camera shop kamera ya
カメラ屋 25d

camping area kyanpujō
キャンプ場 36b

campus kōnai 校内 37c

Can you tell me where...? ...ga
doko ni aru ka oshiete kudasai.
・・・ がどこにあるか教えてくだ
さい。 36c

Can you tell me...? ...o, oshiete
moraemasu ka. ・・・ を、
教えてもらえますか。 9

Canada Kanada カナダ 30b

Canadian Kanadajin カナダ人
30d

canary kanaria カナリア 15b

cancel torikeshi 取り消し 19f

canceled kyanseru sareta
キャンセルされた 32b

cancer gan 癌 40a

Cancer kaniza 蟹座 5d

canine kenshi 犬歯 40b

canoe kanū カヌー 36b

canoeing kanū カヌー 27b

canvas kyanbasu キャンバス
28b

canyon kyōkoku 峡谷 13b

cap bōshi 帽子 25k

capacity yōryō/yōseki/teiin
(persons)
容量／容積／定員（人）3c

cape misaki 岬 13b

capital shuto 首都 13e

capital city shuto 首都 30a

capital letter ōmoji 大文字 19c

capital punishment shikei 死刑
41, 44b

Capricorn yagiza 山羊座 5d

capsule kapuseru カプセル 40a

captain kichō 機長 32c

car jidōsha 自動車 33a

car body bodī ボディー 33e

car radio kārajio カーラジオ 20b

car telephone jidōsha denwa
自動車電話 18a

car window windō ウィンドー
33e

carat karatto カラット 25i

carbon tanso 炭素 13c

carbon dioxide nisanka tanso
二酸化炭素 13c

carbon fiber tanso sen-i
炭素繊維 13c

carbon monoxide issannka tanso
一酸化炭素 13c

carburetor kyaburetā
キャブレター 33e

card kādo カード 19d

cardigan kādigan カーディガン
25k

cardinal number kisū 奇数 1d

career keireki 経歴 11f, 38d

carnation kānēshon
カーネーション 14b

carp koi 鯉 15c

carpenter daiku 大工 38a

carpet, rug jūtan 絨毯 23c

carrot ninjin 人参 14e, 24e

carry hakobu (v) 運ぶ 31

carry-on kinai mochikomi hin
機内持ち込み品 31, 32a

carve kiriwakeru (v) 切り分ける
24o

case kaku 格 8a

cash genkin 現金 26, 35b

cash genkinkasuru (v)
現金化する 26

cash register shiharai basho
支払い場所 25a

cashier shiharaigakari 支払い係
25a

cashier, teller madoguchigakari
窓口係 26

castle shiro 城 36a

cat neko 猫 15a

cataract hakunaishō 白内障 40a

catch toru (v) 捕る 27b

catch tsukamaeru (v) 捕まえる
39b

catch fire hi ga tsuku 火がつく
39a

catcher's mask kyatchā no
masuku
キャッチャーのマスク 27b

caterpillar kemushi 毛虫 15d

catfish namazu ナマズ 15c

cathedral daiseidō 大聖堂 36a

Catholic katorikkukyōto
カトリック教徒 11d

Catholic katorikkukyō no (adj)
カトリック教の 11d

Catholicism katorikkukyō
shinkō カトリック教信仰 11d

cauliflower karifurawā
カリフラワー 14e, 24e

cautious shinchō na (v) 慎重な
21a

cave dōkutsu 洞窟 13b

cavity, tooth decay mushiba
虫歯 40b

CD shīdī シーディー 25j, 42b

ceiling tenjo 天井 23a

celebrate one's birthday tanjōbi
o iwau 誕生日を祝う 11c

celery serori セロリ 14e, 24e

cell saibō 細胞 14a

cello chero チェロ 28c

cellular phone keitai denwa
携帯電話 18a, 42a

Celsius sesshi 摂氏 6c

cement mixer konkurīto mikisā
コンクリートミキサー 33a

censorship ken-etsu 検閲 44b

center chūō 中央 3d

center chūshin 中心 2a

centigrade sesshi 摂氏 6c

centimeter senchi センチ 3a

centipede mukade ムカデ 15d

Central America Chūō Amerika
中央アメリカ 30b

century seiki 世紀 4c

cereal shiriaru シリアル 24i

certified naiyō shōmei no *(adj)*
内容証明の 19e

chain chēn チェーン 25i

chain guard chēn gādo
チェーンガード 33a

chair isu 椅子 23c, 38c

chalk chōku チョーク 37b

chamber music shitsunaigaku
室内楽 25j

champagne shanpen シャンペン
24k

change kaeru *(vt)* 変える 4e

change kawaru *(vi)* 変わる 4e

change kuzusu くずす 25a

change norikaeru *(v)* 乗り換える
34

change (money) otsuri おつり
25a

change clothes kigaeru *(v)*
着替える 25m

change subject wadai o kaeru *(v)*
話題を変える 17a

channel channeru チャンネル
20b

channel suiro 水路 13b

chapter shō 章 28d

character moji 文字 8a

character seikaku 性格 11e

character (in a novel, play) tōjō
jinbutsu 登場人物 28d

characteristic dokutoku na *(adj)*
独特な 11e

characterize seikakuzukeru *(v)*
性格づける 11e

charge genshikaku no yōdenka
原子核の陽電荷 13c

charge kokuhatsusuru *(v)*
告発する 41

charge ryōkin 料金 28a

Charge it to my bill. Watakushi
no kanjō ni, tsukete oite
kudasai. 私の勘定に、
つけておいてください。 35b

charisma karisuma カリスマ 11e

charismatic karisuma no aru
(adj) カリスマのある 11e

charter flight chātā bin
チャーター便 30a

chase oikakeru *(v)* 追いかける
39b

chat chatto チャット 42b

chat zatsudansuru *(v)* 雑談する
17a

cheap yasui *(adj)* 安い 24p

check kogitte 小切手 26

check in (baggage) azukeru *(v)*
預ける 32a

check the oil oiru o chekkusuru
(v) オイルをチェックする 33c

checkbook kogitte chō 小切手帳
26

checker piece chekkā no koma
チェッカーの駒 27a

checkerboard chekkā ban
チェッカー盤 27a

checkers chekkā チェッカー 27a

check-in chekkuin チェックイン
32a

cheek hoo 頬 12a

cheer hagemasu *(v)* 励ます 17a

cheerful akarui *(adj)* 明るい 11e

cheerful yōki na *(adj)* 陽気な
21a

Cheers! Kanpai. 乾杯。 16c, 24l

cheese chīzu チーズ 24g, 24h

chemical kagaku no (adj) 化学の 13c

chemical weapon kagaku heiki 化学兵器 44b

chemist kagakusha 化学者 38a

chemistry kagaku 化学 13c, 37e

cherry blossom sakura no hana 桜の花 14b

cherry sakuranbo サクランボ 14d, 24f

cherry tree sakura 桜 14c

chess chesu チェス 27a

chessboard chesu ban チェス盤 27a

chest mune 胸 12a

chest of drawers (Japanese style) tansu たんす 23c

chest of drawers (western style) yōdansu 洋ダンス 23c, 35c

chestnut tree kuri no ki 栗の木 14c

chestnut kuri 栗 14d, 24f

Chicago Shikago シカゴ 30c

chick hina ひな 15b

chicken chikin チキン 24c

chicken niwatori 鶏 15b

chicken toriniku 鶏肉 24c

chicken pox mizubōsō 水疱瘡 40a

chickpea hiyokomame ひよこ豆 14e, 24e

chief of police keisatsu shochō 警察署長 41

child kodomo 子供 11b

childhood friend osananajimi 幼なじみ 10b

childish kodomoppoi (adj) 子供っぽい 11a

Children's Day (May 5) kodomo no hi 子供の日 5g

chill okan 悪寒 40a

chilled hiyashita (adj) 冷やした 24p

chilled sake reishu 冷酒 24p

chimney entotsu 煙突 23a

chimpanzee chinpanjī チンパンジー 15a

chin ago 顎 12a

China Chūgoku 中国 30b

Chinese character kanji 漢字 8a

Chinese Chūgokugo 中国語 30d

Chinese Chūgokujin 中国人 30d

chisel nomi のみ 25b, 28b

chlorine enso 塩素 13c

chlorophyll yōryokuso 葉緑素 14a

chop kizamu (v) 刻む 24o

chopstick rest hashioki 箸置き 23d, 24l

chopsticks hashi 箸 23d, 24l

Christian kirisutokyōto キリスト教徒 11d

Christianity kirisutokyō キリスト教 11d

Christmas Kurisumasu クリスマス 29a

chrysanthemum kiku 菊 14b

chum nakayoshi 仲良し 10b

church kyōkai 教会 11d, 36a

cicada semi 蝉 15d

cigar hamaki 葉巻 25e

cigarette tabako タバコ 25e

cinnamon shinamon シナモン 24j

circle en 円 2a

circulation hakkō busū 発行部数 20a

circumference enshū 円周 2a

citric kankitsurui no (adj) 柑橘類の 14d

citrus kankitsurui 柑橘類 14d

city shi 市 11f, 13e, 38b

city toshi 都市 30a, 36a

city map toshi chizu 都市地図 36a

civil law minpō 民法 41

clam hamaguri 蛤 15c, 24d

clamp shimegu 締め具 25b

clap of thunder raimei 雷鳴 6a

clarinet kurarinetto クラリネット 28c

class kurasu クラス 30a

class (students) gakkyū 学級 37d, 37f

classical music kurashikku myūjikku クラシックミュージック 25j, 28c

classified ad kōmokubetsu kōkoku 項目別広告 38d

classmate kyūyū 級友 37d

classroom kyōshitsu 教室 37c

clause setsu 節 8a, 19c

clean kirei na/seiketsu na (adj) 奇麗な/清潔な 11a, 25g

clean seiketsu na (adj) 清潔な 12d

clean sōjisuru (v) 掃除する 23f

clean, brush (teeth) ha o migaku (v) 歯を磨く 40b

clear harewatatta (adj) 晴れ渡った 6a

clear senmei na (adj) 鮮明な 25d

clear sukitootta (adj) 透き通った 13d

clear the table atokatazukesuru (v) 後片付けする 23f, 24o

clematis kuremachisu クレマチス 14b

clerk kyokuin 局員 19e

clerk's window madoguchi 窓口 19e

clever kenmei na (adj) 賢明な 11e

client (law) irainin 依頼人 41

cliff zeppeki 絶壁 13b

climate kikō 気候 6a, 13e

climb noboru (v) 登る／上る 3e

clip kurippu クリップ 19d

clock tokei 時計 4d

clone kurōn クローン 42a

close an account kōza o tojiru 口座を閉じる 26

close friend shinyū 親友 10b

closed heiten 閉店 25a

closet oshiire 押し入れ 23b, 35c

closing time heiten jikan 閉店時間 25a

closing musubi no kotoba 結びの言葉 19c

clothes sentakumono 洗濯物 25g

clothes basket sentaku kago 洗濯籠 25g

clothes hanger hangā ハンガー 23d, 35c

clothespin sentakubasami 洗濯バサミ 25g

clothing store yōfuku ya 洋服屋 25k

cloud kumo 雲 6a, 13b

cloudy kumotta (adj) 曇った 6a

club soda (sui) tansan (sui) 炭酸（水）24k

clutch (pedal) kuratchi クラッチ 33e

coach (sports, etc.) kōchi コーチ 27b

coach (transportation) futsū 普通 34

coal sekitan 石炭 13c

coal mine tankō 炭鉱 13c

coal mining tankō 炭坑 13c

coalition rengō/renritsu
連合／連立 43

coast engan 沿岸 13b

coastal engan no (adj) 沿岸の
13b

coat kōto コート 25k

Coca-Cola Kokakōra コカコーラ
24k

cockroach gokiburi ゴキブリ
15d

cod tara タラ 15c, 24d

coed school danjo kyōgaku no
gakkō 男女共学の学校 37a

coffee kōhī コーヒー 24k

coffee machine kōhīmēkā
コーヒーメーカー 23d

coffee pot kōhīpotto
コーヒーポット 23d

cognac konyakku コニャック
24k

coin kōka 硬貨 27a

coin collecting kōka shūshū
硬貨収集 27a

cold kanrei no (adj) 寒冷の 13e

cold kaze 風邪 40a

cold samui (adj) 寒い 6a, 6b

cold tsumetai (adj) 冷たい 24p

cold cuts reiniku no moriawase
冷肉の盛り合わせ 24c

cold front kanrei zensen
寒冷前線 6a

cold medicine kazegusuri
風邪薬 25h

cold water mizu 水 35c

colitis daichōen 大腸炎 40a

colleague dōryō 同僚 10b, 38d

collect call jushinninbarai no
denwa 受信人払いの電話 18b

collection shūshū 収集 27a

collector shūshūka 収集家 27a

collide shōtotsusuru (v)
衝突する 39c

collision shōtotsu 衝突 39c

cologne ōdekoron オーデコロン
25f

colon koron コロン 19c

color iro 色 7c

color iro o nuru (v) 色を塗る 7c

color film karā fuirumu
カラーフイルム 25d

color picture kara shashin
カラー写真 25d

colored iro o nutta (adj)
色を塗った 7c

coloring saishoku 彩色 7c

column koramu コラム 20a

columnist koramunisuto
コラムニスト 20a

comb kushi くし 12d, 25f

comb kushi de tokasu (v)
くしでとかす 12d

come kuru (v) 来る 3e

Come in! Ohairi kudasai.
お入りください。 16b

Come quickly! Isoide kite.
急いで来て。 39b

comedian kigeki yakusha
喜劇役者 28e

comedy kigeki 喜劇 20a, 28e

comet suisei 彗星 13a

comical kokkei na (adj) 滑稽な
11e

comics manga 漫画 20a, 25o

comma konma コンマ 19c

commerce shōgyō 商業 37e, 38d

commercial komāsharu
コマーシャル 20b

commercial radio minkan rajio
民間ラジオ 20b

commercial television minkan terebi 民間テレビ 20b

committee iinkai 委員会 43

communicate tsutaeru (v) 伝える 17a

communication dentatsu 伝達 17a

communism kyōsanshugi 共産主義 43

communist kyōsanshugisha 共産主義者 43

commuter train densha 電車 34

compact car konpakutokā コンパクトカー 33a

compact disc konpakuto disuku/ shīdī コンパクトディスク／ シーディー 20b, 25j, 42a

compact disc player shīdī purēyā シーディープレーヤー 20b

company policy shasoku 社則 38d

company kaisha 会社 38d

compare hikakusuru (v) 比較する 17a

comparison hikaku 比較 8a, 17a

compartment koshitsu 個室 34

compass konpasu コンパス 2b, 37b

compass rashinban/konpasu 羅針盤／コンパス 3d

compatible konpachi (no) (adj) コンパチ（の）42b

competition kyōgi 競技 27b

complain kujō o noberu (v) 苦情を述べる 17a, 21a, 35b

complaint kujō 苦情 17a, 21a, 35b

complementary angle yokaku 余角 2b

complex number fukusosū 複素数 1d

complicated fukuzatsu na (adj) 複雑な 22a

composer sakkyoku ka 作曲家 25j, 28c

composition sakubun 作文 37f

composition (music) sakkyoku 作曲 28c

compound kagōbutsu 化合物 13c

compound interest fukuri 複利 26

computer konpyūta コンピュータ 19d, 37b, 38c, 42b

computer game konpyūta gēmu コンピュータゲーム 27a

computer language konpyūta gengo コンピュータ言語 42b

computer science konpyūta saiensu コンピュータ サイエンス 37e, 42b

concave angle ōkaku 凹角 2b

concept gainen 概念 22a

concert konsāto コンサート 28c

concession baiten 売店 28a

conclude ketsuron o kudasu (v) 結論を下す 17a

conclusion ketsuron 結論 17a

concrete gutaiteki na (adj) 具体的な 22a

concussion nōshintō 脳震盪 40a

conditional mood jōkenhō 条件法 8a

condominium bunjō manshon 分譲マンション 23g

conductor shashō 車掌 34

conductor shikisha 指揮者 25j

cone ensuitai 円錐体 2a

confess jihakusuru (v) 自白する 41

confession jihaku 自白 41

confidential shinten 親展 19e

confirm kakuninsuru (v) 確認する 17a

confirmation kenshinrei 堅信礼 11d

conformist junnōsha 順応者 11e

Confucian jusha 儒者 11d

Confucianism jukyō 儒教 11d

congratulate iwau (v) 祝う 17a

Congratulations! Omedetō gozaimasu. おめでとうございます。 16c, 29c

congratulations! omedetō! おめでとう。 17a

congress gikai 議会 43

congressman/congresswoman giin 議員 43

conjugation dōshi no katsuyō 動詞の活用 8a

conjunction setsuzokushi 接続詞 8a

connection konekushon コネクション 30a, 32a

connection noritsugi 乗り継ぎ 34

conscience ryōshin 良心 11e, 22a

conscientious ryōshinteki na (adj) 良心的な 11e, 22a

conservation shizen hogo 自然保護 44a

conservative hoshuteki na (adj) 保守的な 11e, 43

conservative party hoshutō 保守党 43

conservatory ongaku gakkō 音楽学校 37a

consonant shiin 子音 8a

constant teisū   1f

constipation benpi 便秘 40a

Constitution Day (May 3) kenpō kinenbi 憲法記念日 5f, 5g

construction worker kenchikugenba no sagyōin 建築現場の作業員 38a

consult sōdansuru (v) 相談する 17a

consultant konsarutanto コンサルタント 38a

consumption shōhi 消費 44a

contact lenses kontakuto renzu コンタクトレンズ 40a

continent tairiku 大陸 13b, 13e

continental tairiku no (adj) 大陸の 13b, 13e

continental tairikusei no (adj) 大陸性の 6a

continually tsuzukete (adv) 続けて 4e

continue tsuzukeru (vt) 続ける 4e

continue tsuzuku (vi) 続く 4e

contraception hinin 避妊 44b

contract keiyaku 契約 38d

contradict hininsuru (v) 否認する 17a

contributor kikōsha 寄稿者 20a

convalescence kaifuku 快復 40a

convenience store knobini sutoā コンビニストアー 24n

conversation kaiwa 会話 17a

converse katariau (v) 語り合う 17a

convertible konbāchiburu コンバーチブル 33a

convex angle tokkaku 凸角 2b

convince kakushinsaseru (v) 確信させる 41

convince nattokusaseru (v) 納得させる 22b

cook chōrishi 調理師 38a

cook ryōrisuru *(v)* 料理する 24o

cookbook ryōri no hon 料理の本 25o

cookie kukkī クッキー 24i

cooking ryōri 料理 27a

cooking, cuisine ryōri 料理 24b

cool kakkō ii *(adj)* 格好いい 11a

cool suzushii *(adj)* 涼しい 6a

coordinate zahyō 座標 2b

co-pilot fuku sōjūshi 副操縦士 32c

copper dō 銅 13c

copy kakikata 書き方 37f

copy kopī/utsushi コピー／写し 19d

coral sango 珊瑚 13c

cordial kokoro no komotta *(adj)* 心の籠った 21a

cordless phone kōdoresufon コードレスフォン 18a

corn tōmorokoshi トウモロコシ 14e, 24e, 24i

corn chip kōnchippu コーンチップ 24i

corner (street) kado 角 33c

corner kado 角 36a

corner kōnā コーナー 27b

cornflakes kōnfurēku コーンフレーク 24i

cornflower kōnfurawā コーンフラワー 14b

corona korona コロナ 13a

correction fluid/correction tape shūsei eki/shūsei tēpu 修正液／修正テープ 19d, 25c

correspondence tsūshin 通信 19e

corridor rōka 廊下 23a

cortisone kōchizon コーチゾン 25h

cosecant kosekanto コセカント 2b

cosine kosain コサイン 2b

cosmetics keshōhin/kosume 化粧品／コスメ 12d

cosmetics shop keshōhin ten 化粧品店 25f

cosmos kosumosu コスモス 14b

cosmos uchū 宇宙 13a

cost kakaru *(v)* かかる 24o, 25a

cost nedan 値段 25a

costume ishō 衣装 28e

cotangent kotanjento コタンジェント 2b

cottage cheese kotēji chīzu コテージチーズ 24h

cotton dasshimen 脱脂綿 25h

cotton men 綿 13c

cotton men/momen 綿／木綿 25l

cotton swab menbō 綿棒 25h

cough seki せき 40a

cough seki o suru *(v)* せきをする 40a

cough syrup sekidome shiroppu せき止めシロップ 25h

council chihōgikai 地方議会 43

count kazoeru 数える 1f

countable kazoerareru *(adj)* 数えられる 1f

counter kauntā カウンター 25a

counter mono o kazoeru kotoba 物を数える言葉 8a

country kuni 国 11f, 13e, 30a

country music kantorī mūjikku カントリーミュージック 25j

courage yūki 勇気 11e

courageous yūki ga aru *(adj)*
勇気がある 11e

course kamoku 科目 37f

course kōsu コース 24g

court saibansho 裁判所 41

court music gagaku 雅楽 28c

court of appeal kōsoin 控訴院
41

courteous reigi tadashii *(adj)*
礼儀正しい 11e

courtesy reigi 礼儀 11e

courtroom hōtei 法廷 41

cousin itoko いとこ 10a

cousin itokosan いとこさん 10a

cove irie 入り江 13b

cover hyōshi 表紙 20a

cover charge kabā chāji
カバーチャージ 24m

cow meushi 牝牛 15a

CPR shinpaisoseihō 心肺蘇生法
40a

crab kani かに 15c, 24d

cracker kurakkā クラッカー 24i

crane tsuru 鶴 15b

crash butsukaru *(v)* ぶつかる
3e

crash kurasshu クラッシュ 42b

crash shōtotsu 衝突 39c

crash shōtotsusuru *(v)* 衝突する
39c

crawl hau *(v)* 這う 3e

crayon kureyon クレヨン 7c

crazy, mad kichigaijimita *(adj)*
気違いじみた 11e

cream kurīmu クリーム 24h, 24j

creative sōzōteki na *(adj)*
創造的な 11e, 22a

credit shinyō 信用 26

credit card kurejitto kādo
クレジットカード 26, 35b

credit limit riyō gendogaku
利用限度額 26

crest tosaka とさか 15b

crew tōjōin 搭乗員 32c

crib bebībeddo ベビーベッド
35c

cricket kōrogi コオロギ 15d

crime hanzai 犯罪 39b

criminal hanzaisha 犯罪者 39b

criminal law keihō 刑法 41

critic hyōronka 評論家 20a

critical hihanteki na *(adj)*
批判的な 11e

criticism hihyō 批評 20a

criticism hyōron 評論 28d

crocodile kurokodairu
クロコダイル 15c

cross (over)... ...o yokogiru *(v)*
・・・を横切る 36c

cross the street michi o
yokogiru *(v)* 道を横切る 36c

crossword puzzle kurosuwādo
pazuru クロスワードパズル
27c

crow karasu カラス 15b

crown shikan 歯冠 40b

cruel zankoku na *(adj)* 残酷な
21a

cruise kurūzu クルーズ 36b

crunchy pariparishita *(adj)*
パリパリした 24p

crustacean kōkakurui 甲殻類
15d

cry naku *(v)* 泣く 11e, 21a

cube seirokumentai 正六面体
2a

cube root rippōkon 立方根 1e

cubed sanjō no 三乗の 1e

cubic centimeter rippōsenchi
立方センチ 3a

cubic kilometer rippōkiro 立方キロ 3a

cubic meter rippōmētoru 立方メートル 3a

cubic millimeter rippōmiri 立方ミリ 3a

cuckoo kakkō 郭公 15b

cucumber kyūri キュウリ 14e, 24e

cue tamatsuki no kyū 玉突きのキュー 27a

cultivate saibaisuru (v) 栽培する 14a

cultivation saibai 栽培 14a

Culture Day (November 3) bunka no hi 文化の日 5g

cultured kyōyō no aru (adj) 教養のある 11e

cup (coffee) kōhījawan コーヒー茶碗 23d, 24l

cure ryōhō 療法 40a

cure naosu (vt) 治す 40a

curiosity kōkishin 好奇心 11e

curious kōkishin no tsuyoi (adj) 好奇心の強い 11e

curler kārā カーラー 12d, 25f

curls kāru カール 12d

curly-haired chijirege no (adj) 縮れ毛の 11a

currency tsūka 通貨 26

current denryū 電流 35c

current account tōza kanjō 当座勘定 26

curriculum karikyuramu カリキュラム 37f

curse akkō o haku (v) 悪口を吐く 17a

cursive-style letter hikkitai 筆記体 19c

curtain maku 幕 28e

curtains kāten カーテン 23c, 35c

curve kābu カーブ 33c

curved line kyokusen 曲線 2b

cushion kusshon クッション 27a

customer kokyaku 顧客 26

customer okyaku お客 25a

customs zeikan 税関 31

customs declaration form zeikan shinkokusho 税関申告書 31

customs officer zeikan no kakariin 税関の係員 31

cut kiru (v) 切る 14a, 24o

cut flower kiribana 切り花 14b

cut off kiru (v) 切る 18b

cut one's hair kaminoke o kiru (v) 髪の毛を切る 12d

cute kawaii (adj) 可愛い 11a

cutlery, tableware shokutakuyō shokkigu 食卓用食器具 24l

cyclamen shikuramen シクラメン 14b

cylinder enchū 円柱 2a

cymbals shinbaru シンバル 28c

cypress tree itosugi 糸杉 14c

cyst nōshu 囊腫 40a

D

daffodil suisen 水仙 14b

dahlia daria ダリア 14b

daily mainichi no (adj) 毎日の 4c

daily newspaper nikkanshi 日刊紙 20a

dairy gyūnyū ya 牛乳屋 24n

dairy product nyūseihin 乳製品 24h

daisy dējī デージー 14b

damp jimejime shita (adj) ジメジメした 6a

dance dansu ダンス 28c, 29b

dance odoru *(v)* 踊る 28c

dance music dansu ongaku ダンス音楽 25j

dance-drama (Japanese) Kabuki 歌舞伎 28e

dancer butō ka 舞踏家 28c

dancer dansā ダンサー 28c

Dane Denmākujin デンマーク人 30d

danger kiken 危険 39a

Danish Denmākugo デンマーク語 30d

dark koi *(adj)* 濃い 7b

dark kurai *(adj)* 暗い 6a

dark blue kon 紺 7a

dark-haired kuroi kami no ke no *(adj)* 黒い髪の毛の 11a

dash dasshu ダッシュ 19c

dashboard dasshubōdo ダッシュボード 33e

data dēta データ 42b

data processing dēta shori データ処理 42b

database dētabēsu データベース 42b

date dēto デート 29b

date hizuke 日付 19c

date natsume ナツメ 14d, 24f

date seinengappi 生年月日 38b

date and place of birth seinengappi to shusseichi 生年月日と出生地 38b

date of birth seinengappi 生年月日 11f

daughter musume 娘 10a

daughter ojōsan お嬢さん 10a

daughter-in-law musuko no yome 息子の嫁 10a

daughter-in-law musukosan no oyomesan 息子さんのお嫁さん 10a

dawn yoake 夜明け 4a

day hi 日 38b

day ichinichi/hi 一日／日 4a, 4c

day after tomorrow asatte 明後日 4a

day before yesterday ototoi 一昨日 4a

day care takujisho 託児所 37a

day of the week yōbi 曜日 5a

dead flower kareta hana 枯れた花 14b

deaf mimi no tōi *(adj)* 耳の遠い 12c

dean gakubuchō 学部長 37d

Dear... ...sama ・・・様 19b

dear friend shinyū 親友 10b

Dear Madam haikei 拝啓 19a

Dear Sir haikei 拝啓 19a

Dearest... shinainaru ...sama 親愛なる ・・・様 19b

death shi/shibō 死／死亡 11c

debate tōron 討論 17a, 41

debate tōronsuru *(v)* 討論する 17a, 41

debit kashikata 貸方 26

debt fusai 負債 26

decade jūnenkan 十年間 4c

decagon jukkakukei 十角形 2a

December jūnigatsu 十二月 5b

decent kichin to shita *(adj)* きちんとした 21a

deciduous tree rakuyōju 落葉樹 14c

decimal shōsū 小数 1f

decision hanketsu 判決 41

declarative heijo *(adj)* 平叙 8a

declare sengensuru *(v)* 宣言する 17a

declare shinkokusuru *(v)* 申告する 31

decrease genshō 減少 3c

decrease genshōsaseru *(vt)* 減少させる 3c

decrease genshōsuru *(vi)* 減少する 3c

deer shika 鹿 15a

defecate haibensuru *(v)* 排便する 40a

defend oneself jikobengosuru *(v)* 自己弁護する 41

defibrillator jo saidō ki 除細動器 40a

definite (article) tei *(adj)* 定 8a

definiton gogi 語義 20a

degree (university) gakui 学位 37f

degree do 度 2b, 6c

dehydration dassui shōjō 脱水症状 40a

delete sakujo 削除 19f

delicate sensai na *(adj)* 繊細な 11e

delicatessen derikatessen デリカテッセン 24n

Delighted! Ureshii desu. 嬉しいです。 16b

delivery haitatsu 配達 25a

delivery confirmation haitatsu shōmei 配達証明 19e

democracy minshushugi 民主主義 43

democrat minshushugisha 民主主義者 43

democratic minshushugi no *(adj)* 民主主義の 43

demonstrate hyōmeisuru *(v)* 表明する 22b

demonstration demo デモ 43

demonstrative shiji *(adj)* 指示 8a

Denmark Denmāku デンマーク 30b

dense mitsudo no takai *(adj)* 密度が高い 3b, 13d

density mitsudo/nōdo 密度／濃度 3b

dental hygiene shika eisei 歯科衛生 40b

dentist haisha 歯医者 38a, 40b

dentist's office haisha no shinryōsho 歯医者の診療所 40b

denture, false teeth ireba 入れ歯 40b

deny hiteisuru *(v)* 否定する 17a

deodorant deodoranto デオドラント 25f

department (of a store) uriba 売り場 25a

department store depāto デパート 25a

departure shuppatsu 出発 32a

deposit yokin 預金 26

deposit yokinsuru *(v)* 預金する 26

deposit slip yokinhyō 預金票 26

deposition kyōjutsu 供述 41

depressed yūutsu na *(adj)* 憂鬱な 21a

depression utsubyō 鬱病 40a

depression yūutsu 憂鬱 21a

dermatitis hifuen 皮膚炎 40a

descend kudaru *(v)* 下る 3e

describe noberu *(v)* 述べる 17a

description kijutsu 記述 17a

description ninsōgaki 人相書 39b

descriptive kijutsu *(adj)* 記述 8a

desert sabaku 砂漠 13b

desk tsukue 机 37b

desperate hisshi no (adj) 必死の 21a

dessert dezāto デザート 24g

destroy hakaisuru (v) 破壊する 39a

detain kōryūsuru (v) 拘留する 41

detest kirau (v) 嫌う 21b

develop genzōsuru (v) 現像する 25d

developing country hatten tojōkoku 発展途上国 43

development genzō 現像 25d

dew tsuyu 露 6a

diabetes tōnyōbyō 糖尿病 40a

diagnosis shindan 診断 40a

dial daiaru o mawasu (v) ダイアルを回す 18b

dial daiaru ダイアル 18b

dial mojiban 文字盤 4d

diameter chokkei 直径 2a

diamond anniversary kekkon nanajūgoshūnen kinenbi 結婚七十五周年記念日 11c

diamond daiamondo ダイアモンド 25i

diarrhea geri 下痢 40a

dictate kōjutsusuru (v) 口述する 17a

dictation kakitori 書き取り 37f

dictionary jisho 辞書 20a, 25o, 37b

die nakunaru (v, pol) 亡くなる 11c

die shinu (v) 死ぬ 11c

Diet (Japanese Congress) kokkai 国会 43

Diet member kokkai giin 国会議員 43

diet soda daietto no nomimono ダイエットの飲み物 24k

difference sa 差 1f

difficult muzukashii (adj) 難しい 22a

dig horu (v) 掘る 14a

digestive system shōka keitō 消化系統 40a

digit sūji 数字 1d

digital dejitaru デジタル 18a

digital camera dejitaru kamera デジタルカメラ 25d

digital SLR camera dejitaru ichiganrefu デジタル一眼レフ 25d

digital watch/clock dejitaru no tokei デジタルの時計 4d

digress wakimichi ni soreru (v) 脇道にそれる 17a

diligence kinben 勤勉 11e

diligent, hardworking kinben na (adj) 勤勉な 11e

dimension jigen 次元 3b

dining car shokudōsha 食堂車 34

dining room shokudō 食道 23b

dinner bangohan 晩ご飯 24a

dinner yūshoku 夕食 24a

dioxin daiokishin ダイオキシン 13c

diploma sotsugyōshōsho 卒業証書 11f, 37f

diplomatic gaikōteki na (adj) 外交的な 11e

direct chokusetsu (adj) 直接 8a

direct dialing daiaru chokutsu ダイアル直通 18b

direct train chokutsū ressha 直通列車 34

direction hōkō 方向 3d, 36c

dirty kitanai *(adj)* 汚い 11a, 12d

dirty yogoreta *(adj)* 汚れた 25g

disagree hantaisuru *(v)* 反対する 41

disagree iken o koto ni suru *(v)* 意見を異にする 17a

disagree sansei shinai 賛成しない 21a

disagreement fusansei 不賛成 21a

disagreement iken no sōi 意見の相違 17a

disappoint shitsubōsaseru *(vt)* 失望させる 21a

disappointed gakkarishita *(adj)* がっかりした 21a

disappointment shitsubō 失望 21a

disarmament gunbi teppai 軍備撤廃 43

disco disuko ディスコ 28c, 29b

discount waribiki no *(adj)* 割引の 25a

discount waribiki 割引 26, 30a

discourse wahō 話法 8a

discourteous shitsurei na *(adj)* 失礼な 11e

discrimination sabetsu 差別 44b

discuss rongisuru *(v)* 論議する 17a

discuss sōdansuru *(v)* 相談する 41

discussion rongi 論議 17a

disgust mukamukasaseru *(v)* むかむかさせる 21b

disgusted unzarishita *(adj)* うんざりした 21b

disgusting hakike o moyōsu *(adj)* 吐き気を催す 11e

disgusting mukamuka suru *(adj)* むかむかする 21a

dish antenna parabora antena パラボラアンテナ 42a

dishonest fushōjiki na *(adj)* 不正直な 11e

dishwasher shokkiaraiki 食器洗い器 23d

disingenuous inken na *(adj)* 陰険な 11e

disk disuku ディスク 42b

dislike kirau *(v)* 嫌う 21b

dislocation dakkyū 脱臼 40a

disposable camera tsukaisute kamera 使い捨てカメラ 25d

dissatisfaction fuman 不満 21a

dissatisfied fuman no aru *(adj)* 不満のある 21a

dissolve kaisansuru *(v)* 解散する 43

distance kyori 距離 3d, 33c

dive tobikomu *(v)* 飛び込む 3e

divide waru *(v)* 割る 1e

division warizan 割り算 1e

divorce rikon 離婚 11c

divorce rikonsuru *(v)* 離婚する 11c

divorced rikon 離婚 38b

divorced rikonshita *(adj)* 離婚した 11c, 11f

dizziness memai 目眩 40a

Do you have a vacant room? Heya ga arimasu ka. 部屋がありますか。 35b

doctor igaku hakase 医学博士 16b

doctor isha 医者 38a, 39c, 40a

doctor (direct address) sensei 先生 16b

doctor's instruments shinryō kigu 診療器具 40a

doctor's visit ōshin 往診 40a

doctorate hakasegō 博士号 37f

documentary dokyumentarī ドキュメンタリー 20b

documents shorui 書類 31

dodecahedron jūnimentai 十二面体 2a

does not equal hitoshikunai 等しくない 1f

dog inu 犬 15a

dogwood hanamizuki ハナミズキ 14c

dollar doru ドル 26

dolphin iruka いるか 15c

Don't mention it! Iie, dō itashimashite. いいえ、 どう致しまして。 16c

donkey roba ロバ 15a

door doa ドア 33e

door to 戸 23a

doorbell yobirin 呼び鈴 23a

doorman doaman ドアマン 35b

dormant volcano kyūkazan 休火山 13b

dormitory ryō/kishukusha 寮／寄宿舎 37c

dosage yōryō 用量 25h

dot com dotto komu ドットコム 19f

double daburu no (adj) ダブルの 24p

double nibai ni suru (vt) 二倍にする 3c

double nibai no (adj) 二倍の 3c

double bass kontora basu コントラバス 28c

double bed daburu beddo ダブルベッド 35c

double room daburu no heya ダブルの部屋 35b

doubt utagai 疑い 22a

doubt utagau (v) 疑う 22b

dove kijibato キジバト 15b

down shita ni (adv) 下に 3d

down shita no (adj) 下の 3d

down... ...o kudatta tokoro ni ・・・ を下ったところに 36c

download daunrōdo ダウンロード 42b

downtown toshin 都心 30a, 36a

Dr. (Ph.D. degree) hakase 博士 11f, 16b

draft shitagaki 下書き 19f

draft shitagaki/sōkō 下書き／草稿 19d

draft tegata furidashi 手形振り出し 26

dragonfly tonbo トンボ 15d

drama dorama ドラマ 20a, 28e

draw hikiwake 引き分け 27b

draw hikiwakeru (v) 引き分ける 27b

draw sen o hiku (v) 線を引く 2b

drawer hikidashi 引き出し 23a

drawing instruments seizu kigu 製図器具 2b

drawing sobyō 素描 28b

dream yume ni egaku (v) 夢に描く 22b

dress doresu ドレス 25k

dresser kyōdai 鏡台 35c

dressing room shichakushitsu 試着室 25k

drill (dentist) doriru ドリル 40b

drill (tool) doriru ドリル 25b

drink nomimono 飲み物 24k

drink nomu (v) 飲む 12b, 24o

drive untensuru (v) 運転する 3e, 33b, 33c

driver untenshu 運転手 33b

driver's license unten menkyosho 運転免許書 33b

drizzle kirisame 霧雨 6a

drop out chūtaisuru (v) 中退する 37f

drowsiness nemuke 眠気 40a

drug addiction mayaku chūdoku 麻薬中毒 40a, 44b

drug pusher mayaku mitsubainin 麻薬密売人 44b

drug trafficking mayaku baibai 麻薬売買 44b

drugs mayaku 麻薬 44b

drugstore doraggusutoā ドラッグストア 12d, 25h

drum taiko 太鼓 28c

dry kansōshita (adj) 乾燥した 6a

dry kawakasu (v) 乾かす 12d

dry cleaner doraikurīningu ya ドライクリーニング屋 25g

dryer doraiyā ドライヤー 25g

dryer kansōki 乾燥機 23d

dubbing fukikae 吹き替え 28a

duck ahiru アヒル 15b, 24c

duck dakku ダック 24c

duet nijūshō 二重唱 28c

dull nibui/shizunda (adj) 鈍い／沈んだ 7b

dull taikutsu na 退屈な 11e

dumb gudon na 愚鈍な 11e

dump truck danpukā ダンプカー 33a

dune sakyū 砂丘 13b

during aida ni (adv) 間に 4e

dust pan chiritori ちり取り 23d

duster hataki はたき 23d

Dutch Orandago オランダ語 30d

Dutch Orandajin オランダ人 30d

duty kanzei 関税 31

DVD dībuidī ディーブイディー 20b, 25j, 42b

DVD recorder dībuidī rekōdā ディーブイディーレコーダー 20b

dynamic seiryokuteki na (adj) 精力的な 11e

E

eager nesshin na (adj) 熱心な 21a

eagle washi 鷲 15b

ear mimi 耳 12a

early hayai (adj) 早い 4e, 32b, 34

early hayaku (adv) 早く 4e, 32b

earn kasegu (v) 稼ぐ 38d

earphone iyahōn イヤホーン 18a, 20b

earring iaringu イアリング 25i

earth chikyū 地球 13a

earthquake jishin 地震 13b

easel, tripod īzeru イーゼル 28b

east higashi 東 3d

eastern higashi no 東の 3d

easy yasahii (adj) やさしい 22a

eat taberu (v) 食べる 12b, 24o

eccentric fūgawari na (adj) 風変わりな 11e

eclipse shoku 蝕 13a

ecology seitaigaku 生態学 44a

economics keizai 経済 37e

economy keizai 経済 43

economy class ekonomī kurasu エコノミークラス 30a, 32a

economy seat futsū seki 普通席 34

ecosystem seitaikei 生態系 44a

edge hashi 端 3d

editor henshūsha 編集者 20a, 38a

editorial shasetsu 社説 20a

editor-in-chief henshūchō 編集長 20a

education gakureki 学歴 38b

education kyōiku 教育 11f, 37f

eel unagi ウナギ 15c, 24d

efficient yūnō na *(adj)* 有能な 21a

egg tamago 卵 15b, 24h

eggplant nasu 茄子 14e, 24e

egoism rikoshugi 利己主義 11e

egoist rikoshugisha 利己主義者 11e

egoistic jibun katte na *(adj)* 自分勝手な 21a

egoistic rikoteki na *(adj)* 利己的な 11e

Egypt Ejiputo エジプト 30b

eight hachi 八 1a

eight yattsu 八つ 1a

eight hundred happyaku 八百 1a

eight thousand hassen 八千 1a

eighteen thousand ichimanhassen 一万八千 1a

eighteen jūhachi 十八 1a

eighth daihachi 第八 1b

eighth hachibanme 八番目 1b

eighth yattsume 八つ目 1b

eighty hachijū 八十 1a

eighty thousand hachiman 八万 1a

El Niño eru nīnyo エルニーニョ 6a

elastic danryokusei no aru *(adj)* 弾力性のある 13d

elbow hiji 肘 12a

elder brother ani 兄 10a

elder brother oniisan お兄さん 10a

elder sister ane 姉 10a

elder sister onēsan お姉さん 10a

elderly person nenpai no hito 年配の人 11b

elect erabu *(v)* 選ぶ 43

elected politician giin 議員 43

election senkyo 選挙 43

electric razor denki kamisori 電気カミソリ 12d, 25f

electric stove denki sutōbu 電気ストーブ 23d

electrical denki no *(adj)* 電気の 13c, 25b

electrician denkikō 電気工 38a

electricity denki 電気 13c, 23e

electrocardiograph shindenkei 心電計 40a

electron denshi 電子 13c, 42a

electronic denshi no *(adj)* 電子の 13c

elegance yūga 優雅 11e

elegance yūga/jōhin 優雅／上品 11a

elegant ereganto na *(adj)* エレガントな 25l

elegant yūga na/jōhin na *(adj)* 優雅な／上品な 11a

elegant yūga na *(adj)* 優雅な 11e

elegantly yūga ni *(adv)*/jōhin ni *(adv)* 優雅に／上品に 11a

element genso 元素 13c

elementary school shōgakkō 小学校 11f, 37a, 38b

elephant zō 象 15a

elevator erebētā エレベーター 23g, 35b

eleven jūichi 十一 1a

eleven thousand ichimansen 一万千 1a

eleventh daijūichi 第十一 1b

eleventh jūichibanme 十一番目 1b

elm nire 楡 14c

eloquence yūben 雄弁 11e

eloquent yūben na (adj) 雄弁な 11e

e-mail īmēru Eメール 19f, 38b, 42b

e-mail address ī-mēru adoresu Eメールアドレス 11f, 19f, 42b

embroidery shishū 刺繍 27a

emerald emerarudo エメラルド 25i

emergency exit hijōguchi 非常口 32c, 39a

emergency hospital kyūkyū byōin 救急病院 39c

Emergency Lane kinkyū shasen 緊急車線 33d

emery board tsume yasuri 爪ヤスリ 25f

emotion kanjō 感情 21a

emotional kanjōteki na(adj) 感情的な 21a

emperor tennō 天皇 43

Emperor's Birthday (December 23) tennō tanjōbi 天皇誕生日 5g

emphasis kyōchō 強調 17a

emphasize kyōchōsuru (v) 強調する 17a

employ yatou (v) 雇う 38d

employee jūgyōin 従業員 11f, 38d

employee shain 社員 38d

employee (bank) ginkōin 銀行員 26

employer koyōsha 雇用者 11f, 38d

employment koyō 雇用 11f

employment agency shokugyō shōkaisho 職業紹介所 38d

empress kōgō 皇后 43

empty kara ni suru (v) 空にする 3c

empty kara no (adj) 空の 3c

EMT kyūkyū kyūmei shi 救急救命士 40a

encourage hagemasu (v) 励ます 21a

encouragement gekirei 激励 21a

encyclopedia hyakkajiten 百科事典 20a, 25o, 37b

end owari 終わり 4e

end, finish owaru (v) 終わる 4e

endangered species zetsumetsu kikenshu 絶滅危険種 13c

endorse uragakisuru (v) 裏書きする 26

endorsement uragaki 裏書き 26

enemy teki 敵 10b

energetic enerugisshu na (adj) エネルギッシュな 11e

energy enerugī エネルギー 13c, 44a

energy crisis enerugī kiki エネルギー危機 44a

energy needs enerugī juyō エネルギー需要 44a

energy source enerugī shigen エネルギー資源 44a

energy waste enerugī rōhi エネルギー浪費 44a

engaged konyakushita (adj) 婚約した 11c

engagement konyaku 婚約 11c, 29a

engineer gishi 技師 38a

engineering kōgaku 工学 37e

England Igirisu イギリス 30b

English eigo 英語 30d

English Igirisujin イギリス人 30d

enlarge hikinobasu (v) 引き伸ばす 25d

enlarge ōkikusuru (v) 大きくする 25m

enlargement hikinobashi 引き伸ばし 25d

enough jūbun na (adj) 十分な 3c

enough jūbun ni (adv) 十分に 3c

Enough! (No more!) Mō yoshinasai. もう、よしなさい。 21c

enter hairu (v) 入る 3e, 16b, 36c

enthusiastic nesshin na (adj) 熱心な 21a

entire zentai no (adj) 全体の 3c

entrance iriguchi 入り口 23a, 25a, 35b

Entrance iriguchi 入り口 33d

entrance exam nyūgaku shiken 入学試験 37f

entrance hall (Japanese) genkan 玄関 23b

envelope fūtō 封筒 19d, 19e, 25c

envious urayamashii (adj) 羨ましい 11e

environment kankyō 環境 13b, 44a

environmental protection kankyō hogo 環境保護 13c

envy urayamu (v) 羨む 11e

equality dōtō 同等 1f

equals hitoshii 等しい 1f

equation hōteishiki 方程式 1f

equator sekidō 赤道 13e

equilateral tōhen (adj) 等辺 2a

equinox bunten 分点 5c

erase shōkyo 消去 19f

eraser keshigomu 消しゴム 2b, 19d, 25c, 37b

error machigai 間違い 37f

eruption funka 噴火 13b

escape tōbōsuru (v) 逃亡する 39b

escape, get out nogareru (v) 逃れる 39a

esophagus shokudō 食道 12a

espresso esupuresso エスプレッソ 24k

essay essei エッセイ 20a, 25o, 28d, 37f

esthetician esute biyōshi エステ美容師 12d

esthetics esute / zenshin biyō エステ／全身美容 12d

etching etchingu エッチング 28b

Ethernet Īsanetto イーサネット 42b

Ethernet connection Īsanetto konekushon イーサネットコネクション 35c

e-ticket īchiketto イーチケット 32a

Europe Yōroppa ヨーロッパ 30b

even number gūsū 偶数 1d

evening ban 晩 4a

evening yūgata 夕方 4a

evening paper yūkan 夕刊 20a

evening school yagaku 夜学 37a

evergreen jōryokuju 常緑樹 14c

every time maikai 毎回 4e

every, each dono ~ mo どの～も 3c

Everybody out! Soto e dete kudasai. 外へ出てください。 39a

everyone daremo 誰も 3c, 8i

everything nandemo mina 何でもみな 8i

everywhere doko demo *(adv)* どこでも 36c

evidence shōko 証拠 41

exam shiken 試験 37f

examine shiraberu *(v)* 調べる 40b

examine (medically) shinsatsusuru *(v)* 診察する 40a

exclamation mark kantanfu 感嘆符 19c

exchange kōkan 交換 26

exchange kōkansuru *(v)* 交換する 25a, 26

exchange rates kōkran ritsu 交換率 26

excursion gurūpu tsuā グループツアー 30a

excuse iiwake 言い訳 17a

Excuse me! Sumumasen. すみません。 16c

excuse oneself iiwakesuru *(v)* 言い訳する 17a

exercise renshū mondai 練習問題 37f

exhibition tenjikai 展示会 28b

existence sonzai 存在 22a

exit deguchi 出口 25a, 35b

Exit deguchi 出口 33d

exit, go out deru *(v)* 出る 36c

expensive takai *(adj)* 高い 24p, 25a

explain setsumeisuru *(v)* 説明する 17a, 37f

explanation setsumei 説明 17a, 37f

exponent beki shisū ベキ指数 1f

exposure roshutsu 露出 25d

express noberu *(v)* 述べる 17a

express mail shin tokkyū yūbin 新特急郵便 19e

express train kyūkō 急行 34

expression hyōgen 表現 17a

extension enchō/kakucho 延長／拡張 3b

extension naisen 内線 18b, 38b

extinct volcano shikazan 死火山 13b

extinguish, put out kesu *(v)* 消す 39a

extra copy yakimashi 焼き増し 25d

extract a root (mathematics) kon o hiraku 根を開く 1e

extract, pull nuku *(v)* 抜く 40b

extraction (dentistry) basshi 抜歯 40b

eye me 目 12a

eye doctor meisha 目医者 38a, 40a

eye drops megusuri 目薬 25h

eye shadow aishadō アイシャドー 25f

eyebrow mayuge 眉毛 12a

eyeglasses megane 眼鏡 40a

eyelash matsuge 睫毛 12a

eyelid mabuta まぶた 12a

eyeliner airainā アイライナー 25f

eyesight shiryoku 視力 40a

eyewitness mokugekisha 目撃者 39b, 41

F

fable gūwa 寓話 28d

fabric kiji 生地 25l

fabric softener sofuto shiagezai ソフト仕上がり剤 25g

face kao 顔 12a

face powder oshiroi おしろい 25f

facial biganjutsu 美顔術 12d

faction habatsu 派閥 43

factor (mathematics) insū 因数 1f

factor insū ni bunkaisuru (v) 因数に分解する 1f

factorization insūbunkai 因数分解 1f

factory kōjō 工場 38d

factory worker kōin 工員 38a

Fahrenheit kashi 華氏 6c

fail an exam shaken ni ochiru (v) 試験に落ちる 37f

faint kizetsusuru (v) 気絶する 12b

faint shisshin 失神 40a

fairy tale dōwa 童話 28d

faith shinkō 信仰 11d

faith, trust shinrai 信頼 21a

faithful chūjitsu na (adj) 忠実な 11e

faithful shinkōshin ga atsui (adj) 信仰心が厚い 11e

fake nise no (adj) にせの 13d

falcon hayabusa ハヤブサ 15b

fall aki 秋 5c

fall ochiru (v) 落ちる 3e

fall asleep nekomu (v) 寝込む 12b

fall in love sukininaru (v) 好きになる 11c

false imitēshon no (adj) イミテーションの 25i

family gokazoku ご家族 10a

family kazoku 家族 10a

family friend kazoku no tomodachi 家族の友達 10b

family guest house minshuku 民宿 35a

family name myōji 苗字 11f

family relationship gokazoku kankei ご家族関係 10a

family relationship kazoku kankei 家族関係 10a

fan fan ファン 33e

fantastic subarashii (adj) 素晴らしい 21a

far tōku ni (adv) 遠くに 3d

far tōku no (adj) 遠くの 3d

far (from) tōi (adj) 遠い 36c

fare box ryōkinbako 料金箱 34

Farewell! Gokigenyō. ごきげんよう。 16a

farm nōjō 農場 15a

farmer nōfu 農夫 15a

farmer nōgyō jūjisha 農業従事者 38a

farmland nōchi 農地 13b

fascinate miwakusuru (vt) 魅惑する 11e

fascinating miwakuteki na (adj) 魅惑的な 11e

fascination miwaku 魅惑 11e

fashion fasshon ファッション 25k

fast hayai (adj) 早い 3d

fast hayai (adj) 速い 3e

fast hayaku (adv) 早く 3d

fast hayaku (adv) 速く 3e

fast food fāsuto fūdo ファーストフード 24m

fasten shimeru (v) 締める 32c

fat futotta (adj) 太った 11a

father chichi 父 10a

father otōsan お父さん 10a

father-in-law gifu 義父 10a

father-in-law giri no otōsan 義理のお父さん 10a

fatty abura ga ōi (adj) 脂が多い 24p

faucet jaguchi 蛇口 23a, 35c

fault dansō 断層 13b

fax fakkusu ファックス 18b, 38c

fax machine fakkusu ファックス 18a, 42a

fax number fakkusu bangō ファックス番号 11f, 38c

fear osore 恐れ 21a

feather hane 羽 15b

February nigatsu 二月 5b

feel kanji ga suru (v) 感じがする 40a

feel kanjiru (v) 感じる 21a

feel bad kibun ga warui 気分が悪い 12b, 40a

feel well kibun ga ii 気分がいい 12b, 40a

feeling kanji 感じ 21a

felt-tip pen feruto pen フェルトペン 19d, 25c

female josei 女性 11a

female onna 女 38b

feminine josei 女性 11a

feminine josei no (adj) 女性の 11a

feminine (womanly) joseiteki na (adj) 女性的な 11a

feminism feminizumu フェミニズム 44b

feminist feminisuto フェミニスト 44b

fence kakoi 囲い 15a

fencing fenshingu フェンシング 27b

fencing outfit fenshingu no yunifōmu フェンシングの ユニフォーム 27b

fender fendā フェンダー 33e

fennel uikyō/fenneru ウイキョウ／フェンネル 14e

fertilize hiryō o yaru (v) 肥料をやる 14a

fertilizer hiryō 肥料 14a

fetus taiji 胎児 44b

fever netsu 熱 40a

fiancé konyakusha 婚約者 10b, 11c

fiancée konyakusha 婚約者 10b, 11c

fiber sen-i 繊維 13c

fiction fikushon フィクション 28d

fiction shōsetsu 小説 20a

field kōya 荒野 13b

field kyōgijō 競技場 27b

field nohara 野原 13b

field of study kenkyū bunya 研究分野 37f

fierce hageshii (adj) 激しい 21a

fifteen thousand ichimangosen 一万五千 1a

fifteen jūgo 十五 1a

fifth daigo 第五 1b

fifth gobanme 五番目 1b

fifth itsutsume 五つ目 1b

fifty gojū 五十 1a

fifty thousand goman 五万 1a

fifty-one gojūichi 五十一 1a

fig ichijiku イチジク 14d, 24f

fig tree ichijiku no ki イチジクの木 14c

fight kakutō 格闘 39b

figure of speech hiyuteki hyōgen 比喩的表現 17a

file bunsho fairu 文書ファイル 38c

file bunsho 文書 19f

file fairu ファイル 42b

file yasuri ヤスリ 25b

file card fairu yō kādo
ファイル用カード 38c

file folder shoruibasami
書類ばさみ 25c

fill mitasu (v) 満たす 3c

fill up mantan ni suru (v)
満タンにする 33c

filling tsumemono 詰め物 40b

film fuirumu フイルム 25d

filter firutā フィルター 25d,
33e

fin hire ひれ 15c

final decision saishū kettei
最終決定 41

fine ii (adj) いい 6a

Fine! Junchō desu. 順調です。
16a

fine, ticket ihan no ken 違反の券
33c

fine arts bijutsu 美術 37e

finger yubi 指 12a

fingernail tsume 爪 12a

finish shiagari 仕上がり 25d

finish school gakkō o oeru (v)
学校を終える 11f, 37f

Finland Finrando フィンランド
30b

Finn Finrandojin フィンランド人
30d

Finnish Finrandogo
フィンランド語 30d

fir momi モミ 14c

fire kaji 火事 13c, 39a

Fire! Kaji da. 火事だ。 39a

fire (dismiss) kaikosuru (v)
解雇する 38d

fire alarm kasai hōchiki
火災報知器 39a

fire department shōbōsho
消防署 39a

fire engine shōbōsha 消防車
33a, 39a

fire extinguisher shōkaki 消火器
39a

fire hose shōka yō hōsu
消火用ホース 39a

fire hydrant shōkasen 消火栓
39a

firearm kaki 火器 39b

firefighter shōbōshi 消防士 38a,
39a

firefly hotaru 蛍 15d

fireplace danro 暖炉 23a

fireproof taikasei no (adj)
耐火性の 39a

first daiichi 第一 1b

first hitotsume 一つ目 1b

first ichibanme 一番目 1b

first aid kyūkyūbako 救急箱 25h

first aid ōkyū teate 応急手当
39a, 39c

first class (plane) fāsuto kurasu
ファーストクラス 30a, 32a

first class (train) gurīn sha
グリーン車 30a

first class (train) gurīnsha no
seki グリーン車の席 34

first name mei 名 38b

first name namae 名前 11f, 38b

first person ichininshō 一人称
8a

first third of the month jōjun
上旬 4c

first year ichinen 一年 37a

first-run film fūkiri eiga
封切り映画 28a

fish sakana o tsuru (v) 魚を釣る
15c

fish sakana 魚 15c, 24d

fish store sakana ya 魚屋 24n

fisherman ryōshi 漁師 15c

fishing tsuri 釣り 15c, 27a, 36b

fishing rod tsuriazo 釣り竿 15c

fishmonger sakanaya 魚屋 38a

fission reactor kakubunretsuro 核分裂炉 42a

fit au (v) 合う 25k

five go 五 1a

five itsutsu 五つ 1a

five hundred gohyaku 五百 1a

five thousand gosen 五千 1a

fix naosu (v) 直す 33c

fix, repair shūrisuru (v) 修理する 25i

fixed kotei (no) (adj) 固定（の） 26

fixed price kimatta nedan 決まった値段 24m

fixed price teika 定価 25a

flame honoo 炎 39a

flamingo furamingo フラミンゴ 15b

flash furasshu フラッシュ 25d

flash/bolt of lightning inazuma no hikari 稲妻の光り 6a

flashlight kaichūdentō 懐中電灯 25b

flat-panel TV usugata terebi 薄型テレビ 20b

flatter oseji o iu (v) お世辞を言う 21a

flattery oseji お世辞 21a

flavor aji 味 12c

flea nomi ノミ 15d

flee nigeru (v) 逃げる 3e

Flemish Furandāsugo フランダース語 30d

flight bin 便 32a

flight attendant kyakushitsu jōmuin 客室乗務員 32c

floor yuka 床 23a

floor (level) kai 階 23a, 35b

floor cushion zabuton 座布団 35c

florist hanaya 花屋 38a

flounder hirame 平目 15c, 24d

flour komugiko 小麦粉 24i

flow nagareru (v) 流れる 13b

flower hana 花 14a, 14b

flower arrangement ikebana 活け花 14b

flower bed kadan 花壇 14b

flu ryūkan 流感 40a

fluorescent light keikōtō 蛍光灯 25b

flute furūto フルート 28c

fly hae ハエ 15d

fly tobu (v) 飛ぶ 3e

focus shōten o awaseru (v) 焦点を合わせる 25d

fog kiri 霧 6a

foggy kiri no (adj) 霧の 6a

fold tatamu (v) 畳む 25m

folder forudā フォルダー 19f

foliage ha no shigeri 葉の茂り 14a

folk dance (Japanese) bon odori 盆踊り 28c

folk dance fōku dansu フォークダンス 28c

folk music fōku myūjikku フォークミュージック 28c

folk music minzoku ongaku 民族音楽 25j

follow shitagau (v) 従う 3e

follow tadotte iku (v) 辿って行く 36c

food tabemono 食べ物 24a

food coloring shokumotsu no chakushokuzai 食物の着色剤 7c

food poisoning shokuchūdoku 食中毒 40a

fool bakamono 馬鹿者 11e

foolish, silly bakageta *(adj)* 馬鹿げた 11e

foot ashi 足 12a

foot/feet fīto フィート 3a

football futtobōru フットボール 27b

footnote kyakuchū 脚注 20a

footwear hakimono 履物 25n

for example tatoeba 例えば 44c

for now ima no tokoro 今のところ 4e

for sale uridashichū 売り出し中 25a

for the defense bengogawa no *(adj)* 弁護側の 41

for the prosecution kensatsugawa no *(adj)* 検察側の 41

forehead hitai 額 12a

foreign currency gaikoku tsūka 外国通貨 31

foreign languages gaikokugo 外国語 37e

foreign movie gaikoku eiga 外国映画 28a

foreigner gaikokujin 外国人 31

forest shinrin 森林 13b

forget wasureru *(v)* 忘れる 22b

fork fōku フォーク 23d, 24l

form (to fill out) shoshiki 書式 31

formal dance (Japanese) nihon buyō 日本舞踊 28c

Fortunately! Un yoku. 運良く。 21c

forty yonjū 四十 1a

forty thousand yonman 四万 1a

forty-one yonjūichi 四十一 1a

forty-two yonjūni 四十二 1a

forward tensō 転送 19f

fossil fuel kaseki nenryō 化石燃料 13c, 44a

foul warui *(adj)* 悪い 6a

foul line fāru rain ファールライン 27b

foul weather akutenkō 悪天候 6a

foundation fandēshon ファンデーション 25f

fountain pen mannenhitsu 万年筆 19d, 25c

four shi/yon 四 1a

four yottsu 四つ 1a

four hundred yonhyaku 四百 1a

four thousand yonsen 四千 1a

four-ninths kyūbun no yon 九分の四 1c

four-sided figures shihenkei 四辺形 2a

fourteen jūshi/jūyon 十四 1a

fourteen thousand ichiman-yonsen 一万四千 1a

fourth daiyon 第四 1b

fourth yobanme 四番目 1b

fourth yottsume 四つ目 1b

fox kitsune 狐 15a

fraction bunsū 分数 1d

fractional bunsū no *(adj)* 分数の 1d

fracture kossetsu 骨折 40a

fragile kowareyasui *(adj)* 壊れやすい 13d

France Furansu フランス 30b

Frankfurt Furankufuruto フランクフルト 30c

free climbing furī kuraimingu
フリークライミング 27b

freeze kōru *(vi)* 凍る 6a

freezer reitōko 冷凍庫 23d

freezing point hyōten 氷点 6a,
6c

freezing rain hisame 氷雨 6a

French Furansugo フランス語
30d

French Furansujin フランス人
30d

frequent hinpan na *(adj)* 頻繁な
4e

frequently shibashiba しばしば
4e

fresco painting hekiga 壁画 28b

Friday kinyōbi 金曜日 5a

fried ageta *(adj)* 揚げた 24b

fried egg medamayaki 目玉焼き
24h

friend tomodachi 友達 10b

friendly shitashige na *(adj)*
親しげな 11e

friendly shitashimiyasui *(adj)*
親しみ易い 21a

friendship yūkō 友好 10b

frog kaeru 蛙 15c

from kara から 3d, 8j

from my point of view
watakushi no mikata dewa
私の見方では 44c

from now on korekara これから
4e

front mae 前 3d

front zensen 前線 6a

front page ichimen 一面 20a

frost shimo 霜 6a

frozen kootta *(adj)* 凍った 6a

fruit kudamono 果物 14d, 24f,
24g

fruit store kudamono ya 果物屋
24n

fruit tree kaju 果樹 14c

fuel nenryō 燃料 13c

full ippai no *(adj)* 一杯の 3c

full moon mangetsu 満月 13a

fun, enjoyment tanoshimi
楽しみ 21a

function (mathematics) kansū
関数 1f

function kinō 機能 42b

funny omoshiroi *(adj)* 面白い
11e

fur coat kegawa no kōto
毛皮のコート 25k

furnace danbōro 暖房炉 23e

furniture kagu 家具 23c

furthermore sarani *(conj)* 更に
8k

furthermore sonoue *(conj)*
その上 8k

fuse hyūzu ヒューズ 25b

fusion reactor kakuyūgōro
核融合炉 42a

fussy kourusai *(adj)* 小うるさい
11e

future mirai *(adj)* 未来 8a

future shōrai/mirai 将来／未来
4e

G

gain weight futoru *(vi)* 太る 11a

galaxy ginga 銀河 13a

gallbladder tannō 胆嚢 12a

gallon garon ガロン 3a

gallstones tanseki 胆石 40a

game gēmu ゲーム 27a

game, match shiai 試合 27b

garage chūshajō 駐車場 35b

garage shako 車庫 23a

garbage truck gomi shūshūsha
ゴミ収集車 33a

garden niwa 庭 14e, 23a, 36a

gardening engei 園芸 27a

garlic ninniku ニンニク 14e,
24e, 24j

garment ifuku 衣服 25k

gas gasorin ガソリン 33c

gas gasu ガス 13c, 23e

gas pedal akuseru アクセル 33e

gas pump ponpu ポンプ 33e

gas station gasorin sutando
ガソリンスタンド 33c

gas stove gasu sutōbu
ガスストーブ 23d

gas tank gasorin tanku
ガソリンタンク 33e

gasoline gasorin ガソリン 13c

gate mon 門 23a

gate (airport) gēto ゲート 32a

gather, reap shūkakusuru (v)
収穫する 14a

gauze gaze ガーゼ 25h, 39c

gay dōseiai no (adj) 同性愛の 44b

gay dōseiai no dansei
同性愛の男性 44b

GB gigabaito ギガバイト 25d

gearshift gia shifuto ギアシフト
33c

gearshift shifuto rebā
シフトレバー 33e

Gemini futagoza 双子座 5d

gender sei 性 8a

generator jenerēta
ジェネレーター 33e

generosity kandaisa 寛大さ 11e

generous kandai na (adj) 寛大な
11e

Geneva Junēbu ジュネーブ 30c

genitals gaiinbu 外陰部 12a

genre yōshiki 様式 28d

gentle yasahii (adj) 優しい 11e,
21a

gentleman shinshi 紳士 11a

gentlemanly shinshiteki na (adj)
紳士的な 11a

Gentlemen Haikei 拝啓 19a

geographical chirijō no (adj)
地理上の 13e

geography chiri 地理 13e, 37e

geometrical kika no (adj) 幾何の
2b

geometry kika 幾何 2b

geometry kikagaku 幾何学 37e

geothermal energy chinetsu
enerugī 地熱エネルギー 44a

geranium jeranyūmu
ジェラニューム 14b

German Doitsugo ドイツ語 30d

German Doitsujin ドイツ人 30d

Germany Doitsu ドイツ 30b

gerund dōmeishi 動名詞 8a

get a degree gakui o toru (v)
学位を取る 37f

get a diploma sotsugyō shōsho o
morau (v) 卒業証書をもらう
37f

get a doctor isha o yobu (v)
医者を呼ぶ 39c

get a loan yūshi o ukeru (v)
融資を受ける 26

get cured yokunaru (v) 良くなる
40a

get dressed kiru (v) 着る 25m

get examined shinsatsu o ukeru
(v) 診察を受ける 40a

get hurt kega o suru (v)
怪我をする 12b

get married kekkonsuru (v)
結婚する 11c

get out, exit deru *(v)* 出る 3e

get pregnant ninshinsuru *(v)* 妊娠する 11c

get sick byōki ni naru *(v)* 病気になる 40a

get up, rise okiru *(v)* 起きる 3e, 12b

getaway car tobō yō no kuruma 逃亡用の車 39b

gift gifuto ギフト 25a

gift okurimono 贈り物 11c

gift wrap gifuto hōsō ギフト包装 25a

gigabyte gigabaito ギガバイト 42b

gill era えら 15c

gin jin ジン 24k

ginger shōga 生姜 24j

ginger ale jinjaēru ジンジャエール 24k

ginko tree ichō 銀杏 14c

giraffe kirin キリン 15a

girl onna no ko 女の子 11a

girlfriend onna tomodachi/gāru furendo 女友達／ガールフレンド 10b

give a gift okurimono o ageru 贈り物をあげる 11c

give back the room key kagi o kaesu カギを返す 35b

give birth umu *(v)* 生む 11c

give help tasukete ageru *(v)* 助けてあげる 39a

Give my regards to... ... san ni yoroshiku ・・・さんによろしく 19b

give, hand back kaesu *(v)* 返す 37f

glacier hyōga 氷河 13b

gladiolus gurajiorasu グラジオラス 14b

gland sen 腺 12a

glass (drinking) koppu コップ 23d, 24l

glaucoma ryokunaishō 緑内障 40a

global chikyū zentai no *(adj)* 地球全体の 13e

global warming chikyū ondanka 地球温暖化 13c, 44a

globe chikyū 地球 13e

gloomy inki na *(adj)* 陰気な 11e, 21a

glossy kōtaku no aru *(adj)* 光沢のある 25d

glove tebukuro 手袋 25k

glove (baseball) gurōbu グローブ 27b

glove compartment gurōbu bokkusu グローブボックス 33e

glue nori 糊 37b

glue setchakuzai 接着剤 19d, 25b, 25c

Go ahead! Dōzo. どうぞ。 17b

go away saru *(v)* 去る 3e

go bankrupt hasansuru *(v)* 破産する 38d

go down kudaru *(v)* 下る 36c

go down, descend kudaru *(vt)* 下る 3e

go down, descend sagaru *(vi)* 下がる 3e

go forward zenshinsuru *(v)* 前進する 33c

go on foot aruite iku *(v)* 歩いていく 3e

go out dekakeru *(v)* 出かける 29b

go out (exit) deru *(v)* 出る 3e

go to bed neru *(v)* 寝る 12b

go to school gakkō ni iku *(v)*
学校に行く 11c, 11f, 37f

go up, climb noboru *(vt)* 上る
3e, 36c

go iku *(v)* 行く 3e, 36e

goal gōru ゴール 27b

goal kick gōru kikku
ゴールキック 27b

goalkeeper gōrukīpā
ゴールキーパー 27b

goat yagi 山羊 15a

god kamisama 神様 11d

good, final copy seisho 清書 37f

going through a red light shingō
mushi 信号無視 33c

gold kin 金 13c, 25i

gold kin-iro 金色 7a

golden anniversary kekkon
gojusshūnen kinenbi
結婚五十周年記念日 11c

goldfish kingyo 金魚 15c

golf gorufu ゴルフ 27b

good ii *(adj)* いい 11e

good, delicious oishii *(adj)*
美味しい 24p

Good afternoon! (Hello!)
Konnichiwa. こんにちは。
16a

good at (something) jōzu na *(adj)*
上手な 11e

Good-bye! Sayōnara.
さようなら。 16a

Good evening! (Hello!)
Konbanwa. こんばんは。 16a

Good heavens! Oh my! Oya.
おや。 21c

Good luck! Goseikō o.
ご成功を。 16c

good mood ii kibun いい気分
21a

Good morning! (Hello!) Ohayō
gozaimasu.
おはようございます。 16a

Good night! Oyasuminasai.
おやすみなさい。 16a

good weather ii tenki いい天気
6a

goodness zenryōsa 善良さ 11e

goose gachō ガチョウ 15b

gorge kyōkoku 峡谷 13b

gorilla gorira ゴリラ 15a

gossip uwasabanashi うわさ話
17a

gossip uwasabanashi o suru *(v)*
うわさ話をする 17a

govern tōjisuru *(v)* 統治する 43

government seifu 政府 43

government worker kōmuin
公務員 38a

governor chiji 知事 43

GPS zen chikyū sokui shisutemu
全地球即位システム 13e

graceful yūga na *(adj)* 優雅な
11e

grade gakunen 学年 37a

grade, mark seiseki 成績 37f

grade one ichinen 一年 37a

grade two ninen 二年 37a

graduate sotsugyōsei *(n)* 卒業生
11f

graduate sotsugyōsuru *(v)*
卒業する 11f, 37f

graduate school daigakuin
大学院 11f, 37a, 38b

graft tsugiki 接ぎ木 14a

graft tsugikisuru *(v)* 接ぎ木する
14a

grain kokurui 穀類 14a

gram guramu グラム 3a

grammar bunpō 文法 8a, 37f

grand piano gurando piano
グランドピアノ 28c

grandchildren mago 孫 10a

grandchildren omagosan
お孫さん 10a

grandfather ojiisan おじいさん
10a

grandfather sofu 祖父 10a

grandfather clock hakogata
ōdokei 箱型大時計 4d

grandmother obāsan おばあさん
10a

grandmother sobo 祖母 10a

grapefruit gurēpufurūtsu
グレープフルーツ 14d, 24f

grapes budō ぶどう 14d, 24f

graphic gurafikku グラフィック
42b

grass (field) sōgen 草原 13b

grasshopper batta バッタ 15d

grate orosu (v) おろす 24o

grated ginger (Japanese) oroshi
shōga おろし生姜 24j

grated radish (Japanese) daikon
oroshi 大根おろし 24j

gravitation inryoku 重力 13a

gravity inryoku 引力 13a

gray haiiro/gurē 灰色／グレー
7a

Greece Girisha ギリシャ 30b

Greek Girishajin ギリシャ人
30d

Greek (language) Girishago
ギリシャ語 30d

green midori iro 緑色 7a

green kankyō ni yasashii (adj)
環境に優しい 44a

green pepper pīman ピーマン
14e, 24e

Greenery Day (May 4) midori no
hi 緑の日 5g

greenhouse onshitsu 温室 14a

greenhouse effect onshitsu kōka
温室効果 13c, 44a

greet aisatsusuru (v) 挨拶する
16a

greeting aisatsu 挨拶 16a

greeting card gurītingu kādo
グリーティングカード 19d

grill amiyaki ni suru (v)
網焼きにする 24o

grilled amiyaki no (adj) 網焼きの
24b

grocery store shokuryōhin ten
食品店 24n

groom (bridegroom) hanamuko
花婿 11c

grooming midashinami
身だしなみ 12d

ground floor ikkai 一階 23a, 23g

group gurūpu グループ 25j

group discount dantai waribiki
団体割引 30a

group tour dantai ryokō/gurūpu
tsuā
団体旅行／グループツアー 30a

grow fueru (vi) 増える 3c

grow fuyasu (vt) 増やす 3c

grow up sodatsu (vi) 育つ 11b

growth zōdai 増大 3c

guarantee hoshōsuru (v)
保証する 17a

guide gaido ガイド 36a

guidebook gaidobukku
ガイドブック 25o

guided tour gaido tsuki tsuā
ガイド付きツアー 30a

guilt tsumi 罪 41

guilty yūzai no (adj) 有罪の 41

guilty (verdict) yūzai/kuro
有罪／黒 41

guinea pig morumotto モルモット 15a

guitar gitā ギター 28c

guitarist gitarisuto ギタリスト 28c

gulf wan 湾 13b

gums haguki 歯茎 40b

gun jū 銃 39b

gym jimu ジム 27a

gymnasium jimu ジム 27b

gymnasium taiikukan 体育館 37c

gynecologist fujinnkai 婦人科医 40a

H

habit shūkan 習慣 11e

hail arare ga furu (vi) あられが降る 6a

hail arare あられ 6a

hair kaminoke 髪の毛 12a

hair color heā karā ヘアーカラー 25f

hair conditioner rinsu リンス 25f

hair remover jomōzai 除毛剤 25f

hairbrush heā burashi ヘアーブラシ 25f

hairdresser biyōshi 美容師 12d, 38a

hair dryer heā doraiyā ヘアードライヤー 12d, 25f

hairpin heāpin ヘアーピン 25f

hair spray heā supurē ヘアースプレー 12d, 25f

half hanbun no (adj) 半分の 3c

half century hanseiki 半世紀 4c

halibut ohyō オヒョウ 15c, 24d

hallway rōka 廊下 37c

halve nitōbunsuru (v) 二等分する 3c

ham hamu ハム 24c

hammer kanazuchi 金槌 25b

hand te 手 12a

hand cream hando kurīmu ハンドクリーム 25f

hand lotion hando rōshon ハンドローション 25f

hand luggage tenimotsu 手荷物 31

hand of a clock tokei no hari 時計の針 4d

handcuffs tejō 手錠 39b

handkerchief hankachi ハンカチ 25k

handle (knife) totte 取っ手 23d

handlebar handoru ハンドル 33a

handrail tesuri 手摺 23a

hands-free hanzufurī (adj) ハンズフリー 18a

handshake akushu 握手 16a

handsome (for male) hansamu na (adj) ハンサムな 11a

hang kakeru (v) 掛ける 25m

hang gliding hangu guraidingu ハンググライディング 27b

hang up kiru (v) 切る 18b

happen, occur okoru (vi) 起こる 4e

happiness shiawase 幸せ 11e, 21a

happy shiawase na (adj) 幸せな 11e, 21a

Happy Birthday! Tanjōbi omedetō. 誕生日おめでとう。 11c, 16c, 29c

Happy New Year! Shinnen omedetō. 新年おめでとう。 16c, 29c

Happy to make your acquaintance! Shiriau koto ga dekite ureshii desu.
知り合うことが出来て嬉しいです。 16b

hard katai *(adj)* 堅い 13d

hard disk hādo disuku
ハードディスク 42b

hard-boiled egg yudetamago
ゆで卵 24h

hardware (computer) hādowea
ハードウェア 42b

hardware store daikudōgu ten
大工道具店 25b

hare nousagi 野うさぎ 15a

harmony hāmonī ハーモニー
28c

harp hāpu ハープ 28c

harpsichord hāpushikōdo
ハープシコード 28c

hat bōshi 帽子 25k

hate ken-o 嫌悪 11e

hate nikumu *(v)* 憎む 21b

hate totemo kirau *(v)* とても嫌う
11e

hateful iya na *(adj)* 嫌な 11e

hatred ken-o 嫌悪 21b

have a baby kodomo ga umareru
子供が生まれる 11c

Have a good holday! Oyasumi o, otanoshimi kudasai.
お休みをお楽しみください。
16c, 29c

Have a good time! Tanoshii toki o, osugoshi kudasai.
楽しい時をお過ごしください。
16c

Have a good trip! Ryokō o, otanoshimi kudasai.
旅行をお楽しみください。 16c

have a headache zutsū ga suru
頭痛がする 40a

Have a nice trip! Ryokō o, otanoshimi kudasai.
旅行をお楽しみください。 30a

have a snack kanshoku suru *(v)*
間食する 24o

have a sore throat nodo ga itamu
喉が痛む 40b

have a stomachache i ga itai
胃が痛い 40a

have a toothache ha ga itamu
歯が痛む 40b

have baggage taken to one's room nimotsu o heya e motte itte morau 荷物を部屋へ持っていってもらう 35b

have breakfast asagohan o taberu *(v)* 朝ご飯を食べる 24o

have chills samuke ga suru
寒気がする 6b

have dinner bangohan o taberu *(v)* 晩ご飯を食べる 24o

Have fun! Tanoshinde kite kudasai.
楽しんで来てください。 29c

have fun, enjoy oneself tanoshimu *(v)* 楽しむ 21a, 29b

have lunch hirugohan o taberu *(v)* 昼ご飯を食べる 24o

have white hair shiaga ga aru
白髪がある 11b

hawk taka 鷹 15b

hazard flash hazādo ranpu
ハザードランプ 33e

HDTV haibijon terebi
ハイビジョンテレビ 20b

he kare ga/wa 彼が／は 8c

head atama 頭 12a

head of state genshu 元首 43

head office honten 本店 26

headache zutsū 頭痛 40a

heading midashi 見出し 19c

headline midashi 見出し 20a

headphones heddohōn
ヘッドホーン 20b, 32c

headset heddosetto
ヘッドセット 18a

heal naoru (v) 治る 40a

health kenkō 健康 11a, 40a

health food store
kenkōshokuhinten 健康食品店
24n

health insurance kenkō hoken
健康保険 39c, 44b

**Health-Sports Day (second
Monday in October)** taiiku no
hi 体育の日 5g

healthy kenkō na (adj) 健康な
40a

healthy kenkōteki na (adj)
健康的な 11a

hear kiku (v) 聞く 12c

hearing chōryoku 聴力 12c

heart shinzō 心臓 12a, 40a

heart attack shinzō mahi
心臓麻痺 40a

heartburn muneyake 胸焼け 40a

heat nekki 熱気 6a

heat netsu 熱 13c

heat wave neppa 熱波 6a

heater hītā ヒーター 23d, 33e

heating danbō 暖房 23e

**heavier screen, made of paper or
fabric** fusuma ふすま 23c

heavy omoi (adj) 重い 3b, 11a,
13d, 31

heavy rain ōame 大雨 6a

Hebrew (language) Heburaigo
ヘブライ語 30d

Hebrew, Jewish Yudayajin no
(adj) ユダヤ人の 11d

hectare hekutāru ヘクタール 3a

hectogram hekutoguramu
ヘクトグラム 3a

hedge ikegaki 生け垣 14a

heel kakato かかと 12a, 25n

height se no takasa 背の高さ
11a

height takasa 高さ 3b

Hello! (telephone) Moshi moshi.
もしもし。 18b

helmet herumetto ヘルメット
27b

help tasuke 助け 39a

help tasukeru (v) 助ける 39a

Help! Tasukete. 助けて。 39a,
39c

hemisphere hankyū 半球 13e

hemispheric hankyūjō no (adj)
半球状の 13e

hemorrhage shukketsu 出血 40a

hemorrhoids ji 痔 40a

hen mendori 雌鶏 15b

heptagon nanakakukei 七角形
2a

her kanojo no 彼女の 8d

her kanojo o 彼女を 8e

herb hābu ハーブ 14e, 24j

herbal tea hābutī ハーブティー
24k

here koko ni ここに 36c

here koko ここ 3d

heredity iden 遺伝 11c

hero shujinkō 主人公 28e

heroine onna shujinkō 女主人公
28e

heron sagi 鷺 15b

herpes herupesu ヘルペス 40a

herring nishin 鰊 15c, 24d

herself kanojo jishin 彼女自身 8g

hesitant tameraigachi na *(adj)* ためらいがちな 21a

hesitate tamerau *(v)* ためらう 17a

hesitation tamerai ためらい 17a

hexagon rokkakukei 六角形 2a

Hi! Yā. *(inf)* やー。 16a

hibiscus haibisukasu ハイビスカス 14b

high takai *(adj)* 高い 3b, 6c

high (atmospheric) pressure kōkiatsu 高気圧 6a

high blood pressure kōketsuatsu 高血圧 40a

high definition haidefu/hai definishon ハイデフ／ ハイデフィニション 20b

high school kōkō 高校 11f, 37a, 38b

high school diploma kōkō no sotsugyō shōsho 高校の卒業証書 37f

high tide manchō 満潮 13b

high-heeled shoe haihīru ハイヒール 25n

highway kōsokudōro 高速道路 33c

highway police haiwē patorōru ハイウェーパトロール 33c

hiking haikingu ハイキング 36b

hill oka 丘 13b

him kare o 彼を 8e

himself kare jishin 彼自身 8g

Hindu Hinzūkyōto ヒンズー教徒 11d

hip oshiri お尻 12a

hip-hop hippuhoppu ヒップホップ 28c

hippopotamus kaba 河馬 15a

hire yatou *(v)* 雇う 38d

his kare no 彼の 8d

history rekishi 歴史 37e

hit utsu *(v)* 打つ 27b

HIV eizu uirusu ga yōsei no *(adj)* エイズウイルスが陽性の 44b

HIV eizu uirusu エイズウイルス 40a

HIV-positive eizu uirusu ga yōsei no *(adj)* エイズウイルスが陽性の 40a

hobby shumi 趣味 27a

hockey rink hokkējō ホッケー場 27b

hockey stick sutikku スティック 27b

Hold the line! Kiranaide kudasai. 切らないでください。 18b

hole ana 穴 25g

holiday kyūjitsu 休日 5a, 29a

Holland Oranda オランダ 30b

home base hōmu ホーム 27b

homeless hōmuresu ホームレス 44b

homosexual dōseiai no *(adj)* 同性愛の 44b

homosexuality dōseiai 同性愛 44b

honest shōjiki na *(adj)* 正直な 11e

honesty shōjikisa 正直さ 11e

honey hachimitsu 蜂蜜 24j

honeymoon shinkonryokō 新婚旅行 11c

Hong Kong Honkon 香港 30c

Honolulu Honoruru ホノルル 30c

hood bonnetto ボンネット 33e

hook tsuribari 釣り針 15c

hope nozomu *(v)* 望む 21a

hope nozomi 望み 21a

horizon suihei 水平 3d

horizontal suihei no *(adj)* 水平の 3d

horizontal line suiheisen 水平線 2b

horn horun ホルン 28c

horn keiteki 警笛 33e

horoscope hoshiuranai 星占い 5d

horrible hidokute zotto suru 酷くてゾッとする 11e

horse uma 馬 15a

horse race keiba 競馬 27a

horse racing keiba 競馬 27a

horsefly abu 虻 15d

horsepower bariki 馬力 33e

horseradish (Japanese) wasabi わさび 24j

horseradish (western) hōsuradisshu ホースラディッシュ 24j

horticulture engei 園芸 14a

hospital byōin 病院 39c

hot (spice) karai *(adj)* 辛い 24p

hot (temperature) atsui *(adj)* 熱い 24p

hot (weather) atsui *(adj)* 暑い 6a, 6b

hot and humid mushiatsui *(adj)* 蒸し暑い 6a

hot pepper tōgarashi 唐辛子 14e

hot sake atsukan 熱燗 24p

hot water oyu お湯 35c

hotspot hottosupotto ホットスポット 42b

hotel hoteru ホテル 35a

hotel clerk hoteru no kakariin ホテルの係員 35b

hot-springs resort onsenchi 温泉地 36b

hour jikan 時間 4c

hourglass sunadokei 砂時計 4d

hourly jikangoto ni *(adv)* 時間ごとに 4c

hourly jikangoto no *(adj)* 時間ごとの 4c

house ie 家 23a

House of Councilors (Japanese) sangiin 参議院 43

House of Representatives (Japanese) shūgiin 衆議院 43

House of Representatives (U.S.) kain 下院 43

household Buddhist altar butsudan 仏壇 23c

household Shinto shrine kamidana 神棚 23c

How? Dō yatte. *(inf)* どうやって。 9

How come? Naze. *(inf)* なぜ。 9

How do you get to...? ...niwa, dō yatte ikimasu ka. ・・・には、どうやって行きますか。 36c

How do you say that in Japanese? Nihongo de sore o nan to iimasu ka. 日本語でそれを何と言いますか。 9

How do you say...in Japanese? ...wa, Nihongo de dō iimasu ka. ・・・は、日本語でどう言いますか。 17b

How do you write your name? Onamae wa, dō kakimasu ka. お名前は、どう書きますか。 11f

How have you been? Ogenki desu ka. お元気ですか。 16a

how much dono kurai
どのくらい 3c

how much (money) ikura
いくら 3c

How much do you weigh?
Anata no taijū wa, dono kurai
desu ka. あなたの体重は、
どのくらいですか。 11a

How much? (money) Ikura desu
ka. いくらですか。 9

How much? Dono kurai desu ka.
どのくらいですか。 9

How much does it cost? Ikura
desu ka. いくらですか。 25a

How old are you? Toshi wa,
ikutsu desu ka. 年は、
いくつですか。 11b

How tall are you? Anata no se
no takasa wa, dono kurai desu
ka. あなたの背の高さは、
どのくらいですか。 11a

How's it going? Ikaga desu ka.
いかがですか。 16a

How's the weather? Donna tenki
desu ka. どんな天気ですか。
6a

however keredomo/shikashi/
tokoroga (conj) けれども／
しかし／ところが 8k

human hito no (adj) 人の 15a

human ningen no (adj) 人間の
11d

human being ningen 人間 15a

humanitarian jindōshugi no (adj)
人道主義の 11e

humanities jinbunkagaku
人文科学 37e

humanity ningensei 人間性 11d

humble hikaeme na (adj)
控え目な 11e, 21a

humid shikke ga takai (adj)
湿気が高い 6a

humidity shikke 湿気 6a

humility kenson 謙遜 11e

humor yūmoa ユーモア 11e

humorous kokkei na (adj) 滑稽な
11e

humorous yūmoa no aru (adj)
ユーモアのある 21a

hundredth hyakubanme 百番目
1b

hunger kūfuku 空腹 12b

hunter hantā ハンター 15a

hunting shuryō 狩猟 15a, 27a

hurricane harikēn ハリケーン
6a

hurry isogu (v) 急ぐ 3e, 39b

hurt itamu (v) 痛む 40a

husband goshujin ご主人 10a

husband otto 夫 10a, 11c

hyacinth hiyashinsu ヒヤシンス
14b

hybrid kōhai 交配 14a

hybrid car haiburiddo kā
ハイブリッドカー 33a

hydrangea ajisai 紫陽花 14b

hydrogen suiso 水素 13c

hydrogen bomb suiso bakudan
水素爆弾 44b

hyena haiena ハイエナ 15a

hygiene eisei 衛生 12d

hygienic eiseiteki na (adj)
衛生的な 12d

hyphen haifun ハイフン 19c

hypothesis kasetsu 仮説 22a

I

I watakushi ga/wa 私が／は 8c

I am cold. Samui desu.
寒いです。 6a, 6b

I am hot. Atsui desu. 暑いです。 6b

I am...tall. Watakushi no se no takasa wa,...desu. 私の背の高さは、・・・です。 11a

I believe that... ...to omoimasu. ・・・と思います。 44c

I can't stand the cold. Samusa ni yowai desu. 寒さに弱いです。 6b

I can't stand the heat. Atsusa ni yowai desu. 暑さに弱いです。 6b

I didn't understand. Wakarimasen deshita. 分かりませんでした。 17b

I don't believe it! Shinjiraremasen. 信じられません。 21c

I don't feel like... ... ki ni naremasen. ・・・気になれません。 21c

I don't know if... ... ka dō ka shirimasen. ・・・かどうか知りません。 44c

I don't understand. Wakarimasen. 分かりません。 9, 17b

I doubt that... ... ka dō ka gimon desu. ・・・かどうか疑問です。 44c

I have chills. Samuke ga shimasu. 寒気がします。 6b

I hope you like it. Okuchi ni au to ii no desu ga. お口に合うと良いのですが。 24l

I live... ... ni sunde imasu. ・・・に住んでいます。 11f

I love the cold. Samui no ga suki desu. 寒いのが好きです。 6b

I love the heat. Atsui no ga suki desu. 暑いのが好きです。 6b

I think that ... ... to omoimasu. ・・・と思います。 44c

I was born in 19... Sen kyūhyaku ...nen ni umaremashita. 千九百・・・年に生まれました。 5e

I was born on ... Watakushi wa, ... ni umaremashita. 私は、・・・に生まれました。 11c

I weigh ... Watakushi no taijū wa, ... desu. 私の体重は、・・・です。 11a

I wish! Sō da to iindesu ga. そうだと良いんですが。 21c

I'd like to say... ... to iitai no desu ga. ・・・と言いたいのですが。 44c

I'm... Watakushi wa,...desu. 私は、・・・です。 16b

I'm not sure that... ...ka dō ka tashika dewa arimasen. ・・・かどうか確かではありません。 44c

I'm serious! Honki desu yo. 本気ですよ。 21c

I'm sorry! Sumimasen. すみません。 21c

I'm sure that... ...wa, tashika desu. ・・・は、確かです。 44c

I'm sure that... Tashika ni,... to omoimasu. 確かに、・・・と思います。 17b

ice kōri 氷 6a, 13b

ice cream aisukurīmu アイスクリーム 24g, 24h

ice cream parlor aisukurīmu ya アイスクリーム屋 24n

ice hockey aisu hokkē
アイスホッケー 27b

icon aikon アイコン 42b

icosahedron nijūmentai
二十面体 2a

icy rain hisame 氷雨 6a

icy kōri ga hatta (adj) 氷が張った
6a

idea aidia アイディア 22a

idealism risōshugi 理想主義
11e

idealist risōshugisha 理想主義者
11e

idealistic risōshugiteki na
理想主義的な 11e

identification mibunshōmei
身分証明 11f

identification (paper, card)
mibun shōmeisho 身分証明書
31, 35b

identify shikibetsusuru (v)
識別する 17a

ideology ideorogī イデオロギー
43

ignorant muchi no (adj) 無知の
22a

illustration irasuto イラスト 20a

IM insutantomessenjā
インスタントメッセンジャー
18a

image stabilization tebure bōshi
手ぶれ防止 25d

imaginary number kyosū 虚数
1d

imagination sōzōryoku 想像力
11e, 22a

imaginative sōzōryoku ni tonda
(adj) 想像力に富んだ 11e

imagine sōzōsuru (v) 想像する
22b

imitation imitēshon
イミテーション 25i

impatient kimijika na (adj)
気短な 11e

imperative mood meireihō
命令法 8a

import yunyūsuru (v) 輸入する
31

Impossible! Masaka. まさかあ。
21c

imprison tōgokusuru (v)
投獄する 41

impudence atsukamashisa
厚かましさ 11e

impudent atsukamashii (adj)
厚かましい 11e

impulse shōdō 衝動 11e

impulsive shōdōteki na (adj)
衝動的な 11e

in naka ni (adj) 中に 3d

in naka no (adj) 中の 3d

in ni/de に／で 8j

in black and white shiro kuro de
白黒で 25d

in conclusion ketsuron to
shitewa 結論としては 44c

in front of mae ni 前に 3d

in front of mae no 前の 3d

in front of... ...no mae ni
・・・の前に 36c

in love renai chū 恋愛中 11c

in my opinion watakushi no
iken dewa 私の意見では 22a,
44c

in my view watakushi no kangae
dewa 私の考えでは 44c

in the afternoon gogo ni 午後に
4a

in the country inaka de 田舎で
36b

in the evening ban ni 晩に 4a

in the evening yūgata ni 夕方に 4a

in the latest style/fashion ima hayatte iru 今はやっている 25l

in the meanwhile sono kan ni その間に 4e

in the middle of naka no 中の 3d

in the middle chūkan ni 中間に 3d

in the morning gozenchū ni 午前中に 4a

in the mountains yama de 山で 36b

in time maniatte 間に合って 4e

inbox jushinbako 受信箱 19f

inch inchi インチ 3a

incisor monshi 門歯 40b

income shūnyū 収入 26

incontinence shikkin 失禁 40a

increase zōka 増加 3c

increase zōka/zōdai 増加／増大 3c

increase zōkasaseru (vt) 増加させる 3c

increase zōkasuru (vi) 増加する 3c

indefinite futei (adj) 不定 8a

independent jishuteki na (adj) 自主的な 11e

index sakuin 索引 20a, 25o, 28d

index finger hitosashiyubi 人差し指 12a

India Indo インド 30b

indicate shisasuru (v) 示唆する 17a

indication shisa 示唆 17a

indicative mood chokusetsuhō 直接法 8a

indict kisosuru (v) 起訴する 41

indifference mukanshin 無関心 21a

indifferent mukanshin na (adj) 無関心な 21a

indigestion shōka furyō 消化不良 40a

indirect kansetsu (adj) 間接 8a

individualist kojinshugisha 個人主義者 11e

Indonesia Indoneshia インドネシア 30b

indoor garage okunai chūshajō 屋内駐車場 23e

industrial kōgyō no (adj) 工業の 13c

industrial waste kōgyō haikibutsu 工業廃棄物 13c

industry kōgyō 工業 13c

inexpensive yasui (adj) 安い 25a

infant nyūji 乳児 11b

infection kanō 化膿 40a

infinitive futeishi 不定詞 8a

inflammation enshō 炎症 40a

inflation infure インフレ 43

inform tsugeru (v) 告げる 17a

informal restaurant keishikibaranai resutoran 形式張らないレストラン 24m

information jōhō 情報 18b

information desk annaisho 案内所 32a

infrared light sekigaisen 赤外線 13a

ingenious dokusōteki na (adj) 独創的な 11e, 22a

ingenuity dokusōsei 独創性 11e

inherit (heredity) iden de uketsugu (v) 遺伝で受け継ぐ 11c

injection chūsha 注射 25h, 40a

injure, wound kegasaseru *(vt)*
怪我させる 39b

injury, wound kega 怪我 39b

ink inku インク 19d, 25c

ink stick (calligraphy) sumi 墨
19d

inkstone (calligraphy) suzuri 硯
19d

innocence mujaki 無邪気 11e

innocence muzai 無罪 41

innocent mujaki na *(adj)*
無邪気な 11e

innocent muzai no *(adj)* 無罪の
41

inorganic muki no *(adj)* 無機の
13c

insane shōki dewa nai
正気ではない 11e

insect konchū 昆虫 15d

insecticide satchūzai 殺虫剤 14a

inside naka ni *(adv)* 中に 3d

inside... ... no naka ni *(adv)*
… の中に 36c

insolence ōhei 横柄 11e

insolent ōhei na *(adj)* 横柄な 11e

insomnia fuminshō 不眠症 40a

instant shunji/shunkan
瞬時／瞬間 4c

instrument gakki 楽器 25j, 27a,
28c

insulation (wire) zetsuen 絶縁
25b

insulin inshurin インシュリン
25h, 40a

insurance hoken 保険 19e , 26,
30a, 39c

insurance card hoken sho
保険書 33b

integer seisū 整数 1d

intellectual chishikijin 知識人
11e

intelligence chisei 知性 11e

intelligent chiseiteki na *(adj)*
知性的な 11e

interactive intāakutibu
インターアクティブ 42b

intercom intāhon インターホン
23g

intercom tsūwa sōchi 通話装置
18a

interest kyōmi 興味 22a

interest rishi 利子 26

interest rate riritsu 利率 26

interesting omoshiroi *(adj)*
面白い 22a

interface intāfēsu
インターフェース 42b

interim decision kari kettei
仮決定 41

intermission makuai 幕間 28e

international call kokusai denwa
国際電話 18a

international express mail
kokusai supīdo bin
国際スピード便 19e

international relations kokusai
kankei 国際関係 37e

Internet intānetto
インターネット 35c, 42b

Internet café intānetto kafe
インターネットキャフェ 42b

Internet function intānetto kinō
インターネット機能 18a

Internet telephone intānetto
denwa インターネット電話
18a

interpret tsūyakusuru *(v)*
通訳する 17a

interpretation tsūyaku 通訳 17a

interpreter tsūyaku 通訳 36a

interrogate jinmonsuru (v) 尋問する 17a

interrogative gimon (adj) 疑問 8a

interrogative gimonshi 疑問詞 8a

interrupt saegiru (v) さえぎる 17a

interruption chūdan 中断 17a

intersection kōsaten 交差点 33c, 33d, 36a

interview intabyū インタビュー 20a, 20b

intestine chō 腸 12a, 40a

intransitive verb jidōshi 自動詞 8a

introduce shōkaisuru (v) 紹介する 16b

introduction shōkai 紹介 16b

invertebrate musekitsui dōbutsu 無脊椎動物 15a, 15d

invest tōshisuru (v) 投資する 26

investment tōshi 投資 26

invite maneku (v) 招く 17a

iodine yōso 沃素 13c

Iran Iran イラン 30b

Iraq Iraku イラク 30b

Ireland Airurando アイルランド 30b

iris ayame アヤメ 14b

iron airon o kakeru (v) アイロンをかける 25g, 25m

iron airon アイロン 23d, 25g

iron (metal) tetsu 鉄 13c

ironical hiniku na (adj) 皮肉な 11e

irony hiniku 皮肉 11e

irrational number murisū 無理数 1d

irregular verb fukisokudōshi 不規則動詞 8a

irritable tanki na (adj) 短気な 11e

is equivalent to sōtōsuru 相当する 1f

is greater than yori ōkii より大きい 1f

is less than yori chiisai より小さい 1f

is similar to ruijishiteiru 類似している 1f

Is...(name of person) in? ...wa, irasshaimasu ka. ···は、いらっしゃいますか。 18b

Islam (religion) kaikyō 回教 11d

Islamic kaikyō no (adj) 回教の 11d

island shima 島 13b

Isn't it so? Sō dewanai desu ka. そうではないですか。 17b

isosceles nitōhen (adj) 二等辺 2a

ISP intānetto sābisu purobaida インターネットサービスプロバイダ 42b

Israel Isuraeru イスラエル 30b

Israeli Isuraerujin イスラエル人 30d

It doesn't matter! Kamaimasen. 構いません。 21c

It seems that ... ... mitai desu. ···みたいです。 17b

It seems that ... ... yō desu. ···ようです。 44c

It's 1:00. Ichiji desu. 一時です。 4b

It's 10:00 A.M. Gozen jūji desu. 午前十時です。 4b

It's 10:00 P.M. Gogo jūji desu. 午後十時です。 4b

It's 2:00.

It's 2:00. Niji desu. 二時です。 4b

It's 2:45. Niji yonjūgofun desu. 二時四十五分です。 4b

It's 2:45. Sanji jūgofun mae desu. 三時十五分前です。 4b

It's 3:00. Sanji desu. 三時です。 4b

It's 3:00 on the dot. Sanji kikkari desu. 三時きっかりです。 4b

It's 3:30. Sanji han desu. 三時半です。 4b

It's 5:00 A.M. Gozen goji desu. 午前五時です。 4b

It's 5:00 P.M. Gogo goji desu. 午後五時です。 4b

It's 5:50. Rokuji juppun mae desu. 六時十分前です。 4b

It's a bit cold. Chotto samui desu. ちょっと寒いです。 6a

It's a bit hot. Chotto atsui desu. ちょっと暑いです。 6a

It's awful. Hidoi tenki desu. ひどい天気です。 6a

It's beautiful. Subarashii tenki desu. 素晴らしい天気です。 6a

It's clear that... ...wa, akiraka desu. ・・・は、明らかです。 44c

It's cloudy. Kumori desu. 曇りです。 6a

It's cold. Samui desu. 寒いです。 6a

It's dark already. Mō kurai desu. もう暗いです。 6a

It's exactly 3:00. Chōdo sanji desu. 丁度三時です。 4b

It's fine. Ii tenki desu. いい天気です。 6a

It's foul. Warui tenki desu. 悪い天気です。 6a

It's hot. Atsui desu. 暑いです。 6a

It's humid. Shikke ga takai desu. 湿気が高いです。 6a

It's January second. Ichigatsu futsuka desu. 一月二日です。 5e

It's May third. Gogatsu mikka desu. 五月三日です。 5e

It's mild. Atatakai desu. 温かいです。 6a

It's muggy. Mushiatsui desu. 蒸し暑いです。 6a

It's necessary that ... ... ga, hitsuyō desu. ・・・が必要です。 17b

It's not true! Sore wa, hontō dewa arimasen. それは、本当ではありません。 17b

It's obvious that ... ...koto wa, akiraka desu. ・・・ことは、明らかです。 17b

It's October first. Jūgatsu tsuitachi desu. 十月一日です。 5e

It's pleasant. Kaiteki desu. 快適です。 6a

It's raining. Ame ga futte imasu. 雨が降っています。 6a

It's rainy. Ame ga futte imasu. 雨が降っています。 6a

It's snowing. Yuki ga futte imasu. 雪が降っています。 6a

It's sunny. Hi ga tette imasu. 日が照っています。 6a

It's thundering. Kaminari ga natte imasu. 雷が鳴っています。 6a

It's true! Sore wa, hontō desu.
それは、本当です。 17b

It's 2008. Nisen hachi nen desu.
二千八年です。 5f

It's very cold. Totemo samui
desu. とても寒いです。 6a

It's very hot. Totemo atsui desu.
とても暑いです。 6a

It's windy. Kaze ga tsuyoi desu.
風が強いです。 6a

Italian Itariajin イタリア人 30d

Italian (language) Itariago
イタリア語 30d

italics itarikkutai イタリック体
19c

Italy Itaria イタリア 30b

itch kayumi かゆみ 40a

ivory zōge 象牙 13c

J

Jacket jaketto ジャケット 25k

jaguar jagā ジャガー 15a

Jakarta Jakaruta ジャカルタ 30c

jam jamu ジャム 24j

janitor yōmuin 用務員 37d

January ichigatsu 一月 5b

Japan Nihon/Nippon 日本 30b

Japanese Nihonjin 日本人 30d

Japanese (language) Nihongo
日本語 30d

Japanese cedar sugi 杉 14c

Japanese character kana 仮名 8a

Japanese checkers go 碁 27a

Japanese chess shōgi 将棋 27a

Japanese cypress hinoki 檜 14c

Japanese fencing kendo 剣道
27b

Japanese harp koto 琴 28c

Japanese mandolin shamisen
三味線 28c

Japanese pinball pachinko
パチンコ 27a

Japanese wrestling sumō 相撲
27b

Japanese-style room washitsu
和室 23b

jaw ago 顎 12a, 40b

jay kakesu カケス 15b

jazz jazu ジャズ 25j, 28c

jealous shittobukai (adj)
嫉妬深い 11e

jealousy shitto 嫉妬 11e

jeep jīpu ジープ 33a

jeer azakeru (v) あざける 17a

jelly zerī ゼリー 24j

jellyfish kurage クラゲ 15c

jest karakau (v) からかう 17a

jet-stream jetto kiryū/henseifū
ジェット気流/偏西風 6a

Jew Yudayajin ユダヤ人 11d

jewel hōseki 宝石 25i

jeweler hōsekishō 宝石商 38a

jeweler hōshokuten 宝飾店 25i

Jewish Yudayajin no (adj)
ユダヤ人の 11d

job shigoto 仕事 11f, 38a

job description shokumu naiyō
職務内容 38d

jog jogingu suru (v)
ジョギングする 12b, 27a

jogging jogingu ジョギング 27a

joke jōdan 冗談 17a

Jordan Yorudan ヨルダン 30b

journalism jānarizumu
ジャーナリズム 37e

journalist jānarisuto
ジャーナリスト 20a, 38a

joy yorokobi 喜び 21a

Judaism Yudayakyō ユダヤ教
11d

judge handansuru (v) 判断する
22b

judge hanketsu o kudasu (v)
判決を下す 41

judge saibankan 裁判官 41

judgment handan 判断 22a

judo judo 柔道 27b

juice jūsu ジュース 24k

juicer jūsā ジューサー 23d

July shichigatsu 七月 5b

jump tobiagaru (v) 跳び上がる
3e

June rokugatsu 六月 5b

jungle mitsurin 密林 13b

junior college tandai 短大 11f,
37a, 38b

junior high school chūgaku
中学 11f, 37a, 38b

junk mail meiwaku mēru
迷惑メール 19f

Jupiter mokusei 木星 13a

jury baishin 陪審 41

just now tatta ima たった今 4e

justice seigi 正義 22a, 41

K

kangaroo kangarū カンガルー
15a

karaoke karaoke カラオケ 27a

karate karate 空手 27b

kayaking kayakku カヤック 27b

keep quiet kuchi o hikaeru (v)
口を控える 17a

Kenya Kenia ケニア 30b

ketchup kechappu ケチャップ
24j

kettle yakan やかん 23d

key kagi 鍵 23d, 35b

keyboard kenban 鍵盤 28c

keyboard kībōdo キーボード 42b

keyboard instruments kenban
gakki 鍵盤楽器 28c

kick keru (v) 蹴る 27b

kidney jinzō 腎臓 12a, 24c, 40a

kidney bean ingenmame
いんげん豆 14e

kidney stone jinzō kesseki
腎臓結石 40a

kill korosu (v) 殺す 39b

killer satsujinsha 殺人者 39b

kilogram kiroguramu
キログラム 3a

kilometer kiro キロ 3a

kind shinsetsu na (adj) 親切な
11e, 21a

kindergarten yōchien 幼稚園 37a

kindness shinsetsu 親切 11e

king kingu キング 27a

king kokuō 国王 43

kingfisher kawasemi カワセミ
15b

kiosk kiosuku キオスク 36a

kiss kisu/seppun キス／接吻
11c, 21b

kiss kisusuru/seppunsuru (v)
キスする／接吻する 11c, 21b

kitchen daidokoro 台所 23b

kitchen sink nagashi 流し 23a

kiwi kiwi キーウィー 24f

knee hiza ひざ 12a

knife hōchō 包丁 23d

knife naifu ナイフ 24l, 39b

knight naito ナイト 27a

knitting amimono 編み物 27a

know shiru (v) 知る 22b

know (someone) shitteiru (v)
知っている 16b

knowledge chishiki 知識 22a

knowledgeable yoku shitteiru
(adj) 良く知っている 22a

knuckles kobushi こぶし 12a

Korea Kankoku 韓国 30b

Korean Kankokujin 韓国人 30d

Korean (language) Kankokugo 韓国語 30d

Kuala Lumpur Kuararunpūru クアラルンプール 30c

Kuwait Kuwēto クウェート 30b

Kyoto Kyōto 京都 30c

L

La Niña ranīnya ラニーニャ 6a

label raberu/retteru ラベル／レッテル 19d

label retteru レッテル 25c

Labor Thanksgiving Day (November 23) kinrō kansha no hi 勤労感謝の日 5g

laboratory jikkenshitsu 実験室 13c, 37c

ladder hashigo はしご 25b, 39a

ladle hishaku ひしゃく 23d

lady fujin 婦人 11a

ladybug tentōmushi てんとう虫 15d

laid back nonbirishita (adj) のんびりした 11e

lake mizuumi 湖 13b, 36b

lamb kohitsuji 子羊 15a

lamb kohitsuji no niku 子羊の肉 24c

lamb ramu ラム 24c

lamp ranpu ランプ 23c, 35c

land chakurikusuru (v) 着陸する 32c

land rikuchi 陸地 13b

land mine jirai 地雷 44b

landing gear chakuriku sōchi 着陸装置 32c

landlord yanushi 家主 23g

landscape keshiki 景色 13b

lane (traffic) shasen 車線 33c

language laboratory gaikokugo rabo 外国語ラボ 37c

large ōkii (adj) 大きい 11a, 13d

large bill ōkii osatsu 大きいお札 26

large intestine daichō 大腸 40a

large teapot (Japanese) dobin 土瓶 23d, 24l

lark hibari 雲雀 15b

larva yōchū 幼虫 15d

laryngitis kōtōen 喉頭炎 40a

laser rēzā レーザー 42a

laser beam rēzā kōsen レーザー光線 42a

last mae no (adj) 前の 4e

last saigo no (adj) 最後の 4e

last tsuzuku (vi) 続く 4e

last a long time nagai aida tsuzuku 長い間続く 4e

last a short time tankikan tsuzuku 短期間続く 4e

last day of the month misoka 晦日 4c

last day of the year ōmisoka 大晦日 4c

last month sengetsu 先月 4e

last night yūbe 夕べ 4a

last third of the month gejun 下旬 4c

last year kyonen 去年 4e

late okurete (adv) 遅れて 32b

late osoi (adj) 遅い 4e, 32b, 34

late osoku (adv) 遅く 4e

Latin America Raten Amerika ラテンアメリカ 30b

latitude ido 緯度 13e

laugh warau (v) 笑う 11e, 21a

laughter warai 笑い 21a

laundromat koin randorī コインランドリー 25g

laundry sentakumono 洗濯物 25g

lava yōgan 溶岩 13b

law hōgaku 法学 37e

law hōritsu 法律 41

lawful, legal gōhō no *(adj)* 合法の 41

lawsuit, charge soshō 訴訟 41

lawyer bengoshi 弁護士 38a, 41

laxative gezai 下剤 25h

lay person hirashinto 平信徒 11d

layoff ichiji kaiko 一時解雇 38d

laziness bushō 無精 11e

lazy bushō na *(adj)* 無精な 11e

LCD monitor ekishō monitā 液晶モニター 25d

LCD TV ekishō terebi 液晶テレビ 20b

lead namari 鉛 13c

leaded gas regyurā レギュラー 33c

leaf ha 葉 14a

leap year uruudoshi 閏年 5b

learn narau *(v)* 習う 22b, 37f

lease rīsu リース 23e

leather kawa 皮 13c, 25l

leave, depart hasshasuru *(v)* 発車する 34

leave, depart shuppatsusuru *(v)* 出発する 3e

Lebanon Rebanon レバノン 30b

lecture kōgi 講義 17a, 37f

lecture kōgisuru *(v)* 講義する 17a, 37f

leek naganegi 長ネギ 14e, 24e

left hidari 左 3d

left wing sayoku 左翼 43

leg ashi 足 12a

legislation rippō 立法 43

lemon remon レモン 14d, 24f, 24j

lemonade remonēdo レモネード 24k

length nagasa 長さ 3a, 3b

lengthen nagakusuru *(v)* 長くする 25m

lens renzu レンズ 25d

lentil renzumame レンズ豆 14e, 24e

Leo shishiza 獅子座 5d

leopard hyō 豹 15a

lesbian dōseiai no josei 同性愛の女性 44b

less yori sukunai より少ない 3c

lesson jugyō 授業 37f

Let me introduce you to ... ... san ni shōkai sasete kudasai. …さんに紹介させてくだ さい。 16b

letter moji 文字 8a

letter tegami 手紙 19d

letter (of the alphabet) arufabetto no moji アルファベットの文字 19c

letter carrier yūbin haitatsu 郵便配達 19e

letterhead binsen tōbu no jōhō insatsu 便せん頭部の情報印刷 19d

lettuce retasu レタス 14e, 24e

leukemia hakketsubyō 白血病 40a

level heimen 平面 3d

Level Crossing fumikiri 踏切 33d

liability saimu 債務 26

liar usotsuki 嘘つき 11e, 17a

liberal kakushinshugisha (n) 革新主義者 11e

liberal kakushinteki na (adj) 革新的な 11e, 43

liberal party kakushintō 革新党 43

Libra tenbinza 天秤座 5d

librarian toshokan-in 図書館員 37d, 38a

library toshokan 図書館 37c

license plate nanbā purēto ナンバープレート 33e

lid futa ふた 23d

lie uso o tsuku (v) 嘘をつく 17a

lie uso 嘘 17a

lie down yokotawaru (v) 横たわる 3e

life jinsei 人生 11c

life imprisonment muki chōeki 無期懲役 41

life jacket kyūmeidōgi 救命胴着 32c

life sentence shūshinkei 終身刑 41

lifetime job security shūshin koyō seido 終身雇用制度 38d

lift mochiageru (v) 持ち上げる 3e

light akari 明かり 6a

light akarui (adj) 明るい 7b

light hikari/kōsen 光/光線 13a

light karui (adj) 軽い 3b, 11a, 13d, 31

light (bulb) denkyū 電球 25b

light blue akarui ao 明るい青 7a

light cotton kimono yukata 浴衣 35c

light music kei ongaku 軽音楽 28c

light rain kosame 小雨 6a

light year kōnen 光年 13a

lighter raitā ライター 25e

lightning inazuma 稲妻 6a

lights (car) raito ライト 33e

lights akari 明かり 35c

like konomu (v) 好む 11e, 21b

liking konomi 好み 21b

lily yuri 百合 14b

lily of the valley suzuran 鈴蘭 14b

lima bean rimamame リマ豆 14e

limited express train tokkyū 特急 34

limousine rimujīn リムジーン 33a

line gyō 行 19c

line retsu 列 26

line sen 線 2b

line up narabu (v) 並ぶ 26

linen asa 麻 25l

linen rinneru/asa リンネル/麻 25g

lingerie ranjerī ランジェリー 25k

linguistics gengogaku 言語学 37e

lion raion ライオン 15a

lip kuchibiru 唇 12a, 40b

lipstick kuchibeni 口紅 25f

liqueur rikyūru リキュール 24k

liquid ekitai 液体 13c

liquor store sakaya 酒屋 24n

listen … … o, kiite kudasai. …を聞いてください。 17b

listen to (intently) kiku (v) 聞く 12c

listen to kiku (v) 聞く 17a, 20b, 37f

liter rittoru リットル 3a

literal mojidōri no *(adj)* 文字通りの 17a

literature bungaku 文学 25o, 28d, 37e

litigate soshō o okosu *(v)* 訴訟を起こす 41

litigation soshō 訴訟 41

little chiisai *(adj)* 小さい 3c

little finger koyubi 小指 12a

live sumu *(v)* 住む 11c, 11f

live broadcast nama hōsō/jikkyō chūkei 生放送／実況中継 20b

live in sumikomu *(v)* 住み込む 23f

lively ikiikishita *(adj)* 生き生きした 7b, 11e

lively ikiikito *(adv)* 生き生きと 11e

liver kanzō 肝臓 12a, 24c

liver rebā レバー 24c

livestock kachiku 家畜 15a

living room ima 居間 23b

lizard tokage トカゲ 15c

loan rōn ローン 26

lobby robī ロビー 28a, 35b

lobster robusutā ロブスター 15c, 24d

local call shinai denwa 市内電話 18b

local government worker chihō kōmuin 地方公務員 38a

local time genchi jikan 現地時間 32c

local train kakueki teisha (no kisha) 各駅停車（の汽車）34

locate ichisuru *(v)* 位置する 13e

location ichi 位置 13e

logarithm taisū 対数 1f

logarithmic taisū no *(adj)* 対数の 1f

logic ronri 論理 22a

London Rondon ロンドン 30c

long nagai *(adj)* 長い 3b, 25l, 37f

long-distance call chōkyori denwa 長距離電話 18b

longitude keido 経度 13e

long-term chōkiteki na *(adj)* 長期的な 4e

look nagameru *(v)* 眺める 12c

look yōbō 容貌 11a

look at, watch miru *(v)* 見る 12b

look for something sagasu *(v)* 探す 25a

look forward to kitaisuru *(v)* 期待する 4e

loose yuttarishita *(adj)* ゆったりした 25l

loose change kozeni 小銭 26

loosen yurumeru *(v)* 緩める 25m

loquat biwa 枇杷 14d

Los Angeles Rosanjerusu ロサンジェルス 30c

lose makeru *(v)* 負ける 27b

lose a lawsuit haisosuru *(v)* 敗訴する 41

lose weight yaseru *(v)* 痩せる 11a

loss haiboku 敗北 27b

lot takusan *(adv)* 沢山 3c

lotus root renkon 蓮根 14e, 24e

loudspeaker raudosupīkā ラウドスピーカー 20b

louse (lice) shirami 虱 15d

lovable airashii *(adj)* 愛らしい 11e

love ai 愛 11c, 11e, 21b

love aisuru *(v)* 愛する 11c, 11e, 21b

love affair renai 恋愛 10b

lover koibito 恋人 10b

low hikui 低い 6c

low (atmospheric) pressure teikiaitsu 低気圧 6a

low season isogashikunai toki 忙しくないとき 35b

low tide kanchō 干潮 13b

lowercase komoji 小文字 19c

lowfat milk rōfatto miruku ローファットミルク 24h

luggage nimotsu 荷物 35b

luggage compartment tenimotsu dana 手荷物棚 32c

lukewarm namanurui *(adj)* 生温い 24p

lunar eclipse gesshoku 月蝕 13a

lunar module tsuki chakurikusen 月着陸船 42a

lunch chūshoku 昼食 24a

lunch hirugohan 昼ご飯 24a

lunch break ranchi no kyūkei ランチの休憩 38d

lung hai 肺 12a, 40a

luxury hotel kōkyū hoteru 高級ホテル 35a

lymphatic system rinpasen リンパ腺 40a

M

mackerel saba 鯖 15c, 24d

macro sessha (no) *(adj)* 接写（の）25d

madness kyōki 狂気 11e

magazine zasshi 雑誌 20a, 25o, 37b

maggot uji 蛆 15d

magistrate keihanzai no hanji 軽犯罪の判事 41

magnifying glass kakudaikyō 拡大鏡 19d

magnolia mokuren 木蓮 14c

mahjong mājan 麻雀 27a

maid mēdo メード 35b

mail yūbin 郵便 19e

mail (letters) dasu *(v)* 出す 19e

mail (package) okuru *(v)* 送る 19e

mail delivery yūbin haitatsu 郵便配達 19e

mailbox (home) yūbinuke 郵便受け 23a

mailbox (street) posuto ポスト 19e

main shu *(adj)* 主 8a

main course meinkōsu メインコース 24g

main office jimushitsu 事務室 37c

major senkō 専攻 38b

make a call denwa o kakeru *(v)* 電話をかける 18b

make a movie eiga o seisakusuru *(v)* 映画を製作する 28a

make mistakes machigaeru *(v)* 間違える 37f

make the bed beddo o totonoeru *(v)* ベッドを整える 23f

makeup (o)keshō （お）化粧 12d, 25f

makeup mēkyappu メーキャップ 28e

Malay (language) Marēgo マレー語 30d

Malaysia Marēshia マレーシア 30b

Malaysian Marējin マレー人 30d

male dansei 男性 11a

male otoko 男 38b

malicious akui ni michita *(adj)* 悪意に満ちた 11e

malign, speak badly chūshōsuru *(v)* 中傷する 17a

malignant akusei *(adj)* 悪性 40a

malleable katansei no aru *(adj)* 可鍛性のある 13d

mambo manbo マンボ 28c

mammal honyūrui 哺乳類 15a

man dansei 男性 11a

manager manējā マネージャー 26, 35b, 38d

mandarin orange mikan みかん 14d, 24f

mandarin orange tree mikan no ki みかんの木 14c

mandolin mandorin マンドリン 28c

mango mango マンゴー 14d, 24f

manicure manikyua マニキュア 12d

Manila Manira マニラ 30c

manipulative zurugashikoi *(adj)* ずる賢い 11e

Many thanks! Kansha shimasu. 感謝します。 16c

map chizu 地図 13e, 37b

maple tree kaede 楓 14c

marble sculpture dairiseki no chōkoku 大理石の彫刻 28b

march kōshinsuru *(v)* 行進する 3e

March sangatsu 三月 5b

margarine māgarin マーガリン 24j

margin yohaku 余白 19c

marigold marigōrudo マリゴールド 14b

marinated marine shita *(adj)* マリネした 24b

marine animal kaisei dōbutsu 海棲動物 15c

Marine Day (third Monday in July) umi no hi 海の日 5g

marital status kekkon shikaku 結婚資格 11c, 38b

marker majikku mākā マジックマーカー 19d

market ichiba 市場 24n, 36a

market shijō 市場 38d

marlin kajiki カジキ 15c

marmalade māmarēdo マーマレード 24j

marriage, matrimony kekkon 結婚 11c

married kikon no *(adj)* 既婚の 11c, 11f

married kikon 既婚 38b

marry (someone) ~ to kekkonsuru *(v)* ~と結婚する 11c

Mars kasei 火星 13a

marsh shitchi 湿地 13b

mascara masukara マスカラ 12d, 25f

masculine dansei no *(adj)* 男性の 11a

masculine dansei 男性 8a

mask masuku マスク 27b

masked play (Japanese) Nō 能 28e

masking tape masukingu tēpu マスキングテープ 25b

Mass misa ミサ 11d

mass ryō 量 3b

massage massāji マッサージ 12d

massive tairyō no *(adj)* 大量の 3b, 3c

master shūshigō 修士号 37f

masterpiece meisaku 名作 28b

matches matchi マッチ 25e

material genryō 原料 13c

maternity leave shussan kyūka/sankyū 出産休暇／産休 38d

mathematics sūgaku 数学 37e

matte tsuyakeshi no *(adj)* 艶消しの 25d

matter busshitsu 物質 13c

mauve fuji iro no *(adj)* 藤色の 6a

maximum saidai no *(adj)* 最大の 3b, 31

maximum saidai 最大 3b

maximum saikō (no) *(adj)* 最高 (の) 6c

May gotatsu 五月 5b

May I come in? Haittemo yoroshii desu ka. 入ってもよろしいですか。 16c

May I help you? Otetsudai shimashō ka. お手伝いしましょうか。 16c

mayfly kagerō カゲロウ 15d

mayonnaise mayonēzu マヨネーズ 24j

mayor shichō 市長 43

MB megabaito メガバイト 25d

me watakushi o 私を 8e

meadow sōgen 草原 13b

meal shokuji 食事 24a

mean iji no warui *(adj)* 意地の悪い 21a

mean ijiwaru na *(adj)* 意地悪な 11e

mean imisuru *(v)* 意味する 17a

meaning imi 意味 17a

measles hashika 麻疹 40a

measure hakaru *(v)* 測る 3b

measurement sunpō 寸法 31

measuring cup keiryō kappu 計量カップ 3b

measuring tape tēpumejā テープメジャー 3b

meat niku 肉 24c

mechanic jidōsha shūrikō 自動車修理工 38a

mechanic shūrikō 修理工 33c

mechanical shudō no *(adj)* 手動の 25b

mechanical pencil shāpu penshiru シャープペンシル 19d

medicine igaku 医学 37e

medicine kusuri 薬 25h, 40a

meditate mokusōsuru *(v)* 黙想する 11d

meditation mokusō 黙想 11d

medium chūgurai no *(adj)* 中位の 3b, 13d

medium chūkan no *(adj)* 中間の 3b

medium hōhō 方法 3b

medium midiamu no *(adj)* ミディアムの 24b

medium (average) height chūgurai no se no takasa 中位の背の高さ 11a

meet au *(v)* 会う 16b

meeting room kaigishitsu 会議室 38d

megabyte mebagaito メガバイト 42b

melody merodī メロディー 28c

melon meron メロン 14d, 24f

melt tokeru *(v)* 溶ける 6a

melting point yūten 融点点 6c

membrane genkeishitsumaku 原形質膜 14a

memoir kaikoroku 回顧録 25o

memorize ankisuru *(v)* 暗記する 37f

memorize kiokusuru *(v)* 記憶する 22b

memory kioku 記憶 22a

memory memori メモリー 42b

memory card memorī kādo メモリーカード 25d, 42b

memory stick memorī sutikku メモリースティック 42b

men's shop shinshifuku ten 紳士服店 25k

mend tsukurou *(v)* 繕う 25g

mention noberu *(v)* 述べる 17a

menu menyū メニュー 24g, 42b

merciful nasakebukai *(adj)* 情け深い 21a

merciless zankoku na *(adj)* 残酷な 21a

mercury suigin 水銀 13c

Mercury suisei 水星 13a

Merge gōryū 合流 33d

meridian shigosen 子午線 13e

Merry Christmas! Kurisumasu omedetō. クリスマスおめでとう。 16c, 29c

message dengon 伝言 18b, 35b

metal kinzoku 金属 13c

metamorphosis hentai 変態 15d

metaphor inyu 隠喩 17a

meteor ryūsei 流星 13a

meteorite inseki 隕石 13a

meter mētoru メートル 3a

methane metan メタン 13c

metropolis to 都 11f

Mexico Mekishiko メキシコ 30b

microbe biseibutsu 微生物 15d

microphone maikurohon マイクロホン 20b

microscope kenbikyō 顕微鏡 13c

microtechnology maikuro gijutsu マイクロ技術 42a

microwave chōtanpa 超短波 42a

microwave oven denshirenji 電子レンジ 23d

middle chūkan 中間 3d

middle age chūnen 中年 11b

Middle and Near East Chūkintō 中近東 30b

middle finger nakayubi 中指 12a

midnight mayonaka 真夜中 4a

migratory bird wataridori 渡り鳥 15b

Milan Mirano ミラノ 30c

mild atatakai 温かい 6a

mild karakunai *(adj)* 辛くない 24p

mile mairu マイル 3a

milk gyūnyū 牛乳 24h

milk miruku ミルク 24h

Milky Way amanogawa 天の川 13a

milligram miriguramu ミリグラム 3a

millimeter miri ミリ 3a

millionth hyakumanbanme 百万番目 1b

mime mugon geki 無言劇 28e

mind kokoro 心 22a

mineral kōbutsu 鉱物 13c

mineral water mineraru wōta ミネラルウォーター 24k

minimum saishō no *(adj)* 最小の 3b

minimum saishō 最小 3b

minimum saitei (no) *(adj)* 最低（の） 6c

minister bokushi 牧師 11d

minister daijin 大臣 43

minivan miniban ミニバン 33a

mink minku ミンク 15a

mint minto ミント 14e, 24j

minus mainasu kigō マイナス記号 1e

minus mainasu マイナス 1f, 6c

minute fun 分 4c

mirror kagami 鏡 23c, 25f, 35c

mischievous itazurazuki na *(adj)* いたずら好きな 11e

miss norisokonau *(v)* 乗りそこなう 34

Miss, Ms. san さん 11f, 16b

missile misairu ミサイル 42a

mist kasumi 霞 6a

mistake machigai 間違い 37f

mix mazeru *(v)* 混ぜる 24o

mixer mikisā ミキサー 23d

modal johō no *(adj)* 叙法の 8a

modem modemu モデム 18a, 42b

modern dance modan dansu モダンダンス 28c

modest tsutsushimibukai *(adj)* 慎み深い 21a

moisturizer moisucharaizā モイスチャライザー 25f

molar kyūshi 臼歯 40b

mole mogura モグラ 15a

molecular bunshi no *(adj)* 分子の 13c

molecular formula bunshishiki 分子式 13c

molecular model bunshi kōzō mokei 分子構造模型 13c

molecular structure bunshi kōzō 分子構造 13c

molecule bunshi 分子 13c, 42a

moment shunkan 瞬間 4c

monarchy kunshusei 君主制 43

Monday getsuyōbi 月曜日 5a

money okane お金 26

money order kawase 為替 26

money order (post office) yūbin kawase 郵便為替 19e

monitor monitā モニター 42b

monk shūdōshi 修道士 11d

monkey saru 猿 15a

monkey wrench jizai supana 自在スパナ 25b

monkfish ankō アンコウ 15c

monorail vehicle monorēru モノレール 42a

month tsuki 月 4c, 5b, 38b

month of the year ichinen no tsuki 一年の月 5b

monthly maitsuki no *(adj)* 毎月の 4c, 5b

monthly magazine gekkanshi 月刊誌 20a

Montreal Montoriōru モントリオール 30c

monument kinentō 記念塔 36a

mood (grammar) dōshi no hō 動詞の法 8a

mood kibun 気分 21a

mood kigen 機嫌 11e

moody kimagure na *(adj)* 気まぐれな 21a

moon tsuki 月 5c, 6a, 13a

moon phases tsuki no michikake 月の満ち欠け 13a

moonbeam, ray gekkō 月光 13a

mop moppu モップ 23d

morality dōtoku 道徳 44b

more motto *(adv)* もっと 3c

moreover shikamo *(conj)* しかも 8k

morning asa 朝 4a

morning glory asagao 朝顔 14b

mortgage jūtaku rōn 住宅ローン 26

mortgage teitōken 抵当権 26

Moscow Mosukuwa モスクワ 30c

mosque mosuku モスク 11d

mosquito ka 蚊 15d

motel moteru モテル 35a

moth ga 蛾 15d

mother haha 母 10a

mother okāsan お母さん 10a

mother-in-law gibo 義母 10a

mother-in-law giri no okāsan 義理のお母さん 10a

motion ugoki 動き 3e

motor enjin エンジン 33e

motorcycle ōtobai オートバイ 33a

motorcycling ōtobai オートバイ 27b

mountain yama 山 13b

mountain boot tozangutsu 登山靴 27b, 36b

mountain chain sanmyaku 山脈 13b

mountain climbing tozan 登山 27b, 36b

mountainous yama no ōi 山の多い 13b

mouse mausu マウス 42b

mouse nezumi ネズミ 15a

mouth kuchi 口 12a, 40b

move hikkosu (v) 引っ越す 23f

move ugokasu (vt) 動かす 3e

move ugoku (vi) 動く 3e

move to idōsuru (v) 移動する 19f

movement undō 運動 3e

movie dōga 動画 19f

movie director eiga kantoku 映画監督 28a, 38a

movie star eiga sutā 映画スター 28a

movie theater eiga gekijō 映画劇場 28a

movie, film eiga 映画 28a, 29b

movie(s) eiga kanshō 映画鑑賞 27a

MP3 player emupīsurī purēyā MP3プレーヤー 20b

Mr., Mrs., Ms. san さん 11f, 16b

muffler mafurā マフラー 33e

muggy mushiatsui (adj) 蒸し暑い 6a

mule raba ラバ 15a

multiply kakeru (v) 掛ける 1e

mullet bora ボラ 15c

multiple baisū 倍数 1f

multiplication kakezan 掛け算 1e

multiplication table kuku no hyō 九九の表 1e

mumble bosoboso iu (v) ぼそぼそ言う 17a

mumps otafukukaze おたふく風邪 40a

municipal chihō jichitai no (adj) 地方自治体の 43

murder satsujin 殺人 39b

murder korosu (v) 殺す 39b

murderer satsujinsha 殺人者 39b

murmur tsubuyaku (v) つぶやく 17a

muscle kinniku 筋肉 12a, 40a

museum bijutsukan 美術館 28b, 36a

mushroom kinoko 茸 14e, 24e

music ongaku 音楽 25j, 28c, 37e

music function ongaku kinō 音楽機能 18a

musical myūjikaru ミュージカル 25j

musician ongakuka 音楽家 28c, 38a

Muslim (Moslem) kaikyōto 回教徒 11d

mussel mūrugai ムール貝 15c, 24d

mustache kuchihige 口ひげ 12a

mustard karashi からし 24j

mustard masutādo マスタード 24j

mute gengoshōgai no (adj) 言語障害の 12c

mutton yōniku/maton 羊肉／マトン 24c

mutual sōgoteki na (adj) 相互的な 43

mutual fund tōshi shintaku 投資信託 26

my watakushi no 私の 8d

My God! Komatta. (inf) 困った。 21c

My name is ... Watakushi no namae wa, ... desu. 私の名前は、 ・・・ です。 11f, 16b

My tooth hurts! Ha ga, itai desu. 歯が、痛いです。 40b

myrtle sarusuberi 百日紅 14c

myself watakushi jishin 私自身 8g

mystery misuterī ミステリー 20a, 25o

myth shinwa 神話 11d, 28d

mythology shinwa 神話 28d

N

nag (torment, pester) gamigami iu (v) がみがみ言う 17a

nail (hardware) kugi 釘 25b

nail clippers tsume kiri 爪切り 25f

nail file tsume yasuri 爪やすり 25f

nail polish manikyuaeki マニキュア液 12d, 25f

nail polish remover jokōeki 除光液 25f

name namae 名前 11f, 38b

nap hirune 昼寝 12b

nap hirunesuru (v) 昼寝する 12b

napkin napukin ナプキン 23d, 24l

narcissus suisen 水仙 14b

narrow semai (adj) 狭い 3b

nasty inken na (adj) 陰険な 11a

nasty tachi no warui (adj) 質の悪い 11e

nation kokka 国家 13e

national kokka no (adj) 国家の 13e

national kuni no (adj) 国の 43

National Foundation Day (February 11) kenkoku kinenbi 建国記念日 5g

national government worker kokka kōmuin 国家公務員 38a

nationality kokuseki 国籍 11f, 31, 38b

natural shizen no (adj) 自然の 13b

natural tennen no (adj) 天然の 13d

natural gas tennen gasu 天然ガス 13c

natural number shizensū 自然数 1d

natural resources tennenshigen 天然資源 13c, 44a

natural science shizen kagaku 自然科学 37e

nature shizen 自然 13b

nausea hakike 吐き気 40a

near … no chikaku ni …の近くに 36c

near chikai (adj) 近い 3d

near chikaku ni (adv) 近くに 3d

neat sapparishita (adj) サッパリした 11e

neck kubi 首 12a

necklace nekkuresu ネックレス 25i

nectarine nekutarin ネクタリン 14d, 24f

need iru (v) 要る 21a

need hitsuyō 実用 21a

negative hitei (adj) 否定 8a

negative hiteiteki na (adj) 否定的な 21a

negative number fusū 負数 1d

negotiation(s) kōshō 交渉 38d

nephew oi 甥 10a

nephew oigosan 甥御さん 10a

Neptune kaiōsei 海王星 13a

nerves shinkei 神経 40a

nervous shinkeishitsu na (adj) 神経質な 11e

nest su 巣 15b

net netto ネット 27b

network hōsōmō 放送網 20b

network nettowāku ネットワーク 42b

neuter chūsei 中性 8a

neutron chūseishi 中性子 13c, 42a

never kesshite ~ shinai (adv) 決して…しない 4e

new moon shingetsu 新月 13a

New Year's Day ganjitsu 元日 29a

New Year's Eve ōmisoka no ban 大晦日の晩 5g, 29a

New Year's Day (January 1) ganjitsu 元日 5g

New York Nyūyōku ニューヨーク 30c

New Zealand Nyūjīrando ニュージーランド 30b

newlyweds shinkon fusai 新婚夫妻 11c

news nyūsu ニュース 20a

news report nyūsu bangumi ニュース番組 20b

newscast nyūsu hōsō ニュース放送 20b

newspaper shinbun 新聞 20a, 25o

newsstand shinbun uriba 新聞売り場 34

nice ii (adj) いい 11e

niece mei 姪 10a

niece meigosan 姪御さん 10a

night yoru 夜 4a

nightgown nemaki 寝巻き 25k

nightingale naichingēru ナイチンゲール 15b

nine kokonotsu 九つ 1a

nine ku/kyū 九 1a

nine hundred kyūhyaku 九百 1a

nine thousand kyūsen 九千 1a

nineteen jūku/jūkyū 十九 1a

nineteen thousand ichimankyūsen 一万九千 1a

ninety kyūjū 九十 1a

ninety thousand kyūman 九万 1a

ninth daiku 第九 1b

ninth kokonotsume 九つ目 1b

ninth kyūbanme 九番目 1b

nitrogen chisso 窒素 13c

No! Dame desu. 駄目です。 16c

No. Iie. いいえ。 16c

No Entry shinnyū kinshi 進入禁止 33d

No Left Turn sasetsu kinshi 左折禁止 33d

no one dare mo ~ nai 誰も〜ない 3c, 8i

No Parking chūsha kinshi 駐車禁止 33d

No Passing oikoshi kinshi 追い越し禁止 33d

No problem! Mondai arimasen. 問題ありません。 22a

No Right Turn usetsu kinshi 右折禁止 33d

No smoking kin-en 禁煙 32a

No Stopping teisha kinshi 停車禁止 33d

No Thoroughfare tsūkōdome 通行止め 33d

No U-Turn yūtān kinshi Uターン禁止 33d

nobody daremo ~ nai 誰も〜ない 8i

noise sōon 騒音 12c

noisy yakamashii 喧しい 12c

nonconformist hijunnōsha 非順応者 11e

none daremo ~ nai 誰も〜ない 8i

nonfat milk mushibō gyūnyū 無脂肪牛乳 24h

nonfiction nonfikushon ノンフィクション 20a

nonsmoking kin-en 禁煙 34

nonsmoking room kin-en no heya 禁煙の部屋 35b

noon hiruma 昼間 4a

north kita 北 3d

North America Kita Amerika 北アメリカ 30b

North Pole hokkyoku 北極 13e

northeast hokutō 北東 3d

northern kita no 北の 3d

northern hemisphere kita hankyū 北半球 13e

northwest hokusei 北西 3d

Norway Noruwē ノルウェー 30b

Norwegian (language) Noruwēgo ノルウェー語 30d

Norwegian Noruwējin ノルウェー人 30d

nose hana 鼻 12a

nostril bikō 鼻腔 12a, 40a

nosy sensakuzuki na (adj) 詮索好きな 21a

Not bad! Waruku arimasen. 悪くありません。 16a

not guilty muzai 無罪 41

not guilty shiro シロ 41

not nice, odious iya na (adj) 嫌な 11e

note (music) onpu 音符 28c

note chūshaku 注釈 20a

note mijikai tegami 短い手紙 19e

note nōto ノート 37f

notebook chōmen 帳面 37b

notebook nōto ノート 19d, 25c

notebook computer nōtopasokon ノートパソコン 42b

nothing nani mo ~ nai なにも～ない 3c, 8i

noun meishi 名刺 8a

novel shōsetsu 小説 20a, 25o, 28d

November jūichigatsu 十一月 5b

now ... Ima ... 今 ··· 17b

now ima/genzai 今／現在 4e

now and then tokidoki (adv) 時々 4e

nowadays genzai dewa 現在では 4e

nowhere dokonimo (adv) どこにも 3d

n-sided figures enuhenkei n辺形 2a

nth root enu jō kon n乗根 1e

nuclear energy kaku enerugī 核エネルギー 13c, 42a

nuclear fuel kakunenryō 核燃料 42a

nuclear industry genshiryoku sangyō 原子力産業 42a

nuclear reactor genshiro 原子炉 42a

nuclear war kaku sensō 核戦争 44b

nuclear waste kaku haikibutsu 核廃棄物 13c

nuclear weapon kaku heiki 核兵器 44b

nucleus genshikaku 原子核 13c

nucleus kaku 核 14a

number (address) banchi 番地 38b

number bangō o tsukeru (v) 番号をつける 1d

number kazu/sūji 数／数字 1d, 8a

numeral sūji 数字 1d

numerical kazu no (adj) 数の 1d

nun nisō 尼僧 11d

nurse kangoshi 看護士 38a, 40a

nursery school hoikuen 保育園 37a

nut natto ナット 25b

nylon nairon ナイロン 25l

O

oak tree kashi 樫 14c

oat ōtomugi オート麦 24i

oatmeal ōtomīru オートミール 24i

obesity himan 肥満 11a

obituary shibōkiji 死亡記事 20a

object (grammar) mokutekigo 目的語 8a

object hantaisuru (v) 反対する 17a

object igi o tonaeru (v) 異議を唱える 41

objection igi 意義 41

obnoxious fukai kiwamarinai (adj) 不快極まりない 11e

oboe ōboe オーボエ 28c

obstetrician sankai 産科医 40a

obstinate gōjō na (adj) 強情な 11e

obtuse angle donkaku 鈍角 2b

obtuse-angled donkaku (adj) 鈍角 2a

occasionally tokidoki (adj) 時々 4e

Occidental seiōjin 西欧人 11d

occupation shokugyō 職業 38a

ocean current kairyū 海流 13b

ocean taiyō 大洋 13b

octagon hakkakukei 八角形 2a

octahedron hachimentai 八面体 2a

October jūgatsu 十月 5b

octopus tako タコ 15c, 24d

odd number kisū 奇数 1d

of, ~'s (possessive marker) no の 8j

offend kanjō o kizutsukeru (v) 感情を傷つける 17a

offer mōshideru (v) 申し出る 17a

office ofisu オフィス 38d

office automation ofisu ōtomēshon オフィスオート メーション 42b

office hours shinryō jikan 診療時間 40b

office supplies jimuyōhin 事務用品 25c

office worker (female) ōeru オーエル 38a

office worker (male) sararīman サラリーマン 38a

often yoku (adv) よく 4e

Oh, my! Oya, mā. おや、まあ。 21c

oil oiru オイル 24j, 33e

oil sekiyu 石油 13c

oil filter oiru firutā オイルフィルター 33e

oil paint aburaenogu 油絵の具 28b

ointment nankō 軟膏 25h

OK! Ii desu yo. いいですよ。 16c

old toshitotta (adj) 年取った 11b

old age rōgo 老後 11b

older toshiue no (adj) 年上の 11b

older brother ani 兄 11b

older sister ane 姉 11b

olive orību オリーブ 14d

olive tree orību no ki オリーブの木 14c

omelette omuretsu オムレツ 24h

on ni/de に/で 8j

on ue ni (adv) 上に 3d

on ue no (adj) 上の 3d

on Mondays getsuyōbi ni 月曜日に 5a

on sale sēru セール 25a

on Saturdays doyōbi ni 土曜日に 5a

on Sundays nichiyōbi ni 日曜日に 5a

on the air hōsōchū 放送中 20b

on time jikandōri ni (adv) 時間通りに 34

on time teikoku ni (adv) 定刻に 32b

once katsute (adv) かつて 4e

once in a while tokidoki 時々 4e

once upon a time mukashimukashi 昔々 4e

one hito 人 8i

one hitotsu 一つ 1a

one ichi 一 1a

one (bound object) issatsu 一冊 1a

one (floor) ikkai 一階 1a

one (liquid or dry measure) ippai 一杯 1a

one (long, thin object) ippon 一本 1a

one (person) hitori 一人 1a

one (small object) ikko/hitotsu 一個/一つ 1a

one (thin, flat object) ichimai 一枚 1a

one billion jūoku 十億 1a

one hundred hyaku 百 1a

one hundred and one hyakuichi 百一 1a

one hundred and two hyakuni 百二 1a

one hundred billion sen-oku 千億 1a

one hundred million ichioku 一億 1a

one hundred ten hyakujū 百十 1a

one hundred thousand jūman 十万 1a

one hundred twenty hyakunijū 百二十 1a

one million and one hyakuman-ichi 百万一 1a

one million and two hyakuman-ni 百万二 1a

one million hyakuman 百万 1a

one thousand sen 千 1a

one thousand and one sen-ichi 千一 1a

one thousand ten senjū 千十 1a

one trillion itchō 一兆 1a

one turn (360°) ichi kaiten 一回転 2b

One Way ippōtsūkō 一方通行 33d

one's self jibun 自分 8g

one-fifth gobun no ichi 五分の一 1c

one-fourth yonbun no ichi 四分の一 1c

one-half nibun no ichi 二分の一 1c

one-third sanbun no ichi 三分の一 1c

one-way ticket katamichi ken 片道券 30a

onion tamanegi 玉ねぎ 14e, 24e

online onrain オンライン 42b

only dake だけ 4e

opal opāru オパール 25i

opaque futōmeï na/kusunda (adj) 不透明な／くすんだ 7b, 13d

open kaitensuru (v) 開店する 25a

open an account kōza o hiraku 口座を開く 26

Open your mouth! Kuchi o, akete kudasai. 口を開けてください。 40b

opening hours eigyō jikan 営業時間 25a

opera opera オペラ 25j, 28c

operating room shujutsushitsu 手術室 40a

operation shujutsu 手術 40a

operator kōkanshu 交換手 18b

opinion iken 意見 22a

oppose hantaisuru (adj) 反対する 21a

opposite angle taichōkaku 対頂角 2b

optical fiber hikari faibā 光ファイバー 18a, 20b

optician megane ya 眼鏡屋 40a

optimism rakutenshugi 楽天主義 11e

optimist rakutenshugisha 楽天主義者 11e

optimistic rakutenteki na (adj) 楽天的な 11e

optometrist kengan-i 検眼医 40a

or aruiwa (conj) あるいは 8k

or matawa (conj) 又は 8k

or soretomo *(conj)* それとも 8k

oral kōtō no *(adj)* 口頭の 17a

oral exam mensetsu shiken
面接試験 37f

orally kōtō de *(adv)* 口頭で 17a

orange orenji オレンジ 14d, 24f

orange (color) orenji iro
オレンジ色 7a

orange tree orenji no ki
オレンジの木 14c

orangutan oranūtan
オランウータン 15a

orbit kidō ni noru *(vi)*
軌道に乗る 13a

orbit kidō ni noseru *(vt)*
軌道に乗せる 13a

orbit kidō 軌道 13a

orchestra ōkesutora
オーケストラ 25j, 28c

orchestra conductor ōkesutora
no shikisha オーケストラの
指揮者 28c

orchid ran ラン 14b

order chūmonsuru *(v)* 注文する
24o

order meirei 命令 17a

order meireisuru *(v)* 命令する
17a

ordinal number josū 序数 1d

ordinate coordinate tate zahyō
縦座標 2b

organ naizō 内臓 12a

organ (music) orugan オルガン
28c

organic yūki no *(adj)* 有機の 13c

organism yūkibutsu/yūkitai
有機物／有機体 14a, 15d

Oriental Ajiajin アジア人 11d

original sōsakuteki na *(adj)*
創作的な 11e

orthopedic surgeon seikeigekai
整形外科医 40a

Osaka Ōsaka 大阪 30c

ostrich dachō 駝鳥 15b

others hoka no hito 他の人 8i

otter kawauso カワウソ 15a

ounce onsu オンス 3a

our watakushitachi no 私達の
8d

ourselves watakushitachi jishin
私達自身 8g

out soto e *(adv)* 外へ 39a

out of court settlement jidan
示談 41

out of focus pinboke no *(adj)*
ピンぼけの 25d

outlet autoretto アウトレット
25a

outlet konsento コンセント 25b

outlet sashikomi 差し込み 18a

outside ... ... no soto ni
・・・の外に 36c

outside soto ni *(adv)* 外に 3d

outside soto no *(adj)* 外の 3d

outskirts, suburbs kōgai 郊外
30a

outspokenly enryonaku *(adv)*
遠慮なく 17a

oven ōbun オーブン 23d

over there asoko あそこ 3d

overhead projector ōbāheddo
purojekutā オーバーヘッ
ドプロジェクター 37b

overpopulation jinkō kajō
人口過剰 44b

overtime work zangyō 残業 38d

owl fukurō フクロウ 15b

ox oushi 牡牛 15a

oxtail okkusutēru
オックステール 24c

oxygen sanso 酸素 13c, 40a

oyster kaki 牡蛎 15c, 24d

ozone ozon オゾン 44a

P

P.S. tsuishin 追伸 19c

Pacific taiheiyōsei no *(adj)* 太平洋性の 6a

Pacific Ocean taiheiyō 太平洋 13b

pack (one's bags, luggage) nizukurisuru *(v)* 荷造りする 31

package kozutusmi 小包 10e

package tsutsumi 包み 25a

package tour pakkēji tsuā パッケージツアー 30a

pagan ikyōto 異教徒 11d

page pēji ページ 19c,19d, 20a

pail teoke 手桶 23d

pain itami 痛み 40a

painful itai *(adj)* 痛い 40a

painkiller chintsūzai 鎮痛剤 25h, 40a

paint e o kaku *(v)* 絵を描く 28b

paint (art) egaku *(v)* 描く 7c

paint (houses, rooms) penki o nuru *(v)* ペンキを塗る 7c, 23f

painter (artist) gaka 画家 7c, 28b, 38a

painter (houses, rooms) penkiya ペンキ屋 7c, 38a

painting e/kaiga 絵／絵画 23c, 27a

pair issoku 一足 25n

pair kumi/tsui 組／対 3c

pajamas pajama パジャマ 25k

Pakistan Pakisutan パキスタン 30b

palate kōgai 口蓋 40b

pale aozameta *(adj)* 青ざめた 40a

pale usui *(adj)* 薄い 7b

palette paretto パレット 28b

palm tenohira 手のひら 12a

palm tree yashi no ki 椰子の木 14c

pamphlet, brochure panfuretto パンフレット 20a

pan hiranabe 平鍋 23d

pancreas suizō 膵臓 12a

panda panda パンダ 15a

panoramic panorama (no) *(adj)* パノラマ（の）25d

pansy panjī パンジー 14b

panther hyō 豹 15a

panties pantī パンティー 25k

pantomime pantomaimu パントマイム 28e

pants zubon ズボン 25k

pantyhose pantīsutokkingu パンティーストッキング 25k

papaya papaiya パパイヤ 14d, 24f

paper kami 紙 19d, 25c, 37b

paper clip kurippu クリップ 19d, 25c

paperback pēpābakku ペーパーバック 20a

paprika papurika パプリカ 24j

paragraph danraku 段落 19c

parakeet sekiseiinko セキセイインコ 15b

parallel lines heikōsen 平行線 2b

parallelepiped heikōrokumentai 平行六面体 2a

parallelogram heikōshihenkei 平行四辺形 2a

parcel konimotsu 小荷物 19e

parent oya 親 10a

parents goryōshin 御両親 10a

parents ryōshin 両親 10a

Paris Pari パリ 30c

park chūshasuru (v) 駐車する 33c

park kōen 公園 36a

parking chūsha 駐車 33c

parking lot chūshajō 駐車場 23e

parking meter chūsha mētā 駐車メーター 36a

parliament gikai 議会 43

parliament building gijidō 議事堂 36a

parrot ōmu オウム 15b

parsley paseri パセリ 14e, 24j

part bubun 部分 3c

partial eclipse bubunshoku 部分蝕 13a

participle bunshi 分詞 8a

particle bibunshi 微分子 13c

particle (grammar) joshi 助詞 8a

party pātī パーティー 29b

pass oikosu (v) 追い越す 33c

pass pasusuru (v) パスする 27b

pass a sentence hanketsu o iiwatasu (v) 判決を言い渡す 41

pass an exam shiken ni ukaru 試験に受かる 37f

pass by tōrisugiru (v) 通り過ぎる 3e

passenger dōjōsha 同乗者 33b

passenger jōkyaku 乗客 32c

passenger car jōyōsha 乗用車 33a

Passing Lane oikoshisen 追い越し線 33d

passionate netsuretsu na (adj) 熱烈な 21a

passive shōkyokuteki na (adj) 消極的な 21a

passive ukemi no (adj) 受け身の 8a

passport pasupōto パスポート 30a, 31, 35b

passport control ryoken shinsa 旅券審査 31

past kako (adj) 過去 8a

past kako 過去 4e

past perfect kakokanryōkei 過去完了形 8a

past progressive kakoshinkōkei 過去進行形 8a

pasta pasuta パスタ 24g

pastel pasuteru パステル 28b

pastry pesutorī ペストリー 24i

pastry shop kēki ya ケーキ屋 24n

patience nintai 忍耐 11e, 21a

patient kanja 患者 40a

patient nintaizuyoi (adj) 忍耐強い 11e, 21a

patio nakaniwa 中庭 23a

paulownia kiri 桐 14c

paw ashi 足 15a

pawn pōn ポーン 27a

pay harau (v) 払う 25a, 26, 35b

pay customs/duty kanzei o harau (v) 関税を払う 31

pay off zengaku shiharau (v) 全額支払う 26

pay phone kōshū denwa 公衆電話 18a

payday kyūryōbi 給料日 38d

payment shiharai 支払い 26

PDA keitai jōhō tanmatsu 携帯情報端末 18a

pea endōmame エンドウ豆 14e

peace heiwa 平和 43

peach momo 桃 14d, 24f

peach tree momo no ki 桃ノ木 14c

peacock kujaku 孔雀 15b

peak chōjō 頂上 13b

peak season isogashii toki 忙しいとき 35b

pear (Japanese) nashi 梨 14d, 24f

pear (western) yōnashi 洋梨 14d, 24f

pear tree nashi no ki 梨の木 14c

pearl pāru パール 25i

pearl shinju 真珠 25i

peas endōmame エンドウ豆 24e

pedal pedaru ペダル 33a

pedestrian hokōsha 歩行者 33b

pedestrian crossing ōdanhodō 横断歩道 33c

pediatrician shōnikai 小児科医 40a

peel kawa o muku (v) 皮をむく 24o

pelican perikan ペリカン 15b

pelt kegawa 毛皮 13c

pen pen ペン 2b, 7c, 19d, 25c, 37b, 38c

penalty penarutī ペナルティー 27c

pencil enpitsu 鉛筆 2b, 19d, 25c, 37b, 38c

pencil sharpener enpitsu kezuri 鉛筆削り 25c, 37b

penguin pengin ペンギン 15b

penicillin penishirin ペニシリン 25h

peninsula hantō 半島 13b

penis penisu ペニス 12a

pension nenkin 年金 38d

pentagon gokakukei 五角形 2a

peony shakuyaku 芍薬 14b

pepper koshō 胡椒 14e, 24j

Pepsi-Cola Pepushikōra ペプシコーラ 24k

per hour jisoku 時速 3a

per minute funsoku 分速 3a

per second byōsoku 秒速 3a

perceive chikakusuru (v) 知覚する 12c

percent pāsento パーセント 1f

percentage ritsu 率 1f

perception chikakuryoku 知覚力 12c

percussion instruments dagakki 打楽器 28c

perfection kanzen 完全 11e

perfectionist kanzenshugisha 完全主義者 11e

perfume kōsui 香水 12d, 25f

period shūshiten 終止点 19c

periodical teiki kankōbutsu 定期刊行物 20a

peripherals shūhen sōchi 周辺装置 42b

permanent wave pāmanento パーマネント 12d

perpendicular line suisen 垂線 2b

persimmon kaki 柿 14d, 24f

person (grammar) ninshō 人称 8a

personal ninshō (adj) 人称 8a

personal computer pasokon パソコン 42b

personality seikaku 性格 11e

person-to-person call pāsonaru kōru パーソナルコール 18b

perspire ase o kaku (v) 汗をかく 6b

persuade settokusuru *(v)* 説得する 22b, 41

pessimism hikanshugi 悲観主義 11e

pessimist hikanshugisha 悲観主義者 11e

pessimistic hikanteki na *(adj)* 悲観的な 11e

pesticide satchūzai 殺虫剤 13c

pet petto ペット 15a

petal hanabira 花びら 14b

petal hanabira/kaben 花びら／花弁 14a

petroleum sekiyu 石油 13c, 44a

petunia pechunia ペチュニア 14b

pharmacist yakuzaishi 薬剤師 25h, 38a

pharmacy yakkyoku 薬局 25h

pheasant kiji 雉子 15b

Philippines Firippin フィリッピン 30b

philosophy tetsugaku 哲学 37e

phone book denwachō 電話帳 18a

phone booth denwa bokkusu 電話ボックス 18a

phone outlet denwa no sashikomiguchi 電話の差し込み口 18a

phonetics onpyōmoji 音標文字 8a

phosphate rinsan-en リン酸塩 13c

photo printer fotopurinta フォトプリンタ 25d

photo, picture shashin 写真 19f, 20a, 25d

photocopier fukushaki 複写機 38c

photographer shashinka 写真家 38a

photosynthesis kōgōsei 光合成 14a

phrase ku 句 19c

physical butsuri no *(adj)* 物理の 13c

physical education taiiku 体育 37e

physics butsuri/butsurigaku 物理／物理学 13c, 37e

physiology seirigaku 生理学 37e

pianist pianisuto ピアニスト 28c

piano piano ピアノ 28c

pick flowers hana o tsumu *(v)* 花を摘む 14b

pick up (the phone) juwaki o toriageru *(v)* 受話器を取り上げる 18b

pickle dish okozara お小皿 24l

pickpocket suri すり 39b

picky kuchiyakamashii *(adj)* 口やかましい 11e

picnic pikunikku ピクニック 29a

pie pai パイ 24g

piece shōhen/ko 小片／個 3c

pig buta 豚 15a

pigeon hato 鳩 15b

pill ganyaku 丸薬 25h. 40a

pillow makura 枕 23d, 35c

pillowcase makurakabā 枕カバー 23d

pilot sōjūshi/pairotto 操縦士／パイロット 32c, 38a

pimple nikibi ニキビ 40a

PIN anshō bangō 暗証番号 18a

pinch tsumitoru *(v)* 摘み取る 14a

pine tree matsu 松 14c

pineapple painappuru パイナップル 14d, 24f

Ping-Pong pinpon ピンポン 27b

pink momoiro/pinku 桃色／ ピンク 79

pipe paipu パイプ 25e

Pisces uoza 魚座 5d

pistil meshibe 雌しべ 14a

pitcher pitchā ピッチャー 27b

pixel gaso 画素 25d

place basho 場所 3d

place shusseichi 出生地 38b

place of birth shusseichi 出生地 11f

place of employment koyōsaki 雇用先 11f

plain heiya 平野 13b

plaintiff genkoku 原告 41

plane (tool) kanna 鉋 25b

plane figures heimen zukei 平面図形 2a

plane ticket kōkū ken 航空券 30a

planet wakusei 惑星 13a

plankton purankuton プランクトン 13c

plant shokubutsu 植物 14a

plant ueru (v) 植える 14a

plant (factory) kōjō 工場 38d

plaque shikō 歯垢 40b

plasma display TV purazuma terebi プラズマテレビ 20b

plastic purasuchikku プラスチック 13c

plastic container purasuchikku yōki プラスチック容器 23d

plate sara 皿 23d, 24l

plateau kōgen 高原 13b

platform kōryō 綱領 43

platform purattohōmu プラットフォーム 34

platinum purachina プラチナ 13c, 25i

play ensōsuru (v) 演奏する 28c

play geki/engeki 劇／演劇 20a, 28e

play (a game) shiaisuru (v) 試合する 27a, 27b

play (an instrument) (gakki o) ensōsuru (v) （楽器を）演奏する 27a, 28c

player (music) ensōka 演奏家 28c

player (sports) senshu 選手 27b

playing cards toranpu トランプ 27a

playoff yūshō kettei shirīzu 優勝決定シリーズ 27b

playwright geki sakka 劇作家 28e

plea tangan 嘆願 41

plea for mercy jihi no tangan 慈悲の嘆願 41

plead tangansuru (v) 嘆願する 41

pleasant, likeable tanoshii (adj) 楽しい 11e, 21b

Please give my regards/greetings to... ...san ni yoroshiku otsutae kudasai. さんによろしくお伝えください。 16a

Please! (go ahead) Dōzo. どうぞ。 16c

Please! (request) Onegai shimasu. お願いします。 16c

pliers penchi ペンチ 25b

plot suji 筋 20a, 28e, 28d

plug puragu プラグ 25b

plug sashikomi 差し込み 18a

plum sumomo スモモ 14d, 24f

plumber haikankō 配管工 38a

plumbing haikan 配管 25b

plumbing suidō setsubi 水道設備 23e

plural number fukusū 複数 8a

plus purasu kigō プラス記号 1e

plus purasu プラス 1f, 6c

Pluto meiōsei 冥王星 13a

pneumonia haien 肺炎 40a

poached egg pōchido eggu ポーチドエッグ 24h

pocket poketto ポケット 25g, 27a

pocket book bunkohon 文庫本 20a

pocket radio poketto rajio ポケットラジオ 20b

pocket watch kaichūdokei 懐中時計 4d

poem shi 詩 20a, 25o

poet shijin 詩人 28d

poetry shi 詩 20a, 25o, 28d

point ten 点 2b

point tokuten 得点 27b

point out shitekisuru (v) 指摘する 17a

Poland Pōrando ポーランド 30b

polar bear shirokuma 白熊 15a

Polaris hokkyokusei 北極星 13a

pole kyoku 極 13e

Pole Pōrandojin ポーランド人 30d

police keisatsu 警察 33b, 39b, 39c

police officer (female) fujinkeikan 婦人警官 38a

police officer (male) keikan 警官 38a

police station keisatsusho 警察署 41

policeman keikan 警官 33b, 38a, 39b

policewoman fujin keikan 婦人警官 33b, 38a, 39b

policy seisaku 政策 43

Polish (language) Pōrandogo ポーランド語 30d

political party seitō 政党 43

political power seijiryoku 政治力 43

political science seijigaku 政治学 37e

politician seijika 政治家 38a, 43

politics seiji 政治 43

pollen kafun 花粉 14a

pollution kōgai 公害 44a

pollution osen 汚染 13c

polyester poriesuteru ポリエステル 25g, 25l

polyhedron tamentai 多面体 2a

pomegranate zakuro ザクロ 14d, 24f

pomegranate tree zakuro no ki ザクロの木 14c

pony kouma 子馬 15a

poor misuborashii (adj) みすぼらしい 11e

Poor man! Kawaisō ni. 可哀想に。 21c

Poor woman! Kawaisō ni. 可哀想に。 21c

popcorn poppukōn ポップコーン 24i

poplar tree popura ポプラ 14c

poppy keshi ケシ 14b

popular music popyurā myūjikku ポピュラーミュージック 25j, 28c

porch beranda ベランダ 23a

porcupine yamaarashi ヤマアラシ 15a

porgy tai 鯛 15c, 24d

pork butaniku 豚肉 24c

pork pōku ポーク 24c

pornography poruno ポルノ 44b

portable radio pōtaburu rajio ポータブルラジオ 20b

porter akabō 赤帽 34

porter pōtā ポーター 32a, 35b

portion bubun 部分 3c

portrait pōtorēto ポートレート 28b

Portugal Porutogaru ポルトガル 30b

Portuguese (language) Porutogarugo ポルトガル語 30d

Portuguese Porutogarujin ポルトガル人 30d

position ichi 位置 3d

positive sekkyokuteki na (adj) 積極的な 21a

positive number seisū 整数 1d

possessive shoyūyoku ga tsuyoi (adj) 所有欲が強い 11e

possessive (grammar) shoyū (adj) 所有 8a

post office yūbinkyoku 郵便局 19e

post office box shishobako 私書箱 19e

postage yūbin ryōkin 郵便料金 19e

postal rate yūbin ryōkin 郵便料金 19e

postcard hagaki 葉書 19e

postdate jigohizuke ni suru (v) 事後日付にする 26

pot fukanabe 深鍋 23d

potato jagaimo ジャガイモ 14e, 24e

pottery tōgei 陶芸 27a

pound pondo ポンド 3a

pour tsugu (v) 注ぐ 24o

pouring rain doshaburi 土砂降り 6a

poverty hinkon 貧困 44b

powder konagusuri 粉薬 25h

power brake pawā burēki パワーブレーキ 33e

power steering pawā handoru パワーハンドル 33e

power window pawā windō パワーウィンドー 33e

praise homeru (v) 褒める 17a

prawn kurumaebi 車海老 15c, 24d

pray inoru (v) 祈る 17a

pray oinorisuru (v) お祈りする 11d

prayer oinori お祈り 11d, 17a

praying mantis kamakiri カマキリ 15d

preach sekkyōsuru (v) 説教する 17a

precious stone kiseki 貴石 25i

predicate jutsubu 述部 8a

preface maeoki 前置き 28d

prefecture ken 県 11f, 38b

prefer konomu (v) 好む 21b

preference konomi 好み 21b

pregnancy ninshin 妊娠 11c

pregnant ninshinchū no (adj) 妊娠中の 40a

premiere showing puremia shō プレミアショー 28a

preposition zenchishi 前置詞 8a

prescription shohōsen 処方箋 25h, 40a

present genzai *(adj)* 現在 8a

present genzai 現在 4e

present perfect genzaikanryōkei 現在完了形 8a

present progressive genzaishinkōkei 現在進行形 8a

president daitōryō 大統領 43

president of a university gakuchō 学長 37d

presumptuous buenryo na *(adj)* 無遠慮な 11e

pretentious mie o hatta *(adj)* 見栄を張った 11e

previous mae no *(adj)* 前の 4e

previously mae ni *(adv)* 前に 4e

price nedan 値段 24m, 25a

price tag nedanhyō 値段表 25a

price, rate ryōkin 料金 35b

priest seishokusha 聖職者 11d

primate reichōrui 霊長類 15a

prime meridian honsho shigosen 本初子午線 13e

prime minister shushō 首相 43

prime number sosū 素数 1d

prince ōji 王子 43

princess ōjo 王女 43

principal kōchō 校長 37d

print insatsusuru *(v)* 印刷する 20a

print purinto プリント 25d

print run insatsu busū 印刷部数 20a

Print your name. Onamae o, kaisho de kaite kudasai. お名前を楷書で書いてください。 11f

printed matter insatsubutsu 印刷物 19e

printer purinta プリンタ 19d, 38c, 42b

printing, typography insatsujutsu 印刷術 20a

prism kakuchū 角柱 2a

prison sentence yūkikei 有期刑 41

prison, jail keimusho 刑務所 41

private school shiritsu gakkō 私立学校 37a

probation shikkō yūyo 執行猶予 41

problem mondai 問題 1f, 22a, 37f

problem to solve kaiketsusuru mondai 解決する問題 1f

produce market yasai ichiba 野菜市場 24n

producer seisakusha 制作者 28a

product seihin 製品 25a

product (mathematics) seki 積 1f

production seisakugaisha 制作会社 28a

Prof. kyōju 教授 11f

profession shokugyō 職業 11f, 38a

profession shokureki 職歴 38b

professional puro no *(adj)* プロの 38a

professional puro プロ 27b

professional senmonteki na *(adj)* 専門的な 11f

professor kyōju 教授 37d, 38a

professor's office kenkyūshitsu 研究室 37c

prognosis yogoshindan 予後診断 40a

program puroguramu
プログラム 20b, 42b, 28e

programmer puroguramā
プログラマー 38a, 42b

programming puroguramingu
プログラミング 42b

projection television
purojekushon terebi
プロジェクションテレビ 20b

projector eishaki 映写機 20b

projector purojekuta
プロジェクタ 38c

promise yakusoku 約束 17a

promise yakusokusuru (v)
約束する 17a

promissory note yakusokutegata
約束手形 26

promotion shōshin 昇進 38d

pronoun daimeishi 代名詞 8a

pronounce hatsuonsuru (v)
発音する 17a

pronunciation hatsuon 発音 8a,
17a

proof kōseizuri 校正刷り 20a

proof shōko 証拠 41

proofreader kōseisha 校正者 20a

propose mōshikomu (v)
申し込む 17a

proposition meidai/teiri 命題／
定理 1f

prose sanbun 散文 28d

prostate zenritsusen 前立腺 12a

prostitute baishunfu 売春婦 44b

prostitution baishun 売春 44b

protect fusegu (v) 防ぐ 39a

protest kōgi 抗議 17a, 43

protest kōgisuru (v) 抗議する
17a, 43

Protestant shinkyōto 新教徒 11d

Protestantism shinkyō 新教 11d

proton yōshi 陽子 13c, 42a

protractor bundoki 分度器 2b

proud hokori no takai (adj)
誇りの高い 11e

province shō 省 13e

provincial chihō no (adj) 地方の
43

provocative chōhatsuteki na (adj)
挑発的な 21a

prudent shinchō na (adj) 慎重な
11e

prune senteisuru (v) 剪定する
14a

prune (fruit) hoshisumomo
干しスモモ 14d, 24f

pruning sentei 剪定 14a

psychiatrist seishinkai 精神科医
38a, 40a

psychologist shinrigakusha
心理学者 38a

psychology shinrigaku 心理学
37e

public notices kōji 公示 36a

public parking chūshajō 駐車場
33c

public phone kōshū denwa
公衆電話 36a

public prosecutor kensatsukan
検察官 41

public radio kōkyō rajio
公共ラジオ 20b

public television kōkyō terebi
公共テレビ 20b

public washroom kōshū benjo
公衆便所 36a

publish shuppansuru (v)
出版する 20a

publisher shuppansha 出版社
20a, 25o, 28d

puck pakku パック 27b

pudding purin プリン 24g

pull hipparu (v) 引っ張る 3e

pulse myaku 脈 40a

pumpkin kabocha カボチャ 14e, 24e

punch panchi パンチ 19d, 25b

punctuation kutōten 句読点 19c

pupa sanagi 蛹 15d

pupil seito 生徒 37d

puppet theater (Japanese) Bunraku 文楽 28e

purchase kaimono 買い物 25a

purchase kau (v) 買う 25a

pure junsui no (adj) 純粋の 13d

pure majirike no nai (adj) 混じりけの無い 7b

purple murasaki iro 紫色 7a

pus umi 膿 40a

put oku (v) 置く 3e

put a room in order heya o katazukeru (v) 部屋を片付ける 23f

put down oku (v) 置く 3e

put on kiru (v) 着る 25m

put on (shoes) haku (v) 履く 25n

put on makeup okeshōsuru (v) お化粧する 12d

put on perfume kōsui o tsukeru (v) 香水をつける 12d

puzzle pazuru パズル 27a

pyramid (mathematics) kakusui 角錐 2a

Pythagorean theorem Pitagorasu no teiri ピタゴラスの定理 2b

Q

quail uzura ウズラ 15b

quantity ryō 量 3c

quantum theory ryōshiron 量子論 42a

quart kuōto クオート 3a

quarter century shihanseiki 四半世紀 4c

quartet karutetto カルテット 28c

queen jo-ō 女王 43

queen kuīn クイーン 27a

question shitsumon 質問 37f

question mark gimonfu 疑問符 19c

quickly hayaku (adv) 速く 3e

quiet shizuka na (adj) 静かな 11e

Quiet! Shizuka ni. (inf) 静かに。 21c

Quite well! Umaku itte imasu. うまくいっています。 16a

quotation mark inyōfu 引用符 19c

quotient shō 商 1f

R

rabbi Yudayakyō no rippōhakase ユダヤ教の立法博士 11d

rabbit usagi 兎 15a

raccoon araiguma アライグマ 15a

race minzoku 民族 11d

race (sports) rēsu レース 27b

racism jinshu sabetsu 人種差別 44b

racket raketto ラケット 27b

radiation hōshanō 放射能 13c

radiation hōshasen 放射線 44a

radiator rajiētā ラジエーター 33e

radio rajio ラジオ 20b, 23d, 35c

radio frequency rajio shūhasū ラジオ周波数 20b

radio network rajio hōsōmō ラジオ放送網 20b

radio wave denpa 電波 20b

radioactive hōshasei no (adj)
放射性の 13c

radioactive waste hōshasei
haikibutsu 放射性廃棄物 13c,
44a

radiologist hōshasen-ishi
放射線医師 40a

radish (Japanese) daikon 大根
14e, 24e

radish (western) hatsuka daikon
二十日大根 14e, 24e

radius hankei 半径 2a

railroad tetsudō 鉄道 34

Railway Crossing fumikiri 踏切
36a

rain ame ga furu (v) 雨が降る 6a

rain ame 雨 6a

rain forest urin 雨林 13b

rainbow trout nijimasu 虹鱒 15c

raincoat reinkōto レインコート
25k

rainy season tsuyu 梅雨 6a

raise (someone) sodateru (v)
育てる 11c

raise to a power ruijōsuru (v)
累乗する 1e

raisin hoshibudō 干しぶどう
14d, 24f

rake kumade くま手 25b

ramp intāchenji
インターチェンジ 33c

rap rappu ラップ 28c

rape gōkan 強姦 39b

rape gōkansuru (v) 強姦する
39b

rare (steak) rea no (adj) レアの
24b

rare mare na (adj) 稀な 4e

rarely mare ni (adv) 稀に 4e

rash hasshin 発疹 40a

raspberry kiichigo 木いちご
14d, 24f

rat nezumi ネズミ 15a

ratify hijunsuru (v) 批准する 43

ratio hirei 比例 1e

rational number yūrisū 有理数
1d

ravine kyōkoku 峡谷 13b

raw nama no (adj) 生の 24p

razor kamisori かみそり 12d,
25f

razor blade kamisori no ha
かみそりの刃 12d, 25f

reach tassuru (v) 達する 3e

read yomu (v) 読む 20a, 37f

reader dokusha 読者 20a

reading dokusho 読書 27a

reading (passage) yomikata
読み方 37f

real estate agent fudōsan
assennin 不動産斡旋人 38a

real number jissū 実数 1d

Really? Hontō. (inf) 本当。 21c

rearview mirror bakkumirā
バックミラー 33e

reason riyū 理由 22a

reason ronshōsuru (v) 論証する
22b

rebellious hankōteki na (adj)
反抗的な 11e

receipt reshīto レシート 25a,
35b

receipt uketorishō 受収証 26

Receipt please! Reshīto o onegai
shimasu. レシートをお願い
します。 25a

receive uketoru (v) 受け取る 19e

receiver (audio) reshībā
レシーバー 20b

receiver (telephone) juwaki
受話器 18a

recent saikin no (adj) 最近の 4e

recently chikagoro (adv) 近頃 4e

reception jushindo 受信度 20b

reception (wedding) hirōen
披露宴 11c

rechargeable battery saijūden
kanō denchi 再充電可能電池
25d

recipient jushinnin 受信人 19f

reciprocal number gyakusū 逆数
1d

recommend suisensuru (v)
推薦する 17a

record rokuonsuru (v) 録音する
20b

recover kaifukusuru (v)
快復する 12b, 40a

rectangle chōhōkei 長方形 2a

rectum chokuchō 直腸 40a

rectum kōmon 肛門 12a

red aka 赤 7a

red akai (adj) 赤い 7a

red wine reddo wain
レッドワイン 24g

red-eye fix akame shūsei
赤目修正 25d

red-haired akai kaminoke no
(adj) 赤い髪の毛の 11a

reduced price waribiki nedan
割引値段 25a

referee refurī レフリー 27b

reference book sankōsho 参考書
20a, 25o

references shin-yō shōkaisaki
信用照会先 38b

refined jōhin na (adj) 上品な 11e

reflect shiansuru (v) 思案する
22b

reflexive saiki (adj) 再帰 8a

reflexive verb saikidōshi
再帰動詞 8a

reform kaikaku 改革 43

reform kaikakusuru (v) 改革する
43

refrigerator reizōko 冷蔵庫 23d,
35c

refund haraimodoshi 払い戻し
25a

refund haraimodosu (v)
払い戻す 25a

region chihō 地方 13e

registered letter kakitome yūbin
書留郵便 19e

registration tetsuzuki 手続き
37f

registration fee tetsuzuki ryō
手続き料 37f

registration papers tōrokusho
登録書 33b

regular kisokuteki na (adj)
規則的な 4e

regular verb kisokudōshi
規則動詞 8a

regularly kisokuteki ni (adv)
規則的に 4e

rehab rihabiri sentā
リハビリセンター 44b

reindeer tonakai トナカイ 15a

reject kyozetsusuru (v) 拒絶する
21b

rejection kyozetsu 拒絶 21b

relate kanrenzukeru (v)
関連づける 17a

relative (grammar) kankei (adj)
関係 8a

relatives goshinseki ご親戚 10a

relatives shinseki 親戚 10a

relax kutsurogu (v) くつろぐ 12b

relief anshin 安心 21a

relief ukibori 浮き彫り 28b

religion shūkyō 宗教 11d

religious shinkōbukai 信仰深い 11d

remain nokoru (v) 残る 29b

remember omoidasu (v) 思い出す 22b

remote control rimokon リモコン 20b

rent kariru (v) 借りる 23g

rent yachin 家賃 23g

rental car rentakā レンタカー 33a

repeat kurikaesu (v) 繰り返す 17a, 37f

repetition kurikaeshi 繰り返し 17a

reply henji o dasu (v) 返事を出す 19e

reply henji 返事 19e

reply henshin 返信 19f

reply ōtōsuru (v) 応答する 17a

reply all zenin ni henshin 全員に返信 19f

report hōkoku 報告 17a

report hōkokusuru (v) 報告する 17a

report card seisekihyō 成績表 37f

reporter repōtā レポーター 20a

represent daihyōsuru (v) 代表する 41

representative giin 議員 43

reproach shikaru (v) 叱る 17a

reproduce saiseisuru (v) 再生する 14a

reproduction saisei 再生 14a

reptile hachūrui 爬虫類 15c

republic kyōwakoku 共和国 43

request tanomi 頼み 17a

request tanomu (v) 頼む 17a

request a taxi takushī o tanomu (v) タクシーを頼む 35b

rescue kyūjo 救助 39a

researcher kenkyūin 研究員 38a

reservation yoyaku 予約 24m, 30a, 32a, 35b

reserve yoyakusuru (v) 予約する 30a, 35b

reserved yoyakushitearu (adj) 予約してある 24m

reserved (character) uchiki na (adj) 内気な 1e

reserved seat shitei seki 指定席 34

residence jūsho 住所 11f

resistant teikōsei no aru (adj) 抵抗性のある 13d

Respect for the Aged Day (third Monday in September) keirō no hi 敬老の日 5g

respiratory system kokyū keitō 呼吸系統 40a

rest yasumu (v) 休む 12b

restaurant resutoran レストラン 24m

restless ochitsukanai (adj) 落ち着かない 11e

restore shūfukusuru (v) 修復する 23f

résumé rirekisho 履歴書 38b

retire taishokusuru (v) 退職する 38d

retirement taishoku 退職 38d

retirement money taishoku kin 退職金 38d

return kaeru (vi) 帰る 3e, 29b

return kaesu *(vt)* 返す 3e

return address sashidashinin jūsho 差出人住所 19e

review fukushū 復習 37f

review fukushūsuru *(v)* 復習する 37f

review hyōron 評論 20a, 28d

revolt hanran 反乱 43

revolt hanransuru *(v)* 反乱する 43

revolution kakumei 革命 43

rhetoric shūji 修辞 17a

rhetorical shūjiteki na *(adj)* 修辞的な 17a

rhetorical question hango 反語 17a

rheumatism ryūmachi リューマチ 40a

rhinoceros sai 犀 15a

rhinoceros beetle kabutomushi カブトムシ 15d

rhombus hishigata 菱形 2a

rhythm rizumu リズム 28c

rice (cooked) gohan 御飯 24i

rice (on a plate) raisu ライス 24g

rice (uncooked) kome 米 24i

rice bowl ochawan お茶碗 24l

rice bowl (Japanese) gohanjawan 御飯茶碗 23d, 24l

rice cake (Japanese) mochi 餅 24i

rice cooker suihanki 炊飯器 23d

rice cracker (Japanese) senbei せんべい 24i

rice store okome ya お米屋 24n

rice wine (Japanese) sake 酒 24k

rich yūfuku na *(adj)* 裕福な 11e

ridiculous matomo ja nai *(adj)* まともじゃない 11e

rifle raifuru ライフル 39b

right migi 右 3d

right tadashii *(adj)* 正しい 37f

right angle chokkaku 直角 2b

right away sugu ni *(adv)* 直ぐに 4e

right prism chokkakuchū 直角柱 2a

right to vote futsū senkyoken 普通選挙権 43

right wing uyoku 右翼 43

right, privilege kenri 権利 41

right-angled chokkaku *(adj)* 直角 2a

ring yubiwa 指輪 25i

ring (phone) naru *(vi)* 鳴る 18b

ring finger kusuriyubi 薬指 12a

rinse kuchi o susugu *(v)* 口をすすぐ 40b

riot bōdō 暴動 43

ripe jukushita *(adj)* 熟した 14a

ripen jukusu *(v)* 熟す 14a

rite gishiki 儀式 11d

ritual gishiki 儀式 11d

river kawa 川 13b, 36b

road michi 道 33c

road map dōro chizu 道路地図 33b

roast rōsuto ロースト 24b

rob ubau *(v)* 奪う 39b

robber gōtō 強盗 39b

robbery gōtō 強盗 39b

robin komadori コマドリ 15b

robot robotto ロボット 42a

robust ganjō na *(adj)* 頑丈な 13d

rock rokku ロック 28c

rock iwa 岩 13b

rock climbing rokku kuraimingu ロッククライミング 27b

rock music rokku ロック 25j

roll rōrupan ロールパン 24g

roller rōrā ローラー 25b

rollerblading rōrāburēdo
ローラーブレード 27b

Roman numerals Rōma sūji
ローマ数字 1d

romance renai 恋愛 20a

romance (novel) renaishōsetsu
恋愛小説 25o

romantic romanchikku na *(adj)*
ロマンチックな 11e

Rome Rōma ローマ 30c

roof yane 屋根 23a

roof (car) rūfu ルーフ 33e

rook rūku ルーク 27a

room heya 部屋 23b, 35b

room with two beds tsuin no
heya ツインの部屋 35b

rooster ondori 雄鶏 15b

root ne 根 14a

root (dentistry) shikon 歯根 40b

rope (mountain climbing) zairu
ザイル 27b

rose bara バラ 14b

rosemary rōzumarī
ローズマリー 14e, 24j

rotten kusatta *(adj)* 腐った 14a

rough kime ga arai *(adj)*
きめが粗い 13d

rough soya na *(adj)* 粗野な 11e

rough copy, draft shitagaki
下書き 37f

round-trip ticket ōfuku ken
往復券 30a

row retsu 列 28a

rowing sōtei 漕艇 27b

rubber band wagomu 輪ゴム
25c

ruby rubī ルビー 25i

rude burei na *(adj)* 無礼な 11e

ruler jōgi 定規 2b, 19d, 25c, 37b,
38c

rum ramu ラム 24k

rumor uwasa うわさ 17a

run hashiru *(v)* 走る 3e, 12b, 27b

run into (someone) deau *(v)*
出会う 16b

runway kassōro 滑走路 32c

rush hour rasshu awā
ラッシュアワー 33c

Russia Roshia ロシア 30b

Russian (language) Roshiago
ロシア語 30d

Russian Roshiajin ロシア人 30d

rye raimugi ライ麦 24i

S

sable ten テン 15a

sad kanashige na *(adj)* 悲しげな
11e

sad kanashii *(adj)* 悲しい 21a

sadness kanashimi 悲しみ 21a

safe kinko 金庫 26

safe deposit box kashikinko
貸金庫 26

saffron safuran サフラン 24j

Sagittarius iteza 射手座 5d

sailing sēringu セーリング 27b

sailor sen-in 船員 38a

sake cup sakazuki 杯 24l

sake jug tokkuri 徳利 24l

sake on the rocks sake no on za
rokku 酒のオンザロック 24p

salad sarada サラダ 14e, 24g

salad dressing doresshingu
ドレッシング 24g

salamander sanshōuo 山椒魚
15c

salami sarami sōsēji
サラミソーセージ 24c

salary sararī/kyūryō
サラリー／給料 26, 38d

sale hanbai 販売 25a

sales representative hanbaiin/
ten-in 販売員／店員 38a

salmon sake 鮭 15c, 24d

salt shio 塩 13c, 24j

salty shiokarai *(adj)* 塩辛い 24p

salutation aisatsu no kotoba
挨拶の言葉 19c

salvia sarubia サルビア 14b

samba sanba サンバ 28c

San Francisco Sanfuranshisuko
サンフランシスコ 30c

sand suna 砂 13b

sandal sandaru サンダル 25n

sandpaper kamiyasuri 紙ヤスリ
25b

sandpiper isoshigi イソシギシギ
15b

sandwich sandoitchi
サンドイッチ 24g

sanitary napkin seiri napukin
生理ナプキン 25h

sapling wakagi 若木 14c

sapphire safaia サファイア 25i

sarcasm hiniku 皮肉 11e

sarcastic hiniku na *(adj)* 皮肉な
11e

sardine iwashi 鰯 15c, 24d

sash (for kimono) obi 帯 35c

satellite eisei 衛星 13a, 20b

satellite jinkōeisei 人工衛星 42a

satellite broadcasting eisei hōsō
衛星放送 20b

satellite dish eisei antena
衛星アンテナ 20b

satisfaction manzoku 満足 21a

satisfied manzokushita *(adj)*
満足した 21a

Saturday doyōbi 土曜日 5a

Saturn dosei 土星 13a

saucer ukezara 受け皿 23d, 24l

Saudi Arabia Saujiarabia
サウジアラビア 30b

sausage sōsēji ソーセージ 24c

sautéed sotē ni shita *(adj)*
ソテーにした 24b

save chokinsuru *(v)* 貯金する 26

save hozon 保存 19f

savings chokin 貯金 26

saw nokogiri のこぎり 25b

saw nokogiri de kiru *(v)*
のこぎりで切る 14a

saxophone sakisofōn
サキソフォーン 28c

say, tell iu *(v)* 言う 17a

scale uroko うろこ 15c

scalene futōshen/sha *(adj)*
不等辺／斜 2a

scallop kaibashira 貝柱 15c,
24d

scanner sukyana スキャナ 19d,
38c, 42b

scarf sukāfu スカーフ 25k

scene bamen 場面 28e

scenery haikei 背景 28e

scenic route nagame no ii kōsu
眺めのいいコース 36b

schedule jikokuhyō 時刻表 34

schedule yoteihyō/sukejūru
予定表／スケジュール 4e

scheming zurui *(adj)* ずるい 11e

school gakkō 学校 37f

school bag tsūgaku kaban
通学カバン 37b

school yard kōtei 校庭 37c

school year gakunen 学年 5b

schoolmate gakuyū 学友 37d

science fiction saiensu fikushon
    サイエンスフィクション 20a,
    25o

sciences kagaku 科学 37e

scientific research kagaku
    kenkyū 科学研究 42a

scientist kagakusha 科学者 38a

scissors hasami はさみ 12d, 19d,
    25c, 38c

scooter sukūtā スクーター 33a

score tokuten 得点 27b

score (music) gakufu 楽譜 28c

Scorpio sasoriza 蠍座 5d

scorpion sasori サソリ 15d

Scotch whiskey sukotchi
    スコッチ 24k

screen sukurīn スクリーン 25d,
    28a, 42b

**screen with paper and wooden
    grid** shōji 障子 23c

screw neji ねじ 25b

screwdriver nejimawashi
    ねじ回し 25b

sculpt chōkokusuru (v) 彫刻する
    28b

sculptor chōkokuka 彫刻家 28b

sculpture chōkoku 彫刻 28b

sea umi 海 6a, 13b, 36b

sea bass suzuki 鱸 15c, 24d

sea lion todo とど 15a

Sea of Japan Nihonkai 日本海
    13b

sea otter rakko ラッコ 15a, 15c

sea urchin uni ウニ 15c

seafood gyokairui 魚介類 24d

seagull kamome カモメ 15b

seahorse tatsu no otoshigo
    タツノオトシゴ 15c

seal azarashi アザラシ 15c

seal azarashi/ashika/ottosei
    アザラシ／アシカ／オットセイ
    15a

season kisetsu 季節 5c

seat seki 席 28a, 34, 32c

seat (bicycle) sadoru サドル 33a

seat (car) shīto シート 33e

seat belt shītoberuto
    シートベルト 32c, 33e

secant sekanto セカント 2b

second byō 秒 4c

second daini 第二 1b

second futatsume 二つ目 1b

second nibanme 二番目 1b

second person (grammar)
    nininshō 二人称 8a

second third of the month
    chūjun 中旬 4c

second year ninen 二年 37a

secretary hisho 秘書 37d, 38a

security system keibi shisutemu
    警備システム 23e

sedative chinseizai 鎮静剤 40a

seduction yūwaku 誘惑 11e

seductive miwakuteki na (adj)
    魅惑的な 11e

see miru (v) 見る 12c, 30a

See you! Soredewa, mata.
    それでは、又。 16a

See you later! Soredewa,
    nochihodo. それでは、
    後ほど。 16a

See you soon! Soredewa,
    chikaiuchi ni.
    それでは、近いうちに。 16a

See you Sunday! Soredewa,
    nichiyōbi ni.
    それでは、日曜日に。 16a

seed tane o maku (v) 種を蒔く
    14a

seed tane 種 14a

seedling naegi 苗木 14c

segment line senbun 線分 2b

segment kyūkei 弓形 2b

selfish rikoteki na (adj) 利己的な 11e

self-service serufu sābisu セルフサービス 24m, 33c

self-sufficient jiritsu shiteiru (adj) 自立している 11e

sell uru (v) 売る 25a

semicolon semikoron セミコロン 19c

senate jōin 上院 43

senator jōin giin 上院議員 43

send okuru (v) 送る 3e, 19e

sender sashidashinin 差出人 19e, 19f

senior discount kōreisha waribiki 高齢者割引 30a

senior discount shinia waribiki シニア割引 28a

seniority system nenkōjoretsu sei 年功序列制 38d

sense kankaku 感覚 12c

sense of humor yūmoa no kankaku ユーモアの感覚 11e

sense, feel kanjiru (v) 感じる 12c

sensitive binkan na (adj) 敏感な 11e, 12c

sensitive kanjiyasui (adj) 感じやすい 21a

sent sōshinzumi 送信済み 19f

sentence (court) hanketsu 判決 41

sentence bun 文 8a, 19c

sentimental kanshōteki na (adj) 感傷的な 11e

Seoul Souru ソウル 30c

separate bekkyosuru (v) 別居する 11c

separated bekkyoshita (adj) 別居した 11f, 11c

separation bekkyo 別居 11c

September kugatsu 九月 5b

series renzoku bangumi 連続番組 20b

serious majime na (adj) 真面目な 11e

serious shinken na (adj) 真剣な 21a

serious accident daijiko 大事故 39c

sermon sekkyō 説教 17a

serve (food or drink) dasu (v) 出す 24o

serve a sentence keiki ni fukusuru (v) 刑期に服する 41

service sābisu サービス 24m

service charge sābisu ryō サービス料 24m

services sābisu サービス 35b

set shūgō 集合 1f

set of drums taiko no setto 太鼓のセット 28c

set the table tēburu o totonoeru (v) テーブルを整える 23f, 24o

settlement wakai 和解 41

seven nanatsu 七つ 1a

seven shichi/nana 七 1a

seven hundred nanahyaku 七百 1a

seven thousand nanasen 七千 1a

seventeen jūshichi/jūnana 十七 1a

seventeen thousand ichimannanasen 一万七千 1a

seventh dainana 第七 1b

seventh nanabanme 七番目 1b

seventh nanatsume 七つ目 1b

seventy nanajū 七十 1a

seventy thousand nanaman 七万 1a

several ikutsuka no (adj) いくつかの 3c

sew nuu (v) 縫う 25g

sewage osui 汚水 44a

sewing machine mishin ミシン 23d

sex sei 性 11a

sex seibetsu 性別 38b

shabby misuborashii (adj) みすぼらしい 11a

shadow, shade kage/kage 影／陰 6a

shake yureru (vi) 揺れる 3e

shake hands akushusuru (v) 握手する 16a

shame haji 恥 21a

shameless hajishirazu no (adj) 恥知らずの 21a

shampoo shanpū シャンプー 12d, 25f, 35c

shark same サメ 15c

shave hige o soru (v) ひげを剃る 12d

shaving cream shēbingu kurīmu シェービングクリーム 25f

shawl shōru ショール 25k

she kanojo ga/wa 彼女が／は 8c

sheep hitsuji 羊 15a

sheet (bed) shītsu シーツ 23d, 35c

shelf tana 棚 23a, 23c

shellfish ebi, kani, kairui エビ、カニ、貝類 24d

sherbet shābetto シャーベット 24g

shingles taijōhōshin 帯状疱疹 40a

Shinto priest kannushi 神主 11d

Shinto shrine jinja 神社 11d

Shintoism shintō 神道 11d

Shintoist shintō no shinja 神道の信者 11d

shirt shatsu シャツ 25k

shiver furueru (v) 震える 12b

shock shokku ショック 39c

shoe kutsu 靴 25n

shoe department kutsu uriba 靴売り場 25n

shoe polish kutsuzumi 靴墨 25n

shoe repair shop kutsu no shūriya 靴の修理屋 25n

shoe store kutsu ya 靴屋 25n

shoehorn kutsubera 靴べら 25n

shoelace kutsu himo 靴ひも 25n

shoot utsu (v) 撃つ 39b

shop kaimonosuru (v) 買い物する 25a

shop mise 店 25a

shop for food shokuryōhin o kau (v) 食料品を買う 24o

shopping shoppingu ショッピング 29b

shopping bag kaimonobukuro 買い物袋 23d

shopping mall shoppingu mōru ショッピングモール 25a

short mijikai (adj) 短い 3b, 25l, 37f

short se ga hikui 背が低い 11a

short story tanpen shōsetsu 短編小説 20a, 25o, 28d

shorten mijikakusuru (v) 短くする 25m

shorts hanzubon 半ズボン 25k

shorts shōtsu ショーツ 25k

short-term tanki no *(adj)* 短期の 4e

shoulder kata 肩 12a

shout sakebi 叫び 39a

shout, yell sakebu *(v)* 叫ぶ 17a, 39a

shovel shaberu シャベル 25b

show shō bangumi ショー番組 20b

show shō ショー 28b

Showa Day (April 29) shōwa no hi 昭和の日 5g

shower niwakaame にわか雨 6a

shower shawā o abiru *(v)* シャワーを浴びる 12d

shower shawā シャワー 12d, 23a

shower cap shawā kyappu シャワーキャップ 25f

shredder shureddā シュレッダー 19d, 38c

shrewd nukemenonai *(adj)* 抜け目の無い 11e

shrimp ebi 海老 15c, 24d

shrine jinja 神社 36a

shrine assistant (female) miko 巫女 11d

shrub kanboku 灌木 14c

shut up damaru *(vi)* 黙る 17a

Shut up! Damare. *(inf)* 黙れ。 17a, 21c

shy uchiki na *(adj)* 内気な 11e

sick byōki no *(adj)* 病気の 11a, 40a

sick leave byōki kyūka 病気休暇 38d

sickness, disease byōki 病気 11a, 40a

side hen 辺 2b

side mirror saido mirā サイドミラー 33e

sideboard shokki todana 食器戸棚 23c

sigh of relief ando no tameiki 安堵のため息 21a

sight shikaku 視覚 12c

sign shomeisuru *(v)* 署名する 11f, 19c, 26

signal shigunaru シグナル 33c

signature shomei 署名 11f, 19c, 26, 38b

signs of the zodiac jūnikyūzu no sain 十二宮図のサイン 5d

silence chinmoku 沈黙 17a

silent (person) mukuchi na *(adj)* 無口な 17a

silk kinu 絹 13c

silk shiruku シルク 25l

silk shiruku/kinu シルク／絹 25g

silkworm kaiko 蚕 15d

silly oroka na *(adj)* 愚かな 21a

silver gin 銀 13c, 25i

silver (color) gin-iro 銀色 7a

silver anniversary kekkon nijūgoshūnen kinenbi 結婚二十五周年記念日 11c

simple tanjun na *(adj)* 単純な 11e, 22a

simple interest tanri 単利 26

simultaneous dōji no *(adj)* 同時の 4e

simultaneously dōji ni *(adv)* 同時に 4e

since kara から 4e

since Monday getsuyōbi kara 月曜日から 4e

since yesterday kinō kara 昨日から 4e

sincere seijitsu na *(adj)* 誠実な 11e, 21a

sine sain サイン 2b

sing utau *(v)* 歌う 28c

Singapore Shingapōru シンガポール 30b

singer kashu 歌手 25j, 28c, 38a

singer shingā シンガー 25j

single dokushin 独身 38b

single mikon no *(adj)* 未婚の 11f

single shinguru no *(adj)* シングルの 24p

single room shinguru no heya シングルの部屋 35b

singular number tansū 単数 8a

sink, wash basin senmendai 洗面台 23a, 35c

siren sairen サイレン 39a

sister-in-law giri no ane 義理の姉 10a

sister-in-law giri no imōto 義理の妹 10a

sister-in-law giri no imōtosan 義理の妹さん 10a

sister-in-law giri no onēsan 義理のお姉さん 10a

sisters goshimai ご姉妹 10a

sisters shimai 姉妹 10a

sit down suwaru *(v)* 座る 3e, 32c

six muttsu 六つ 1a

six roku 六 1a

six hundred roppyaku 六百 1a

six thousand rokusen 六千 1a

sixteen jūroku 十六 1a

sixteen thousand ichimanrokusen 一万六千 1a

sixth dairoku 第六 1b

sixth muttsume 六つ目 1b

sixth rokubanme 六番目 1b

sixth sense dai rokkan 第六感 12c

sixty rokujū 六十 1a

sixty thousand rokuman 六万 1a

size saizu サイズ 3b, 25a, 25k, 25n

skate sukēto de suberu *(v)* スケートで滑る 27b

skateboarding sukētobōdo スケートボード 27b

skating sukēto スケート 27b

sketch suketchi スケッチ 28b

ski sukī o suru *(v)* スキーをする 27b

ski resort sukījō スキー場 36b

skiing sukī スキー 27b, 36b

skim milk sukimu miruku スキムミルク 24h

skin hifu 皮膚 12a

skinny yasekoketa *(adj)* 痩せこけた 11a

skinny, thin yaseta *(adj)* 痩せた 11a

skip a class jugyō o saboru *(v)* 授業をサボる 37f

skip school, play hooky gakkō o saboru *(v)* 学校をサボる 37f

skirt sukāto スカート 25k

skull zugaikotsu 頭蓋骨 12a

skunk sukanku スカンク 15a

sky sora 空 6a, 13b

slacks surakkusu スラックス 25k

slash shasen/surasshu 斜線／スラッシュ 19c

sleep nemuru *(v)* 眠る 12b

sleeping bag surīpingubaggu スリーピングバッグ 36b

sleeping car shindaisha 寝台車 34

sleet mizore みぞれ 6a

sleeve sode 袖 25g

slender hossorishita (adj)
   ほっそりした 11a

slice usugiri ni suru (v)
   薄切りにする 24o

slide suberu (v) 滑る 3e

slide suraido スライド 25d

slide projector suraido eishaki
   スライド映写機 37b

sliding door hikido 引き戸 35c

slim, slender hossorishita (adj)
   ほっそりした 11a

slip surippu スリップ 25k

slipper surippa スリッパ 25n

sloppy, disorganized darashinai
   (adj) だらしない 11e

slow osoi (adj) 遅い 3e, 4e

slow down gensokusuru (v)
   減速する 33c

slowly osoku (adv) 遅く 3e, 4e

slug namekuji ナメクジ 15d

sly warugashikoi (adj) 悪賢い
   11e

small chiisai (adj) 小さい 3c, 25l

small, little chiisai (adj) 小さい
   3c, 11a, 13d, 25l

small bill chiisai osatsu
   小さいお札 26

small intestine shōchō 小腸 40a

small letter komoji 小文字 19c

small teapot (Japanese) kyūsu
   急須 23d, 24l

smart rikō na (adj) 利口な 11e

smart phone sumātofon
   スマートフォン 18a

smell nioi 匂い 12c

smell niou (v) 匂う 12c

smelt wakasagi ワカサギ 15c,
   24d

smile hohoemi 微笑み 11e, 21a

smile hohoemu (v) 微笑む 11e,
   21a

smoke kemuri 煙 13c, 39a

smoking kitsuen 喫煙 34

smoking room kitsuen dekiru
   heya 喫煙出来る部屋 35b

smooth nameraka na (adj)
   滑らかな 13d, 24p

snack kanshoku/oyatsu
   間食／おやつ 24a

snack sunakku スナック 24a

snack bar sunakku スナック 24m

snail katatsumuri カタツムリ
   15d

snake hebi 蛇 15c

sneaker sunīkā スニーカー 25n

sneeze kushami o suru (v)
   クシャミをする 40a

sneeze kushami クシャミ 40a

snobbish kidotta (adj) 気取った
   11e

snow yuki ga furu (v) 雪が降る
   6a

snow yuki 雪 6a

snow accumulation sekisetsu
   積雪 6a

snow goggles gōguru ゴーグル
   27b

snowboarding sunōbōdo
   スノーボード 27b

snowfall kōsetsu 降雪 6a

snowflake seppen 雪片 6a

snowstorm fubuki 吹雪 6a

So? Sorede. それで。 9

So, so! Māmā desu.
   まあまあです。 16a

so, therefore shitagatte (conj)
   従って 8k

so, therefore sorede それで 8k

soap sekken 石鹸 12d, 25f, 35c

soap powder konasekken 粉石鹸 25g

soccer sakkā サッカー 27b

sociable shakōteki na (adj) 社交的な 21a

social worker sōsharu wākā ソーシャルワーカー 38a

socialism shakaishugi 社会主義 43

socialist shakaishugisha 社会主義者 43

sociology shakaigaku 社会学 37e

sock sokkusu ソックス 25n

sodium natoriumu ナトリウム 13c

sofa sofā ソファ 23c

soft yawarakai (adj) 柔らかい 13d

soft drink sofuto dorinku ソフトドリンク 24k

soft-boiled egg hanjuku 半熟 24h

software sofutowea ソフトウェア 42b

soil dojō 土壌 13b

solar cell taiyō denchi 太陽電池 44a

solar eclipse nisshoku 日蝕 13a

solar energy taiyō enerugī 太陽エネルギー 13c, 44a

solar system taiyōkei 太陽系 13a

soldier heishi 兵士 38a

sole ashi no ura 足の裏 12a

sole shitabirame 舌平目 15c, 24d

sole (shoe) kutsu zoko 靴底 25n

solid kotai no (adj) 個体の 13c

solid figures rittai 立体 2a

solo dokushō (singing)/dokusō (instrumental) 独唱（歌）/独奏（楽器）28c

solstice shiten 至点 5c

soluble yōkaisei no aru (adj) 溶解性のある 13d

solution kaiketsuhō 解決法 1f

solve kaiketsusuru (v) 解決する 1f

solve a problem mondai o toku (v) 問題を解く 37f

some ikuraka no (adj) いくらかの 3c

some (people) aru hito ある人 8i

someone dareka 誰か 8i

something nanika 何か 8i

somewhere dokoka どこか 3d

son musuko 息子 10a

son musukosan 息子さん 10a

song uta 歌 25j, 28c

son-in-law musume no otto 娘の夫 10a

son-in-law ojōsan no goshujin お嬢さんのご主人 10a

soon mōsugu (adv) もうすぐ 4e

sooner or later sonouchi その内 4e

sore back kata no kori 肩のこり 40a

sore throat inkōen 咽喉炎 40a

sore/stiff neck kubi no kori 首のこり 40a

sorrow kanashimi 悲しみ 21a

soul tamashii 魂 11d

sound oto 音 12c

soundtrack saundotorakku サウンドトラック 28a

soup sūpu スープ 24g

soup bowl (Japanese) owan お椀 23d, 24l

sour suppai *(adj)* 酸っぱい 24p

south minami 南 3d

South Africa Minami Afurika 南アフリカ 30b

South America Minami Amerika 南アメリカ 30b

South Pole nankyoku 南極 13e

southeast nantō 南東 3d

southern minami no *(adj)* 南の 3d

Southern Cross minamijūjisei 南十字星 13a

southern hemisphere minami hankyū 南半球 13e

southwest nansei 南西 3d

souvenir shop omiyageya お土産屋 36a

sow tane o maku *(v)* 種を蒔く 14a

soy bean daizu 大豆 14e, 24e

soy sauce shōyu 醤油 24j, 24l

soy sauce dish okozara お小皿 24l

soy sauce pitcher shōyusashi 醤油差し 24l

space kūkan 空間 2b, 13a

space shuttle supēsushatoru スペースシャトル 42a

spacecraft uchūsen 宇宙船 42a

spaghetti supagetti スパゲッティ 24g

Spain Supein スペイン 30b

Spaniard Supeinjin スペイン人 30d

Spanish Supeingo スペイン語 30d

spare tire supea taiya スペアタイヤ 33e

spark hinoko 火の粉 39a

spark plug supāku puragu スパーグプラグ 33e

sparrow suzume 雀 15b

spasm, talk keiren 痙攣 40a

speak, talk hanasu *(v)* 話す 17a

speaker supīkā スピーカー 20b

special delivery sokutatsu 速達 19e

special skills tokugi 特技 38b

specialist senmonka 専門家 40a

species hinshu 品種 14a

species shu 種 13c

speech, talk hanashi 話 17a

speed sokudo 速度 3a, 33c

Speed Limit sokudo seigen 速度制限 33c, 33d

speed up kasokusuru *(v)* 加速する 33c

speedometer sokudokei 速度計 33e

spelling tsuzuri 綴り 19c

spend (money) tsukau *(v)* 使う 4e, 25a

spend (time) sugosu *(v)* 過ごす 4e

sphere kyūkei 球形 2a

spice yakumi 薬味 24j

spicy piritto shita *(adj)* ぴりっとした 24p

spider kumo 蜘蛛 15d

spinach hōrensō ほうれん草 14e, 24e

spine, backbone sebone 背骨 12a

spirit seishin 精神 11d

spiritual seishinteki *(adj)* 精神的 11d

splint fukuboku 副木 39c

spoke supōku スポーク 33a

spoon supūn スプーン 23d, 24l

sporadic tokiori no *(adj)* 時折の 4e

sporadically tokiori *(adv)* 時折 4e

spore hōshi 胞子 14a

sports supōtsu スポーツ 27a, 27b

sports car supōtsukā スポーツカー 33a

sports fan supōtsu fan スポーツファン 27b

spot, stain shimi シミ 25g

spouse haigūsha 配偶者 11c

sprain nenza 捻挫 40a

spray fukikakeru *(v)* 吹きかける 14a

sprig koeda 小枝 14a

spring haru 春 5c

spring onion, scallion hosonegi 細ネギ 14e, 24e

Sprite Supuraito スプライト 24k

square hiroba 広場 11f, 36a

square seihōkei 正方形 2a

square bracket kaku kakko 角カッコ 19c

square centimeter heihōsenchi 平方センチ 3a

square foot heihōfīto 平方フィート 3a

square inch heihōinchi 平方インチ 3a

square kilometer heihōkiro 平方キロ 3a

square meter heihōmētoru 平方メートル 3a

square mile heihōmairu 平方マイル 3a

square millimeter heihōmiri 平方ミリ 3a

square root heihōkon 平方根 1e

squared nijō no 二乗の 1e

squash sukasshu スカッシュ 27b

squid ika イカ 15c, 24d

squirrel risu リス 15a

stable anteishita *(adj)* 安定した 13d

stadium sutajiamu スタジアム 27b

stag beetle kuwagatamushi クワガタ虫 15d

stage butai 舞台 28e

stainless steel sutenresu suchīru ステンレススチール 13c

stairs kaidan 階段 23a, 35b

stamen oshibe 雄しべ 14a

stamp kitte 切手 19e, 27a

stamp collecting kitte shūshū 切手収集 27a

stand tachiagaru *(v)* 立ち上がる 3e

staple hotchikisu no hari ホッチキスの針 19d, 25c, 38c

stapler hotchikisu ホッチキス 19d, 25c, 38c

star hoshi 星 6a

star kōsei 恒星 13d

starch sentaku nori 洗濯のり 25g

starling mukudori 椋鳥 15b

start (car) enjin o kakeru *(v)* エンジンをかける 33c

starting salary shoninkyū 初任給 38d

state kokka 国家 43, 38b

state noberu *(v)* 述べる 17a

state shū 州 11f, 13e

statement seimei 声明 17a

station eki 駅 34

station (broadcasting)
hōsōkyoku 放送局 20b

station wagon wagonsha
ワゴン車 33a

stationary front teitai zensen
停滞前線 6a

stationery binsen 便せん 25c

stationery store bunbōgu ten
文房具店 25c

statistical tōkei no (adj) 統計の
1f

statistics tōkei/tōkeigaku
統計／統計学 1f, 37e

statue zō 像 28b

steal nusumu (v) 盗む 39b

steam musu (v) 蒸す 24o

steamed mushita (adj) 蒸した
24b

steel tekkō 鉄鋼 13c

steering wheel handoru
ハンドル 33e

stem kuki 茎 14a

stereo sutereo ステレオ 20b

stethoscope chōshinki 聴診器
40a

still mada (adv) まだ 4e

stingy kechi na (adj) ケチな 11e

stir kakimawasu (v) かき回す
24o

stitch nuime 縫い目 25g

stitch nuu (v) 縫う 40a

stock market kabushikishijō
株式市場 26

stock, share kabuken 株券 26

stockbroker kabu no burōkā
株のブローカー 38a

stocking sutokkingu
ストッキング 25n

stomach i 胃 12a, 40a

stomachache fukutsū 腹痛 40a

stone ishi 石 13b

Stop teishi 停止 33d

stop tomaru (vi) 止まる 3e, 34

stop tomeru (vt) 止める 3e

Stop thief! Dorobō. 泥棒。 39b

stopwatch sutoppuwotchi
ストップウォッチ 4d

store mise 店 25a

store clerk ten-in 店員 25a, 38a

store hours eigyō jikan 営業時間
25a

store/shop window shōwindō
ショーウィンドー 25a

storekeeper tenshu 店主 38a

stork kōnotori コウノトリ 15b

storm bōfūu 暴風雨 6a

stormy arashi no (adj) 嵐の 6a

story monogatari 物語 17a

stove renji レンジ 23d

straight ahead kono mama
massugu このまま真っすぐ
36c

straight angle heikaku 平角 2b

straight line chokusen 直線 2b

straight sake (Japanese) hiya
冷や 24p

strawberry ichigo 苺 14d, 24f

street michi 道 36a

street tōri 通り 11f

street tōri/gai 通り／街 38b

street sign dōro hyōshiki
道路標識 36a

streetcar romendensha 路面電車
33a

strength chikara/tsuyosa
力／強さ 11a

stress sutoresu ストレス 40a

strict genkaku na (adj) 厳格な
21a

string himo 紐 19d, 25c

string bean sayaingen 菜隠元 14e, 24e

string (music) gen 弦 28c

stringed instruments gengakki 弦楽器 28c

stroke nōsotchū 脳卒中 40a

strong genki na (adj) 元気な 40a

strong takumashii (adj) たくましい 11e

strong tsuyoi (adj) 強い 11a, 13d, 24p

stubborn ganko na (adj) 頑固な 11e

student gakusei 学生 37d

student discount gakusei waribiki 学生割引 28a, 30a

study benkyōsuru (v) 勉強する 37f

study manabu (v) 学ぶ 22b

stuff shizai 資材 13c

stupid oroka na (adj) 愚かな 11e

style buntai 文体 19c, 28d

stylish iki na (adj) 粋な 11a

styrofoam happōsuchirōru 発泡スチロール 13c

subject gakka 学科 37e

subject (grammar) shugo 主語 8a

subjunctive mood kateihō 仮定法 8a

submit teishutsusuru (v) 提出する 37f

subordinate buka 部下 38d

subordinate jūzoku (adj) 従属 8a

subscription teiki kōdoku 定期購読 20a

substance busshitsu 物質 13c

subtitles jimaku 字幕 28a

subtract hiku (v) 引く 1e

subtraction hikizan 引き算 1e

suburb kōgai 郊外 36b

subway chikatetsu 地下鉄 34

subway station chikatetsu no eki 地下鉄の駅 34

sudoku sudoku スドク 27a

sue uttaeru (v) 訴える 41

suede suēdo スエード 25l

suffer kurushimu (v) 苦しむ 40a

sufficient jūbun na (adj) 十分な 3c

sugar satō 砂糖 24j

suggest teiansuru (v) 提案する 17a

suicide bombing bakudan jisatsu 爆弾自殺 44b

suit sūtsu スーツ 25k

suitcase, piece of luggage sūtsukēsu スーツケース 31

sulphur iō 硫黄 13c

sulphuric acid ryūsan 硫酸 13c

sum gōkei 合計 1f

sum up gōkeisuru (v) 合計する 1f

summarize yōyakusuru (v) 要約する 17a

summary yōyaku 要約 17a

summer natsu 夏 5c

summer solstice geshi 夏至 5c

summons shōkanjō 召喚状 41

sun taiyō 太陽 5c, 6a, 13a

Sunday nichiyōbi 日曜日 5a

sundial hidokei 日時計 4d

sunflower himawari ヒマワリ 14b

sunlight nikkō 日光 13a

sunny jōtenki no (adj) 上天気の 6a

sunray taiyō kōsen 太陽光線 13a

sunrise hinode 日の出 4a

sunset hinoiri 日の入り 4a

sunspot taiyō no kokuten
太陽の黒点 13a

sunstroke nisshabyō 日射病 40a

superintendent kanrinin 管理人
23g

supermarket sūpā スーパー 24n

superstitious meishinbukai (adj)
迷信深い 11e

supplementary angle hokaku
補角 2b

suppository zayaku 座薬 25h,
40a

supreme court saikō saibansho
最高裁判所 41

surface hyōmen 表面 3d

surface mail funabin 船便 19e

surfing sāfin サーフィン 27b

surgeon gekai 外科医 38a, 40a

surgery shujutsu 手術 40a

surname, family name myōji
苗字 11f, 38b

surname, family name sei 姓
38b

surprise odoroki 驚き 21a

surprise odorokasu (vt) 驚かす
21a

surveyor sokuryōshi 測量士 38a

suspect yōgisha 容疑者 39b

SUV tamokuteki supōtsusha
多目的スポーツ車 33a

swallow tsubame ツバメ 15b

swamp shitchi 湿地 13b

swan hakuchō 白鳥 15b

swear (in court) chikau (v) 誓う
17a

swear (profanity) kitanai
kotobazukai o suru (v)
汚い言葉遣いをする 17a

sweat ase o kaku (v) 汗をかく
12b

sweater sētā セーター 25k

sweatshirt torēnā トレーナー
25k

Swede Suwēdenjin
スウェーデン人 30d

Sweden Suwēden スウェーデン
30b

Swedish (language) Suwēdengo
スウェーデン語 30d

sweet amai (adj) 甘い 24p

sweet (character) yasashii (adj)
優しい 11e

sweet potato satsumaimo
サツマイモ 14e, 24e

swim oyogu (v) 泳ぐ 27b

swimming suiei 水泳 27b

swimming pool pūru プール
27b, 35b

switch suitchi スイッチ 23a, 35c

Switzerland Suisu スイス 30b

swollen hareta (adj) 腫れた 40a

swordfish kajiki カジキ 15c, 24d

symbol shōchō 象徴 17a

symbol (mathematics) kigō 記号
1f

sympathetic dōjōteki na (adj)
同情的な 21a

sympathy dōjō 同情 21a

symphony shinfonī
シンフォニー 25j, 28c

symptom shōjō 症状 40a

synagogue Yudayakyō jiin
ユダヤ教寺院 11d

synthesizer shinsesaizā
シンセサイザー 28c

synthetic gōsei no (adj) 合成の
13c, 13d

syphilis baidoku 梅毒 40a

syringe chūshaki 注射器 40a

syrup shiroppu シロップ 24j, 25h

T

Tabasco tabasuko タバスコ 24j

table tēburu テーブル 23c, 24l, 35c

table clock okidokei 置き時計 4d

table of contents mokuji 目次 25o, 28d

tablecloth tēburukurosu テーブルクロス 23d, 24l

tablespoon ōsaji 大さじ 23d

tablet jōzai 錠剤 25h, 40a

tableware shokutakuyō shokkigu 食卓用食器具 23d

tadpole otamajakushi オタマジャクシ 15c

tail shippo しっぽ 15a

tailor shitateya 仕立て屋 25k, 38a

Taipei Tapiei 台北 30c

take (purchase) kau (v) 買う 25a

take a bath ofuro ni hairu (v) お風呂に入る 12d

take a course/subject kamoku o toru (v) 科目を取る 37f

take a picture shashin o toru (v) 写真を撮る 25d

take a trip ryokō ni iku 旅行に行く 30a

take a walk sanpo ni iku (v) 散歩に行く 3e

take an exam shiken o ukeru (v) 試験を受ける 37f

take an excursion gurūpu tsuā ni sankasuru (v) グループツアーに参加する 36a

take attendance shusseki o toru (v) 出席を取る 37f

take back kaesu (v) 返す 25a

take drugs mayaku o tsukau (v) 麻薬を使う 44b

take notes nōto o toru (v) ノートを取る 37f

take off (clothing) nugu (v) 脱ぐ 25m

take off (plane) ririkusuru (v) 離陸する 32c

take off (shoes) nugu (v) 脱ぐ 25n

take one's temperature netsu o hakaru (v) 熱を計る 40a

take out (food to go) mochikaeru (v) 持ち帰る 24m, 24o

take place okoru (vi) 起こる 4e

take/catch the train, etc. noru (v) 乗る 34

take-home pay tedori no kyūryō 手取りの給料 38d

takeoff (plane) ririku 離陸 32c

talcum powder shikkarōru シッカロール 25f

talk hanasu (v) 話す 17a

talkative oshaberi na (adj) おしゃべりな 11e

tall se ga takai 背が高い 11a

tall takai (adj) 高い 3b

tambourine tanbarin タンバリン 28c

tame hito ni nareta (adj) 人に慣れた 15a

tame kainarasu (v) 飼いならす 15a

tampon tanpon タンポン 25h

tangent sessen 接線 2a

tangent tanjento タンジェント 2b